Investing in Innovation

Investing in Innovation

Creating a Research and Innovation Policy That Works

edited by Lewis M. Branscomb and James H. Keller

The MIT Press, Cambridge, Massachusetts, and London, England

Library of Congress Cataloging-in-Publication Data

Investing in Innovation : creating a research and innovation policy
  that works / edited by Lewis M. Branscomb and James H. Keller.
     p.   cm.
  Includes bibliographical references and index.
  ISBN 0-262-02446-2 (hardcover : alk. paper)
   1. Technological innovations—Economic aspects—United States.
  2. Technology and state—United States.   3. United States—Economic
  policy—1993–   I. Branscomb, Lewis M., 1926–   . II. Keller, James H.
  HC110.T4I58   1998
  338'.064—dc21   97-36969
                                                                    CIP

Contents

Preface

There is broad agreement among Americans that rapid progress in science and technology is an essential requirement for innovation and productivity growth in both the private and public sectors. In an increasingly competitive global economy, technical creativity and efficiency are essential ingredients of a vibrant economy and the fulfillment of such public needs as a clean environment, a strong defense, and a healthy and well-educated population. The consensus fails, however, on the question of the extent to which market forces will induce sufficient private investment in research and innovation to ensure the attainment of these worthy goals. There is a debate over the role of government in the assurance of a healthy scientific and technological enterprise and an innovative, productive private sector.

The absence of a non-partisan consensus on the role of the federal government in promoting innovation and fostering the creation, accessibility, and use of new technology deprives public technology policy of continuity, increases the temptation for political manipulation of public investments, and fails to deliver the value Americans should expect from a $75 billion annual investment in government-funded research and development. This book explores the dimensions of a research and innovation policy that might earn that broadly based support and increase the effectiveness of public investments, without impinging on the great power of competitive markets to induce innovation.

We begin this examination with the technology policy declaration that President Clinton and Vice President Gore issued on

February 22, 1993. This policy statement represented the logical culmination of over twenty years of debate on how the United States should respond to the challenge posed by foreign competition in high-technology industries and by the investments of other governments in support of their industries' ability to innovate. The administration anticipated a broader role than simply public financing for research and development. Theirs was to be a strategy of investment—in technical knowledge, in human skills, and in research institutions—carried out through a variety of public-private partnerships. But, as documented in the 1993 Harvard University study *Empowering Technology*,[1] there were serious economic and political issues involved in such a strategy. The 104th Congress raised these issues and challenged the administration's insistence that competitively motivated private investment would not be adequate and that government was competent and trustworthy as a partner of the private sector.

In response to these questions, and believing that an effective consensus policy could be defined, we assembled in the fall of 1996 a national team of experts to make a non-partisan examination of the Clinton-Gore administration's first-term experience with technology policy. To ensure the study's independence, the bipartisan, congressionally established Competitiveness Policy Council agreed to sponsor it. Under the leadership of the Council's director, J. Fred Bergsten, the Council's executive director, Howard Rosen, made a major contribution to the project leading to this book. He organized a two-day workshop in November 1996, in Washington, D.C., at which about 100 experts discussed with senior government officials the full range of issues that had been raised in the technology policy debates. The steering committee for the project— Lewis M. Branscomb (chairman), Darin Boville, Richard Florida, David Hart, and James Keller (project director)—then prepared a report, entitled *Investing In Innovation: Toward A Consensus Strategy for Federal Technology Policy*. This report was presented and released at a combined session of the annual Colloquium of the American Association for the Advancement of Science entitled "Toward a Strategic View of Science and Technology," and the Princeton University Conference on "Organizing for Research and Development in the 21st Century," which took place in Washington on April 24, 1997. This report, posted on the project web site for public comment, was also reviewed by many of the government officials who had participated in the November workshop, and by members of the Committee on Civilian Industrial Technology of the president's National Council for Science and Technology. We particularly appreciate the assistance of the undersecretary of commerce for technology, Mary Good, and her deputy undersecretary, Gary Bachula, and of Jack Gibbons, director of the Office of Science and Technology Policy and his acting associate director for technology, Henry Kelly, for arranging for access by our authors to official sources in the government.

The steering committee's report and this book of the same title, not surprisingly, reach essentially consistent conclusions. Authors of the individual chapters were given the opportunity to criticize the report as it was being written, and they exerted significant influence on it. The editors of this book, as authors of its last chapter, drew substantially on the report and on each chapter. The chapters represent the independent views of their authors, but they also reflect a consistent set of policy themes from which the six principles discussed in the final chapter are drawn.

We are pleased to acknowledge a grant from the Alfred P. Sloan Foundation, which supported the editing of this book and the research on science policy described in Chapter 5. We are especially indebted to Darin Boville, who headed the project staff, participated in the editing, and supported all of the authors with research and access to sources. Teresa J. Lawson and Miriam Avins, our copy editors, with the help of Research Assistant Dean Berlin, provided highly professional assistance to the editors and to the authors, helping to make this book both coherent and readable. The project was undertaken under the aegis of the Science, Technology and Public Policy program (directed by John Holdren, who is also author of Chapter 12), which is part of the Belfer Center for Science and International Affairs of Harvard's John F. Kennedy School of Government.

Note

1. Lewis M. Branscomb, ed., *Empowering Technology: Implementing a U.S. Strategy* (Cambridge, Mass.: The MIT Press, 1993).

About the Authors

R. Darryl Banks (darrylb@wri.org) is the Director of the World Resources Institute's Program in Technology and the Environment. Prior to joining WRI, he served as the Deputy Commissioner for the New York State Department of Environmental Conservation. He has also worked at RAND, EPA, the American Association for the Advancement of Science, and the Office of Technology Assessment.

Michael Borrus (mborrus@violet.berkeley.edu) is co-director of the Berkeley Roundtable on the International Economy (BRIE) and adjunct Professor at the University of California, Berkeley.

Lewis M. Branscomb (Lewis_Branscomb@harvard.edu) is Aetna Professor (Emeritus) of Public Policy and Corporate Management at Harvard University's John F. Kennedy School of Government. Former Director of the school's Science, Technology, and Public Policy project, he previously served as Vice President and Chief Scientist of IBM, Director of the National Bureau of Standards, and Chairman of the National Science Board. He is editor and an author of *Empowering Technology* (MIT Press).

Harvey Brooks (care of nora_o'neil@harvard.edu) is Benjamin Peirce Professor of Technology and Public Policy, emeritus, at Harvard University's John F. Kennedy School of Government, where he headed the Science, Technology, and Public Policy Program from 1975 until his retirement in 1986. He received his PhD in physics from Harvard in 1940, served as Dean of the Division of Engineering and Applied Physics at Harvard from 1957 to 1975, and was Gordon McKay Professor of Applied Physics from 1950 to 1982. He served on the President's Science Advisory Committee from 1957 to 1964; was a member of the National Science Board from 1962 to 1974; and was chairman of the Committee on Science and Public Policy (COSPUP) at the National Academy of Sciences from 1966 to 1971.

Duncan M. Brown (dbrown@nas.edu) is a Washington, D.C.-based science writer and consultant. He has also served as a staff officer of the National Research Council.

Christopher M. Coburn (coburnc@battelle.org) is Vice President of the Technology Partnership Practice at Battelle Memorial Institute. He has served as Staff Director of the States Task Force of the Carnegie Commission on Science, Technology and Government; Executive Director of Ohio's Thomas Edison Program; Science and Technology Advisor to Ohio Governor Richard F. Celeste; and as a Director of the United States Enrichment Corporation.

Linda R. Cohen (lrcohen@uci.edu) is Professor of Economics at the University of California at Irvine. She received her bachelor's degree in mathematics from the University of California, Berkeley, and her doctorate in social science at the California Institute of Technology. She has also taught at Harvard and the University of Washington, and been a member of the research staff of the Brookings Institution and the RAND Corporation. She is the co-author of *The Technology Pork Barrel*, analyzing U.S. commercial research and development programs.

Frank Field (furd@mit.edu) is a Senior Research Engineer at MIT's Center for Technology, Policy, and Industrial Development. He is Director of the Materials Systems Laboratory, a research program studying the strategic implications of materials choice, and is a Research Director for the International Motor Vehicle Program (IMVP).

Richard Florida (rlflorida@aol.com) is the Heinz Professor of Economic Development and co-director of the Center for Economic Development at Carnegie Mellon University's Heinz School of Public Policy and Management. He recently was a visiting professor in the Science, Technology, and Public Policy program at Harvard's Kennedy School. He is the co-author of *Beyond Mass*

Production (Oxford University Press, 1993) and *The Breakthrough Illusion* (Basic Books, 1990), and is currently completing *For Knowledge and Profit* (Oxford University Press) on university-industry research relations and *Financiers of Innovation* (Princeton University Press) on the American venture capital system.

Jane E. Fountain (Jane_Fountain@harvard.edu) is Associate Professor of Public Policy at Harvard University's John F. Kennedy School of Government, and a core member of the university-wide Organizational Behavior faculty. She co-edited *Proposition 2 1/2: Its Impact on Massachusetts* and co-authored *Service Excellence: Using Information Technologies to Improve Service Delivery in Government.* She consults widely on public management and technology issues to governments in the United States and abroad, and is on the faculty of several of Harvard's executive programs including Senior Managers in Government.

David H. Guston (guston@rci.rutgers.edu) is Assistant Professor of Public Policy in the Bloustein School of Planning and Public Policy at Rutgers, The State University of New Jersey, and an associate of the Center for Science and International Affairs of Harvard University's John F. Kennedy School of Government. He is a co-author of *Informed Legislatures: Coping with Science in a Democracy* (University Press of America); and co-editor of *The Fragile Contract: University Science and the Federal Government* (MIT Press).

David M. Hart (David_Hart@harvard.edu) is Assistant Professor of Public Policy at the Kennedy School of Government, Harvard University. He is the author of *Forging the "Postwar Consensus": Science, Technology, and Economic Policy in the United States, 1921–1953* (forthcoming, Princeton University Press).

George R. Heaton (grheaton@aol.com) teaches law and public policy at the Worcester Polytechnic Institute in Worcester, Mass. In the 1970s, he began to study the impact of regulation on technological change, and has published frequently on this topic. He consults widely on issues of environmental and technology policy.

Christopher T. Hill (chill2@osf1.gmu.edu) is Vice Provost for Research and Professor of Public Policy and Technology at George Mason University, Fairfax, Virginia. He has served as Senior Specialist in Science and Technology Policy at the Congressional

Research Service, and has held positions at RAND, the National Academy of Engineering, MIT, the Congressional Office of Technology Assessment, Washington University, and Uniroyal.

John P. Holdren (John_Holdren@harvard.edu) is Teresa and John Heinz Professor of Environmental Policy and Director of the Program in Science, Technology, and Public Policy in the Center for Science and International Affairs, John F. Kennedy School of Government, and Professor of Environmental Science and Public Policy in the Department of Earth and Planetary Sciences, Harvard University. He is also Professor Emeritus of Energy and Resources at the University of California, Berkeley, Visiting Distinguished Scientist at the Woods Hole Research Center, and a member of President Clinton's Committee of Advisors on Science and Technology (PCAST). The views expressed herein are the author's, not necessarily those of these organizations.

Adam B. Jaffe (ajaffe@stanley.feldberg.brandeis.edu) is Associate Professor of Economics at Brandeis University, and Project Coordinator for the National Bureau of Economic Research Project on Industrial Technology and Productivity.

Brian Kahin (Brian_Kahin@harvard.edu) is a consultant to the White House Office of Science and Technology Policy (OSTP). He was the co-founder, with Lewis M. Branscomb, of the Harvard Information Infrastructure Project, and he served as Director of the project until 1997. Kahin served as General Counsel for the Interactive Multimedia Association from 1987 to 1997. He is a graduate of Harvard College and Harvard Law School. His contribution to this book was written at Harvard independently of his work for OSTP.

James H. Keller (James_Keller@harvard.edu) is the Associate Director of the Harvard Information Infrastructure Project, and a Research Associate in the Center for Science and International Affairs of Harvard University's John F. Kennedy School of Government.

James Neely (jneely@mit.edu) is a Ph.D. candidate in MIT's Technology, Management, and Policy Program. He previously worked in management consulting, with a focus on the assessment of business opportunities stemming from emerging technologies.

Lucien Randazzese (Lucien_Randazzese@harvard.edu) works at the strategic management consultancy of Dean & Company in Vienna, Virginia. He has been a post-doctoral fellow at the Center for Science and International Affairs of Harvard University's John F. Kennedy School of Government, and has also worked at IBM and the RAND Corporation. He is co-author of *For Knowledge and Profit: University-Industry Research Centers in the United States* (tentative title, forthcoming, Oxford University Press).

Daniel Roos (drdr@athena.mit.edu) is a Professor of Civil Engineering at the Massachusetts Institute of Technology, and Director of its Center for Technology, Policy, and Industrial Development. He is also the Director of the International Motor Vehicle Program (IMVP).

Philip Shapira (philip.shapira@pubpolicy.gatech.edu) is an Associate Professor in the School of Public Policy at Georgia Institute of Technology, where he teaches and conducts research on technology policy, industrial restructuring, and economic and regional development. He co-directs the Georgia Tech Policy Project on Industrial Modernization.

Jay Stowsky (jay.stowsky@ucop.edu) is Director of Research Policy and Development for the University of California system. He served from 1993–95 as Senior Economist for Science and Technology on the staff of President Clinton's Council of Economic Advisers. He is co-author of *The Highest Stakes: The Economic Foundations of the Next Security System* (Oxford University Press, 1992).

Scott J. Wallsten (wallsten@leland.stanford.edu) is a doctoral candidate in economics at Stanford University, where he was awarded an Alfred P. Sloan Foundation dissertation fellowship. He has been a staff economist at the President's Council of Economic Advisers, where he focused on industrial organization, regulation, and science and technology policy.

Acronyms

Web addresses are given in italics.

AMTEX   The American Textile Partnership (DOE)
amtex.sandia.gov

ARPA   Advanced Research Projects Agency (see DARPA)

ATP   Advanced Technology Program (NIST, DOC)
www.atp.nist.gov

CEA   Council of Economic Advisors (EOP)
www.whitehouse.gov/WH/EOP/CEA/html/CEA.html

CRADA   Cooperative Research and Development Agreement

CTI   Critical Technologies Institute
www.rand.org/centers/cti

DARPA   Defense Advanced Research Projects Agency (DoD)
(formerly ARPA) *www.darpa.mil*

DOC   Department of Commerce *www.doc.gov*

DoD   Department of Defense
www.dtic.dla.mil/defenselink/index.html

DOE   Department of Energy *www.doe.gov*

DOT   Department of Transportation *www.dot.gov*

DUAP   Dual Use Applications Program (DARPA, DoD)
www.jdupo.darpa.mil/jdupo/index.html

EOP	Executive Office of the President *www.whitehouse.gov/WH/EOP/html/EOP_org.html*
EPA	Environmental Protection Agency *www.epa.gov*
ETI	Environmental Technology Initiative (EPA) *www.epa.gov/oppe/eti/eti.html*
GAO	General Accounting Office *www.gao.gov*
GOCO	Government-owned, contractor-operated
GOGO	Government-owned, government-operated
GPRA	Government Performance and Results Act (OMB) *www.whitehouse.gov/WH/EOP/OMB/Special_Emphasis/ gpra2cov.html*
HPCC	High Performance Computing and Communications Program *www.hpcc.gov*
IPR	Intellectual property rights
IR&D	Independent research and development
ITS	Intelligent Transportation System (DOT) *www.its.dot.gov*
MEP	Manufacturing Extension Partnership (NIST, DOC) *www.mep.nist.gov*
MTC	Manufacturing Technology Center (NIST, DOC)
NASA	National Aeronautics and Space Administration *www.nasa.gov*
NBS	National Bureau of Standards (now NIST)
NEC	National Economic Council (EOP) *www.whitehouse.gov/WH/EOP/nec/html/main.html*
NEMI	National Electronics Manufacturing Initiative *www.nemi.org*
NGA	National Governors Association *www.nga.org*
NIH	National Institutes of Health *www.nih.gov*
NII	National Information Infrastructure *nii.nist.gov*
NIST	National Institute of Standards and Technology (DOC) (formerly NBS) *www.nist.gov*
NOAA	National Oceanographic and Atmospheric Administration (DOC) *www.noaa.gov*

NSF   National Science Foundation *www.nsf.gov*

NSTC   National Science and Technology Council (EOP)
*www.whitehouse.gov/WH/EOP/OSTP/NSTC/html/
NSTC_Home.html*

OMB   Office of Management and Budget
www.whitehouse.gov/WH/EOP/OMB/html/ombhome.html

ORTA   Office of Research and Technology Applications
(national laboratories)

OSTP   Office of Science and Technology Policy (EOP)
*www.whitehouse.gov/WH/EOP/OSTP/html/
OSTP_Home.html*

PCAST   President's Committee of Advisors on Science and
Technology (EOP) *www.whitehouse.gov/WH/EOP/
OSTP/NSTC/PCAST/pcast.html*

PICS   Platform for Internet Content Selection
www.w3.org/PICS

PNGV   Partnership for a New Generation of Vehicles
www.ta.doc.gov/pngv and *www.USCAR.org*

SBA   Small Business Administration *www.sba.gov*

SBIR   Small Business Innovation Research program (SBA
and other agencies)
www-wsmr.army.mil/docpage/pages/sbir.htm

TA   Technology Administration (DOC) *www.ta.doc.gov*

TRP   Technology Reinvestment Project (DoD) (see DUAP)

USDA   U.S. Department of Agriculture *www.usda.gov*

USIP   United States Innovation Partnership

I
The Changing Environment for Technology Policy

1

Challenges to Technology Policy in a Changing World Economy

Lewis M. Branscomb and Richard Florida

"The economy, stupid," James Carville wrote on a white board in the campaign headquarters of candidate Bill Clinton during his run for the White House in 1992.[1] Shortly after taking office, President Clinton and Vice President Gore issued a major report on technology policy, "Technology for America's Economic Growth: A New Direction to Build Economic Strength." Reflecting themes outlined in an earlier campaign statement, the president outlined a new direction and role for the federal government to build economic strength and spur economic growth:

American technology must move in a new direction.... We cannot rely on the serendipitous application of defense technology to the private sector. We must aim directly at these new challenges and focus our efforts on the new opportunities before us, recognizing that government can play a key role helping private firms develop and profit from innovations.[2]

To what degree has the Clinton administration delivered on these promises? Is it even appropriate for the federal government to help "private firms develop and profit from innovations?" Do the 1993 policy directions adequately reflect the changes sweeping over private industry in an increasingly global economy? What are the most appropriate and effective lines of action for both the administration and the Congress to build a more effective technology policy for the future? What lessons should be taken from the experience of the last four years?

This book takes up these questions. It reflects the analyses and assessments of a broadly based group of experts who have examined the successes and disappointments of the administration's implementation of its first term technology policy. The experts do not always agree, except on one point: there is no single right answer—no "one size fits all" technology policy that would best serve the nation.

The chapters provide assessments of key Clinton administration programs and initiatives. The book also offers suggestions for policy directions that take advantage of what has been learned. The aim of this book is to define a set of policies, and principles to guide them, that are both timely for action now and also might endure over the time scales necessary for research and innovation incentives to bear economic fruit.

In addition, this book seeks to shed light on some of the broader, more conceptual issues surrounding government intervention in science and technology. What should be the guideposts for federal scientific and technological intervention in the nation's economic life? What should be done at the federal level, and what should and can be done by the states? What are the most appropriate and effective policy tools and mechanisms? What is the proper mix of policy tools?

Taking office with great hopes and a grand vision, the Clinton administration made technology policy a front-burner issue. It unveiled a host of so-called new (but in many cases repackaged) technology programs as the cornerstone of its investment strategy for the economy.[3] In a relatively short time (certainly short for action in Washington, D.C.) a torrent of programs was pushed forward. In the Commerce Department, these included the Advanced Technology Program (ATP) to accelerate development of new technology in high-tech industry; the Manufacturing Extension Partnership, helping states assist small firms to use the best production tools and methods; and the Partnership for a New Generation of Vehicles (PNGV) to accelerate the introduction of new, less fuel-consuming power plants in automobiles. In the Defense Department, the Technology Reinvestment Project (TRP)[4] introduced the idea of dual-use (civilian and military) technology and promised to aid in defense conversion. The Environmental Protection Agency (EPA) initiated the Environmental Technology Initiative (ETI) to help industry generate more efficient and less polluting manufacturing processes. The most controversial of these programs has been ATP, which broke new policy ground as the only federal program providing funds to commercial firms for the sole purpose of accelerating economic progress, not tied to any specific technology of special interest to the government.

One of the key elements of the Clinton-Gore approach to technology policy was an attempt to reallocate technology spending from defense to commercial purposes. The president declared his intention to rebalance the ratio of civilian to military R&D from about 40:60 to 50:50. This would require an increase of over $8 billion in civilian R&D, from $27.9 billion in 1993 to $36.6 billion by 1998, while defense R&D expenditures declined.[5]

Even more dramatic, those programs specifically devoted to private sector incentives for research-based innovation—such as the ATP, the TRP, and the multi-agency Small Business Innovation and Research (SBIR) program—were so small compared to defense spending that extraordinary growth rates would be necessary to bring R&D spending aimed at economic progress to a level equal to that for defense. The political problems this effort might entail were understood to be significant, but few anticipated the backlash from conservatives that came with the election of a Republican majority to the 104th Congress in 1994.

Ideological objections to what conservatives call "industrial policy" and "corporate welfare" removed any doubts that the 104th Congress would reject a rapid shift in R&D spending from military to the administration's civil technology initiatives. Social liberals also opposed "corporate welfare" as a diversion of resources from traditional welfare; indeed they had invented the phrase, only to see it co-oped by conservatives as a signal of opposition to government expenditures seen as wasteful. The boldness of the Clinton-Gore plan and the budget priority assigned to it may have had the effect of politicizing technology policy. From the conservative perspective, the administration's desire for rapid increases in these programs stood in the way of tax reductions and budget balancing. More importantly, there were some basic issues related to the nature and scope of government interventions in technology that were of great concern to many in Congress.

Nonetheless, the 105th Congress, elected in the fall of 1996, seems much more willing to search for common ground on many of these issues. An opportunity to build a new consensus based on sound principles that meet the legitimate concerns of both the administration and the Congress seemed to be at hand in the spring of 1997.

The commitment of both political parties to a balanced federal budget requires that government extract the maximum value from every dollar invested in the research and development of technology. These new fiscal realities are also shaping a rethinking of how government can most effectively support innovation, both in the private sector and in its own operations. Such a rethinking creates the opportunity to develop new models and strategies for technology policy which can overcome existing ideological and partisan differences. A bipartisan strategy is essential to the long-term stability needed to foster technology and the economic benefits that flow from technological leadership.

Looking Forward

The limitations of the research and innovation policies of the Cold War period are clear, but what will replace them? What relationships will foster science and technology in the new age of distributed and global innovation? What level of investment is required and how can global investment priorities be determined? What kinds of institutions must be crafted? How will these changes be brought into being? These are the questions that are likely to define technology policy into the twenty-first century, and they are the subjects of this book.

Americans should not assume that the scientific and technical achievements of the past, so effective in winning the Cold War, will be sufficient to sustain rising living standards in the future. "High-tech" was once a description of research-intensive industries such as computers, biotechnology, and aircraft. Today, high-tech is a style of work applicable to every business, however simple its products or services may appear. Skill, imagination, and knowledge, together with new forms of institutional collaboration between firms, universities, and government, can make products and services more effective and productive. Thus, technology policy must be user-centered and demand-based, in contrast to a supply-side approach.

If employing the full range of available policy tools and working in collaboration with state governments enables the federal government to help firms become more innovative, the private sector will not only increase its own investment in technology but will express its demand for expanded federal investment in research and education. That expressed appreciation for the value of public investments in research could then create the conditions for a business-based political constituency in both parties in support of a farsighted technology policy.

Building a bipartisan consensus for technology policy requires a recognition that science and technology are deeply intertwined and often indistinguishable, in contrast to research and development, which are quite distinct activities calling for different institutional settings and different expectations from their sponsors. The government's sphere is research, along with education, and the building of a knowledge-based infrastructure; industry's sphere is development, along with production, and delivery of user benefits. If the sharing of costs in public-private partnerships reflects the relative expectations for public and private benefits; if the participating firms are encouraged to share the fruits of the government's investment (but not necessarily of their own); if the government uses rigorously professional and fair merit-based review as the basis for performer selection, then the use of public-private partnerships can join publicly funded research in universities and national laboratories as a powerful institutional mechanism for innovation.

This new way of working with the private sector puts heavy demands on government officials. It was easy to run a technology policy when government decided what research was needed, agreed to pay for it, and picked the people to do it. Now government must work more by indirection and must understand the way the new economy works, sector by sector, much more profoundly. If it succeeds, the public and the business community can build their confidence in a new kind of relationship between government and the institutions and people in our society. This will be liberating for innovation, just as it is liberating for personal freedom.

This first chapter explores the roots of the political conflict over technology policy, and traces the evolution of both the debate and the policies that emerged from it. The political pressure for policy change flowed from perceived weaknesses in the U.S. economy—lagging personal incomes, layoffs in high-wage employment, and sales of U.S. industrial assets to foreign investors—as American firms faced increasing competition from abroad in the 1970s and 1980s. The chapter then explores the changes that firms have made in the way they innovate and how they relate to sources of technology outside the firm, as they have restored their manufacturing competitiveness. These changes, especially the move toward less hierarchical and more collaborative relationships among firms, their suppliers, and sources of technical knowledge and skill, call for additional changes in the way government tries to help empower innovation in the economy. We then discuss the importance to firms of sources of technical knowledge for which government has a special responsibility, including university ties to industrial firms, which government has encouraged. Finally we address the implications for policy of the rapid globalization of innovation activities. The chapter closes with a brief synopsis of each of the chapters of the book.

The Roots of Political Controversy over Technology Policy

To understand what kinds of policies might be both appropriate in the new world economy and also politically acceptable within the American system of government, we must begin by reviewing the roots of the political and ideological differences that characterize the debate, and then search for common ground.

Just at the time when the new American economy is in a position to use much more technical knowledge, the sources of private support for the basic scientific and technological research formerly carried out in big corporate laboratories appear to be shrinking. The new patterns of private sector innovation depend more on reaching outside the firm to partnerships and alliances, searching out technical knowledge wherever it may be found. These trends appear to call for government policy that supports alliances among firms, universities, and national laboratories, and that compensates with long-term approaches for the increasingly short-term investments large firms and their suppliers are making.

Furthermore, large firms seeking collaborative innovation from their supply chains are not confining their search for innovation to local suppliers. If the United States should fade as a leader in technical creativity, just at the time Japan, Korea, and China are dramatically accelerating their public investments in scientific and technical infrastructure, the big companies will simply look to foreign sources for those innovative suppliers. For the United States to remain the most attractive location for innovation and advanced research requires renewal of the basic technological research on which innovation rests. Those who support the Clinton-Gore strategy believe this is a proper, even urgent, role for government.

Presidents Reagan and Bush did not totally disagree with this. President Bush endorsed federal cost-shared investments in private firms to create "precompetitive, generic" technology in his administration's technology policy declaration of September 1990.[6] These two qualifying adjectives, which appear in the 1988 Omnibus Trade and Competitiveness Act creating the Advanced Technology Program (ATP) in the Department of Commerce, were intended to make sure that any commercial technology funded by government was precompetitive (not yet ready for commercialization) and was generic (of interest to many users).[7] But President Bush's willingness to accept the Democrats' ATP program at a modest level of funding was not shared by the activists who controlled the Congress in 1995. The Clinton-Gore technology program, off to such an auspicious start in 1993, was in trouble two years later.

The political battle over balancing the federal budget provided an opportunity for conservatives in the contentious 1995–96 Congressional sessions to raise ideological as well as fiscal objections to the Clinton administration's technology policy priorities and programs. Although one might expect conservatives to support efforts aimed at improving the performance of U.S. companies, many opposed these programs as "corporate welfare." There were calls for the abolition of the Commerce Department's Technology Administration (and the Department itself), and some criticized the administration's high-profile R&D partnerships with the private sector. The vehemence of the attacks came as a surprise to many observers.[8] The bipartisan policy for U.S. science and technology that had seemed to be emerging by the end of the Bush administration had collapsed. However, by 1997, the extreme nature of some of the attacks on government funding of technological research seems to have produced a reaction from moderates in both parties, who appreciate the importance of sorting out the issues and searching for common ground.

Forging a New Non-partisan Consensus on Research and Innovation Policy

Early in the 105th Congress a new flurry of bipartisanship seems to have gripped the president and the Congress. Despite concerns about government distortions of a free market and the necessity to cut the discretionary budget, almost everyone in Congress believes that U.S. ingenuity and research have made the nation strong and prosperous. The Republicans' first-day legislative package for the 1997 congressional session included an unexpected and widely praised authorization bill introduced by Senator Phil Gramm (R-Texas) that would double government expenditures in nominal dollars on non-defense basic scientific and medical research over the next ten years, implying an annual growth rate of some 7 percent (before inflation). This would be a significant change from the 1996 projections by both the president and Congress, which called for federal nonmilitary R&D to shrink, in constant dollars, by as much as 20 to 30 percent in the outer years of their budget-balancing plans. There was other evidence of a common interest in resolving science and technology policy issues by leaders within both parties. A group of highly respected, influential legislators have formed a bipartisan Science and Technology Caucus in the Senate. In the House Science Committee, Chairman James Sensenbrenner and ranking minority member George Brown are working well together. There is a sense among key legislators that if agreement can be reached on the management of the Advanced Technology Program, many other program issues will be more easily resolved. The Congress now has a unique opportunity to set a new course that could endure for at least a decade and make a huge contribution to American capability and well-being.

Given that a willingness to compromise is shared by members of both parties, what are the basic differences in Republican and Democratic views of civilian technology policy? Conservatives have greater confidence in the power of competition to induce firms to invest in technology in pursuit of their commercial interests, which firms understand in far greater detail than does the government. Most conservatives would agree that market failures may require government to supplement private investment in special cases. They strongly support federal R&D to develop military and other systems the government wishes to purchase for its own use. But where there are market failures that lead to private under-investment, they raise warnings about "government failure" to remedy a market failure competently, and the temptation to use public R&D funds for partisan political purposes.

Conservatives and liberals generally agree that government should support basic research in science. They understand that scientific research entails uncertainties about what may be learned, how quickly progress can be made, and how new knowledge might be used in a practical application. The serendipitous discoveries that emerge from science suggest that scientific research is best performed under conditions that allow a lot of freedom to researchers to follow nature's lead in the quest for knowledge. Indeed, scientific research is more about finding good questions than turning out predictable answers.

However, the bipartisan agreement that government should support scientific research tends to break down when one moves from more theoretical science disciplines such as astronomy and mathematics to fields seen as more practical, such as chemistry, oceanography, or engineering. In these fields, much more is assumed to be known in advance about how research results might be used. Politicians are tempted to treat research in these fields as "applied research" and, because the work is assumed to have economic value, conservatives may expect the market to motivate firms to pay for it. Thus, most of the argument centers on the more useful kinds of research, especially when government chooses to fund that research through partnerships with private firms. When commercial firms are invited to share the cost of research with the government, the market failure that justified the public expenditure appears to be modest at best, adding to conservative doubts about its necessity.

The line that divides basic scientific research from more immediately useful technological research is quite unclear. So too is the line that divides technological research from commercial product development. Between science (which has bipartisan support) and commercial product development (which neither party would have government subsidize) lies a large part of the most intellectually exciting and economically useful research. The political controversy about government subsidies to research concerns primarily this gray area between "pure" science and development, in the area we call "basic technology research" (see Chapter 5).

Challenges Facing a New Research and Innovation Policy

This book starts from the premise that managing a technology policy in support of economic growth is much more complex than implementing the traditional national security-oriented policies of the preceding four decades. This is so, not only because of ideological differences over the appropriateness of government activities in private markets, but because, for the new policies to be successful, much of the success must come by indirection. In a defense-oriented R&D economy, government is the customer for the fruits of most of its R&D investment, but when government research is to be picked up by private firms and used to compete in world markets, government is no longer the primary customer. In its economic context, technology is always embedded in a larger business context of production, marketing, and finance. Technology policy, if it is to contribute to the economy, must in turn be linked to economic policy. It was for this reason that the administration in 1993 created, in deliberate parallel to the National Security Council, a National Economic Council (NEC) to "monitor the implementation of the new [technology] policies and provide a forum for coordinating technology policy with the policies of the tax, trade, regulatory, economic development, and other economic factors."[9]

Technology policy must derive at least part of its legitimacy from the mainstream national concerns about productivity and growth and from the capacity of the private sector to contribute more to public ends, such as environmental protection, public health, and the like. It should not be seen as simply the "applied" component of science policy. The institutions for policy-making in the White House and the Executive Office will have to learn how to marry the function of economic policy-making, with its political salience and high stakes, to the traditionally apolitical, low-visibility function of science and technology policy support. (The White House role is discussed in Chapter 17 by David Hart.)

The Importance of Reaching Bipartisan Agreement

Why is it important for the Congress and the administration to try to find common ground for a new policy direction? U.S. firms are competing globally against industrious people in market economies whose governments are making massive investments in research and innovation incentives; Americans must agree on how our government should respond.

There are other reasons for rethinking technology policy: new approaches to public-private partnerships may be the right strategy for defense and environment too. The new direction for defense acquisition, already begun in the last year of President Bush's term, is to seek to utilize the innovative capacity of commercial firms to a greater extent (as Linda Cohen explains in Chapter 7). This entails co-investing with private firms in "dual-use" technology (applicable to both military and civil uses) so that the government's investment is leveraged by private funds driving towards similar technological goals. Thus defense will, more and more often, ask of industry, "how close can you come to meeting my requirements with your technology and the limited funds we have available?" instead of saying, "here are my requirements; what will it cost?" Partnerships become the appropriate institutional relationship, replacing the command economy that characterized a dedicated defense-only industry.

Similarly, the new policy path for dealing with environmental pollution (as discussed in Chapter 11 by George Heaton and Darryl Banks) will be to supplement end-of-pipe controls with incentives to modify process technologies so that less offensive effluent is produced without adding much, if any, cost to the product being

made. Even the delivery of health care, now being rapidly commercialized in the quest for cost containment, will have its influence on
technology policy in the health sector, a trend that has shown up
first in the extensive use of Cooperative Research and Development Agreements (CRADAs) by the National Institutes of Health
(NIH) and collaborating medical industry firms (discussed in
Chapter 9 by David Guston).

Government is learning how to leverage research investments
and other policies to empower private innovation and to induce
behavior in commercial markets so as to reduce the need for
federal regulatory intervention. The administration can claim
some success with this kind of enabling policy in its effort to
enhance the National Information Infrastructure (see Chapter 13
by Brian Kahin). This is the path to achieving public ends at lowest
cost, to building a strong economic base for the future, and for
gaining the support of the U.S. public for the long term commitment to science and technical innovation on which our future
depends.

The Evolution of U.S. Technology Policy after World War II

To understand the opportunities and constraints on policy for the
future, it is important to see the current scene in historical context.
During the first four decades after World War II, the United States
attained the highest level of scientific and technological achievement in history.[10] With the world's largest economy and the strongest armed forces, it helped to defend the cause of free societies
and demonstrated the strength of market economies. There was
little foreign competition for the new defense-based high-tech U.S.
industries. The nation met the security threat from the Soviet
Union with massive commitments to technological superiority.
When, in 1957, the Soviet Sputnik rattled public confidence in this
strategy the nation put on a spectacular demonstration of its
capability to mobilize and deploy technology, by going to the
moon. The period from the early 1950s to about 1968, after which
the growth of government investments in R&D came to a halt for
ten years, is often called the golden age of American science and
technology.[11]

Despite the success of these policies in containing Soviet expansionism and demonstrating technical prowess, there were early indications, as Japan and Germany recovered from the war, that the defense-based science and technology policies might not be sufficient to assure a strong economy. In 1968, Michael Boretzky, a Commerce Department economic analyst, began to document for a succession of Commerce secretaries and for the intelligence committees of the Congress the erosion, already visible by 1968, of the previous highly favorable balance of trade in high technology goods.[12] President Nixon entertained a presentation from his special trade representative, Peter G. Peterson, documenting the situation. Nixon's Secretary of Commerce Maurice Stans made a strong appeal to Congress for investment in research to reverse this high-tech trend.[13] President Carter, during his last year in office, chartered a major study of how the federal government might enhance innovation rates in the private sector. The study, completed for the secretary of commerce by Assistant Secretary for Science and Technology Jordan Baruch, was presented to Congress, but with the election of President Reagan it lost any opportunity to influence policy.[14]

It was President Reagan who introduced concern about competitiveness into the political discourse by declaring an administration "competitiveness" strategy.[15] But high-tech erosion continued, and in 1986 the U.S. high-tech trade balance went negative for the first time. Thus the government's concern with ensuring a competitive commercial economy against technologically sophisticated competition from abroad began to provoke policy responses long before the fall of the Berlin Wall in 1989.

In the first two decades after World War II, both mission-based technology and general scientific research were supported by the mission agencies, primarily the Department of Defense. Budgets of the National Science Foundation (NSF) and the National Institutes of Health were relatively modest. As a guarantee against central political control over scientific and engineering activities, American policy after the war called for a highly decentralized responsibility for investing in research and development by federal agencies. All federal agencies were to develop the technology needed for their assigned tasks and were also to support a proportionate share of the country's basic research, as a kind of "mission overhead" re-investment in the basic knowledge on which their technology depended.[16] The autonomy of academic science was to be preserved by competitive selection, through peer review of proposals.

The two main elements of postwar technology policy, then, were government support for research in basic science, and active development of advanced technology by federal agencies in pursuit of their statutory missions.[17] The assumption that these activities would sustain a competitive private economy was derived from a supply-side picture of how the process of innovation works in high-technology industries. This postwar technology policy approach, followed by France and Britain as well as the United States, has been characterized by Henry Ergas as mission-oriented technology policy, in contrast to the diffusion-oriented policies of Germany, Switzerland, and Sweden.[18]

The bipartisan support for science in the postwar period rested on two assumptions. The first was acceptance of the "pipeline model" of the process by which social return arises from scientific research in the form of industrial innovations. Innovations, in this model, arise from scientific research and invention, followed sequentially by product development and production. While this is not a bad description of how new industries arise from new science—a process that usually takes a decade or more—it is inapplicable to the way existing industries compete through rapid incremental progress in which product and process development, driven by market opportunity, provide the stimulus to research.[19] The pipeline model is an even less appropriate description of how high-technology firms compete in the 1990s.

The second assumption was that technology created in pursuit of governmental missions, especially defense, space, and nuclear energy, would automatically flow to industry and make for prosperity. The process through which this is presumed to happen is called "spinoff."[20] A key reason for its appeal is that spinoff, like the pipeline from basic science to innovation, is assumed to be automatic and cost-free. Both of these assumptions have the attractive feature that if these processes are automatic and cost-free, the government does not have to "pick winners and losers" in order for the economy to gain the benefits. Government can then claim that its policies achieve the goals of economic growth without interference with the autonomy of private firms. This argument still constitutes the core of the conservative opposition to active governmental interest in the diffusion and commercialization of government research, and even stronger objections to government R&D investments to meet commercial requirements for new technology.

In short, U.S. policy after the Second World War, with its pipeline and spinoff images, sought to avoid the business community's abhorrence of industrial policy and the scientists' abhorrence of centrally planned science, while still retaining the benefits of technological stimulation of the economy. The political attractiveness of this policy helps explain its persistence, despite the fact that its assumptions are no longer realistic today. But the alarms first sounded by Michael Boretsky in the late 1960s suggested that there were flaws in the assumption that the pipeline from science and the spinoff from technology to commercial markets was either automatic or free.

The first response of Congress to the rising concerns about U.S. high-tech competitiveness was to try to accelerate the spinoff of government technology to the commercial sector, beginning with the Bayh-Dole Patent Act in 1980, which allowed agencies to grant exclusive licenses for inventions made with the agency's funds. It was followed by the Stevenson-Wydler Act of 1980, encouraging university-industry collaboration. The National Cooperative Research Act of 1984 reduced the risk of civil anti-trust prosecution of firms collaborating in R&D, a response to the view that Japanese consortia of competing firms gave them a competitive advantage. The Technology Transfer Act of 1986 (amendments to Stevenson-Wydler) provided a variety of specific incentives for government agencies and national laboratories to enter into Cooperative Research and Development Agreements (CRADAs, discussed in Chapter 9 by David Guston).

In 1988, with President Reagan in the White House but with Democrats in control of both the House of Representatives and the Senate, the Congress passed and the president signed the Omnibus Trade and Competitiveness Act. This statute, in which Senator Hollings of South Carolina played an important role, represented the first important institutional change in federal agency structure for addressing the technological dimensions of economic performance. It added new goals and missions to the Commerce

Department's National Bureau of Standards (NBS) and changed its name to National Institute for Standards and Technology (NIST). A few weeks later, Congress created a Technology Administration (TA) in the Department of Commerce with an undersecretary at its head. Subsequently both President Bush and President Clinton sought to strengthen the capabilities of the Executive Office to coordinate science and technology matters, most recently by the creation of the National Science and Technology Council (NSTC). Despite strong Republican opposition to many of the policy innovations embodied in the Omnibus Trade and Competitiveness Act, even after they won control of the Congress in 1994, none of the legislative authorizations for these institutional changes has been repealed. The recent fight has been over budgets and appropriations to implement the authorized activities.

Until 1988, it was reasonable to suppose that the Department of Defense (DoD) would continue to focus its main effort on neutralizing the strategic threat from the Soviet Union, even as it began to rely more on dual-use technologies as a means of shortening defense systems development cycles, reducing acquisition costs, and indirectly making a contribution to the defense industrial base. The Department of Energy (DOE) still placed top priority on its nuclear weapons program, even as it began to broaden its technical activities into the Human Genome project and high-performance computing in support of new opportunities for the computer industry.

The Commerce Department, until the 1988 law, had been the main focus of debates about federal roles in support of industrial competitiveness, but there had been little change in its agency structure or functions. Indeed, the Reagan administration attempted to disestablish much of the activity in fire research, building technology, and computer engineering at the National Bureau of Standards. These were among the NBS activities directed most specifically at assistance to industry. Only a sympathetic Congressional ear to objections from industry trade associations kept these activities in place.

During the 1980s, the National Science Foundation (NSF) had begun to build up its investment in fundamental engineering research in the universities. It initiated two new programs (the Engineering Research Centers and the Science and Technology Centers) intended to promote interdisciplinary research in universities in which industry participation would be required. Further evidence of interest in associating NSF with industrial interests was a brief (and abortive) effort by Congress to restructure the Commerce Department by merging the National Bureau of Standards with the National Science Foundation, and to redefine the mission of the Department as a "Department of Trade and Industry."[21]

The assumption that government R&D in pursuit of agency missions such as defense was what commercial firms needed to remain competitive could no longer be sustained when the Berlin Wall fell in 1989. U.S. self-interest then shifted rapidly from a first priority on Cold War security to a first priority on economic performance and domestic issues. Studies of competitiveness issues showed that where foreign industries seemed to have better performance, it was not in R&D but in downstream functions of quality and cost of manufacturing and in the quick pace of product cycles.[22] Congress, with Senator Jeff Bingaman from New Mexico in the lead, began to shift its focus from research and development to technology, asking the administration for a series of studies of critical technologies and establishing the Critical Technologies Institute (CTI) as a Federally Funded Research and Development Center (FFRDC) supporting the Office of Science and Technology Policy (OSTP).[23] At this point, major changes in U.S. policy began to appear, as outlined in Table 1-1.

The break with reliance on the spinoff model was now clear, and was reflected, or at least implied, in the Clinton-Gore technology policy announced on February 22, 1993. The pace and scale of these proposals and the administration's implicit confidence in their efficacy marked a dramatic change from the policy proposals of the 1970s and 1980s. Central was a proposed shift in the balance between military and civil R&D expenditures requiring spectacular growth in the civil R&D programs. The political difficulties associated with executing this plan were clearly identified at the time.[24] The resulting intense and often emotional debate between the Republican-controlled Congress and the administration has displayed radically different views about how the U.S. government

Table 1-1 Changes in the Policy Environment for Government Technology Programs

New program environment	Cold War era environment
Consensus management by cooperative agreement	Federal financing and control by contract
Technology adoption by internalization of R&D	Technology transfer to industry assumed or required
Expanded scope; goal is industry transformation	Single goal defined by engineering objective
Complementary assets are important to success	Principal risks are technical or market uncertainty
Recursive innovation model	Pipeline innovation model
Technologies for design, process, and quality are important	Emphasis placed on precompetitive research, plus development for government uses
Difficult to create constituency for program	Danger of constituency capture of program
Firms are selected by competitive negotiation on likelihood of commercialization	Firms are selected by contract competition on fulfillment of government specifications

should deal with the competitive challenge to U.S. industry that emerged in the 1980s.

It is a thesis of this book that many of these political difficulties could be resolved with careful attention to what is known and indisputable about the role of government activities in the innovation process and the language used to discuss it. However, while the effort to resolve these ideological differences proceeds—and it is making progress in the 105th Congress—the world economy is hurtling into new territory. Any forward-looking technology policy must deal with the world of innovation as it will be in the next decade, not as it was in the last.

A Moving Target for Policy: New Patterns of Innovation and Research

The search for a bi-partisan agreement on the nation's civilian science and technology policies is chasing a rapidly moving target.

The extraordinary changes that are sweeping over private industry all around the world call for a new role for government—one that exerts less authority over private activities, listens better to research requirements coming from the private sector, and focuses more on enabling innovation and building capacity than on creating new things for government use. New patterns of innovative activity and new multi-firm industrial structures are emerging. The focus of innovation is shifting from the multinationals and their university-like central laboratories to the dozens of hungry firms in their supply chains. This is unleashing a wave of opportunity for creativity and entrepreneurship in the smaller firms, but their sights tend to be set on much closer time horizons. At the same time that government has been struggling to find a new set of policy principles for technology appropriate to a shift in priorities from public to private innovation, sweeping changes have been affecting both the economy and the American system of innovation.

American corporations have come to realize—now more than ever—that the playing field is on longer national but global. That goes not only for markets, but for technology development as well. Firms are seeking out sources of technology on a global basis, developing alliances with foreign competitors, and establishing laboratories in foreign nations. Foreign companies are doing the same in the United States. These sweeping changes in the economic environment have made the old technology policies even less effective than they already were in the waning years of Cold War. Thus the need for a new perspective on government's role arises not only from the transition from military security to economic and domestic security, but from the need to reflect these sweeping transformations and leverage them to American advantage.

Transformation of Industrial R&D

Responding to these and other changes in the global economic landscape, research-based innovation in the United States and around the world is undergoing a fundamental shift. The dimensions are of this change include the increasing pace of technological change; the rise of new technology-intensive sectors, such as information technologies, advanced materials, and biotechnology; the increasing knowledge-intensity of industry; the relentless pressure for shorter development cycle times; the globalization of technology; and increasingly complex relationships and interdependencies between corporations, government, and university.

Underlying and driving these changes is the increasingly distributed and decentralized nature of technology. Industry is shifting from the central R&D laboratory to the global R&D network. In the past, corporations could internalize research and technology development, but as the sources of technology have become more decentralized and distributed, the challenge has become how to manage external sources of technology. To cope with these changes, corporations are developing new collaborative relationships, alliances, and partnerships; relying more upon their suppliers, customers, and users as sources of technology; establishing overseas R&D labs; and increasing their partnerships with universities and government laboratories.

Industrial R&D is extending its focus, monitoring the external environment for potential sources of technology, and seeking to forge the partnerships required to gain access to them. Corporations have increased their reliance on outside suppliers both as sources of goods and service and as sources of innovation. In doing so, many companies have reduced, downsized, and in some cases eliminated their central R&D laboratories, once the much-admired centerpiece of the American innovation system.[25] Some have shifted their technology development work to more applied activities, while others have increased their reliance on universities for both pioneering and applied activities.

New strategies are emerging to meet these challenges. In the past, the large central corporate laboratories of companies like IBM, AT&T, General Electric, RCA, DuPont, and Xerox served as important contributors to the national and international science base, as well as being sources of commercial technology and industrial leadership within their own companies. That is now unsustainable. A number of corporations have cut back, and in some cases eliminated, their centralized research laboratories, RCA's Sarnoff Laboratories being the most notable example. Between 1986 and 1993, the average annual growth in industrial R&D was just slightly better than 1 percent, compared to a 6.7 percent annual growth rate between 1976 and 1985.[26] Tighter research and development budgets are driving industry's quest for more efficient R&D, perhaps with a greater realization that no company can keep pace with technology by itself, and that technology is not the only key to economic success.

To cope with this new environment, corporations are developing new strategies which focus R&D resources on core strengths, tie R&D more closely to manufacturing and marketing, and leverage outside sources of technology. Illustrative of this shift are GE's new priorities for its central R&D laboratory, which include educating and training people, coordinating work across business units, transferring best practices across the company, and only last, developing and solving new problems.

Reaching out to Universities for Technology

The rise in collaborative research and development efforts among corporations, their suppliers, universities, and even government labs is a clear indicator of the trend toward ever more dependence on distributed, external sources of technology. R&D managers across the advanced industrial world are decentralizing and globalizing R&D efforts, developing ways to collaborate fruitfully with other companies, suppliers, universities, and government labs while focusing their internal efforts on core products and competencies. For example, IBM, Toshiba, and Siemens are collaborating on the development of 256-megabit memory chips. Such collaboration is even extending to the fiercest direct competitors: witness the Big Three car manufacturers' joint USCAR consortium, supported by the federal government's "Clean Car" (PNGV) effort. Collaboration reduces cost, spreads risk, and promotes cross-fertilization of ideas, while allowing companies to monitor constantly the external sources of technology. It also places new demands on public support for the research infrastructure that creates new technological opportunities.

The distributed nature of innovation has also resulted in an explosion in university-industry research relationships. Universities have become an important component of the R&D system over the past two decades, registering significant gains in the share of research they conduct (see Chapter 14 by Harvey Brooks and Lucien Randazzese). The university share of total research and development increased between 1970 and 1993 from 8.9 percent to 12.8 percent. Universities performed $20.6 billion in R&D in 1993, $10 billion more in real terms than in 1970.[27] Industrial funding of university research has also increased dramatically in recent years, providing a further indication of industry's growing reliance on external sources of technology. It grew by nearly 600 percent in real terms between 1970 and 1993, from $176 million to $1.2 billion. Industry's share of the total expenditures on academic research grew from 2.6 to 7.3 percent over the same period.[28]

Relationships between university and industry have grown more extensive over the past decade or so, as universities have sought to cope with federal funding patterns that have not kept pace with demand, and have responded to changes in federal policy that made federal funding contingent on industry funding. The explosion of university-industry research relationships has been even larger than anticipated. There are now more than 1,000 university-industry research centers (UIRCs) on more than 200 U.S. university campuses.[29] They spent an estimated $4.1 billion on research and related activities in 1990, $2.5 billion of which was devoted explicitly to research and development. University-industry centers provide government with a mechanism for accelerating the diffusion of useful technical knowledge to industry while concentrating public resources on advanced research accessible to a broad range of potential users.

Decentralized Innovation

A recent survey by the Industrial Research Institute indicates that firms are indeed increasing linkages with the external corporate environment.[30] According to the IRI study, 49 percent of laboratories expect to increase their joint ventures and alliances, while just four percent expect this to decrease. Additionally, 34 percent of R&D labs expect to increase licensing to others, while 22 percent expect to increase licensing from others. These findings are reinforced by a broad international survey of technology managers in

North America, Europe, and Japan, which indicate that corporations are relying more heavily than ever on external sources for both basic research and product development.[31] Firms in Europe, North America, and especially Japan see themselves as increasingly dependent on external sources of technology. The study further indicates that corporations utilize different external sources for basic research and for product development. Universities are the primary external source for basic science, while, for product development, corporations rely much more on joint ventures and suppliers. Even as corporations increase their reliance on external sources of technology, however, internal sources—both central R&D labs and divisional R&D units—are still the dominant sources of technology.

The shift toward distributed technology has been followed by decentralization of technology management responsibilities. The United States has undergone a rapid decentralization of technology over the past three years, from the central R&D laboratory to business divisions. Roughly 60 percent of the U.S. research managers in the survey indicated that they were shifting responsibility for R&D budgets and activities from central laboratories to business units.[32] This shift in corporate structures and relationships poses important challenges for American technology policy. It must begin to rely less on the research talents in the largest firms, such as IBM, AT&T, and Dupont, and less on the linkage to universities and national laboratories which the corporate research laboratories provided historically. This illustrates an important new dimension to technological innovation: innovation entails organizational change as well as advances in technology. Second, technology policy has long failed to give highly innovative small and medium-sized firms the central role that they deserve. Part of the reason for this reluctance was the fact that, by necessity, small and medium firms had a short-term perspective on research. But, as the center of industrial innovation shifts to these firms and away from fundamental, long-term, high-risk research, technology policy must find a way to compensate for this short-term perspective.

Other nations trail the United States in the decentralization of R&D. Japanese and European corporations continue to move control up the hierarchy from the business-unit level toward more centralized corporate control. Nevertheless, foreign-based firms are also increasing their reliance on suppliers as a source of technology and innovation. Japanese companies have long depended upon their suppliers as a key source of innovation. German corporations are increasing their use of suppliers as a source of technology. The trend to new strategies and structures referred to variously as "lean production," the "knowledge-based firm," or the "high-performance organization" is worldwide, even though the models differ from one country to the next. This transformation has altered the internal structure of the firm, with new emphasis on the use of teams, a high degree of task integration, decentralized decision-making, continuous innovation, organizational learning, and a blurring of the sites of innovation and production.

The Globalization of Innovation

Globalization of markets, production, and technology is another defining feature of the new economy. Goods are increasingly produced where they are sold. The sales of goods produced in the global factories of multinational enterprises now totals some $6 trillion, an amount which far exceeds the $3.5 to $4 trillion generated by international trade.[33] The exports from foreign subsidiaries of multinational firms now exceed the total exports from the home countries in which those multinationals are based.

The past decade has seen the sweeping globalization of R&D, as corporate innovation systems have become international in scope. Today, U.S. multinational enterprises invest nearly $15 billion per year, roughly 10 percent of their total R&D spending, in R&D laboratories located in foreign nations.[34] Foreign companies account for more than 15 percent of all R&D conducted in the United States, and constitute large and significant shares of the American technology base in fields like chemicals and pharmaceuticals. In fact, foreign direct investment (FDI) in R&D by foreign enterprises comprises the most rapidly growing segment of U.S. R&D.

U.S. corporations are the world's leaders in global R&D. According to a recent survey of the overseas R&D activities of world's largest 500 corporations, U.S. companies maintained the largest global R&D network, accounting for more than a third of all overseas laboratories.[35] The leading centers for foreign R&D investment by U.S. companies are Germany ($2.5 billion), the United Kingdom ($1.6 billion), and Canada ($1 billion). The notable exception to the pattern of aggressive U.S. foreign investment is Japan, where government barriers limited investment in R&D by American firms to just $595 million, roughly the same amount as they invested in Ireland ($573 million).[36]

Japanese companies have expanded their global R&D networks substantially in recent years and currently operate more than 200 R&D laboratories abroad. Japan's international R&D laboratories are concentrated in North America (98) and Asia (81) with a smaller number (25) located in Europe.[37] European companies, which have long operated cross-national networks in Europe, are establishing new laboratories and expanding existing ones in the United States and Japan. For example, a leading producer of electrical power systems, Asea Brown Boveri, has organized its extensive network of European laboratories along matrix lines, under which R&D projects are coordinated across laboratories in different nations, rather than being undertaken by individual laboratories.

The United States has also become the center for the global R&D explosion. Over the past decade, overseas corporations have invested more than $10 billion in 400 research and development centers in the United States. Two thirds of this spending is concentrated in three sectors: chemicals, drugs, and electronics.[38] R&D spending by foreign affiliates grew from $6.5 billion in 1987 to $11.3 billion in 1990, an increase of nearly 75 percent. Furthermore, the proportion of total U.S. R&D provided by foreign companies has grown significantly over the past few years. Foreign affiliates devote roughly 2.5 percent of sales to R&D, and 6.5 percent of value-added, comparable to spending by U.S. owned firms. The foreign share of total corporate R&D grew from roughly 9 percent in 1985 to 15.4 percent in 1990. Foreign R&D accounted for one out of every five dollars of U.S. high-technology R&D in 1990.[39]

Building a National Capacity for Innovation

These changes affect the way government intervenes in the areas of science and technology policy. Some economists, including former

Chairman of the Council of Economic Advisors Joseph Stiglitz, have come to believe that science and some aspects of technology are increasingly taking on the characteristics of what they refer to as an "international public good," a good that tends to flow across national borders and whose shared benefits are enjoyed by all. If true, this raises a series of important questions, especially about the extent to which a national government can offer sufficient incentives for investment in science and technology assets that may then flow away beyond its borders.

Globalization challenges some of most fundamental assumptions of U.S. technology policy. Foremost among these is the notion that technology policy can somehow act upon self-contained "national systems of innovation."[40] To the extent that all highly industrialized economies are tightly linked through the flow of technology, components, and services, U.S. technology policy must take into account the investments of other governments in domestic technological resources and capacity. The policy must shift to systematic concern for the quality of the U.S. workforce, the depth and breadth of new technical knowledge, the American spirit of entrepreneurship—in short, to the infrastructure for innovation and productivity that will make America the most attractive place for innovation. Thus, while the nation-state may not be the natural unit within which the system of innovation is best understood, the proper concern of public policy is for the national capacity for innovation. How the U.S. government can and should contribute to this national capacity is the primary focus of this book.

Capturing Benefits of Technology Policy for Americans

Unfortunately for the prospects of consensus technology policy, the globalization of R&D and of innovation raises very uncomfortable political questions about where the U.S. interest lies. Strong voices within both of the dominant political parties are skeptical of the advantages of open markets, lowered barriers to foreign investment, and accelerating diffusion of technical knowledge. Concerns are expressed about free-riding on U.S.-funded basic and advanced research, about the exportation of jobs when American firms invest abroad, about foreign control of U.S. R&D assets when foreign firms invest here. It is true that governments try, usually with limited success, to capture the benefits of their technology investments domestically. They erect barriers to participation in national technology programs by foreign-owned corporations, and barriers to foreign purchases of controlling interests in domestic firms seen as critical assets for national security.

However, we believe that attempts by government to manipulate the flow of benefits from public investments in R&D against the tide of global markets is both fruitless and potentially destructive. Once the innovations have been internalized in a firm, it must be free to deploy these assets in the best way it can, including the possibility that it might sell the assets to a foreign owner at some time in the future. To do otherwise abrogates to government the very market power to which those who believe in private enterprise most object. As a result, current policy seeks a reasonable and moderated response to these political concerns. Foreign-owned firms are allowed to participate in most government programs if their own governments accord similar benefits to U.S. subsidiaries in their country. Barriers to foreign direct investment have been raised only in rare cases. The American government is trying to find ways to enhance the respect for U.S. intellectual property abroad and to express concern about importation of goods produced by child or prison labor, or produced under conditions of severe environmental degradation. As the world economy becomes more open, and with the entry of former communist states into world markets and the growth of third world production, these political concerns may be expected to rise.

It will take new international understandings and perhaps institutional innovations to resist political pressures to attempt to stem the tide of globalization. A positive, investment-based strategy is the best antidote to projectionist pressures. Government should try to help U.S. firms respond to the competitive challenge of a fast-changing global marketplace and should be able to do it without meddling in domestic markets or favoring selected competitors. There does seem to be reason to believe that this investment strategy may find support on both sides of the political aisle, constrained as it is more by budget deficits than by economic ideology.

The New Role for Government in Research and Innovation

In recent years, economists have begun to revise their view on the appropriate nature and role of government involvement in science and technology. Writing in the late 1950s and early 1960s, Kenneth Arrow and Richard Nelson provided a compelling economic logic for greater government support of R&D.[41] R&D offered tremendous potential social returns, they argued, but it was often just too risky for private firms to make the required investments. Government support was required to close the gap, and to ensure that sufficient levels and types of R&D investment were undertaken.

Recent economic research on the process of technological innovation and on the government's role in support of science and technology note the importance of so-called "spillovers" of two kinds.[42] Knowledge spillovers derive from the public good nature of knowledge, combined with the difficulty of keeping economically useful knowledge secret when it is profitably exploited. Such spillovers can be derived from reverse engineering, when some aspects of a competitor's technology may be discovered by examining how his product is made. Even negative information, the abandonment of a line of work by a respected competitor, for example, can be a useful spillover of his decision.

Consumer surplus spillovers result from the creation of new goods or the improvement of existing ones. The innovator captures only part of the consumer value in the sales price; there may be a social surplus that exceeds the innovator's profit. Research tends to generate more knowledge spillovers, which is a reason for government support, but research, by itself, cannot generate consumer surplus spillovers. These come from product and process development. Private firms have inadequate incentives (to varying degrees, depending on market structure and other considerations) to take new ideas to market. Furthermore, the transfer of potentially useful ideas from the government or university sector to the private sector does not happen costlessly or automatically. For better or worse, if government or university scientists are not given any incentive to transfer their commercially useful ideas to the for-profit sector, many of these ideas will languish.

Economists who study innovation also note that there are complementarities among research, development, and human capital. A major reason firms do research is to develop the internal capability to absorb and utilize others' research.[43] The ability of a firm to appropriate knowledge spillovers to its advantage is limited by its absorptive capacity. Thus, from a public policy perspective, nations whose firms do very little research may find it difficult to appropriate the "international public goods" represented by U.S. research investments. To maximize the social return on public research investments, preference should be given to research where the spillovers to the intended beneficiaries—primarily U.S. firms—are greatest, providing the research is intrinsically promising.

Pavitt and Patel have also called attention to the importance of the institutional efficiency and creativity with which an economy responds to competitive pressures and opportunities. The economic theory prevailing in the 1960s, they argue, predicted that buoyant demand and an open trading system would allow the international (and domestic) diffusion of technology and this would lead to equalization of technological performance at the national level.[44] Pavitt and Patel argue that this prediction was based on a flawed model of science-based development and of technological change. It supposed that: a) "embodied" technical change would derive from investment in better machinery: imported machines incorporate process technology within their designs, available to all who purchase; b) "unembodied" change would arise from the relatively costless diffusion of knowledge that is codified as "information" in books, journals, drawings, patents, etc.; c) unembodied change also is assumed to be acquired as "tacit" knowledge, resulting from relatively costless "learning by doing."

If this model were equally applicable to all countries in a similar state of development, it would follow that through markets for machinery, free access to codified technical knowledge, and a rapid process of learning by doing, the gaps between the U.S. economy, and those of Japan, the U.K., Germany, and France should have closed during their recovery from World War II. It did not happen. Japan and Germany have moved ahead, while the U.K. and France have fallen behind. In three decades Taiwan, Korea, Singapore have leapt ahead from a very backward state, while Brazil, Mexico, and India have failed to do so (although they show signs of progress).

All three of those assumptions are elements of the technology diffusion process, but the efficiency of each of these processes appears to vary strongly from one institutional setting to another. Patel and Pavitt conclude that technology diffusion, productivity learning, and transfer of embodied technology are vulnerable to cultural, managerial, and institutional barriers. Thus they focused attention on the importance of investments in education, training, R&D, and efficient inter-institutional collaboration. These are the attributes of a society that Jane Fountain describes as social capital in Chapter 4.

Government efforts—which helped to create the broad institutional contours of the postwar R&D system—must now be strategically recast to inform the new institutional relationships between industry, government, and university required for a new system of research-based innovation to emerge, prosper, and flourish. The role of the extensive network of government laboratories, which consumes more than $25 billion in federal R&D spending per year, must be reexamined in light of changing economic and technological realities. The federal government must develop clear and measurable goals for innovation-based economic progress so that the private sector can gauge the effectiveness of new institutions, policies, and programs. Federal science and technology initiatives must be aligned with broader economic, trade, and regulatory policy initiative and goals. All of this must be consistent within its global context.

Outline of the Book

This book is presented in three parts. The first part explores the changing environment for technology policy. It tackles the big picture, providing insights on the key questions of technology and economic growth, the role of social capital in facilitating innovation, and appropriate measures of technology policy effectiveness. It also outlines appropriate areas for direct federal investment in scientific and technological research. Chapter 2 by Michael Borrus and Jay Stowsky shows how technology policy contributes to economic and productivity growth. In Chapter 3, Adam Jaffe discusses how to measure the effectiveness of technology policy. He concludes from his review of the models of analysis underlying current legislation that new and more effective measures are badly needed. He also advances the notion of using experimental designs to test the efficacy of technology policy interventions. Chapter 4 by Jane Fountain explores the role of social capital in innovation and technology policy. Social capital describes the capacity of individuals and economic institutions to innovate with high levels of productivity. Key attributes of social capital include "trust, norms, and networks that can improve the efficiency of society by facilitating coordinated actions."[45] The last chapter in this first part, written by Lewis Branscomb, explores the nature of scientific and technological research and the opportunities it presents for federal investment. Branscomb argues that technological research often includes work that is fundamental and precompetitive in the same way that basic scientific research can be, and that what the nation needs is not a "technology policy" to go with its science policy, but a more broadly defined "research policy" that provides knowledge and skills to support a policy for promoting innovation.

The second part of the book assesses seven specific technology programs promoted by the Clinton-Gore administration. In Chapter 6, Christopher Hill reviews the history and current controversies surrounding the Advanced Technology Program (ATP) in the National Institute for Standards and Technology. Hill describes the need and justification for this program, and recommends a series of steps that would strengthen and expand it. Linda Cohen, in Chapter 7, examines the Technology Reinvestment Project (TRP) and its successor, the Dual-Use Applications Program (DUAP), which embodies the Defense Department's new approach to acquiring technology for military use through collaboration with commercial firms in research leading to dual-use applications, those with both commercial and government markets. Cohen identifies a number of institutional factors in the defense department and in industry that have presented barriers to the TRP program goals and concludes with recommendations on other means of achieving TRP dual-use objectives.

In Chapter 8, Scott Wallsten reviews the role of the federal government's Small Business Innovation Research Program (SBIR), which supports commercial R&D among small firms through an obligatory set-aside of agency R&D appropriations. His review of

SBIR suggests that there may be more effective ways to stimulate small firm innovation. David Guston examines the effectiveness of Cooperative Research and Development Agreements (CRADAs) as a technology transfer strategy in Chapter 9. He focuses primarily on the industry cooperation agreements formed at the National Institutes of Health and identifies areas of opportunity for maximizing CRADA effectiveness as a technology transfer tool. Philip Shapira, in Chapter 10, looks at the record and achievements of federal efforts to spur manufacturing modernization through the use of the manufacturing extension centers, funded by NIST as the Manufacturing Extension Partnership (MEP) with state governments. This effort is viewed by many as the most successful of the Clinton administration programs. Shapira finds that the centers are indeed effective and concludes that the administration might consider expanding their missions to include a variety of economic goals.

Chapter 11, authored by George Heaton and Darryl Banks, reviews the intriguing issue of technology policy for the environment. In recent years, sophisticated analysts of environmental policy have increasingly concluded that reliance on sanctions for violation of regulatory pollution limits should be supplemented, and to a degree supplanted, by new approaches that leverage process innovation so as to reduce effluents while sustaining or even increasing productivity. Heaton and Banks chronicle the record of the Clinton-Gore Environmental Technology Initiative (ETI) and discuss the importance of an environmental technology strategy, and the reduction of legislative and other barriers to environmentally beneficial industrial innovation. In Chapter 12, John Holdren argues for the critical importance of the federal role in energy R&D and decries the minimal attention and support it has received from the federal government in the recent years.

The third and final part of the book turns to policy tools and institutions in the American system of innovation. In Chapter 13, Brian Kahin explores the history of the administration's information infrastructure initiatives. Information and communications technology issues illustrate the importance of using the broad spectrum of policy tools that, if thoughtfully applied in a coordinated manner, can leverage private investment to enhance national innovative capability and productivity. Kahin reflects on the experience of the first Clinton term and the new challenges information infrastructure presents as an area of technology policy. He recommends priorities for the continued advancement of the Internet as a powerful vehicle for competition and growth. Harvey Brooks and Lucien Randazzese, in Chapter 14, review the experience of university-industry cooperation, encouraged over the past decade or so by government policy in the expectations of returns to the U.S. economy. The authors discuss those expectations as well as the effect that these relationships tend to have on the universities as scholarly institutions. The chapter suggests policy measures designed both to preserve the strengths of the university system and to benefit technological advance and economic growth.

Industry is the key player in the advance of technology, and a key message of this book is that technology policy must take differences among industry sectors into account. This critical issue is picked up in Chapter 15, by Daniel Roos, Frank Field, and James Neely, who explore the role of industry-level analysis in the development of technology programs and consortia. Other key issues are the appropriate division of responsibility between the federal government and the states, and the best coordinating mechanisms, and Chapter 16, by Christopher Coburn and Duncan Brown, explores these questions and the opportunities for the U.S. Innovation Partnership (USIP). This federal-state coordinating body is managed for the president by the Commerce Department's Technology Administration (TA) and for the states by the National Governors' Association (NGA). The creation of USIP is an achievement of the administration acting on the advice of the State-Federal Technology Partnership Task Force.[46] Chapter 17, by David Hart, tackles the difficult questions surrounding the way the Executive Office of the President (EOP) is structured to provide and coordinate national policies for which science and technology policy are important inputs. In his review of policy-making mechanisms, Hart examines not only the OSTP and the National Science and Technology Council but also the key White House policy bodies that deal with economic, domestic, and security issues that should be informed by technology policy. Hart suggests that additional resources for analysis and industry input and stronger linkages to other major areas of policy development including security and economic policy, are needed.

The concluding chapter, by Lewis Branscomb and James Keller, provides a summary of key findings and outlines a series of principles and policy guidelines for the future.

Notes

1. Popularly, but erroneously, remembered as "It's the economy, stupid," the sign actually had four messages: "Change vs. More of the same," "the economy, stupid," "don't forget health care," and "the debates, stupid." See the final frames of the documentary motion picture *The War Room* (October Films, 1993).

2. William J. Clinton and Albert Gore Jr., "Technology for America's Economic Growth, A New Direction to Build Economic Strength" (Washington, D.C.: White House, February 22, 1993), p. 1.

3. The Clinton-Gore program proposals were almost all extensions or expansions of programs already initiated by the Congress and approved by President Bush. This fact left many Democrats unprepared for the Republican opposition that was mobilized in 1995.

4. The acronym TRP is often interpreted as the "Technology Reinvestment Program" and, occasionally, as the "Technology Reinvestment Partnership." The proper name of the program is the "Technology Reinvestment *Project.*"

5. In fact, the administration's FY 1998 budget for outlays, as submitted to Congress, has 53.9 percent devoted to defense and nuclear weapons, which represents significant progress toward the 50 percent goal, but much of this was achieved through defense cuts, rather than civil increases. On the civil side, the growth has been in health research, not in R&D devoted to economic growth. *Physics Today*, April 1997, p. 47.

6. Allan Bromley, *The U.S. Technology Policy* (Washington, D.C.: The Executive Office of the President, September 26, 1990).

7. The history of the ATP program is discussed in some detail in Chapter 6.

8. An analysis of the 1993 Clinton-Gore policy statement, "Technology for America's Economic Growth," made at the time pointed out many of the political pitfalls inherent in the new commercially oriented policy, but did not foresee the strength of the Republican opposition that emerged in 1994. Lewis M. Branscomb, ed., *Empowering Technology: Implementing a Technology Policy* (Cambridge, Mass.: The MIT Press, 1993).

9. Clinton and Gore Jr., "Technology for America's Economic Growth," p. 4.

10. In 1960 the U.S. Department of Defense funded one-third of all R&D in the Western world. This investment comprised about 80 percent of all federal R&D

spending. John Alic, Lewis M. Branscomb, Harvey Brooks, Ashton B. Carter, and Gerald Epstein, *Beyond Spinoff: Military and Commercial Technologies in a Changing World* (Boston: Harvard Business School Press, 1992), p. 5.

11. Bruce L.R. Smith, *American Science Policy Since World War II* (Washington, D.C.: Brookings Institution, 1990), pp. 48–52, and 164–166.

12. Branscomb, *Empowering Technology*, p. 65.

13. "The magnitude of the problem is such that we cannot rely upon normal forces to maintain our advantage in technology. We are at the forefront in many technological areas. The costs of breaking new ground in some of these areas are high—higher than private companies or perhaps even private consortia are able to justify because the risks are so great. We have recognized this fact in space, defense, and atomic energy areas. Other trading nations have recognized it in the area of civilian R&D and have taken steps to assist technological development. If we are to maintain our advantages in this area we must first of all accept the idea that it has become a proper sphere of governmental action." Maurice Stans, Hearing of the House of Representatives Committee on Science and Astronautics on "Science, Technology, and the Economy" (Washington, D.C., U.S. Government Printing Office [U.S. GPO], July 27–29, 1971), p. 17; quoted in Harvey Brooks, "What's Happening to the U.S. Lead in Technology?" *Harvard Business Review*, May–June 1972.

14. *Public Papers of the Presidents of the United States: Jimmy Carter 1979, Book II, June 23–December 31, 1979* (Washington, D.C.: U.S. GPO, 1980), pp. 2068–2974.

15. Ever since, economists have debated the meaning of "competitiveness" as applied to nations rather than to firms. In technology policy debates, competitiveness has come to mean the ability of the economy to sustain full employment and stable or rising personal incomes in a global system of open trading. See Cal Clark and Danny Lam, "The Competitiveness Debate," *Business and the Contemporary World*, Vol. 7, No. 2 (1995), pp. 12–27.

16. The principles advocated by Vannevar Bush in *Science, the Endless Frontier* (Washington, D.C.: Office of Scientific Research and Development, July 1945; repr. National Science Foundation, 1960, 1980, 1990) were given specific form in John R. Steelman, Chairman, President's Scientific Research Board, *Science and Public Policy: Administration for Research*, 3 vols., (U.S. G.P.O, 1947), Vol. 1, p. 26, usually referred to as the "Steelman Report." President Eisenhower ordered these recommendations to be carried out in Executive Order 10521, March 17, 1954.

17. Lewis M. Branscomb, "America's Emerging Technology Policy," *Minerva*, Vol. 30, No. 3 (Autumn, 1992), pp. 317–336.

18. Mission-oriented policy features heavy government investment in advanced technologies supporting government program commitments in space and defense as a stimulus to industrial innovation, while diffusion-oriented policy features investments to expand the utilization of technology throughout the economy. Henry Ergas, "Does Technology Policy Matter?" in Bruce R. Guile and

Harvey Brooks, *Technology and Global Industry: Companies and Nations in the World Economy* (Washington, D.C.: National Academy Press, 1987), p. 192.

19. Ralph Gomory, "From the 'Ladder of Science' to the Product Development Cycle," *Harvard Business Review*, November–December 1989, pp. 99–105.

20. Alic, Branscomb, Brooks, Carter, and Epstein, *Beyond Spinoff.*

21. This somewhat curious proposal was intended to strengthen the Commerce Department's role in competitiveness by gathering together under its roof most of the elements of trade policy, but it would have removed from the department its capability to understand industrial technology. It would thus have been a pale copy of Japan's Ministry of International Trade and Industry (MITI) despite the fact that the proposed name, DITI, seemed intended to call MITI to mind.

22. Michael L. Dertouzos, Richard K. Lester, and Robert M. Solow, *Made in America: Regaining the Productive Edge* (Cambridge, Mass.: The MIT Press, 1989).

23. Lewis M. Branscomb, "Targeting Critical Technologies." in Branscomb, ed., *Empowering Technology*, chap. 2, pp. 36–63.

24. Branscomb "Empowering Technology Policy," chap. 9 in *Empowering Technology*, pp. 266–294.

25. Richard Nelson, ed., *National Innovation Systems: a Comparative Analysis* (New York: Oxford University Press, 1993).

26. National Science Board, *Science and Engineering Indicators 1993* (Washington, D.C.: National Science Foundation, 1994).

27. Ibid.

28. Ibid.

29. Wesley Cohen, Richard Florida, and W. Richard Goe, "University-Industry Research Centers in the United States," Carnegie Mellon University, Pittsburgh, July 1994. An initial survey was sent to all 437 universities and colleges that were recipients of industry-sponsored research between 1981 and 1988; it identified 1,056 university-industry research centers. A second, more detailed survey was sent to all 1,056 university-industry research centers, generating 511 responses, for an adjusted response rate of 48.4 percent.

30. The Industrial Research Institute (IRI) sent questionnaires to the official representatives of 253 IRI members in the United States. The survey generated responses from 158 companies for a response rate of 62 percent.

31. Edward Roberts surveyed 244 global firms that perform approximately 80 percent of worldwide R&D. Completed surveys were provided by 95 firms, of which 46 were from the United States, 27 were from Europe, and 22 were from Japan. The response from German firms was low; the remaining Western European companies, however, had an overall response rate of 51 percent. Edward Roberts, "Strategic Benchmarking of Technology," Sloan School of Management, MIT, Cambridge, Mass., 1994.

32. Ibid.

33. United Nations Division on Transnational Corporations and Investment, *World Investment Report 1995, Transnational Corporations and Competitiveness* (New York: United Nations, 1995.

34. Donald Dalton and Manuel Serapio, *Globalizing Industrial Research and Development* (Washington, D.C.: U.S. Department of Commerce, Office of Technology Policy, 1995). Also see Richard Florida, "The Globalization of R&D: Foreign-Affiliated Laboratories in the U.S.," *Research Policy,* Vol. 26 (1997), pp. 85–103.

35. Robert D. Pearce and Satwinder Singh, *Globalizing Research and Development* (New York: St. Martin's Press, 1992).

36. Dalton and Serapio, *Globalizing Industrial Research and Development.*

37. MITI, *Fourth Annual Survey on Japanese Overseas Activities* (Tokyo: MITI, 1994).

38. In 1990, foreign R&D affiliates accounted for 58.9 percent of industrial chemical R&D, 42 percent of pharmaceutical R&D, and 7–10 percent of the R&D in consumer electronics, in computers and office equipment, and in electronic components. Dalton and Serapio, *Globalizing Industrial Research and Development.*

39. Ibid.

40. Nelson, *National Innovation Systems.*

41. Kenneth J. Arrow, "Economic welfare and the allocation of resources for invention," in *The Rate and Direction of Inventive Activity: Economic and Social Factors, A Report of the National Bureau of Economic Research* (Princeton, N.J.: Princeton University Press, 1962). Richard R. Nelson, "The simple economics of basic research," *Journal of Political Economy,* Vol. 67 (1959), pp. 297–306.

42. We are indebted to Adam Jaffe of Brandeis University for his contributions to this discussion of spillovers.

43. Wesley M. Cohen, and Daniel A. Levinthal, "Innovation and Learning: The Two faces of R&D," *The Economic Journal,* Vol. 99, No. 397, 1989, pp. 569–596.

44. Pari Patel and Keith Pavitt, "The Nature and Economic Importance of National Innovation Systems," *STI Review,* No. 14 (1994), pp. 9–32.

45. Robert Putnam, *Making Democracy Work: Civic Traditions in Modern Italy* (Princeton, N.J.: Princeton University Press, 1993), p. 167.

46. *The State-Federal Technology Policy Task Force—Final Report,* September 5, 1995.

2
Technology Policy and Economic Growth

Michael Borrus and Jay Stowsky

Technology policy is obscured in deep shadow: the idea America preaches is to let the market decide industrial fortunes, but a half century of government sponsorship of new technology industries from jet aircraft to electronics and biotechnology suggests a different reality. Unacknowledged U.S. practice often contradicts what is preached, and does so to enormous economic benefit. With the cover of the Cold War gone, it is time to move technology policy into the light—not to the patchy fluorescence of Bill Clinton's first term, but to the bright spot of center-stage. In what follows, we suggest why and how this should be done.

Technology and Productivity

A nation's standard of living is the most significant indicator of its economic performance. Productivity growth (the rate of growth in output per unit of input, usually output per worker), income distribution, and the unemployment rate are the three variables that most directly affect the standard of living of large numbers of people.[1] Over the past several decades, the United States has been doing especially poorly on productivity growth and income equality compared to its past domestic performance, to the performance of the major economies of Europe and Asia, and to what our own resources ought to permit. Relative to these indicators, U.S. performance remains poor even after five straight years of reasonable economic growth, despite the widely held perception that America's mid-1980s problems with competitiveness have been solved. While many U.S.-owned firms are indeed prospering again on world markets, the nation's long-run economic prospects remain troubled. Persistent income inequality and slow productivity growth threaten to undermine the nation's relative standard of living and ultimately its political influence abroad, while setting the stage for domestic social unrest.[2]

Essentially all economists agree that productivity growth is the key to doing better over the long term, but they can neither explain why productivity growth has slowed in the United States nor what to do to make it grow faster.[3] Most would agree that the answer lies in some combination of a higher level and an altered composition of investment—investment in capital formation (including infrastructure), in people (including training and education), and in technical progress (including new technologies and corresponding new ways of organizing industrial activities). Of these variables, better technology is usually deemed the most significant. Even economists skeptical about technology policy admit that "technological progress is a vital source of economic growth and R&D a vital source of technological progress."[4] According to the widely cited growth-accounting literature, traditional factor inputs like capital and labor cannot account for at least one-quarter and perhaps as much as one-half of the total U.S. growth rate since the end of World War II. This large residual is attributable to advances in technical know-how.[5]

Other strands of the economics literature also emphasize the relationship of technological progress to economic performance. "New growth theory" emphasizes that the rate of economic growth is driven by the total stock of human capital: the collection of knowledge or innovative "ideas" held at any one time by people in businesses, universities, and governments. This approach contends that new ideas are the source of growth because they lead to technological innovation and hence to productivity improvements. Thus, if too few resources are dedicated to education and scientific research and development (which both increase the stock of human capital or new ideas), then the rate of economic growth will be lower than it could be.[6]

Compounded over generations, a 1 or 2 percent reduction in the overall growth rate could be the difference between the standard of living merely doubling or surging five-fold over a hundred-year period. For countries with similar standards of living today, small differences in the rate of growth could lead to very different economic outcomes in the future. In addition, studies by economic historians and theorists of increasing marginal returns suggest that, once an economy sets out on a high-growth or low-growth path, both high growth and low growth may be self-reinforcing over time.[7] For example, Argentina and the United States had roughly similar levels of economic performance during the 1860s, but the United States managed to launch itself on a high-growth path while Argentina became mired in low growth which reinforced itself over time. Thus, rather than try to evolve from low growth to high growth through rapid industrialization—a strategy which would typically focus on the development of basic industries and a capacity for low-cost mass production—a relatively poorer country might do better to invest resources in higher education and high-tech R&D—that is, try to jump quickly onto a high-growth path. Indeed, that appears to be the new strategic focus of developmental strategies in emerging Asian economies such as Malaysia, the region around India's Bangalore, and the coastal provinces of mainland China.

Finally, a recent review of efforts to measure the rates of return on investments in new technology in a variety of industries found that the private rates of return to firms performing R&D often vary from 20 to 30 percent. In comparison, the average rate of return to investment in the business sector as a whole is about 10 percent. Estimated rates of return from R&D to society as a whole, due to beneficial spillovers to consumers and to other firms from an initial R&D investment, vary from 20 percent to well over 100 percent in a variety of industries, with an average near 50 percent.[8] The channels of diffusion of the spillovers vary considerably, and their effects on productivity growth are sizable. These results also suggest that private firms may substantially under-invest in R&D because they can not internalize the significant returns that would accrue to others, including competitors.

In sum, various economic approaches that use disparate methods all acknowledge a strong link between advances in knowledge, technical progress, and long-term growth in productivity and gross domestic product (GDP). There is also general consensus that high rates of investment in broad-based R&D across a wide technical frontier are essential, and that a modern technical infrastructure and a skilled, technically competent work force are crucial complements to achieving sustained productivity growth.

Beyond the consensus on goals, however, economists do not agree on how to craft policies to meet these goals. First, there is broad disagreement about the composition of investment, whether public or private. There is no consensus about what the proper balance of investment ought to be between industry, government, and academia. There is no agreement about whether government's role should include direct R&D dollars or be limited to investment incentives for private R&D spending (as with R&D tax credits). There is no agreement about whether public funding should be limited to cases of private market failure (as when private returns to R&D spending are small relative to social returns, providing little incentive for investment by private market actors), or if it should include a focus on government missions (e.g., defense) and social needs (e.g., health).

Second, there is substantial contention over whether on balance new technologies create or displace jobs. The evidence is highly contingent on which period is studied, but the bulk of the evidence suggests that over the long term, new technologies are capital saving, require the labor force to become more skilled, and thus create more challenging, higher paying jobs.[9] In general, economists presume that new technology will generate more jobs than it eliminates, as it leads to new products and services, lower prices, and expanded markets. Unfortunately, there may be prolonged lags between job losses and new job creation, and the new jobs may not be appropriate for those displaced by technological change. In that adjustment process, income inequality can be greatly exacerbated. For example, the Industrial Revolution in Great Britain eventually produced a large and unprecedented middle class, but only after creating a decline in the real wages of most workers—and tremendous resistance to change—during its first half-century. The consensus answer to the time lag problem— and it is the Clinton administration's answer as well— is that the compensating demand effects that offset job loss from technological change come more quickly when overall economic growth is strong and when markets for both labor and capital are flexible. Government can help by avoiding recessions and making workers more adaptable through improvements in education and training.

Third, although there is basic agreement that the vast bulk of social benefits from technology flow from its application and widespread diffusion, it is unclear whether an economy the size of the U.S. economy must be a leading-edge producer of a new product or a new piece of production equipment in order to reap the full benefits from its use. Technology policy proponents typically argue that the initial establishment of a dominant position in markets for an advanced technology can lock in control of a long stream of follow-on product and process innovations, making market entry much harder for technology "followers." This locked-in position constitutes what game theorists and business analysts refer to as a "first-mover advantage." This means that a temporary market advantage can turn into a more enduring technological advantage. A more conventional argument holds that it might actually be to the economic advantage of manufacturers to be *second*: to absorb the spillovers from investments made initially by competitors (foreign or domestic), and thus start production further along the technological learning curve. In practice, there are good examples of both strategies succeeding (and failing).

Such issues are likely to remain unsettled. For the foreseeable future, there is no algorithm or formula that can identify the best balance of choices and optimize the economic returns. Where one stands is ultimately a normative judgment about the role of government, the virtue of certain ends, and the relative efficacy of different means. Thus, the current debate pits both conservatives, who oppose an aggressive technology policy as too interventionist, and liberals, who think government should intervene to serve different ends, against various groups of so-called moderates, economic nationalists, and self-interested industry trade associations who favor it.

These political stances should not be permitted to obscure the real stakes in the debate over technology policy. In light of the probably central role technical progress plays in long-term economic performance, much is at risk if either the conservatives' hands-off prescriptions are followed or liberals do not include technological development among the objectives for which they believe government should intervene in the economy. If such intervention is either forbidden outright or simply sloughed off in favor of other worthy goals, we will risk a significant sacrifice of opportunities for long-term national economic growth and productivity advance. We will risk, that is, a permanent inability to extract ourselves from precisely the conditions we are now experiencing.

There is surely cause for long-term concern. Both Europe and Japan project significant increases in civilian R&D over the next few years, with Japan proposing to double R&D spending between 1995 and the year 2000. U.S. spending, particularly federal spending, may be headed in the opposite direction. Recent proposals, from both Congress and the president would cut federal R&D spending between 10 and 30 percent over the next seven years. Other proposals would skew federal spending toward basic R&D while eschewing an active technology policy. The United States could enter the next century spending less on technological innovation than its major competitors—less in absolute dollars as well as in percentage of GDP—for the first time in the postwar era.[10]

Picking Winners and Losers

The public debate on technology policy is typically truncated into the issue of "picking winners and losers," leading to two facile conclusions: first, that markets do that most effectively; and second, that porkbarrel politics is more likely to support the losers anyway. This neat two-step eliminates from the role of technology policy everything for which government is institutionally well-suited, from infrastructure building and investment incentives to support of skills training. It then notes that what is left is, of course, institutionally more appropriate for the market. The argument is legitimated simultaneously by our ancient faith in markets and our recent cynicism about politics.

In fact, however, even accepting the critics' definition of the issue, there are limiting cases in which the reductionist conclusion about picking winners and losers is not defensible. The most important is the development of new technologies, for which markets are not entirely adequate institutions. As previously noted, empirical evidence suggests that as a result of spillovers of all kinds, the social returns to R&D spending on new technologies far exceed the private returns, perhaps by as much as 50 to 100 percent.[11] Appropriability problems lead to over-investment in some technologies and under-investment in others relative to the social optimum.[12]

Markets also deal inadequately with technological progress because of the highly contingent nature of innovation. Rather than being preordained by scientific logic, technology development is contingent upon the actions of developers, producers and users, as they perform their respective roles, interact, and accrue different kinds of know-how over time. The contingent nature of technical progress means that perfect information is impossible; neither innovators nor the private capital markets that fund them are fully capable of accurately evaluating the risks involved. Therefore, private capital markets and innovators alike inevitably misallocate their investment and effort. Some bets will pay off big; some not at all. Winners and losers can only be positively identified in the revealing gaze of hindsight.

This is as true for private as for public investment. For every Apple Macintosh there are normally several Altairs and Amigas. For every IBM there are several GEs and RCAs whose technological bets on mainframe computers failed to pay off. For every Intel there are defunct Molectros and AMEs. For every winner in a venture portfolio, there are untold losers that get nowhere near the publicity. Indeed, there is absolutely no evidence, beyond the economist's leap of faith, that private investment is any more capable than public investment of separating the winners from the losers before the fact. The major difference is that private losers exit the market, while publicly backed losers are held to the higher standard of wasting taxpayers' money.

In short, picking winners and losers is the wrong metaphor to characterize the government's socially useful and necessary activity of supporting the process of innovation. Government is actually placing bets on our collective future. From the public standpoint, the magnitude of the potential social gains is sufficiently large to provide a comfortable margin for error in choosing among technologies to back.[13]

The Case in Favor

The case against aggressive technology policy thus falls short of damning a significant government role in support of new technology development. But this does not by itself justify government support. Two related rationales, one political and the other economic, accomplish that. First, the government is a significant consumer of technology as it provides for our common needs. In areas ranging from national defense to infrastructure, the government must open taxpayers' wallets to get the technology it needs. Very often that means sponsoring research and procurement that launch new industrial capabilities.

As consumer, the government's demands are usually determined through the political process rather than the market. Those who acknowledge all of the flaws of politics but none of the market are extremely leery of this. They dismiss it by labeling it porkbarrel politics.[14] To be sure, this process can involve substantial time-honored earmarking of public funds to favored projects in favored Congressional districts, with little regard for overall social benefits. As we discuss below, however, it can also be organized in ways that limit earmarking and maximize the likelihood for public gain. As a process in its own right, American politics may fail to satisfy the economist's dream of perfect efficiency, but the government can hardly fail to respond to constituents' demands.

It is quite possible that politics does effectively what the market does not, namely aggregate the demand of numerous dispersed customers (citizens) who would otherwise have no other way of expressing their collective influence over technological development. In that way, a broader portfolio of socially useful technologies is undoubtedly explored and screened than the market would ever normally permit. Those who see this process as porkbarrel are often lamenting not the economic inefficiency but the lack of expert influence.

The pure economic case in favor of public support for new technologies must rest on the disproportionate importance to economic well-being of high-tech industries that produce substantial domestic value-added. Industries may be strategic for economic welfare in at least three ways: they may contribute a major share of the technological progress that is central to long-term growth; they may provide a higher return to factors of production than could be earned elsewhere in the economy; or they may provide externalities like technological spillovers that broadly benefit the rest of the economy.[15] High-tech industries do all three. First, as suppliers of producer goods (and service inputs), high-tech industries are primary carriers of technological progress. Second, high-tech industries fund a disproportionate amount of industrial R&D, offering innovations that pervasively spill over to the economy as a whole.[16] In the early 1990s, high-technology industries accounted for only about 20 percent of the nation's manufacturing output and 24 percent of its manufacturing value-added, but nearly 60 percent of its private industrial R&D. Third, high-technology industries are high-productivity industries that pay higher compensation than other manufacturing industries. By the early 1990s, value-added per worker in all high-technology industries was one-third higher than the average for all manufacturing, and two-thirds higher if only production workers are included. These differentials are significant and persistent.[17] In short, the production of a dollar's worth of silicon chips really is more important than that of potato chips for many principal determinants of economic well-being such as wages, skill formation, productivity, investment, and R&D.

Equally important, the pervasive economic and technological spillovers generated by high-tech industries appear mostly to accrue locally: domestic production is necessary if the nation is to enjoy many of their economic benefits. While some technical knowledge is footloose—embodied in products, blueprints, or open technical forums like published research—much is generated only in the processes of development and production. That kind of technical knowledge accumulates in specialized local assets like labor pools and supplier networks. It is embodied in them and does not diffuse easily.

When U.S. personal computer assemblers go to Taiwan for design and development of notebook computers, when U.S. disc drive assemblers go to Singapore for processes and volume manufacturing, when IBM moves microsystem development out of the United States to Japan, they are seeking access to such specialized and local know-how in components and microsystems design, processes, and manufacturing. Such domestic capabilities are the probable basis for product differentiation and new technology generation. They help to attract footloose technological know-how originating abroad, and ensure that it can be exploited domestically. In other words, without such domestic capabilities, an economy has no enduring potential to operate at the technological frontier, with all that this implies for maintaining national well-being.

This localization of technology's economic benefits is strongly reinforced by the imperfect nature of technological competition. Modern high-technology markets are characterized by extreme scale economies, oligopoly, persistent entry barriers, and often, strong first-mover advantages. Firms or nations that establish an initial advantage—whether through private competence or government support—can enjoy those advantages long enough for the economic benefits to accrue domestically rather than abroad. This happened with Japan's concerted efforts to dominate semiconductor memory and display technologies, and Europe's Airbus program.

A bigger national share of global high-tech output can thus mean a bigger share of good jobs and a higher level of economic well-being at the expense of others. That is why international competition in technology-intensive industries often generates beggar-thy-neighbor trade disputes. An aggressive technology policy that aims at sponsoring the development and launch of new technology industries may be a necessity for the United States merely to counter the efforts of other nations both to eliminate U.S. technological leadership and to force U.S. firms to remove domestic capabilities from the domestic economy and transplant them abroad.

What Works and What Does Not

How effective has the U.S. government's sponsorship of new technologies been? In the postwar period, federal support to new technology crystallized around defense, the development of nuclear energy, and later space exploration. The spending model was premised on the belief that pouring investments in to science at the front end of the development pipeline would produce technology out the other end. Public spending supported the enormous development costs of relevant new technologies. Initial applications were developed for and procured by the military, and later "spun off" into commercial use.[18] For example, U.S. defense spending promoted the rapid development of jet aircraft and engines, silicon chips, computers and operating systems, complex machine tools, data networks, data compression, optoelectronics, and advanced ceramic and composite materials.

In these cases, government underwrote the relevant basic science research at universities and labs; direct R&D contracts accelerated the development of the technology; and defense procurement at premium prices constituted a highly effective initial launch market. Very often, the military funded varied technological approaches to the same goals, prudently spreading its bets under conditions of uncertainty. The successful approaches were judged according to strict cost-performance criteria, and then were launched through procurement and strongly supported. A variety of mechanisms, ranging from patent pooling and hardware leasing (such as machine tool pools) to loan guarantees for building production facilities, helped to lower entry costs, diffused technology widely among competitors, and set the stage for commercial market penetration. Aspects of this support model were adapted for government investment in other sectors, notably for public health, and produced similarly beneficial results in the form of new drugs, diagnostics, medical equipment, and biotechnologies.

The overall key to the successful cases of government sponsorship was the successful launch and diffusion of a technology development path—a trajectory—whose characteristics corresponded to the requirements of the commercial marketplace. For example, when the military pushed silicon chips toward high reliability, miniaturization, high performance, and low costs, it was helping to create a trajectory that the commercial computer industry could ride. Similarly, when it turned to the national community of scientists and engineers in their roles as users to define the characteristics for the ARPANet, the Defense Department was launching a data networking trajectory that would also meet that community's commercial needs, as the ARPANet metamorphosed into today's Internet.

The historical experience strongly suggests that the U.S. government's direct R&D sponsorship has often been far less important for commercial success than has its support for diffusion and use. Its procurement of new technologies and other indirect supports for application launched fledgling technologies and helped to diffuse them into widespread use. Although some of the winners generally credit their parallel civilian R&D efforts for the relevant technological advances, they all acknowledge the benefit of procurement, of know-how spilling over from defense R&D, of defense funding of graduate education and research in the relevant technical disciplines, of funding of prototype systems that demonstrated the efficacy of new technologies, and of the variety of other mechanisms that supported diffusion and use.

The strategy of public support was not a simple stepchild of the technological successes of World War II. Indeed, before the recent ideological purity set in, the U.S. government was occasionally an active public risk-taker. For example, government support to aeronautics began in earnest with the creation of NASA's precursor, the National Advisory Commission on Aeronautics (NACA). NACA was a vital source of the R&D and testing during the 1920s and 30s that led to the modern passenger airliner. Similarly, RCA grew out of Woodrow Wilson's concern that British dominance of radio technology would limit America's commercial rise, and was created to establish a commercial U.S. presence in radio.[19] With the guarantee of Navy contracts providing R&D funding, the launch market, and the lure, RCA was formed as a patent-pooling consortium among the Navy, GE, and eventually AT&T, Westinghouse, and United Fruit.

However, the most elaborate and arguably most successful U.S. program of public support to commercial innovation is the Agricultural Research and Extension System, a network of interdependent institutions from the federal to the local level, including land-grant colleges, the state experiment stations, and research and extension services.[20] Dating from the Morrill Act in 1862, the evolving system has provided focused education and training, long-term R&D, and widespread diffusion of new technology to America's farms. Although not without controversy—e.g., over its neglect of organic farming and pest-control methods—it is still widely credited with a major role in making American agriculture the world's most productive.

While such successes are suggestive, there is as much to learn from the failures. These include outright flops like the supersonic transport (SST), synfuel plants, and the fast breeder reactor, as well as more ambiguous cases like the development of photovoltaics or numerical control (NC) for machine tools. For example, the Air Force sponsored the development of NC technology for machine tools to build advanced aircraft. The programming language proved too complex for general commercial use; diffusion was slow and civilian application costly. The resulting technological development path produced only a commercially vulnerable U.S. industry that was squeezed by Japanese competitors from the low end and German firms from the high.[21] Similarly, the supersonic transport failed because the commercial airliner market was aiming at short-haul and wide-body aircraft rather than supersonic speeds.[22] The fast breeder reactor and synfuel programs were far more expensive than commercial alternatives, particularly after the oil shocks abated. In each case there were problems of both conception and execution: performance objectives were narrowly construed and alternative technological paths were not sufficiently explored. Demonstrations and pilots proceeded despite experimental evidence of failure. In some cases, like photovoltaics, political considerations killed development prematurely.

Public support to technology thus runs into trouble mostly when it pursues development paths that diverge from commercial market cost-performance requirements, particularly when it over-specifies an exotic technical solution in the form of a particular product.[23] Thus, the first requirement of government technology development is that it must be sensitive to the needs of commercial market diffusion, like the need for manufacturability of designs or for customer-defined cost and performance. Second, it must support multiple experimental approaches to achieve cost-performance goals, letting the specific technical solution emerge from the resulting competition. Such requirements should not be difficult to build in to future programs, particularly if the public risk is shared jointly with private investment, as it has been with more recent forays into industrial policy like SEMATECH, the semiconductor industry's manufacturing technology program.

Technology Policy during the First Clinton Administration

The Clinton administration came into office committed to an aggressive technology policy in the service of long-run economic growth. The scope and ambition of the effort, if not the rhetoric defending it, were soon scaled back in deference to the growing popularity of efforts to eliminate the federal budget deficit. [24] Many of the Clinton administration's higher-profile technology efforts had actually been launched by a reluctant Bush administration under pressure from the Congress. Nevertheless, even though, as expected, the new administration gave the initiatives more resources and more public exposure, the combined efforts continued to represent a minuscule claim on the federal R&D budget. In fiscal 1994, when Democrats still controlled both the Congress and the White House, the technology initiatives taken over or launched by the Clinton administration accounted for less than $3 billion (roughly 4 percent) out of a total federal R&D budget of $71 billion. Defense ($38.3 billion), NIH ($10.4 billion), and NASA ($9.4 billion) retained the largest share of federal R&D spending in their traditional programs. [25] Despite the creation of two overarching policy coordination councils at the White House—the National Economic Council (NEC) and the National Science and Technology Council (NSTC)—it has been difficult for the Clinton administration to graft its expanded agenda for technology policy onto entrenched prerogatives of the traditional agency-based R&D programs. And as David Hart implies (Chapter 17), this persistent difficulty has undermined the effectiveness of the administration's overall efforts.

As the Clinton administration's technology investment strategy was put in place early in 1993, policy designers consciously attempted to prevent new instances of "government failure"—the public sector analog of the market failures these projects were trying to correct—by building several programmatic features into the projects to ensure that they would not dampen market signals. First, to avoid backing the wrong technologies, the Clinton technology initiatives relied on industry to participate in the design of the research agenda for each project. This ensured that project awards would target technologies that were also thought likely to be commercially viable once technical bottlenecks were overcome.

Second, investments were made in an array of technical fields to ensure that the champions of any particular technology or industry did not exercise undue influence. The programs also required grant applicants to compete in teams (e.g., defense and commercial firms with universities or government labs) for a finite flow of federal funds. The competitions were to be judged on technical and economic criteria by a panel of government technical experts or by some other independent peer-review process. Applicants were typically required to provide evidence that the technology at hand could be commercially sustained within five years without further federal funding.

Third, to prevent the subsidies from reducing the efficiency-inducing effects of competition, private sector participants were required to cover at least 50 percent of the project's costs. (Later, to make it easier for small companies to participate, companies were allowed to use federal funds from other government programs, such as Small Business Innovation Research grants, to pay for part of their "cost share.") To prevent the creation of technology pork barrels, government program managers were committed at the outset to rigorous program evaluations and could typically make only time-limited grants. Technical milestones and other performance metrics were established up front. It was also felt that the 50 percent matching requirement would make private sector partners eager to abandon technological approaches that were not working.

After four years, the various Clinton technology initiatives have demonstrated progress: as documented in the chapters by Christopher Hill (Chapter 6), David Guston (Chapter 9), and Philip Shapira (Chapter 10), the Clinton efforts have fostered new industry-led R&D partnerships in a number of technical fields and have encouraged defense and commercial firms to work together on the commercial development of a number of military-relevant technologies. By playing midwife to consortia or teams of companies, universities, and national labs, these initiatives appear to be facilitating more rapid technology transfer and innovation, though at a small scale. In some cases, the government's involvement appears to have helped public and private research and development performers to overcome the "collective action" problems that otherwise prevent them from exploiting potentially significant economic and technological opportunities. Indeed, many recipients of the awards—and even some teams that failed to win—report that the programs have facilitated beneficial organizational relationships that would not have existed had the programs not existed. In effect, as suggested in the chapter by Jane Fountain (Chapter 4), the Clinton efforts have helped to build "social capital."

Significantly, the features these programs incorporated to avoid government failure also appear to have worked. It is too early to judge the effect of time-limited grants, but other features of these programs—government-industry cost-sharing, competitive selection, and the requirement that applicants be made up of industry-led teams—have combined to render these efforts nearly free of political pork.

Ironically, the very success of those features has reduced opportunities for supporters to cultivate stable political constituencies for continuing these programs, never mind expanding them. For example, three of the major technology initiatives begun under Bush and expanded under Clinton have been scaled back or essentially eliminated: the Commerce Department's Advanced Technology Program (geared toward promoting private-sector competitiveness and economic growth and discussed in Chapter 6 by Christopher Hill); the Pentagon's Technology Reinvestment Project (geared toward promoting the commercial development of technologies with both civilian and military applications and discussed in Chapter 7 by Linda Cohen),[26] and the Department of Energy's severely curtailed program of Cooperative Research and Development Agreements (CRADAs) between DOE's national laboratories and industry. In contrast, the Clinton administration's National Flat Panel Display Initiative, discussed in Chapter 15 by Daniel Roos, Frank Field, and James Nealy, and the "Clean Car" program (officially the Partnership for a New Generation of Vehicles) have survived Congressional scrutiny so far, down-sized but intact, due to the focused efforts of their specific and therefore readily-organized industrial constituencies. More tellingly, the Commerce Department's Manufacturing Extension Partnership (MEP) which, as Shapira describes in Chapter 10, placed more than 70 manufacturing extension centers in, fortuitously, all 50 states (and thus in at least that many congressional districts), is actually being expanded by the Republican-led Congress.[27]

Equally significant, the Clinton projects suffer from two important political deficiencies. One is the lack of programmatic objectives tied to clearly defined government missions; they rely on more amorphous goals like "competitiveness" and "growth," which most Americans assume to be primarily the responsibility of the private sector. Success may be possible where competitiveness is clearly defined in terms of a specific, tangible mission such as the broader diffusion of technological advances and best practice to small manufacturers, a main goal of the MEP. But historically, competitiveness—comparatively long-run productivity growth and a rising standard of living—is best pursued indirectly: it results when federal spending develops new technology industries through sponsored research and through procurement in mission areas where government itself can serve as the initial launch market.

The second flaw of the Clinton initiatives is their lack of sufficient scale and scope: it is fine to fund small-scale projects, but only so long as they are clearly connected, as a group, to a larger set of public purposes. And the public purposes to which they are connected must be understood and approved broadly enough to inspire strong support from a wide range of political constituencies. Instead, the Clinton initiatives spread limited resources across too many projects that, taken in the aggregate, are still too small in overall scale to have a major impact on most large industry sectors or any pressing national problems. In addition, the projects have typically failed to exploit the potential for more stable budgetary support that could have been provided had they been designed as part of the regular R&D programs of the various mission-oriented agencies of the federal government. The lack of scale is largely a consequence of President Clinton's political inability to sell his "investment" program in the political debates over deficit reduction early in his first term. The lack of scope reflects the Clinton administration's tactical preference for funding stand-alone initiatives that are easier to "market" and for which it is easier to claim political credit when they go well, but that are also more vulnerable to budget cutters both in and outside the administration. This tactic has diverted the administration's attention from the more arduous and important work of integrating the expanded reliance on industrial partnerships for technology development into the standard operating procedures of the traditional mission agencies.

The New Reality

Difficult as it will continue to be to create political and budgetary support to enlarge technology policy efforts in scale and scope to the point where they would have significant impacts in launching new technology industries, this would be a most inopportune moment for the United States to confine its role only to R&D instead of comprehensive technology sponsorship, or to rely blindly on the invisible hand. Until the 1980s, when the absolute lead U.S. industry enjoyed in most high-technology sectors began to evaporate, the federal government could be certain that the domestic economy would enjoy the lion's share of the broad social gains generated by its vast R&D budget. As the strongest and most advanced economy, the United States was always the launch market for the new technologies fostered by public spending. U.S. industry typically commercialized and produced the innovations at home, and then exported abroad. Initial and leading customers—those who shaped the new technology's initial development and its path of diffusion—were also typically domestically based. Local R&D, production, and advanced use meant that most of the spillovers that generated the broad social benefits would occur within U.S. borders.

During the past decade, however, several trends have converged to challenge the easy identity between federal R&D and domestic spillovers. Foreign competitors have caught up with and in some cases surpassed U.S. producers. Foreign governments followed the U.S. lead to sponsor high and rising levels of R&D spending. Foreign markets became effective launch markets for their own new technologies, such as the European Airbus's pioneering of fly-by-wire and other aeronautical innovations. Available time for spillover from U.S. defense spending shrank as foreign producers caught up with U.S. innovation. And as international competition intensified, so did the costs and risks of private R&D investment, so that even U.S. firms chose to spread them across global markets by producing abroad and finding foreign partners.

As a result, technologies pioneered in the United States now flow rapidly across the national borders, sometimes to be commercialized, produced, and exploited more effectively there than in the United States. Conversely, more and more innovations now originate abroad, but because foreign economies are rarely as open as the United States, a reverse flow of innovation into the United States has not fully materialized. Indeed, international technological specialization is increasing: new technical skills that are essential to the commercialization of innovation are arising in new places around the globe, especially in Asia, and are not readily duplicated back in the United States.[28]

Thus the relationship between federal R&D spending and domestic spillovers and social benefits has been significantly attenuated. This makes it all the more important for government to focus its own sponsorship in areas where spillovers are most likely to be generated and captured locally. Because know-how developed through production and use, and embedded in local assets like labor pools, supplier networks, and infrastructure, is less likely to diffuse readily across borders, the government should focus on helping to bring such assets into being. Such assets will be created whenever comprehensive government sponsorship of new technologies helps to develop the domestic market as the principal launch market for those technologies.

In the current era of tight budget constraints, this means that government must focus its scarce resources, not squander them in piecemeal sponsorship of small projects with at best modest impacts. It also means that the government cannot focus on the amorphous goal of directly supporting commercial competitiveness, for in most cases, the market dynamics of commercial industries are already developed, and policy intervention is unlikely to alter them significantly in ways that create new domestic capabilities. Rather, federal sponsorship can most effectively launch local capabilities only by focusing on wholly new technological possibilities linked tightly to a government mission (so that the government itself becomes the initial launch market for new technologies for which commercial markets have yet to develop).

Two prime possibilities are environmental stewardship and infrastructure. The environmental opportunity, explored in greater detail in Chapter 11 by George Heaton and Darryl Banks, is to move beyond existing efforts aimed at regulating waste reduction and mandating clean-up. Sponsorship should instead be directed to replacing existing industrial production with technologies that generate no waste or pollution in the first place. Government procurement, from automobile fleets to office supplies, should favor industrial processes that boost pollution prevention, resource sustainability, and efficient resource usage. Policy should set performance standards only, inviting different competitive approaches to determine the most effective means of meeting those standards.

Similarly, there is an acknowledged need to rebuild much of the nation's eroding networks for transportation, power, sewage, and water, and to upgrade the infrastructure for communications. Sponsorship of innovation to meet modern infrastructure needs would spur a host of new technologies from low-maintenance concretes to optical control systems. Emphasis would be on seeding and then procuring new technological approaches that, while more costly up-front, hold the promise of reducing total life-cycle costs.

U.S. public support for government investments such as these remains weak, even though they are critical to raising long-run living standards. To many Americans, the Clinton administration's investments in technological innovation have appeared to benefit only the multibillion-dollar corporations and high-tech professionals who are already doing well in the global information-age economy. Most middle-class voters, concerned about the impact of new computer-based technologies on their own jobs, uncertain and impatient about the economic future, see no evidence that these policies are actually working, let alone that larger scale projects might work.

Nevertheless, a broad consensus both about national needs and the legitimacy of government's role persists in two areas—national security and public health. A set of small technology development and demonstration projects connected to these and other larger purposes—aggregated, that is, into a set of large, high-profile efforts to address easily demonstrated national needs such as protecting the environment and improving mass transportation— might finally attract a broader, more stable constituency for government investments in technological progress.

Where possible, government procurement should help to provide launch markets for new technologies that provide promising solutions to national needs, as long as deadlines and benchmarks for commercialization and the eventual withdrawal of government subsidy are established up front. But government technology development programs, to which such procurement should be tied, must incorporate the features that have proved critical to ensuring that recent initiatives such as ATP and TRP remained responsive to commercial market demand: industry must be involved in setting research agendas, applicants must compete for individual grants, and there must be strict time limits on government support. The necessity of involving profit-seeking firms in the development of commercially sustainable technologies means that the public is always likely to remain ambivalent about government's proper role. Nevertheless, a set of programs modelled on ATP but established within the various mission agencies (e.g., the Department of Transportation, the Environmental Protection Agency, the Department of Energy) might help establish a standard mechanism (and a set of political constituencies) to ensure that the United States can routinely explore technological innovation to address national needs, while at the same time enlisting the private sector in partnerships to accelerate the invention and eventual commercialization of any novel technologies that result.

Notes

1. If productivity growth is accomplished simply by corporate "downsizing," then at least in the short run it may come at the expense of progress on income inequality and unemployment.

2. Income inequality and slow productivity growth are equally important factors in determining the standard of living, but because the way that new technology enables workers to earn higher real wages is by first making them more productive, we focus here on the direct link between technological progress and productivity growth.

3. Prior to his recent vituperative attacks on popular concepts of relative economic performance, Paul Krugman made this point most succinctly for non-

economist policy audiences in Krugman, *The Age Of Diminished Expectations* (Cambridge, Mass.: MIT Press, 1990).

4. The quote is from Linda R. Cohen and Roger G. Noll, *The Technology Pork Barrel* (Washington, D.C.: Brookings, 1991), p.11.

5. See, e.g., Edward F. Denison, *Accounting for United States Economic Growth, 1929–1969* (Washington, D.C.: Brookings, 1974). The role of technology and R&D has been studied by economists for more than forty years. The earliest studies almost stumbled upon the importance of technology-spawned productivity improvements as an explanation for economic growth. One, which examined the U.S. economy over the period 1909–49 when gross output per household doubled, estimated that only 12.5 percent of this increased output was due to increased use of capital (i.e., more machines). More importantly, the residual growth of 87.5 percent could only be explained by technical change, i.e., new machines and better ways of organizing industrial activities. Robert M. Solow, "Technical Change and the Aggregate Production Function," *Review of Economics and Statistics*, No. 39 (1957), pp. 312–320. Attempting to overcome many restrictive assumptions of these initial studies, a recent study by Boskin and Lau examined economic growth in the five largest industrial economies and found that, consistent with the earlier work, technological progress is by far the most important source of economic growth. Michael J. Boskin and Lawrence J. Lau, "The Contribution of R&D to Economic Growth: Some Issues and Observations," American Enterprise Institute, conference paper, October 3, 1994. For a nice summary of the growth-accounting and return-on-investment literature, see Gregory Tassey, *Technology and Economic Growth: Implications for Federal Policy* (Washington, DC: U.S. Department of Commerce, Technology Administration, October 1995).

6. Paul M. Romer, "Increasing Returns and Long-Run Growth," *Journal of Political Economy*, Vol. 94, No. 4 (October 1986), pp. 1002–37; and "Endogenous Technological Change," *Journal of Political Economy*, Vol. 98, No. 5 (1990), pp. S71–S102.

7. Brian Arthur, *Increasing Returns and Path Dependence in the Economy* (Ann Arbor: University of Michigan Press, 1994). See, in particular, Chapter 7, pp. 111–132.

8. Ishaq Nadiri, "Innovations and Technological Spillovers," National Bureau of Economic Research, Working Paper No. 4423 (August 1993).

9. Richard M. Cyert and David C. Mowery, eds, *Technology and Employment: Innovation and Growth in the U.S. Economy* (Washington, D.C.: National Academy Press, 1987); Paul Krugman, "Technology's Revenge," *Wilson Quarterly* (Autumn 1994), pp. 57–64; David R. Howell, "The Skills Myth," *The American Prospect*, No 18 (Summer 1994), pp. 81–89; "Technology and Unemployment," *The Economist* (February 11, 1995), pp. 21–23.

10. Department of Commerce, *Building the American Dream* (August 1996).

11. In addition to Nadiri, "Innovations and Technological Spillovers"; see Martin Neil Baily and Alok K. Chakrabarti, *Innovation and the Productivity Crisis* (Washington, D.C.: Brookings Institution, 1988); Edwin Mansfield "Social Returns

from R&D: Findings, Methods, and Limitations," *Research and Technology Management* (November–December 1991); and Zvi Griliches, "The Search for R&D Spillovers," *Scandinavian Journal of Economics*, Vol. 94, supplement (1992), pp. 29–47.

12. For a concise summary, see Cohen and Noll, *The Technology Pork Barrel* at pp.18–22; and Richard R. Nelson, ed., *Government and Technical Progress* (New York: Pergamon Press, 1982), pp. 2–5 and pp. 480–481.

13. Gene M. Grossman, "Promoting New Industrial Activities: A Survey of Recent Arguments and Evidence," *OECD Economic Studies*, No. 14 (Spring 1990), pp. 87–125.

14. Cohen and Noll, *The Technology Pork Barrel*, are illustrative.

15. The latter two ideas originated in the so-called new trade theory literature; see, e.g., Paul R. Krugman, ed., *Strategic Trade and the New International Economics* (Cambridge, Mass.: MIT Press, 1986).

16. This and the following data are drawn from Laura D'Andrea Tyson, *Who's Bashing Whom: Trade Conflicts in High Technology Industries* (Washington, D.C.: Institute for International Economics, 1992).

17. See, e.g., William T. Dickens and Kevin Lang, "Why It Matters What We Trade: A Case for Active Trade Policy," in William T. Dickens, Laura D'Andrea Tyson, and John Zysman, eds., *The Dynamics of Trade and Employment*, (Cambridge, Mass.: Ballinger, 1989).

18. For a fuller elaboration of the successes and failures of this technology development model, see chapter by Jay Stowsky, "From Spin-Off to Spin-On: Redefining the Military's Role in American Technology Development," in Wayne Sandholz, Michael Borrus, et al., *The Highest Stakes: The Economic Foundations of the Next Security System* (New York: Oxford University Press, 1992), pp. 114–140.

19. For details, see Eric Barnouw's classic history of broadcasting, *A History of Broadcasting in the United States* (New York: Oxford University Press, 1966).

20. For an evaluation, see "Agriculture" by R.E. Evenson in Nelson, *Government and Technical Progress*.

21. See Stowsky, "From Spin-Off to Spin-On," pp. 122–126.

22. For details, see the relevant chapters in Cohen and Noll, *The Technology Pork Barrel*.

23. Even in those cases, there are likely to be important technical spillovers, especially when generic research is funded as part of the program.

24. The decision to scale back the technology initiatives was made even before the new president officially assumed his office, in a series of internal debates detailed by journalist Bob Woodward, in *The Agenda* (New York: Simon and Schuster, 1994). The initiatives were scaled back further in bruising, early-term battles with Congress over spending priorities and deficit reduction.

25. Figures from American Association for the Advancement of Science, *Congressional Action on Research and Development in the FY 1997 Budget*, special table, "Trends in R&D, FY's 1994–97"; and National Science Foundation, *Science and Engineering Indicators, 1996*, Text Table 4–5.

26. For additional discussion of the political dynamics underlying TRP and the Pentagon's other dual-use technology initiatives, see Jay Stowsky, "The Dual-Use Dilemma," *Issues in Science and Technology*, Vol. 13, No. 2 (Winter 1996–97), pp. 56–64.

27. For a discussion of the history and fate of CRADAs at the Department of Energy (DOE) labs, see "DOE to Industry: So Long, Partner," *Science* (Vol. 274), October 4, 1996. For more on the National Flat Panel Display Initiative, see Kenneth Flamm, "Flat-Panel Displays: Catalyzing a U.S. Industry," *Issues in Science and Technology*, Vol. 11, No. 1 (Fall 1994). For more on the Clean Car Initiative, see Daniel Sperling, "Rethinking the Car of the Future," *Issues in Science and Technology* Vol. 13, No. 2 (Winter 1996–97), pp. 29–34.

28. For evidence, see e.g., Daniele Archibugi and Jonathan Michie, "The Globalization of Technology: Myths and Realities," *Cambridge Journal of Economics*, No. 19 (1995); and Keith Pavitt and Parimal Patel, "The International Distribution and Determinants of Technological Activities," *Oxford Review of Economic Policy*, No. 4 (1988), pp. 35–55.

3

Measurement Issues

Adam B. Jaffe

Arguments regarding the desirability of federal science and technology programs are often based on strongly-held views about the "proper" role of government. No doubt this will always be the case to some extent. But the effect that specific programs have on society and the economy, and the relative efficacy and cost-effectiveness of different policy approaches, cannot be determined on the basis of theoretical or philosophical arguments. These are empirical questions. It is the thesis of this chapter that systematic efforts to measure and assess the effects of specific programs can produce useful information that can improve policy-making in the long run.

The first section of the chapter briefly reviews the statutory mandate for performance assessment, and some previous federal efforts to implement measurement and assessment of science and technology programs. The second describes a conceptual framework for measurement in this area, emphasizing clarity in understanding the relationship between unobservable effects and proxies or correlates of those effects. The third section discusses existing measures, and issues that arise in identifying good indicators of success. Many existing benefits studies over-count or double-count project benefits; I suggest that agencies be open-minded and creative in devising new indicators, and urge the use of multiple indicators at multiple levels of aggregation to counter the inherent limitations of any one measure.

The chapter concludes with a discussion of the data needs for long-term research on the advantages and disadvantages of different generic science and technology policy approaches. Unlike short-term assessment carried out for management purposes, such long-term research requires data across multiple agencies and contexts. Further, the results of this kind of research could be much clearer if performance assessment were made an explicit consideration in the design of programs. In particular, if we really desire to know how effective programs are, then the programs need to incorporate elements of experimental design into their ongoing operation, in the same way that the efficacy of drugs is determined by scientifically-designed clinical trials.

The Government Performance and Results Act and Related Measurement Efforts

The Government Performance and Results Act ("GPRA"), passed in 1993, mandates that every federal agency prepare a strategic plan by September 1997, and then regularly assess its performance relative to that plan and report the results to Congress. The plans must contain specific *performance goals,* expressed as measurable objectives against which the success of the agency can be objectively assessed. The plans must also identify the *performance indicators* that will measure the agency's success in achieving its goals. Thus the GPRA is an ambitious attempt to ensure that government programs are successful and cost-effective. Science and technology agencies view the GPRA as a major challenge.

The GPRA distinguishes between *outputs* and *outcomes.* Outputs are the direct production of agency activities and effort; outcomes are the effects or consequences that the program is intended to have. The Act mandates that performance objectives be specified for both outputs and outcomes, and that performance indicators be tracked for both. It is clear, however, that the intent of the Act is to cause agencies to establish goals with respect to outcomes, and develop indicators that will permit them to determine if these outcomes are being achieved.[1]

The Act requires that performance goals be specified in objective, tangible form, and be evaluated quantitatively. However, if an agency, in consultation with the Office of Management and Budget (OMB), determines that it is not feasible to express the performance goals for a particular program in quantifiable form, then the director of OMB may authorize an alternative form, so long as the alternative would still allow for an accurate and independent determination of whether performance is meeting the goal.

Beginning before GPRA, and accelerating in response to it, there have been a number of interagency efforts within the science and technology agencies to develop performance metrics or indicators. In 1992, the Interagency Committee on Federal Technology Transfer established a working group, chaired by the Commerce Department, on Technology Transfer Measurement and Evaluation. The group was charged with "a coordinated effort to develop a system to measure the effectiveness of Federal technology transfer and to assess the impact of Federal technology transfer programs on U.S. industry and the economy." The Working Group issued a draft report in November 1994.[2]

The working draft proposed a "matrix" for characterizing technology transfer activities and measuring their impacts. The matrix allows for activities to be described and data to be collected using a set of terms and categories that (it is hoped) could be standardized across agencies. The four dimensions of the analysis are: the nature of the R&D; the development phase; the technology application area; and the transfer mechanism. The Draft Report includes a proposed standard reporting form, in which technology transfer activities would be categorized along these dimensions, and a set of common data collected. The data to be collected includes some items that would be collected for all activities (mainly identifying information and the characterization along the four dimensions, as well as a description of the private-sector transferee), and also specific data to be collected for the different kinds of transfer mechanisms.

The thrust of this effort, which preceded GPRA, was to develop data across agencies on a comparable basis. In contrast, agencies' implementation efforts under GPRA do not seem to have emphasized comparability. As discussed further below, however, determining what really works and what does not in technology policy will require data that permits systematic study across agencies, whether it satisfies GPRA requirements or not.

The National Science and Technology Council (NSTC), in response to the GPRA mandates, established the Committee on

Fundamental Science "to establish a broad framework for GPRA implementation in assessment of fundamental science programs."[3] Since this committee was working in direct response to GPRA, its framework mirrors that of the Act. It begins by describing performance goals at several levels. It describes "improved health and environment, national security, economic prosperity and quality of life" as the "overarching goals" of science in the national interest. In support of these overarching goals, the committee identifies "leadership across the frontiers of scientific knowledge" as "an enabling or intermediate objective."

Having identified these goals, the document states that for the purpose of evaluating specific programs in individual agencies, "merit review based on peer evaluation will continue to be the primary vehicle for assessing the excellence and conduct of science at the cutting edge." The document does not advocate specific quantitative measures to be used in GPRA assessment of fundamental science, arguing that existing measures of research results (e.g., publication counts, citation counts, and rate of return and related economic measures) were developed for other purposes and capture only a subset of the spectrum of research outputs and outcomes.[4]

NASA Administrator Daniel Goldin has been particularly aggressive in pursuing quantitative measures of the impact of NASA research and technology development. This has led to the publication of some dubious claims, such as a report from the Marshall Space Flight Center that uses simplistic multiplier effects to conclude that the center has produced economic benefits of some $350 million at a benefit/cost ratio of 60:1.[5] But it has also led to a systematic agency-wide effort to come up with quantitative indicators of all aspects of the agency's activities. More than other agencies, NASA seems to have resisted the temptation to conclude that impacts cannot be quantified, and has instead pushed to develop multiple quantitative indicators.

The Advanced Technology Program (ATP) of the National Institute of Standards and Technology (NIST) in the Department of Commerce is in the unique position of funding the development of new commercial technology in the private sector with no specific government mission orientation. (See Chapter 6 by Christopher Hill in this volume.) Slated for dramatic funding increases in the first Clinton budget, the ATP has faced severe scrutiny from Congressional skeptics of support of industrial technology. Presumably in response to this pressure, the ATP has undertaken an ambitious effort to measure its economic impact. Its Economic Assessment Office in 1994 convened a group of outside experts to provide guidance in the development of evaluation and impact studies.[6] This group was organized and chaired by Zvi Griliches, past president of the American Economic Association and a leading expert on the economics of new technology. The first meeting saw extensive discussion of the difficulty of using existing data and models to construct reliable estimates of the economic benefits of ATP projects. In response, the ATP has undertaken a significant long-run research effort with the multiple objectives of beginning preliminary evaluation of ATP projects where feasible, developing the methodologies and data necessary for more long-term evaluation, and improving understanding of the underlying social and economic processes as a foundation for better assessment.[7] In this context, the ATP has developed an extensive database of information about all of its projects,[8] and has funded a series of studies by outside investigators.[9]

Inputs, Outputs, and Outcomes

The first step in designing systematic data collection is to define the various elements of the process that we wish to measure, and the nature of different kinds of measurements. The GPRA established a framework in which agencies use "inputs" to produce specific program "outputs," which should have intended "outcomes" in the broader economy and environment. Agencies are expected to develop and then collect "performance indicators" for both outputs and outcomes. This section discusses generically what this might mean for science and technology programs, using the terminology of the GPRA, while defining somewhat more precisely the underlying concepts and their relationship to measurements.

A framework for the analysis of these concepts is represented in Table 3-1. Any program will have *inputs*, namely the resources consumed by the operation of the program that otherwise could have been put to another use. It will also have *outputs*, which the

Table 3-1   Conceptual Framework for Performance Measurement

Concepts	Proxies	Correlates
Inputs		
Person-years, equipment-years	Expenditures	
Outputs		
Ideas, discoveries	Papers, prizes	
Inventions	Patents, invention-disclosures	
Human capital	Degrees awarded	
Technology transfer	CRADAs, licenses	Cost-shared dollars
Outcomes or Impacts		
Broad advance of human knowledge	Papers, citations, expert evaluations	
New products	Patents, citations	Licenses, license royalties, product announcements, new product sales
Productivity improvements	Measured productivity growth	
Income growth	Benefit/cost ratio or rate of return	New firms, induced investment
Excitement about science		Science News articles
Health, environment, etc.	New drug applications	Emissions levels
Cooperation and knowledge flow	CRADAs	

program is designed to produce directly. In general, these direct outputs may not be the policy reason for the program; rather, the goal is that these outputs have some impact on the economy or broader environment. The GPRA calls this latter concept *outcomes*. Impacts or outcomes are defined by social and economic objectives, and they are realized only when the direct outputs of the program interact with society and the economy.

Outputs may be desirable in and of themselves, but need not be. Further, outputs are typically produced relatively soon after the use of inputs, while outcomes may take much longer to develop. While the GPRA does not clearly distinguish between outputs and outcomes, the defining difference is that outputs can be produced by the program itself without significant interaction with the broader world, while outcomes result only when those outputs interact with the economy and nongovernment agents. For example, specific research results and the human capital of post-doctoral researchers are outputs; government programs can produce these things essentially on their own.[10] But a broad advance in scientific understanding, increased productivity or economic growth, or increased excitement about science only come about when these outputs merge and interact with other forces.[11]

Thus, for basic research programs like those of National Science Foundation (NSF) and some Department of Energy (DOE) programs, the outputs are typically discoveries and new ideas, as well as human capital created in researchers operating at the frontier of their fields, and the graduate students and others they employ. These things are desirable themselves, but as an additional impact, we hope that the spread of the new ideas will, eventually and on average, provide the basis for commercial innovation that creates new products and improves productivity. In addition, the trained researchers will utilize their knowledge and skills in subsequent work, at least some of it in the broader economy.

For mission-oriented research, or technology programs like the ATP, the outputs are solutions of specific technical problems, demonstrations of feasibility of certain processes, the development of commercial prototypes, and the like. These outputs are typically less valued in and of themselves than the scientific discoveries produced by basic research.[12] The motivation for these programs lies almost entirely in their ultimate impacts on the broader economy, such as clean-coal technology installed in utility generating stations, new standards or equipment that increase the productivity of industry, or new products that create consumer satisfaction and successful exports.

An important category of outcomes is the creation and enhancement of social capital (see Chapter 4 by Jane Fountain in this volume). For example, increasing public awareness about science and technology and public excitement about scientific break-throughs foster a social and cultural milieu in which knowledge can move forward, and concerns about the risks of new technologies can be addressed constructively. The importance of cooperation in the scientific and engineering enterprise means that the creation of institutions supporting cooperation (e.g., Cooperative Research and Development Agreements, or CRADAs) can be thought of as a social capital outcome as well as an output.

The GPRA expects agencies to track both outputs and outcomes, and assess their performance in meeting well-defined goals for both measures. But because outcomes depend on the complex interaction of outputs with the broader society and economy, it is virtually impossible to set performance goals for outcomes that can be tracked on a short-term basis. As discussed below, one cannot assess a program's success in producing the intended *outcomes* and *outputs* in the same way. While assessing outputs can realistically be carried out as a more or less routine internal activity, assessing outcomes is a long-term research task.

Table 3-1 indicates the kinds of performance indicators that might be collected to assess both outputs and outcomes. In almost all cases, outputs and outcomes themselves are largely unobserv-able. Instead, we measure observable constructs that we hope bear some relationship to the desired but unobservable concept. A "proxy" indicator is a data element that we believe measures, imperfectly, the output or impact we care about. A "correlate" indicator is a data element that measures something other than what we really care about, but which we believe (based on some model of the relevant social and economic processes) is correlated with the thing we care about.[13] This distinction is often fuzzy; patents, for example, are a proxy for commercially-useful inven-tions, but are also a correlate because we know that, on average and over time, there tends to be a correlation between the rate of patenting and the rate of commercially successful invention. The number of new firms, however, is a correlate measure but not a proxy. New firm formation tends to be correlated with growth in economic output and income, but we do not care about the number of new firms in and of itself.

Evaluating Available Proxies, Correlates and Other Indicators

Since an indicator, by definition, is an imprecise measure of the underlying concept, its validity must be evaluated. Some criteria for a good indicator are characteristics of the indicator itself. For example, it should not be too expensive to collect and it should be reproducible or verifiable by independent observers. But most issues in evaluating an indicator pertain to the relationship between the indicator and the underlying concept of interest. Since this underlying concept is unobservable, reliance on an indicator is inevitably somewhat a matter of faith. Nonetheless, it is useful to understand the issues.

First, an indicator should be as precise as possible; that is, it should bear a tight relationship with the underlying concept, or have a high "signal-to-noise ratio."[14] Second, the indicator should be unbiased, meaning that the relationship between the indicator and the underlying concept does not vary systematically with particular characteristics. For example, if NSF-funded researchers get a disproportionately high number of citations simply because they are well known, citations would be a biased indicator of broad scientific impact. Third, the relationship between the indicator and the underlying concept should be stable over time. For example, if the widespread diffusion of computer-searchable databases tends to increase the number of citations made in every paper, then the relationship between citations and impact will not be stable over time, implying that reliable conclusions about the changing performance of programs over time cannot be drawn from citations data.

Fourth, an indicator should be comparable across agencies or environments. Note that an attribute can be precise without being comparable, and it can be comparable without being precise. Suppose that, on average, each paper in physics contains ten "ideas," while each paper in economics contains on average one idea. Then the number of papers as an indicator for ideas is not comparable across these fields, but it might be precise if the variation around the mean within a field is small. Conversely, it could be that the average number of ideas per paper is the same in both fields, but the variation is enormous. In this case the indicator is comparable but not precise.

Fifth, indicators should not be susceptible to manipulation. Since indicators are to be the basis for assessment, and assessment may be the basis of individuals' promotion and agencies' budgets, we must be concerned about the possibility that the act of measurement may influence the process being observed. Specifically, it is fine if basing the assessment of a program's creation of new ideas on publications induces scientists to produce more ideas and therefore more papers, but it is not fine if it induces scientists to publish more papers with fewer ideas per paper.

Finally, an indicator should be subject to aggregation. Since we desire to assess the performance of individual projects, programs, and entire agencies simultaneously, we want the indicator for the whole to equal the sum of the indicators for the constituent parts. This is partly an issue of comparability—adding physics papers and economics papers to get total NSF papers makes little sense if papers do not constitute comparable indicators in their fields—but it is also an issue of the relationship between the indicator and the underlying concept. Suppose, for example, we estimate the rate of return to NASA satellite research by measuring the economic value of commercial satellites, subtracting an estimate of all non-NASA investment that has contributed to the industry, and then compare the resulting net economic value to NASA expenditures. (Put aside the heroic data problems that would have to be solved to do this.) Suppose we then undertook the analogous exercise for the Defense Department. Individually, these might be sensible proxies for the economic benefit of each agency's program. Their combined estimate for the overall rate of return to federal satellite research, however, is clearly too high, because it double-counts the extent to which total economic benefits exceed the total investments of all parties.

Of course, no indicator satisfies all these criteria. There are often tradeoffs, such as the likelihood that indicators that measure output in a particular area with high precision will not be comparable across areas. Further, the criteria are not of equal consequence, because some issues can be handled by appropriate statistical techniques. For example, with appropriate external information, corrections can be made for instability over time or sometimes even for noncomparability across contexts. Finally, the significance of different problems will depend on the use to which the assessment is to be put. An agency tracking its own performance for internal management purposes should care a lot about stability over time but might not care much about comparability, while a researcher or congressional staffer who is trying to figure out if the rules governing cost-sharing affect the rate of return to cooperative research will need performance indicators that are comparable across different programs and agencies.

Output Indicators

Counts of publications have long been used as a performance measure for research enterprises[15] and are widely used in nongovernment research settings. Paper counts are inexpensive to track and are independently verifiable. Further, since scientists in essentially all fundamental research environments publish papers, output and efficiency as measured by papers can be compared across government and other non-profit and for-profit institutions.

However, the measure also has well-known limitations. Papers vary greatly in their significance, and the use of counts for assessment can lead to an increase in publishing of marginal results. It is also clear that publication counts are not typically comparable across fields of science or engineering. Papers can be made a more reliable output indicator by using one or more methods to control for their varying quality. Looking only at peer-reviewed papers and papers in "high-impact" journals or using citation-weighted paper counts can greatly increase the signal-to-noise ratio, and, at the same time, minimize the incentive to generate marginal papers to inflate the count.

Patents and invention disclosures have many of the same advantages and disadvantages as measures of invention that papers have as measures of scientific output. They are public, computerized, and represent a disinterested decision by an examiner that a non-obvious and potentially commercially useful invention has occurred. On the other hand, patents vary enormously in their significance; indeed, the majority are never commercialized. Further, the difficulty of patenting varies across fields, making patent counts noncomparable across different types of technologies. In addition, there have been significant changes in patent rates over time, requiring statistical adjustments when examining patent rates over time, even for a given institution.[16]

Proxies also exist for the human capital outputs of science and technology programs. In addition to degrees and numbers of post-doctoral researchers and other trainees supported, agencies can count outside researchers who spend time in government labs under various programs. Obviously, none of these measures controls for the quality of the training, but it is not clear that there are systematic biases as a result.

Technology transfer raises special issues for performance measurement;[17] the activity itself can be considered the output. Just as we typically assume without further verification that a graduate research assistant or a post-doctoral researcher learns something by participating in funded research, we can assume that a commercial firm that participates in a CRADA or licenses a government technology gains something in the process. Of course, CRADAs vary greatly in significance; a compound measure such as CRADA-staff-hours is probably more appropriate than a simple count. Such measures are probably as valid as indicators of outputs as papers and patents are in their realms, although there is less research justifying this conclusion than with older measures.

Outcome Indicators

Because outcomes tend to be less tangible than outputs, it can be more difficult to find proxies for outcomes than for outputs. However, the interaction of firms and other agents from the broader environment may generate correlates that can be observed and from which inferences can be drawn about likely outcomes. In particular, to the extent that productivity improvement and income growth are desired outcomes, it is possible to exploit known relationships between these outcomes and measurable quantities such as royalties, sales, investment, and firm formation.

The greatest difficulty in measuring performance with respect to outcomes is in reliably relating observed outcomes to government programs. Because outcomes depend on the interaction of government activities with the wider environment, it is by definition difficult to determine accurately when and to what extent desired outcomes are traceable to specific government programs or agencies.

While the specific problems that must be solved to connect outcomes convincingly to particular government activities vary with the activity being considered, there are a number of common issues. First, in economists' jargon, what matters most for evaluation is the marginal effect of the government activity, not the average effect. That is, we usually want to know what would happen if we increased or decreased the activity a little bit, not what would happen if we shut it down entirely. Unfortunately, it is often much easier to measure the average effect than to measure the marginal effect. Further, we expect that most activities are subject to diminishing marginal returns, so a demonstration that average returns are high is not sufficient to conclude that marginal returns are high.

Thus, for example, time-series statistical techniques have been used to demonstrate that aggregate productivity growth over a span of decades can be traced to aggregate social investments in basic research.[18] It is a little harder to prove that the aggregate federal investment in basic research has been productive, although federal spending is such a large share of the total that this is almost surely true. Similarly, no one needs to do a study to convince us that the general state of our knowledge about physical, biological, and social systems would be much less today if the government had not been involved in fundamental research in the postwar period. On the basis of these findings, one can conclude (assuming the past can be extrapolated into the future) that shutting down the federal research establishment would be a very bad thing. One cannot use this evidence to conclude, however, that reducing the scale or scope of that establishment by 5, 10, or 25 percent would necessarily be a bad thing.

A second important issue is the need to examine net economic returns, not gross returns. Even if a project is a "success," it is necessary to assess how much of that "success" would have occurred in the absence of any government action.[19] Only the incremental benefits that would not otherwise have existed are properly attributable to the government action. Further, to the extent that the success is based partly on costs incurred by private parties, those costs must be added to the public costs in determining the overall economic return. Finally, in considering the overall economic return to a program, we must include the costs of administering the program itself, and the costs incurred by private parties to compete for the program awards.

These problems are common in existing evaluation studies. As a result, the claimed benefits are so large that it is likely that if similar studies were done for all government programs, the total estimated benefits from the aggregate of all programs would exceed total Gross Domestic Product (GDP). While some of the excess is no doubt the result of conscious boosterism, a big part is surely due to assuming that average effects are the same as marginal effects, and that net benefits equal gross benefits. The result is systematic double-counting and over-counting of the true benefits.

Both of these problems are mitigated when measurement occurs at the smallest level of detail. A specific project is by definition marginal, so there is no confusion of average and marginal. Further, when examining a specific project, it is much easier to identify systematically both the parties who benefit and those who are hurt, so it is possible, in principle, to construct a true estimate of net benefits.[20] However, it is usually difficult to determine the extent to which measurements for a single project can be extrapolated to an entire program or agency. Sometimes the bias is systematic: the most successful projects are often the ones chosen for measurement. Even without such bias, however, it may be very difficult to perform the "all else equal" analysis that is necessary to draw general conclusions from case studies of specific projects.

I do not believe that it is possible to perform a reliable and comprehensive measurement of the outcomes of science and technology programs. This does not mean, however, that measurement is pointless. By looking at multiple indicators, captured and evaluated at multiple levels of aggregation (individual projects, individual programs, agencies, the economy as a whole), we can draw reasonably reliable conclusions. Further, the use of multiple indicators reduces the need to be overly concerned about the limitations of any one. We should encourage imagination and experimentation to identify new proxies for hard-to-measure concepts. For example, NASA has proposed tracking articles in the journal *Science News* about its activities as a proxy to measure its success at generating excitement about science. Francis Narin has analyzed citations in patent applications of scientific papers, and then identified the sources of funding for the researchers who wrote the cited papers, as a proxy for the impact of science research funding on the development of commercial technology.[21] Rather than bemoan the inadequacy of existing measures and the inherent fuzziness of performance goals, we should expand the range of measures that we consider.

Assessment, Evaluation and Policy Research

What should we do with performance indicator data once we have it? The GPRA makes it sound simple. The performance plans will specify clear goals for outputs and outcomes, and then the performance indicators will provide clear measures of success and failure, improvement and deterioration. Presumably, programs that perform poorly or whose performance is deteriorating will be restructured or otherwise reformed; agencies whose overall performance is poor or deteriorating will see their budgets cut by Congress.

One does not have to be excessively cynical to doubt that this will happen in practice, partly due to human nature and politics, but partly because it is hard to figure out what works and what does not, and how to change programs that do not work into programs that do. GPRA's formulaic approach masks this reality. The Act makes it sound like it is just a matter of passing out grades and then doing something about the students who get D or F. Anyone who has taught knows that passing out the grades is the easy part.

In reality, determining which programs and policies work and which do not involves several different activities that utilize data on performance indicators in different ways. On a short-run basis, program managers need data that allow them to assess ongoing operations. Such assessment can provide early warning of management problems, or programs that are unexpectedly performing poorly, so that adjustments can be made. In the medium term, agencies evaluate individual projects and programs to make decisions regarding the allocation of incremental resources. In the long run, social scientists research the effects of government on society and the economy, and try to draw generalizable conclusions about the efficacy of different policy approaches.

Assessment, evaluation, and research must all draw on performance indicators, but their needs are quite different. The kinds of data that will be generated by the GPRA—agency-specific, internally generated, and oriented toward stated performance objectives—are most appropriate for assessment, and probably somewhat useful for evaluation. They are less useful for research, however.

First, and most important, effective research needs data that are comparable across different environments. Since each agency's GPRA effort is aimed at its own internal goals process, comparability across agency environments is not a priority. Yet it would not be difficult to publish a significant number of common indicators for multiple agencies; many of the basic indicators (papers, patents, license royalties) would be common to many agencies. Indicators that are more complicated and require more methodological assumptions (such as new product sales) could also be compiled, along with agency statements about methodology. Indeed, if such methodologies could be tested and compared by outside researchers, the results would be far more likely to be credible. Where feasible, as envisioned by the Working Group on Technology Transfer Measurement and Evaluation,[22] agencies could jointly agree on definitions and items for data capture. All of these data could be tabulated and published as part of the NSF publication *Science & Engineering Indicators*.[23]

A second and related need is for some body or agency to be charged with common analysis of science and technology program performance. It is a good thing that the ATP is funding research to develop methods for evaluating government support of technology programs, but since related activity occurs in many places in the government, it would be much more effective for a small evaluation staff to be charged with the overall responsibility for developing methodology and examining disparate programs from a shared perspective. Given the role assigned to it by the GPRA, the OMB should have an interest in such research, but developing methodology has not traditionally been an OMB function. The White House Office of Science and Technology Policy (OSTP) could

coordinate an inter-agency effort at developing common approaches, picking up the work of the 1994 inter-agency committee,
and supported by the Critical Technologies Institute.

Finally, our ability to truly trace outcomes to programs and
policies would be greatly enhanced if programs were designed with
evaluation in mind. This is particularly crucial for programs like
ATP and TRP that aim to elicit certain specific behaviors from
nongovernmental agents. Evaluation of these programs as they
currently operate is tremendously complicated by the need to use
statistical techniques to control for the nonrandom selection of
firms for participation in the programs. Much clearer conclusions
about their efficacy could be drawn if some firms were randomly
accepted and denied for these programs, just as the efficacy of
drugs is determined by experiments in which randomly chosen
groups are given a new drug or a placebo.

The notion of randomly granting or denying research contracts
is considered by many to be politically unfeasible. Yet imagine the
Food and Drug Administration's reaction if, in demonstrating the
efficacy of a new AIDS treatment, scientists first attempted to
determine which patients were most likely to benefit from the drug,
and then administered the drug to such patients, and compared
their "outcomes" to those of patients who did not get the drug
(because they were judged less likely to benefit). Such a test would
be considered a travesty in the medical context. Yet this is precisely
the context in which we are trying to evaluate technology programs. Why is it acceptable (indeed, mandatory) to give only some
sick people a real drug, but not acceptable to give only some eligible
projects a real research grant?

The introduction of randomization into the grants process would
have to be undertaken judiciously. We could start with NSF. How
could scientists object to the idea that the collection of experimental data is required to validate the theory that government support
advances science? As it is, if NSF-supported scientists have more
papers (or any other output measure) than those who are not
supported, we cannot distinguish whether the funding allowed the
scientists to do research that otherwise they would not have done.
This may be because NSF funds the best scientists, and the best
scientists always produce more output; or because NSF funding

creates a "halo" that allows the scientists to get funding from other sources, or to participate in activities that would otherwise be closed to them. If, after the peer review process were completed, a small number of "winning" proposals were denied funding, and a small number of "losing" proposals were funded, we could answer these questions. If the feasibility of this approach (and its value in demonstrating a program's effectiveness) can be established with NSF, then it could be expanded to technology programs like the ATP.

Obviously, the analogy with drug trials cannot be taken too far. Drug trials are typically "double blind," meaning that neither the researchers nor the subjects know who is getting the treatment and who the placebo. In science or technology funding, the projects that are given a "placebo"—that are identified as "winning" but not given any money—will obviously know that they have not gotten the "treatment." This complicates the analysis, but still renders the data from such a trial far more useful than if no randomization occurs. Indeed, comparing the performance of unfunded winners with true "losers" will provide evidence on the existence of a "halo" effect whereby government recognition makes it easier for projects to get funding from other sources.

Would such a process be unfair to the unfunded winners? As with any human experimentation, subjects would have to be notified in advance that there was a chance of this occurring. Given the inherent randomness of the grant processes, this change need not increase greatly the perceived risk from the point of view of project proponents. With respect to putative "losers" that are funded anyway, it would be appropriate to apply a minimal quality screen before selecting these, so that the randomly-funded projects would be close in quality to those chosen on merit.

The desirability of experimental data illustrates a more general point about the data needs of research compared to those of assessment and evaluation. Experiments are probably considered politically unfeasible because the cost to stakeholders would be immediate, while the benefit—a better understanding of how these programs work—would come only in the future. While agency activities are driven by short-run pressures from OMB and Congress, it is in the long run that conclusions about effective and ineffective policy change the policy debate. In the 1950s and 1960s, economists began to study the adverse impacts of regulation of airlines, trucking, and other potentially competitive industries; in the 1970s and 1980s that research changed policy. Similarly, it took decades for market-based incentives for environmental cleanup to move from research into legislation. Sometime in the first decade of the next century, if we continue to collect the necessary data being produced now, we will understand the circumstances under which programs like ATP work well. The current Congress may not care about that, but future Congresses will.

The data needs for effective long-term research are not effectively addressed by the current GPRA-inspired performance measurement initiatives. With some modification, however, the collection of performance data could be augmented to satisfy these long-term needs. If a better understanding of what works and what does not in science and technology policy is truly our performance goal, such augmentation is crucial.

Acknowledgments

Tim Brennan, Jack Carpenter, Sylvia Kraemer, Rosalie Ruegg and Loren Yager provided helpful comments on this chapter, but are of course not responsible for any remaining errors or the chapter's policy recommendations.

Notes

1. "While the Committee believes a range of measures is important for program management and should be included in agency performance plans, it also believes that measures of program outcomes, not outputs, are the key set of measures that should be reported to OMB and Congress." United States Senate, "Government Performance and Results Act of 1993," 103rd Congress, Report 103–58, 1993, p. 29.

2. Interagency Committee on Federal Technology Transfer, Working Group on Technology Transfer Measurement and Evaluation, "Collective Reporting and Common Measures" (Draft for Comment), November 1994. This draft has never been finalized.

3. Committee on Fundamental Science, "Assessing Fundamental Science," <http:\\www.NSF.gov>, undated. (Participants in its development tell me it was completed in the fall of 1996.)

4. The Committee Report also contains case studies of individual agency assessment efforts.

5. See Randy Barrett, "Will Metrics Really Measure Up?" *Technology Transfer Business,* Spring 1995, pp. 34–36.

6. The author was one of these experts, and continues on an ongoing basis to advise ATP on its evaluation research. In addition, through the National Bureau of Economic Research, I am coordinating a series of research projects funded by the ATP as part of its evaluation effort.

7. See Rosalie Ruegg, "Guidelines for Economic Evaluation of the Advanced Technology Program" (Gaithersburg, Md.: Economic Assessment Office, Advanced Technology Program, November 1996).

8. See Jeanne W. Powell, *The ATP's Business Reporting System: A Tool for Economic Evaluation* (Gaithersburg, Md.: Economic Assessment Office, Advanced Technology Program, September 1996).

9., Edwin Mansfield, *Estimating Social and Private Returns from Innovations Based on the Advanced Technology Program: Problems and Opportunities,* for The Advanced Technology Program, National Institute of Standards and Technology, U.S. Department of Commerce, January 1996.

10. Of course, some involvement of the outside world is required, as in the willingness of university researchers to accept research grants, or of companies to form CRADAs. But this involvement is in the form of direct participation in the agency programs, as opposed to interaction of the agencies' activities with parties other than program participants.

11. For a discussion of this point in the context of fundamental research, see Susan E. Cozzens, "The Knowledge Pool: Measurement Challenges in Evaluating Fundamental Research Programs," Julia Melkers and J. David Roessner, eds., *Evaluation and Program Planning,* forthcoming.

12. I distinguish between outputs and outcomes based on whether they are direct or indirect consequences of the program. An alternative formulation would define outputs as anything produced by the program that is a means to a subsequent end but is not valued for its own sake, and an outcome as any valued product, whether direct or indirect. Under this formulation, new knowledge might be an output for some programs and an outcome for others, depending on the program's goals.

13. Carpenter and Carr use the word "indicator" for the concept that I am labeling "correlate." I have assigned "indicator" a broader meaning since the term is used explicitly in the GPRA with this broader meaning. See Jack Carpenter and Robert K. Carr, "Measurement and Evaluation of Technology Transfer from U.S. Dual-Use and Technology Programs," based on Robert K. Carr, "Measurement and Evaluation of Federal Technology Transfer," *Technology Commercialization and Economic Growth,* the Proceedings of the Twentieth Annual Meeting of the Technology Transfer Society, July 16–19, 1995, Washington, D.C.

14. Formally, if we think of the indicator as the sum of the underlying concept and an unobserved random error, we wish the variance of that error to be as small as possible.

15. See Cozzens, "The Knowledge Pool."

16. Changes over time in patenting behavior can be controlled for, if one is willing to make assumptions about the extent to which these changes are common across different patenting institutions. See Adam B. Jaffe and M. Trajtenberg, "Flows of Knowledge from Universities and Federal Labs: Modelling the Flow of Patent Citations over Time and Across Institutional and Geographic Boundaries," *Proceedings of the National Academy of Science*, Vol. 93 (November 1996), pp. 12671–12677.

17. See Carr, "Measurement and Evaluation of Federal Technology Transfer."

18. See James D. Adams, "Fundamental Stocks of Knowledge and Productivity Growth," *Journal of Political Economy*, Vol. 98, No. 41 (1990), pp. 673–702.

19. See United States General Accounting Office (GA0), "Measuring Performance: Strengths and Limitations of Research Indicators" (Washington, D.C.,U.S. GAO, March 1997).

20. See Mansfield, *Estimating Social and Private Returns from Innovations Based on the Advanced Technology Program.*

21. See Francis Narin, et al., *Linkage Between U.S. Patents and Public Science* (Haddon Heights, N.J.: CHI Research, Inc., January 9, 1997).

22. Working Group on Technology Transfer Measurement and Evaluation, "Collective Reporting and Common Measures."

23. See National Science Board, *Science & Engineering Indicators—1996*, NSB 96–21 (Washington, D.C.: U.S. Government Printing Office, 1996). The 1993 edition contained a table presenting four indicators of technology transfer from federal labs, by agency, for the years 1987–91. This table does not appear in the 1996 edition.

4

Social Capital: A Key Enabler of Innovation

Jane E. Fountain

The trend toward inter-organizational linkages in the form of partnerships and consortia has contributed to a strong resurgence of the U.S. economy. Many firms, industries, and regions that are currently successful have formed productive collaborative relationships with a variety of other firms, laboratories, universities, and governments at both state and federal levels in order to leverage the benefits of cooperation. These benefits include shared resources, shared staff and expertise, group problem-solving, multiple sources of learning, collaborative development, and diffusion of innovation.

The contribution to institutional effectiveness of all these relationships measured in terms of economic performance and innovative capacity—horizontally among similar firms in associations, vertically in supply chains, and multidirectional links to sources of technical knowledge, human resources, and public agencies—I refer to as "social capital." This form of capital, as powerful as physical and human capitals, is the "stock" that is created when a group of organizations develops the ability to work together for mutual productive gain.[1] The concept is drawn from research that demonstrates the effect of institutional and social arrangements on economic development. It has more recently been extended to explain differences in innovation rates among countries with similar capital, labor, and national resources.[2]

In this chapter, I explain the relationship between social capital and innovation in science and technology. I argue that social capital is a necessary, although not sufficient, enabler of effective public-private partnerships, for devolution of some science and technology responsibilities to the states, and for a new, more collaborative style of government policy. The fundamental significance of social capital for innovation, and thus for science and technology policy, while noted by observers at the forefront of thinking in this area, has yet to be assimilated by policy-makers and captured in the design of policy tools.[3] So far, almost no explicit attention has been directed toward the effect of social capital on innovation. But the relationship is important and has serious implications for science and technology policy.

In contrast to political and economic perspectives that emphasize individualism, closely held information, and autonomy, social capital is derived from those perspectives in which cooperation paradoxically enhances competitiveness, information sharing leads to joint gains, and the importance of reputation and trust ensure reciprocity and fair play within a given network. Adam Smith and other classical economists of the nineteenth century recognized that any firm needs an underlying fabric of shared values and understanding to make division of labor meaningful. Smith's observation is no less true today. When partnerships and consortia succeed, the glue that holds them together is not simply in the form of contracts that detail every aspect of these complex and dynamic relationships (although contracts are, of course, important). Nor is cohesion to be found exclusively in the information systems that link networks of organizations. The glue in the new political economy is the trust, or enlightened self-interest, among decision-makers that makes collaboration feasible.

The dramatic changes that have occurred in private industry throughout the world constitute a highly compelling challenge to the United States to craft a consensus policy that will strengthen civilian science and technology.[4] An effective science and technology policy should aid the ability of the private sector to reconfigure itself in ways that advance rapid technological change and diffuse innovation. It should recognize and support the fact that business and industry are now conducted on the basis not only of strategic alliances and partnerships but also on the basis of networks of learning and innovation. Although some aspects of science and technology policy already support organizational and institutional arrangements to increase research-based productivity in innovation, the pace of institutional innovation by government has slowed dramatically during a time of rapid and fundamental restructuring of the private sector. Inadequate attention has been paid by policymakers to those arrangements that contribute to social capital.

In the next section of this chapter I define social capital in some detail. I then extend the concept to explain how social capital affects innovation in science and technology. I present two cases of "best practice," the biotechnology industry and the regional-based industrial system in Silicon Valley. Both are highly innovative networks that demonstrate the importance and pervasiveness of external firm relationships to innovation. I describe two federal programs that make evident the growing importance of consortia development: the Advanced Technology Program (ATP) and the Manufacturing Extension Partnership (MEP). The final section of this chapter develops a set of recommendations designed to enhance national innovative capacity through the formation of social capital.

What Is Social Capital?

Like "physical capital and human capital—tools and training that enhance individual productivity—'social capital' refers to features of social organization, such as networks, norms, and trust, that facilitate coordination and cooperation for mutual benefit."[5] The notion of social capital extends our understanding of "cooperation" or "collaboration" in two significant ways. First, linking cooperation to the economic concept "capital" signals the investment or growth potential of a group's ability to work jointly. Second, the concept identifies the *structure* created from collaborative effort as capital. Well-functioning partnerships, consortia, and networks are in and of themselves "a form of social capital."[6] Capital is located both in the sharable resources held by individual institutions in a network and in the overall structure—the relationship—among the institutions in a network. For example, a group of scientists who have collaborated on a relatively small scientific project may then use their collaborative ability to propose and to complete larger, riskier research projects. They may then further use their network to address the economic revitalization of their community. Their originally small network may be extended to members of the political and business community: small cooperative ventures may grow into more ambitious undertakings as parties learn how to collaborate productively and develop reputations for trustworthiness. Social capital, like other forms of capital, accumulates when used productively. Traditional economic perspectives that focus on short-term self interest and individual transactions ignore the accretion, or growth, opportunities of cooperation.[7] Closely related to accretion is the self-reinforcing cyclic nature of social relations. Trustful relations tend to be self-reinforcing in the positive direction. Mistrust tends to cycle in the negative direction.

The concept of social capital is relatively simple, yet its opposite was viewed until recently as the common, if unfortunate, order of most economic relations. Consider the eighteenth century Scottish philosopher David Hume's pessimistic account of human nature:

Your corn is ripe today; mine will be so tomorrow. 'Tis profitable for us both that I should labour with you today, and that you should aid me tomorrow. I have no kindness for you, and know you have as little for me. I will not, therefore, take any pains upon your account; and should I labour with you upon my own account, in expectation of a return, I know I should be disappointed, and that I should in vain depend upon your gratitude. Here then I leave you to labour alone; You treat me in the same manner. The seasons change; and both of us lose our harvests for want of mutual confidence and security.[8]

Hume wrote of the dilemma economists typically refer to as the problem of "collective action." Although in most situations all parties would be better off were they to cooperate, collective action theory argues that, in the absence of an overarching authority to enforce appropriate behavior or clear mechanisms to ensure commitment, individuals will tend not to take the risks of cooperation. None achieve the gains from cooperation and all are worse off.

Policy experts, drawing on collective action theory, have long argued that the coordination costs associated with interorganizational and interjurisdictional arrangements often exceed the benefits.[9] They have stressed the need for clear lines of authority and strong, centralized governance structures to monitor behavior and to enforce sanctions against inappropriate actions. But during the past decade or so, social scientists from a variety of disciplines, as well as an increasing number of policy experts, have noted and have sought to explain the proliferation and success of collaborative arrangements in a variety of policy settings. The broad term "social capital" captures many of the salient properties that allow these arrangements to prosper.

The constituent elements of social capital are trust, norms, and networks. Trust is developed over time as individuals gain confidence in the reliability of others in a series of interactions.[10] A key property of social capital rests on the transitivity of trust: A trusts C because B trusts C and A trusts B. Thus, relatively large networks may exhibit generalized trust without close personal contact among all members. Norms of appropriate behavior develop as a social contract is negotiated among actors. Experts have noted that the norm of reciprocity is fundamental to productive relationships. In politics and bureaucratic behavior this norm is well known as the "favor bank."[11] Closely linked to reciprocity is a norm that actors will forego their immediate self-interest to act not only in the interest of the group but in their own long-term self-interest.[12] Thus, a reputation for trustworthiness, so important in politics and government, is also essential to actors within collaborative networks. Social capital is preserved by careful selection of network players and strict sanctioning of inappropriate (network-destroying) behaviors. A network develops when a group of individuals or organizations develop reliable, productive communication and decision channels and a more or less permeable boundary to define members.

It is important to note in any discussion of the concept that social capital—like its constituent elements, trust, norms, and networks—is inherently neither good nor bad. It is a tool that may be employed for legal or illegal purposes, for good or ill. Trust allows actors to engage in productive collaboration, but trust also provides a necessary condition for fraud and other illegal activities. Norms decrease transaction costs and regulate behavior, but when improperly used, they may stifle the creativity and diversity of opinion necessary for solving novel and complex problems. Networks of firms collaborating to produce new technologies or applications widely report the benefits of cooperation; cartels, unfortunately, also understand the benefits of network approaches to production and distribution. The important point is that social capital is a powerful resource that develops from productive social ties. Its use depends entirely upon the values and objectives of the actors involved.[13] The benefits that flow from social capital far outweigh the dangers, given present levels of government scrutiny of potential collusive activity.

In fact, within the public policy community, after decades of failure and billions of lost dollars invested in the impoverished nations of the world, development experts have come to appreciate the importance of social capital as the foundation for economic development. Policy experts have documented the importance and extent of rotating credit associations—informal collective savings and loan plans—that prosper throughout the world.[14] Others researchers have studied the collaborative stewardship of common-pool resources, such as water supplies and grazing areas, that are managed for long-term collective benefit.[15] Experts on urban development in the advanced industrial nations have made the formation of social capital a fundamental element of policies to build and strengthen the social and economic fabric of cities. International relations scholars have documented the extent to which international agreements of many types are developed and adhered to in the absence of overarching authority.

Empirical research on the characteristics of successful cooperative arrangements indicates a set of conditions that aid the formation of social capital. When actors form relationships over a period of time long enough to establish a series of transactions, reputations for fairness and reliability may be built which lead to trustful relations.[16] Successful cooperative arrangements tend to have a limited number of players, which makes it easier for information about reputations and transactions to be shared within the network. Successful formation of social capital requires that actors value the long-run relationship highly enough to forego immediate gains for future benefits. The boundaries and objectives of the network must be clearly defined. In some cases, it has been important for participants in the network to define the rules under which they will cooperate. Graduated sanctions must be in place to punish inappropriate actions without destroying the network. Similarly, well-performing networks must develop conflict resolution mechanisms in order to resolve inevitable disagreements.[17]

How Social Capital Increases Innovation

As the pace of technological change has intensified, as economic resources have become more scarce, and as information technologies have made linkages among geographically dispersed actors commonplace, the predominant form of economic organization has been changing. Large, centralized bureaucracies emphasizing division of labor and functional specialization have given way to smaller, leaner organizations in which team-based structures cross functional lines, disrupt traditional hierarchical chains of command, and focus on core functions while contracting with outside firms for other tasks.

As an adjunct to internal restructuring, large manufacturers have turned to long-term external supplier relationships for many inputs to the production process as well as a variety of operational and administrative functions. Thus, specialized technological knowledge—and innovation—increasingly reside in small and medium suppliers whose "research and development" takes place in team-based configurations on the shop floor rather than in corporate laboratories staffed with scientists working on long-range basic research. Roos, Field, and Neely note in Chapter 15 of this volume that the base of technology offerings has increased to the point that it has outstripped the capacity of single firms to remain competent in the technology fields relevant to their business. In addition, the investments necessary to sustain technology development and deployment have increased to the point that single firms usually cannot undertake the level of risk necessary for innovation. For these reasons, supplier relationships have grown in importance. For complex products, suppliers function both as partners with lead firms and independently to develop and deploy new technologies.[18]

Another change is found in the relationship of firms to an array of government agencies with jurisdiction over regulation, research and development funding, standards setting, procurement, and other functions that shape the capacity of firms to innovate. (See Chapter 11, "Towards A New Generation of Environmental Technology," by George Heaton and Darryl Banks in this volume.) A significant effort is being made to reduce the extent of mandatory regulations enforced by primitive sanctions and to replace them with a growing array of incentives and disincentives intended to induce firm behavior that satisfies public needs while allowing firms to optimize their economic performance. If government-industry relationships also contribute to the formation of social capital necessary to innovation in science and technology, then government must continue to modernize its management, rules, and behavior to contribute. The criticality of innovation to economic performance and competitiveness is one powerful reason to move away from a market economy bounded by hard walls of government regulation to one with permeable boundaries of government incentives and disincentives.

The presence of a network of institutions in no way assures collaboration. Many networks are highly conflictual, mired in contractual disputes and lack of coordination.[19] However, high-performing networks are able to learn to collaborate. Firms leverage their information-processing capacity through the network form. Unless the network that provides firms with new sources of efficiency and opportunities for innovation is open in structure and efficient in information exchange, little advantage can be gained. Thus the transformation in information networks from hierarchically structured and centrally controlled to highly efficient and flexible peer-to-peer (mesh) network structures has been a key factor in enabling the formation of new sources of social capital.

Compared to large, hierarchical structures, network structures can more effectively scan the environment for changes, more accurately interpret environmental change, and more creatively and adaptively craft responses to change. Better scanning means stronger capacity for timely and accurate problem recognition. Greater effectiveness of interpretation enhances policy and problem formulation, estimation of parameters, and selection from alternative policy choices. Greater adaptability translates into timely innovation and enhanced alignment of firms, practices, and products with environmental conditions.

It should be clear from this discussion that social capital is entirely different from "informational capital."[20] Many observers have noted the importance of shared information to entrepreneurship and economic growth. Although open access to information, notably in recent times through the Internet, provides a variety of opportunities, informational capital is not a replacement for social capital. Social capital provides decision-makers with far more important information benefits than access to the Internet. Useful access involves understanding who will benefit from specific information. It also involves screening information for accuracy, importance, and implications. Collaborative networks perform this critical screening function.[21] Social capital encompasses not only shared access to vast amounts of timely information but many positive properties of interdependence: shared values, goals, and objectives; shared expertise and knowledge; sharing of work, decision-making, and prioritization; shared risk, accountability, and trust; and shared rewards.[22] Social capital increases the ability to build and use informational capital because trustful relationships increase information flows and bring richer meaning to information.

Actors in a collaborative network exhibit an efficient form of collective learning. They learn of new technologies, opportunities, the outcome of transactions, and challenges more quickly because of density of interaction within the network. Learning is of a higher quality because it is subject to discussion and debate among horizontal counterparts whose perspectives and backgrounds may differ. For this reason, geographic regions that include highly adaptive industry networks have been termed "learning regions."[23]

By contrast, vertically organized firms and their supply chains with few horizontal connections tend toward characteristics that adversely affect information-processing capacity: inward, insular focus; unproductive levels of vertical integration within large firms and bureaucracies; unproductive levels of secrecy and organizational loyalty that dampen information sharing within and across professions; norms of institutional stability and autonomy that fit poorly with a turbulent economic, technological, globally competitive environment; authority centralized at unproductive levels; and predominantly vertical flows of information, which tend to be slower, biased, and thus less reliable. Regions characterized by firms with these properties cannot as effectively innovate. In fact, attempts at partnerships and consortia under these conditions of low trust lead either to failure or to poorly performing, noncollaborative networks.

Understanding the differences in information processing in large, vertically integrated hierarchies versus more horizontal network structures is critical to understanding how social capital is built and maintained in the latter and how it leads to greater innovation potential. Differences in environmental scanning, information flows, and relative lack of bias aggregate to a greater capacity to innovate in the network form than within a hierarchy. Dense social networks can encourage experimentation and entrepreneurship among actors because of the mix of collaboration and competition within the network. Network members compete fiercely but also collectively process and share information about environmental changes including markets, regulations, technologies, and opportunities.

Interorganizational networks, partnerships, and consortia could not function to the extent and at the levels of interaction now typical without an electronic interface. However, the promise of information technologies for bringing about vast changes in the structure, systems, and management of business and industry—far beyond those discussed in this chapter—has yet to be achieved.[24] Researchers consistently note the resistance of systems and structures to change even in the face of the great potential for increased efficiency offered by new information technologies. The ability to collaborate both within and among firms and other organizations appears to be a necessary condition for firms to take advantage of new technologies rather than resisting change.

The explosive growth of Internet use prompts another question: Does social capital have to be built face-to-face? Currently, experts disagree regarding the importance of face-to-face interaction for the formation of trust and collaboration. Technology researchers celebrate the ability of information technology to make distance and time constraints virtually meaningless. However, most of the research that has been conducted on industry networks notes the importance of geographic proximity. More empirical study is required to understand the potential for developing social capital in geographically dispersed networks.

In spite of the need for continuing research efforts, the responsibility of the federal government to invest in information infrastructure is clear and relates importantly to the ability of researchers in science and technology to collaborate in a variety of ways. (See Chapter 13, "Beyond the National Information Infrastructure Initiative," by Brian Kahin in this volume.) The more difficult investments in information infrastructure are not hardware but software and institution-building to enable industry restructuring and partnerships, to enhance education and training at all levels, and to make the national network of libraries and information services available throughout the nation.[25]

The Dynamics of Collaboration in Networks

The two illustrations that follow present examples of high-performing network structures that have developed significant levels of trust. The first describes the ways in which firms in the biotechnology industry partner to remain at the forefront of research and development. The second case outlines the dynamics that undergird regional industrial systems, exemplified in this case by the semiconductor industry in Silicon Valley, California.

The Biotechnology Industry: Learning Networks

The biotechnology industry provides a cutting-edge example of new forms of industry operation that demand an intensive level of external collaboration. The traditional view of technological development and industry structure holds that technologies follow a typical life cycle whose character shapes the form of an industry. In industries as diverse as high technology, heavy manufacturing, and utilities, the trajectory of technological development and change and its effect on industry structure have been viewed by scholars as roughly similar. Within an early experimental period during which technologies are young, many firms compete and exhibit high turnover rates. As the dominant technologies for the industry take shape, those firms that best exemplify the leading technologies build economies of scale and are able to leverage the most efficient

process technologies and market-scale economies, thereby blocking new entrants to the field. As the industry matures, less efficient
firms are driven out of business by market forces, while a small
number of leading firms, traditionally viewed as the most efficient,
remain.[26]

However, under conditions where "new discoveries create technological discontinuities, or [there are] radical breaks from previously dominant methods," leading firms may lose their advantage,
and new ways of doing business may emerge that better exploit the
new technologies.[27] Biotechnology is an industry characterized by
radical, or discontinuous, technological advances. "Biotechnology
represents a competence-destroying innovation because it builds
on a scientific basis (immunology and molecular biology) that
differs significantly from the knowledge base (organic chemistry)
of the more established pharmaceutical industry."[28] Thus, one
would expect that the traditional model would not hold, but that
instead many firms would continue to compete over a longer
period of time.

Many experts regard strategic alliances to be the foundation for
inter-firm collaboration in business and industry. Whereas large
firms in the past maintained in-house research and development
laboratories in order to retain dominance in their core technologies, firms increasingly have externalized this function through
cooperative agreements with other firms, research laboratories,
and universities. Most experts explain the rise in consortium
activity as attempts to reduce the cycle time of innovation, to reach
new markets and technologies, to share risks and gain complementary competencies.[29]

But other researchers have argued that when the knowledge
base of an industry is hard to comprehend, not complete, and
highly dispersed across organizations, then collaboration among
firms, universities, and national laboratories will reflect a strong
and fundamental interest in access to knowledge rather than
simply with strategic calculation, resource sharing, or transaction
cost reduction.[30] Internal expertise remains necessary to evaluate
external research and development, but external relations facilitate access to new information and expertise that is not easily built
within the firm. The biotechnology industry exemplifies this concern with knowledge access. The shape of the industry provides

strong evidence for the effect of social capital on innovation.

The birth and early development of the biotechnology industry occurred during the 1980s and early 1990s. The National Institutes of Health (NIH) played a vital role in the formation of the industry by its support of $65 billion of scientific research through universities and their buffer institutions. (See Chapter 14, "University-Industry Relations: The Next Four Years and Beyond," by Harvey Brooks and Lucien Randazzese in this volume.) Federal support comprised the funding source of initial biotech firms and remains a continued source of sustenance.

One of the striking aspects of this industry is the range and number of formal interorganizational collaborations among firms, research laboratories, and universities. (See Chapter 9 by David Guston.) For example, a detailed study of collaboration in the most research-intensive segment of the industry, human therapeutics and diagnostics, found that the percentage of firms with formal ties to other biotech firms increased from 74 percent in 1990 to 86 percent in 1994.[31] Measurement of formal ties underestimates the extent to which these firms collaborate. A complete portrayal of the degree of extra-firm associations would have to include not only formal interorganizational arrangements but also informal alliances and professional interactions among scientists from different organizations. Such informal, professional interactions are numerous.

In the biotechnology industry, older firms possess a greater number of formal collaborative relationships than younger firms. Those firms that collaborated externally tended to be older and much larger than firms without ties, and the disparity in size grew slightly during this time period. Firms with no external ties tended to be very small and the percentage of isolated firms decreased by 50 percent, from 62 to 31 firms, during the five-year period.[32] Although the number of formal external relationships grows only slightly, on average, network measures of centrality and closeness indicate that firms strengthened their existing connections substantially during this time period. As firms age and grow in size, they do not decrease the number and diversity of external ties although they are clearly large enough to move several R&D activities in-house. But although network centrality appears to be necessary for firm success, it is not a sufficient condition. In other words, all of the successful biotech firms in this study are highly active collaborators and none of the isolated firms were successful. However, there are actively collaborative firms that do not succeed. In general, however, the more network R&D activity engaged in by a firm, the greater the likelihood that the firm becomes a central—and highly successful—player in the industry network.[33]

In fields in which knowledge is distributed across a wide range of organizations and where scientific and technological knowledge is critical to competitiveness, innovation is located in the network rather than within individual firms. A zero-sum depiction, in which a firm gains only at the expense of others, inaccurately portrays the situation of most industries affected by the rapid pace of technological and scientific change. It is far more accurate to view the external relationships in terms of a positive-sum game in which joint gains, or wins, are realized which disadvantage no firm in the network. Few would suggest that the biotechnology industry is not characterized by fierce competition. Nevertheless, the basis for competition is more accurately described in terms of competing networks of firms rather than rivalries among individual firms. The collaboration required to stay abreast of technological and process advances, rather than diminishing competition, merely changes its character.

Finally, one cannot fully understand the structure and development of this knowledge network without reaching far beyond the small biotech firms into the universities and the NIH government laboratories (discussed by David Guston in Chapter 9, "Technology Transfer and the Use of CRADAs at the National Institutes of Health"). The government role in positioning universities and NIH to spin off biotech firms is critical. Decades of biotech research funded by NIH (10 percent in-house, 90 percent outside contracts) created the capability and strongly influenced the institutional structure described in this section.

Regional Network-Based Industrial Systems: The Case of Silicon Valley

Many other industries have developed social capital through external relations with other organizations in order to increase their ability to innovate and to absorb innovations. Experts have documented the unprecedented competitive success of networked systems of industrial production.[34] To date, proximity has provided a powerful aid to realizing these advantages. Examples of such systems are found in Silicon Valley, California; Triangle Park, North Carolina; in the textile firms of northern Italy; and as the predominant industrial form in Japan.

One of the best-known examples of a high-performing industry network is the computer industry of Silicon Valley, California. The professional culture is highly collaborative. Non-proprietary professional and technical information is regularly shared among employees and companies. Professionals regularly telephone and e-mail one another for assistance concerning specific technical problems. Professionals meet socially and discuss technical issues. Employment mobility of professional employees is unusually high relative to other industries. Nevertheless, among competing firms and professionals, the level of competition is fierce.[35]

Three different, but highly interrelated, structures—firm, industry, and institution—work together in Silicon Valley and explain the high levels of efficiency, adaptability, and innovation within this setting.[36] The system exhibits congruence, or alignment, among the internal firm structure, the organization of the network, and the wider institutional structure in the region that supports the industry. At the level of the firm, one typically finds management structures aligned with the use of advanced information technologies. These include de-layering the chain of command and greater use of horizontal coordination through the formation of cross-functional teams, a more fluid division of labor, decision-making that is pushed down the organization, task specialization that reflects the job enrichment available through the use of workstations and reengineered business processes, and organization by business unit rather than by function. These structural characteristics at the level of the organization enable greater flexibility, increased capacity to absorb innovation, and more efficient use of human and technical resources.

At the industry level, networked systems exhibit low levels of vertical integration because of the high degree of outsourcing for inputs that occurs. In addition, one finds a greater number and type of linkages among producers, suppliers, and customers within and across related sectors, forming a rich system of interconnections among network nodes.

The broader institutional structure in which the industry network is embedded plays a critical role in the economic viability of the network. Stanford University plays a much more central role in this network than simply as supplier of research and researchers to industry. Stanford spawned Hewlett-Packard, one of the Valley's central firms, as well as many other firms. Firm leadership, as well as several venture capitalists, have strong ties to the university and, thus, to one another. In many ways, Stanford University is the chief influence on the culture of Silicon Valley. Similarly, the Massachusetts Institute of Technology and the banks of Boston played similar roles in shaping the culture of the high-tech industry along Route 128 in Massachusetts.[37]

Some, but not all, of the norms that comprise social capital have been codified into legal arrangements. Contracting devices critical for scientific and technical innovation in a network environment include cross-licensing, second-sourcing arrangements, technology agreements, and joint ventures. The federal government has played a key role here. It catalyzed cross-licensing through judicial decisions made during the anti-trust suit against AT&T. Second-sourcing arrangements were originally required by the Department of Defense to ensure supply. The arrangements, however, quickly spread beyond military contracts and some of the second-source firms became innovators in their own right. These legal instruments spread innovation and risk by pooling resources.

Educational systems at all levels ensure a supply of skilled labor and provide training, retraining, and development of technical staff. At the graduate school level, these systems produce basic and applied research and researchers. The inclusion of a first-rate research university or laboratory in the network, like Stanford University in Silicon Valley, greatly strengthens the potential for scientific innovation. Strong networks or partnerships among government, universities, and industry help to ensure the supply of scientists and technical experts, a critical component of national competitiveness. These partnerships also ensure the continued high quality of scientists and technical experts by translating new ideas, technologies, and methods from universities to industry and from industry to universities. In the case of Silicon Valley, the system benefits from the strong supporting role played by other institutions of higher learning. State and community college systems, through strong, focused engineering and technical training programs, supply and sustain high-quality technical employees able to function effectively in a networked environment.

The case of Silicon Valley, an exemplar of a regional network-based industrial system, exhibits many of the properties that underlie national advantage. The firms and other players within the network tend to become mutually reinforcing, with beneficial interactions flowing in all directions. The ability of a well-functioning network exceeds the aggregate abilities of the individual nodes. The network attracts related industries and grows into a "cluster" of associated industries. Research comparing national advantage in a variety of industry sectors demonstrates that this clustering of industries, with all the benefits of collaboration associated with the network form, is highly correlated with national competitive advantage.[38]

Building Social Capital through Science and Technology Policy

Many aspects of federal science and technology policy advance interorganizational relationships. The components of two federal programs that build social capital are summarized in the next section. Although neither the Advanced Technology Program (ATP) nor the Manufacturing Extension Partnership (MEP) have as their primary focus the construction of collaborative efforts, both programs contribute to linkage in substantial ways.

Enabling Cooperation through the Advanced Technology Program

Many benefits of network-based arrangements have been produced as positive, if largely unintended, consequences of the U.S. Department of Commerce's Advanced Technology Program. (See Chapter 6, "The Advanced Technology Program: Opportunities for Enhancement," by Christopher Hill.) The ATP funds, on a cost-shared basis, research to create industrial technology that is considered too risky for firms to fund on their own but which, if successfully developed, would be of net benefit not only to the firm but also to the nation.

The program selects awardees by a competitive process using well-defined criteria, none of which is meant to favor consortia over single firms. [Editors' note: while this book was in press, ATP changed its criteria in ways that now favor consortia.] Advanced Technology Program projects are selected on two criteria. First, they must be technically sound and promise high value if successful and, second, if technically successful they must be judged likely to possess low business risk. Consortia typically pool business risk, and technologies of interest to more than one firm tend to be of broader interest than those pursued by single firms. For these two reasons, indirect incentives in ATP would tend to give joint ventures a broadly based advantage over single firms, although single firms are by no means excluded.

As this chapter and many others in this volume argue, the development of new technologies increasingly comes about through broad-based, multi-party cooperation. If social capital inheres in the *structures* that are developed through consortium efforts, then the long-term benefits to the nation in terms of increasing innovative capacity should accrue more strongly through support to consortia rather than to single firms. In each case evaluated by ATP, some value should be estimated for the potential long-term benefits of creating collaboration that extend beyond the estimated direct value of the proposed project.

A survey of 115 ATP awardees who received their awards during the 1990–92 period provides insights into the benefits of ATP as perceived by firms in the program. One of the key benefits, from the perspective of participant firms, was the stimulus to collaborate provided by the program. The joint venture projects included, on average, six formal participants. Moreover, during the course of the contract, 35 out of 85 joint venture participants established subcontracts with five other companies, on average. All but one of the consortia were newly formed as a result of ATP.

One might argue that many firms would develop external ties even in the absence of ATP, given the obvious leverage achieved through partnerships. But the survey results indicate otherwise. A participant in a large joint venture which brought together competitors as joint researchers observed:

Collaboration, cooperation, and learning to operate in a consortium with competitors were key outcomes of the ATP. We saw and experienced the value of working together with competitors. The ability to leverage knowledge has been so tremendous. It has broken invisible barriers.[39]

Another respondent noted, "We gain the leverage of working together with the companies. The money is not the actual benefit, but the leverage."[40] One of the most important indirect effects of ATP may be attitudinal change. A participant in a joint venture reported:

The ATP award has opened the eyes of management that technological projects like this one are valuable. Our company used to turn away from outside collaborations. We had a history of zero; we were an inward-looking company. We were skeptical at first of collaboration, but not now.[41]

ATP awardees responded overwhelmingly that the chief benefit of collaboration has been the stimulation of creative thinking by pooling expertise. The two other benefits rated most highly by participants relate to time savings. Firms value the ability to commercialize products more quickly and to save time in general.[42]

The chief difficulties reported concern the start-up period and the multi-party negotiations required to integrate different cultures for the purposes of the joint venture. Learning to collaborate equates to learning to trust, or establishing credibility among the parties. This process necessarily involves a series of interactions over time. But in spite of these difficulties, 92 percent of the participants surveyed reported that the ATP experience heightened their interest in external collaboration. Moreover, 96 percent of the joint venture participants said that their ATP experience had motivated them to seek out future joint ventures.[43]

It is widely observed, although the evidence remains anecdotal at this time, that many firms not awarded funds have also found great value in the process of building consortia in order to apply for an ATP award. The existence of ATP creates a forum within which firms can identify potential partners and ventures. These spillover effects merit systematic evaluation in order to more fully identify the incentives and outcomes produced by programs that play a role in restructuring industry. The favorable social, economic, and technological context for collaboration—plus the obvious benefits—suggest that even a relatively small incentive from the government can foster the development of networks of firms and universities, and thus increase the rate and quality of technological innovation. For these reasons, the authors of Chapter 18 urge that ATP be focused primarily on networks of firms, and in appropriate cases, networks in which universities, national laboratories, and perhaps state governments participate. The incentive that ATP could offer for formation of such networks or consortia might be the program's most valuable economic contribution.

Revitalizing Manufacturing through the Manufacturing Extension Partnership

The benefits of partnership and collaboration in networks are not confined to high-tech industries. The revitalization of manufacturing depends to a great extent on the capacity of manufacturers to develop external relationships. A limiting factor for many older manufacturing firms is the requirement for an attitudinal shift on the part of manufacturers to recognize the benefits, indeed the necessity, of working collaboratively in order to modernize and to remain abreast of technological developments that affect the business.

The key to state-of-the-art manufacturing is close integration throughout the supply chain. At the core of such integration of systems and operations are advanced manufacturing technologies such as electronic data interchange (EDI) and just-in-time (JIT) inventory control. Advanced technologies are necessary for the success of advanced manufacturing settings. Studies demonstrate that effective manufacturing systems tend to implement state-of-the-art human resource practices in order to enable and support cross-functional teams and systematic, decentralized problem-solving at all levels of the operation.[44] Externally, those manufacturing firms that have successfully implemented product and process data exchange across firms have had to develop the ability to cooperate in order to evolve shared goals, resources, and incentives that provide a basis for smooth communication among firms.[45]

A key success of federal technology policy during the 1990s has been the revitalization of manufacturing by means of policies that support both new technologies and the state-of-the-art business practices that allow new technologies to be implemented.[46] The Manufacturing Extension Partnership (MEP) comprises a broad network of federal and state governments, non-profit organizations, industry groups, and educational institutions. The MEP is itself a collaborative network. It links a host of management and technology assistance providers to small and medium-size manufacturing firms. (See Chapter 10, "Manufacturing Extension: Performance, Challenges, and Policy Issues," by Philip Shapira.) Most of the services provided by MEP are focused on individual firm needs. However, MEP also helps firms to develop external relationships to promote integration and information processing capacity.[47] Given the importance of external relationships to innovation, the ability of MEP to promote linkages within more mature industries is a critical element in the revitalization of manufacturing.

The delivery mechanism used by MEP also builds social capital. Awards stimulate public and private organizations to collaborate in order to work with local manufacturers in a systematic, integrated fashion. Typically, MEP centers form an integral part of local networks of service providers. A national network of more than 300 local MEP offices has links to more than 750 service delivery organizations. This vast and growing network includes a wide variety of players: "non-profit technology or business assistance centers, economic development groups, universities and community colleges, private consultants, utilities, federal laboratories, and industry associations."[48]

In many aging manufacturing settings and in some urban settings, the key obstacle to development of strategic alliances, networks of innovation, and consortia lies in outmoded ways of interacting. Information is closely held. There are few institutionalized opportunities for discussion and dialogue across functions and firms. Joint problem-solving skills have not been developed as they have been in larger, more profitable firms that experimented with quality programs, team-based problem-solving, and the formation of consortia during the 1980s and 1990s. These basic skills are necessary for collaborative efforts to work. Training and development programs, as well as exposure to the criticality of network linkages in order to gain access to innovations, could foster development of these skills. The Manufacturing Extension Partnership provides a model to manufacturers for networked approaches to innovation.

Recommendations and Conclusions

This chapter closes with a set of recommendations for government action, using a more complete set of policy tools to foster linkages and the trust that would enable accelerating innovation and productivity growth. First, the federal government should aggressively provide incentives and information to promote the use of networks and consortia in order to connect firms to universities, national labs, and state and federal partnership programs. Second, it should examine closely the potential use of the Internet to diffuse power of regional agglomerations to distance-independent ones.

Third, consensus building is an indirect policy tool that government can use to advance the objectives of technology policy. The federal level can explicitly seek to build social capital among key stakeholders by providing a forum for dialogue and discussion to search for and establish consensus as a basis for collaboration.

Fourth, the urgent need for collaboration and integration suggests the need for a less adversarial relationship between government and business. Government is an indispensable part of the national network of innovation, both through its incentive programs and through its regulatory constraints. Therefore, the need for trust within the national network is essential. This recommendation does not imply that government should weaken control mechanisms, but instead suggests that it should make full use of modernized, more flexible, and more powerful controls, using advanced information and communication technologies.

Fifth, greater decentralization within science and technology policy programs would allow for greater responsiveness without loss of control. For government actions to fit the needs of industry and of regions, government must better understand the needs of different industries and different states. The tendency to adopt "one size fits all" policies and overly standardized programs has been a problem.

Finally, the research needs to support social capital formation are great. Mapping of industry clusters as well as regions that remain relatively insular is needed. The actual potential of the Internet to foster linkages the transcend geographic boundaries has yet to be explored. The dynamics of the start-up period for consortia demand study. If the initial negotiations among parties can be made more efficient and effective, resources could move toward innovation more quickly and at lower cost.

The current political, economic, and technological environment in the United States forces government to invest less money more wisely in higher-leverage policy instruments. Rather than simply "doing more with less," policy-makers must identify and use more advanced and powerful policy tools to yield the best return on investment of tax dollars. Policy design that reflects the importance of institutional arrangements to technological innovation has the potential to yield substantial return on government investment.

In sum, federal policies must be adapted to the extraordinary structural changes taking place in industries as firms develop and maintain competencies by forming alliances and overlapping collaborative relationships. The key enabler to strengthening innovation, and its dissemination and absorption, may lie as much in increasing the social capital of our productive sectors as in direct investments in science and technology.

Acknowledgments

The author gratefully acknowledges the helpful comments of Darin Boville, Cary Coglianese, David Hart, Christopher Hill, and Robert Putnam.

Notes

1. James S. Coleman, *Foundations of Social Theory* (Cambridge, Mass.: Harvard University Press, 1990), pp. 300–321; Robert Putnam, *Making Democracy Work: Civic Traditions in Modern Italy* (Princeton, N.J.: Princeton University Press, 1993), chap. 6.; Putnam, "The Prosperous Community: Social Capital and Public

Life," *The American Prospect*, No. 13 (Spring 1993). Glenn Loury first introduced the term "social capital" and noted its importance to economic development. See Glenn Loury, "A Dynamic Theory of Racial Income Differences," in P.A. Wallace and A. LeMund, eds., *Women, Minorities, and Employment Discrimination* (Lexington, Mass.: Lexington Books, 1977); Loury, "Why Should We Care about Group Inequality?" *Social Philosophy and Policy*, Vol. 5 (1987), pp. 249–271.

2. Lewis M. Branscomb, "Social Capital: The Key Element in Science-Based Development," *Science-Based Economic Development: Case Studies around the World*, Annals of the New York Academy of Sciences, Vol. 798; Lewis M. Branscomb and Young-Hwan Choi, "A Framework for Discussing Korea's Techno-Economic Future," in Branscomb and Choi, eds., *Korea at the Turning Point: Innovation-Based Strategies for Development* (Westport, Conn.: Praeger, 1996).

3. Branscomb, "Social Capital"; Branscomb and Choi, "A Framework for Discussing Korea's Techno-Economic Future"; Branscomb and Choi, "The Next Stage: The Road to an Innovation-Led Korea," chapter 15 in Branscomb and Choi, *Korea at the Turning Point*; Lewis M. Branscomb and Henry Ergas, "Contrasting Models: Brazil and Small European Countries," chap. 11 in ibid.; and see also Richard R. Nelson, ed., *National Systems of Innovation: A Comparative Analysis* (New York: Oxford University Press, 1993).

4. Lewis Branscomb, et al., "Investing in Innovation: A Strategy for U.S. Technology Policy," Science, Technology, and Public Policy Program Discussion Paper, Harvard University, 1997.

5. Putnam, "The Prosperous Community."

6. Ronald S. Burt, *Structural Holes: The Social Structure of Competition* (Cambridge, Mass.: Harvard University Press, 1992), p. 12.

7. Elinor Ostrom, *Governing the Commons: The Evolution of Institutions for Collective Action* (New York: Cambridge University Press, 1990).

8. David Hume (1740), Book 3, Part 2, Section 5, quoted in Robert D. Putnam, *Making Democracy Work: Civic Traditions in Modern Italy* (Princeton, N.J.: Princeton University Press, 1993), p. 163.

9. See, for example, Jeffrey Pressman and Aaron Wildavsky, *Implementation* (Berkeley: University of California Press, 1973); Eugene Bardach, *The Implementation Game* (Cambridge, Mass.: The MIT Press, 1977).

10. For micro-level explanations of the development of interorganizational arrangements see Peter Smith Ring and Andrew Van de Ven, "Developmental Processes of Cooperative Interorganizational Relationships," *Academy of Management Review*, Vol. 19, No. 1 (1994); Jane E. Fountain, "Trust as a Basis for Interorganizational Forms," paper delivered at conference on "Network Analysis and Innovations in Public Programs," University of Wisconsin at Madison, September 30, 1994.

11. See, for example, Christopher Matthews, *Hardball* (New York: Simon & Schuster, 1988), chap. 3.

12. See Coleman, *Foundations of Social Theory*.

13. See Alejandro Portes and Patricia Landolt, "The Downside of Social Capital," *The American Prospect*, No. 26 (May–June 1996).

14. A rotating credit association consists of a network of carefully selected participants, each of whom make monthly contributions and each of whom receive the "pot" in sequence. Failure to pay, even after receiving the combined contributions, is exceedingly rare. Members typically use the funds to begin or develop small businesses or to make home improvements. See Robert Putnam, *Making Democracy Work*, pp. 167–169; T. Besley, S. Coate, and G. Loury, "The Economics of Rotating Savings and Credit Associations," *American Economic Review*, Vol. 83, No. 4 (September 1993), pp. 792–811; Carlos G. Velez-Ibanez, *Bonds of Mutual Trust: The Cultural Systems of Rotating Credit Associations among Urban Mexicans and Chicanos* (New Brunswick, N.J.: Rutgers University Press, 1983); Clifford Geertz, "The Rotating Credit Association: A 'Middle Rung' in Development," *Economic Development and Cultural Change*, Vol. 10 (April 1962).

15. Elinor Ostrom has conducted systematic comparative studies of common-pool resource management in order to determine why some collective action arrangements succeed while others fail to achieve cooperative, and hence, successful outcomes, in order to develop recommendations regarding institutional design. See Ostrom, *Governing the Commons*.

16. Robert Axelrod, *The Evolution of Cooperation* (New York: Basic Books, 1984); D. Fudenberg and E. Maskin, "A folk-theorem in repeated games with discounting and with incomplete information," *Econometrica*, Vol. 54 (1986).

17. Ostrom, *Governing the Commons*.

18. Daniel Roos, Frank Field, and James Neely, "Industry Consortia," chap. 15 in this volume.

19. Robert G. Eccles and D.B. Crane, *Doing Deals: Investment Banks at Work* (Cambridge: Harvard Business School Press, 1988), p. 119ff.

20. The author is grateful to Christopher Hill for noting the importance of this distinction to policy-makers.

21. Burt, *Structural Holes*, p. 13ff.

22. John F. Rockart and James E. Short, "The Networked Organization and the Management of Interdependence," in Michael S. Scott Morton, ed., *The Corporation of the 1990s* (New York: Oxford University Press, 1991), p. 192.

23. Richard Florida, "Toward the Learning Region," *Futures*, Vol. 27, No. 5 (June 1995), pp. 527–536.

24. Jane Fountain, "Enacting Technology," Faculty Research Working Paper Series, John F. Kennedy School of Government, Harvard University, 1995; Michael S. Scott Morton, "Introduction," in Morton, *The Corporation of the 1990s*.

25. Information Infrastructure Task Force, *The National Information Infrastructure: Agenda for Action* (Washington, D. C.: U.S. Department of Commerce, September 15, 1993).

26. Tushman and L. Rosenkopf, "Organizational Determinants of Technological Change: Towards a Sociology of Technological Evolution," in B. Staw and L. Cummings, eds., *Research in Organizational Behavior*, Vol. 14, pp. 311–347; Richard R. Nelson, "Capitalism as an Engine of Progress," *Research Policy*, Vol. 19, No. 3 (June 1990), pp. 193–214; Michael Tushman and Philip Anderson, "Technological Discontinuities and Organizational Environments," *Administrative Science Quarterly*, Vol. 31, No. 3 (September 1986), pp. 439–465; M. Gort and S. Klepper, "Time Paths in the Diffusion of Product Innovations," *The Economic Journal*, Vol. 92 (September 1982), pp. 630–653.

27. The discussion of learning networks in the biotechnology industry summarizes research reported in Walter W. Powell, Kenneth Koput, and Laurel Smith-Doerr, "Interorganizational Collaboration and the Locus of Innovation: Networks of Learning in Biotechnology," *Administrative Science Quarterly*, Vol. 41, No. 1 (March 1996), p.116.

28. Ibid., p. 117.

29. Ibid., pp. 116–120.

30. Ibid., pp. 118–120.

31. Powell, Koput, and Smith-Doerr created a database to measure network activity of all biotech firms dedicated to research and development in human therapeutics from 1988–93. The researchers counted 230 dedicated biotech firms in human therapeutics in 1988, of which 118 firms had formal ties to other biotech firms. In 1990, 144 out of 226 firms had developed formal external relationships to other biotech firms; in 1991, it was 162 out of 222; in 1992, 167 out of 206; in 1993, 176 out of 199. See ibid., Table 1.

32. Ibid.

33. Ibid.

34. Michael Piore and Charles Sabel, *The Second Industrial Divide: Possibilities for Prosperity* (New York: Basic Books, 1984); Charles Sabel, "Flexible Specialization and the Reemergence of Regional Economies," in Paul Hirst and Jonathan Zeitlin, eds., *Reversing Industrial Decline? Industrial Structure and Policy in Britain and Her Competitors* (Oxford: Berg, 1988); AnnaLee Saxenian, *Regional Advantage: Culture and Competition in Silicon Valley and Route 128* (Cambridge, Mass.: Harvard University Press, 1994).

35. Saxenian, *Regional Advantage*.

36. Ibid., p. 7ff.

37. See ibid. for detailed histories of the industry networks in Silicon Valley and Route 128 and for a provocative argument that accounts for deep cultural differences between the two networks.

38. Michael Porter, *The Competitive Advantage of Nations* (New York: Free Press, 1990), pp. 149–154.

39. Silber & Associates, "Survey of Advanced Technology Program 1990–1992 Awardees: Company Opinion about the ATP and Its Early Effects," January 30,

1996, pp. 21–22.

40. Ibid, p. 21.

41. Ibid, p. 24.

42. Ibid, pp. 27–30.

43. Ibid, p. 33–36.

44. Scott A. Snell and James W. Dean, Jr., "Integrated Manufacturing and Human Resource Management: A Human Capital Perspective," *Academy of Management Journal*, Vol. 35, No. 3 (1992), pp. 467–504.

45. Harvard University, John F. Kennedy School of Government, Center for Science and International Affairs, Science, Technology and Public Policy Program, "Manufacturing Partnerships in the Digital Environment: Best Practices in CALS Implementation," December 1996.

46. Philip Shapira, "Manufacturing Extension Services: Performance, Challenges, and Policy Issues," chap. 10 in this volume.

47. Ibid.

48. Ibid.

5

From Science Policy to Research Policy

Lewis M. Branscomb

Technology policy serves to stimulate both public and private innovation. During the Cold War, when government interests in technical superiority were paramount, public investments in research formed the cornerstone of technology policy. Few questioned the appropriateness of government support for applied or technological research for national security. Today, it is commercial innovation in service to the economy that increasingly drives technology policy. Does government still need to support the development of new technologies? If so, when, if ever, is it appropriate to fund research in private commercial firms? What kinds of technical research are deserving of a subsidy? In what institutional settings should such research be performed? How should government decide?

These questions lie at the heart of the debate in Congress over the Clinton administration's science and technology initiatives. In the political debate, few quarrel with government support for basic science, but technology is often seen as the province of commercial firms. Thus arguments about appropriate government roles seek to draw distinctions between science and technology. The discussion becomes more tractable if, instead of debating the boundaries of "science and technology policy," we address the requirements for "research policy," to create technical knowledge, and "innovation policy," to cover the important subject of incentives for innovation.

This chapter advances the idea that one should distinguish between research—understood as an activity aimed at creating and informing scientific and technical choices for the use of many potential (and often unknown) beneficiaries—and narrow problem-solving, understood as the accomplishment of specific, obtainable objectives in the service of an identified beneficiary.

This distinction leads to a simple policy proposition: The decision on the appropriateness of federal funding of research should rest on the identification of the expected beneficiaries of the work, not the level of abstractness or the practicality of the work or the motives of the investigator in undertaking it. When the public is the primary intended beneficiary, public investment is appropriate, provided the work is done under highly creative, intellectually competitive conditions and the results are widely diffused and appreciated.

In other cases, the intended beneficiaries should normally pay for the work, and the results may be kept proprietary. The idea that those who will primarily benefit should pay also applies to the government, when it intends to buy the products made possible by the research, and when national security may require that the results be kept secret. The criteria for public investment in research are not directly related to how "basic" or abstract the work is, nor to its likely utility, but rather to its net public value. However, this does not necessarily imply that publicly funded work must be placed in the public domain; sometimes assigning proprietary rights to the performer may be the most effective way of assuring both the production of value and its eventual diffusion to the public at large.

Research, in this definition, may create both new understanding of nature and new technical opportunities. Some of those opportunities may be immediately accessible. Others may not mature for decades. But in general both scientific research and technological research may be contribute to public value. Thus basic technology research is a natural companion of basic scientific research. Indeed the two are often interdependent and even indistinguishable. Like science, engineering and medical research also contribute to the public stock of knowledge and skill.

Technological as well as scientific research aimed at building national capability, creating new opportunities, and guiding technological decisions should motivate the government's investment in research. When science itself is the driver to create new opportunities and new understanding, the research community should have the primary voice in setting goals and priorities. When, on the other hand, it is public needs that drive the research, the political process, informed by research, provides the funding and the overall goals. But in both cases, researchers need an environment that favors risk-taking and allows them considerable latitude in setting research strategies.

This public investment in intellectual infrastructure creates knowledge, skills, and institutions. It responds to the intellectual challenges both of unraveling the mysteries of nature and of imagining the uses for the knowledge gained. Scientists, engineers, physicians, and others participate in it. Universities, government-funded laboratories, and firms all contribute to this kind of research, which we call "basic technological research," a companion to the more widely understood and accepted "basic scientific research" to which the U.S. government has contributed so effectively over the years. (I discuss just what we mean by "basic technological research" after addressing some reasons for caution in such public investments.)

This is a better way of thinking about the world of research in which the U.S. government plays such an important role. Americans believe in the importance of research to keep the nation smart, strong, and capable, and to provide the right kinds of incentives for a competitive, private economy. A research policy that creates new understanding of technology as well as new science is a key to realizing that goal and resolving some of the political conflicts over how public dollars should be spent.

This chapter begins by seeking terminology to discuss research policy that better reflects the criteria that should be used in distinguishing public from private responsibilities for investment. It then addresses the market failures that call for government incentives, and the government failures than may frustrate otherwise justified public expenditures. Next I discuss the selection of publicly-funded research performers and the conditions under which basic scientific and technological research should be performed. I conclude that the nature of research opportunities and needs will determine the relative influence the political process and the research community should have in setting the levels and priorities for public investments in research.

What Is Research?

Many people lump together all kinds of technical activity into "research and development." The shorthand "R&D" is often taken as if it were one word, despite the fact that its two components are very different kinds of activities. Scientific and technological research are intensely intellectual and creative activities with uncertain outcomes and risks, performed in laboratories where the researchers have a lot of freedom to explore and learn. Development, by contrast, is a highly focused activity aimed at producing a design or a process that can be realized in a specified time using specifically allocated resources. It is typically tightly managed to minimize risks and to achieve neither more nor less than the specified objective.

When government officials gather statistics on different kinds of technical activities in order to make policy on budgeting and managing government R&D, distinctions as to the purpose and nature of the work are needed and programs are divided into "basic research," "applied research," and "development." At one end of the spectrum, basic research is most often assumed to refer to scientific investigations, most likely in a university or independent laboratory; at the other end, development is assumed to be an activity of engineers, most often in an industrial setting.

Any of these three categories of technical work may be aimed at building society's knowledge and skill base, or creating products for the government's use, or exploring new product or process opportunities for a commercial market. But basic research depends primarily on public funding, while development is almost always driven by markets, private or public. Applied research is an ambiguous category, usually defined as research of identifiable utility, placed somewhere in the middle of the intellectual spectrum between speculative theories of science at one end and predictable application of well-verified knowledge on the other. Since most of the confusion about the government's role in research funding concerns this gray area of applied research, this category is not very useful for policy makers. To call a research program "applied" is not enough to tell us whether it is appropriate for government funding. Thus we must find a set of categories for technical activities that better lend themselves to the discussion of the government's role.[1] This is the task of the next section.

Defining Research

Scientific research embraces inquiry into the workings of nature without regard to the motivation of the scientist or the investor in the scientist's work.[2] Within this conception of research lies all of what is commonly called "basic" or "fundamental" research, plus much of what some people choose to call "applied" (because it is likely to be useful). "Research" does not normally encompass development, testing, design, or product simulation. Research is an activity for which the doctorate is often the appropriate training. It is carried out primarily in laboratories managed for the purpose of conducting scientific research and is funded by agencies or bureaus experienced at research investment and management.

We all know that some basic research is highly abstract and speculative, far from any kind of practical application or economic value. No one is going to commercialize theories about black holes any time soon. But must basic research be useless to qualify as "basic"? Surely that would be an absurdity. Basic research is best thought of as research to create knowledge that expands human opportunities and understanding and informs human choices. It may lead to a new scientific observation that raises new questions. If black holes are found at the centers of galaxies, including our own, what does that tell us about the ultimate fate of our own solar system? Surely that is an important question, but only experts will be able to see how the work might, some day, inform more "practical" science.

Research may also lead to understanding that suggests a technological possibility or informs a choice among alternative technologies. What does science tell us about the chemical reactions in the earth's stratosphere from which we might predict whether a fleet of supersonic transports might deplete the protective ozone layer? President Nixon asked his science advisor, Dr. E. E. David, this question when considering whether to ask the Senate to reconsider its negative vote (by a margin of one) on the Supersonic Transport (SST). The president's decision not to try to gain that extra vote turned, in part, on quite basic questions of free-radical chemistry.[3] It does not take decades for basic research to have value when it informs technological choices, as in this case.

Research might lead to the discovery of a new material, the understanding of a new process, or the creation of an idea leading to a new kind of instrument. If materials can be made that are offer no electrical resistance at room temperature (i.e., are high-temperature superconductors), could world demands for energy be greatly reduced in the future? What other applications for electric current that flows without resistance might we imagine? Such basic research may lead to scientific or technological progress, or both.

Most often, scientific and technological research go hand in hand.[4] A scientist might invent a new kind of scientific instrument to explore a poorly understood area of natural phenomena. Her colleagues build similar instruments in their laboratories. One of them, perhaps a bit more entrepreneurial than her fellows, decides to make a more reliable version of the instrument, manufacture it, and sell it to other scientists in the field. Soon this instrument is in widespread use for analysis, and someone, perhaps an engineer, realizes the instrument can be used in reverse to control a process rather than measure it. Thus an instrument designed for analysis becomes a tool for synthesis.

Consider, for example, the electron microscope. It was invented to enable scientists to *see* very small things. It is now used in reverse to *make* very small things, not only in the laboratory but in electronics factories. In this example, science created the need for the instrument. The resulting instrument business enabled more rapid scientific progress. Soon the electron microscope instrument was used in reverse as an electron-beam lithography tool for making tiny structures on computer chips. The computers using these tiny chips are faster and provide a more powerful tool for the advance of other fields of science. In this example, it is very difficult to sort out whether science was driving the technology or technology was driving science: both were happening concurrently.

Basic Technological Research

The justification for federal support of research that is investigator-initiated (that is, not driven by sponsor-defined needs or applications) is not restricted to science. Harvey Brooks points out that "pure technology" may be as appropriate for public investments as "pure science." There are many examples of successful public investments in technology that preceded identification of market-supported applications. Brooks cites as examples the development by the Atomic Energy Commission of radio-isotopes and stable-isotope tracers—now used for both diagnosis and treatment of disease and for fundamental biological research—well before the medical and biology communities had learned how to use them or defined a need and a market. This investment enabled much of the molecular biology revolution that followed.

The public investment in computer networking that led to the Internet is a contemporary example. (See Chapter 13 by Brian Kahn.) When Robert Kahn first developed the Internet Protocol for computer networking at the Defense Research Projects Agency, no one imagined that within a few years, billions of dollars would be invested in information services offered through the World Wide Web.

Good examples of basic technological research can be found in academic engineering research, such as might be funded in the National Science Foundation (NSF) Engineering Research Centers, or in much of the Department of Defense (DoD) budget category called "exploratory development," such as the quest for efficient operating systems for massively parallel computers. Other examples are the fusion energy program in the Department of Energy (DOE) or the search for practical materials that exhibit room temperature superconductivity. Within the civilian technology programs, such as the Advanced Technology Program (ATP) of the National Institute of Standards and Technology (NIST), one also finds examples of high-risk science-based industrial research, such the search for solid state lasers that radiate in the ultra-violet, which would permit greater information storage capacity on compact-disk-based media.

The phrase "basic technological research" is meant to direct our attention to work that creates new capabilities as well as new understanding, and is not simply focused on narrow problem-solving or product development. Thus "basic technological research" takes its place beside "basic scientific research," forming two arms of intellectual investment into a vital capability of human society. The appropriate public policies for investment in them are not based on attempts to distinguish these activities by their intellectual content, which is fortunate since they are highly interdependent and overlapping. Rather, policies for resource allocation should derive from a weighing of opportunities and needs, and from provisions for diffusion and use of the information produced. The right public policy for supporting research should not require rigid distinctions to be made between basic scientific and basic technological research.

Distinguishing Research from Narrow Problem-Solving

The criteria for public funding of basic technological research are similar to those for basic science. Technological and scientific research should be understood to be complementary and should receive bipartisan support for the same reasons. Yet politicians are typically more comfortable with advocating funding for scientific rather than technological research, perhaps because the implicit utility of technological research may suggest that there is—or might be—an identifiable beneficiary who should be footing the bill. If there were such a beneficiary, then the work, they might say, should be called "applied research" and the government should keep hands off.

The culprit, as noted above, is the ambiguous phrase "applied research." Much of the basic and exploratory research funded by the Departments of Defense and Energy and by the National Aeronautics and Space Administration (NASA) is neither specific to government procurement nor commercially proprietary; rather it is devoted to enhancing the U.S. capability to innovate broadly. But in government statistics such work may be labeled "applied research" if the research is said to be working toward a well-defined, utilitarian objective. What matters for public policy, however, is the objective of the investor, and its expectations of return from the investment. The fact that work may have a useful application does not tell us whether the government should fund it. The opposite syllogism, surely, we must reject; government should not decline to fund research simply because it might have a practical application.

The usual distinctions between "basic research," "applied research," and "development," used for many years in the formal government statistics kept by the National Science Foundation are, unfortunately, insufficient for discussions of policy for government investment in technical activities. Indeed, definitions are the source of much of the confusion over the appropriate role for government in the national scientific and technical enterprise.[5]

One cannot distinguish in any meaningful way "basic" from "applied research" by observing what a scientist is doing. A scientist engaged in testing a steel pipe for leaks—a rather routine "applied" task—may insist his work is "basic" because his leak-free pipe might allow a measurement of the second-order Doppler shift predicted by relativity theory. Another scientist working on extensions to the quantum theory of collisions of electrons with atoms—a highly sophisticated and apparently abstract activity—may say she is engaged in "applied research," because the use of her theory to predict collision cross sections might be of practical assistance to fusion energy engineering.[6]

"Applied research" should not be used to mean "purposeful and demonstrably useful basic research," and one should be wary of the use of the term in government statistics.[7] In corporate research laboratories, such as the T.J. Watson Research Laboratories of IBM, all of the work is referred to simply as "research." There is no need to attempt a distinction between "basic" and "applied" research. All of the company's research investments are motivated by corporate interests. All of the research has a purpose. All of it is conducted under highly creative conditions. None of it is so "pure" that there are no expectations of value from the research investment.

We should reserve the words "applied research" for those narrowly defined tasks in which limited time and resources are devoted to a specific problem for an identified user who gets all the benefit and should pay all the costs. To make this view of applied research clear in this discussion, I use the words "problem-solving research" instead.

Narrow problem-solving and development are activities initiated by someone who wishes to apply research methods purposefully to exploit an identified opportunity or solve a problem.[8] They involve the application of technical resources to achieve an identified goal for a specified beneficiary, usually the investor in the work. It is a reasonable assumption that those who engage in such activities expect to benefit from them, and to benefit by a sufficient margin over the cost to accommodate the technical risk that is ever-present in research. The investor in problem-solving may be a government agency, but is more likely to be a private firm. In most cases that firm would be expected to be able to appropriate sufficient benefits to need no government subsidy to take those risks.

Public investment in the creation of new technology (technological development, whether by research or as a product of problem-solving) is a critical link between societal goals and the scientific research that is pursued by virtue of society's commitment to those goals. Thus the desire for technology is an important—perhaps the most important—source of demand for science.[9] The way scientific research is used to further technological goals may profoundly affect policies for allocating funds to science and determining the institutional settings in which scientific research is performed. In fact, the way innovations are brought about in industry, and the role of science in support of innovation and productivity growth, have both substantially changed. Thus, any discussion of technology policy must address research policy as well.

The Search for Useful Language in the Public Debate

These questions of definition may seem highly academic. But they lie at the heart of public policy debates about technology policy, not only because science is both a source and a product of technology, but because the boundaries between research that leads to new technical knowledge and research that leads to scientific understanding are obscure and often misunderstood. Before one can create a policy for public investment in research, one must know more about the goals of the work, who its intended beneficiaries might be, and how these results might reach those who can use them beneficially. These are the attributes that should determine the role of government in funding technical work, not the narrow distinctions between science and technology.

As Neal Lane, director of the National Science Foundation (NSF) said in testimony to Congress:

To my mind, the question is not, where the dividing lines are between science and technology, or between basic and applied research, but rather how do we take better advantage of the interrelationships in order for the nation to reap the full benefits of its integrated investment in science and technology?[10]

Lane quoted Donald E. Stokes:

The annals of research so often record scientific advances simultaneously driven by the quest for both understanding and use, that we are increasingly led to ask how it came to be so widely believed that these goals are inevitably in tension and that the categories of basic and applied science are radically separated.[11]

Conservatives in Congress are searching for the right language through which to express their support for what they understand to be basic research, while making clear their objections to public funding of private goods. Congressman F. James Sensenbrenner, chairman of the House Committee on Science, made this distinction in explaining the Committee's report:

Federal R&D should focus on essential programs that are long term, high risk, non-commercial, cutting edge, well-managed and have great potential for scientific discovery. Funding for programs that do not meet this standard should be eliminated or decreased to enable new initiatives.[12]

To make clear what the Committee majority does not like, Sensenbrenner added:

Beyond the demonstration of technical feasibility, activities associated with evolutionary advances or incremental improvements to a product or a process, or the marketing or commercialization of a product or process, should be left to the private sector.

Representative Sensenbrenner's views as expressed here probably do not conflict with the consensus in both the technical and the political communities. But it should not require six qualifying adjectives to describe the research the government should support, and it complicates the issue to try to restrict approval to *scientific* discovery. Sensenbrenner's apparent restriction to scientific discovery implies that he would not be equally enthusiastic about technological discovery, even if it were "long term, high risk, noncommercial, cutting edge, [and] well-managed." A simpler way to distinguish appropriate opportunities for public funding from those better left to the private sector is to focus on the intended beneficiaries of the research.

Identifying the Intended Beneficiaries of Publicly Funded Research

The rule is simple: let the primary intended beneficiary pay for the research. The careful circumscriptions of the precise kinds of research that government should and should not support, described above, are a way of implementing this principle by describing what kind of research the speaker believes best serves the public interest.

Research to serve a firm's commercial interest will be recouped in profits from that commercialization; no government funds should be employed. The company pays. When the government makes the market (as in defense procurement), the government pays. When the government invests in the nation's skills and knowledge, going far beyond the private investments justified by market rewards, the people benefit, and the people's government pays. And, where firms under-invest in relation to a defined public interest, such as reducing environmental risk or accelerating medical progress, government and the private sector may share the costs. As discussed in the final chapter of this book (Chapter 18 by Lewis Branscomb and James Keller), the cost-sharing ratio should reflect the best understanding of the likely distribution of public and private benefits.

We have argued that public funds should be invested when the public interest outweighs private gain, and that basic technological research can contribute as much as basic science to national capability and need. But that leaves a number of questions still to be answered about the nation's research policy: What provisions should be made for insuring that research outcomes reach intended beneficiaries? Who should do the research? How much autonomy should be accorded investigators in universities, national laboratories, or independent laboratories in order to ensure a creative environment? Who sets the priorities for different research programs? What motivations should drive allocation of resources to different research objectives? These will be subject of the remainder of the chapter.

Conditions for Gaining Value from Research

If research, whether in the more abstract science disciplines or in the more "practical" fields of science and engineering, is to provide public value, it must be conducted under conditions that ensure a high level of creativity, accountability to sponsors of the work, and effective access by potential users.

A Creative Environment for Research

Research is most fruitful when pursued by highly trained people who are accorded freedom to decide what are the most important scientific questions and how to pursue them. When engaged in research, scientists need latitude to set research strategies and need the feedback that comes from exposure of their work to the praise and criticism of their peers. Development and narrow, task-oriented problem-solving also benefit from a creative environment, but the explicit nature of the goals and the time pressure to reach them substantially reduces the freedom to shift directions in response to unexpected opportunities for discovery. Thus the circumstances under which the work is performed help to distinguish "basic scientific and technological research" from "problem-solving," "testing," and "development."

Researchers insist that the need for academic autonomy, balanced with accountability, is indeed legitimate when the work is research and the goal is to maximize learning.[13] A government agency may lay out its view of the areas of research it believes most fruitful and in which it is prepared to invest. A policy of responding to unsolicited proposals from scientists with good ideas in response to the agency's challenge creates a wealth of valuable research opportunities. Selecting from among these ideas by submitting them to the critical review of other scientists knowledgeable in the same field and by technically expert users who can assess the likely value of the work sustains the quality of the work, its likely value to society, and the fairness of the allocation of government funds. The peer review process also expands awareness of the work and promotes its subsequent diffusion. The primary diffusion mechanisms are horizontal, to others in the same or nearby fields. The employment of recent graduates trained in research, the secondary literature, and various conferences and study groups are relied upon to diffuse the work to practitioners such as engineers, clinicians, and scientists in "downstream" disciplines.[14]

This system of selection of projects and of performers is strongly defended by the scientific community, and for good reasons. One of these arguments seeks to tie the need for autonomy to the unpredictable nature of science in pursuit of understanding and new possibilities. Scientists fear that Congressional pressure for immediately useful results from publicly supported research may lead to a loss of the conditions necessary for creative work. If research is treated like problem-solving or like development, they fear, micromanagement and unrealistic expectations for quick results cannot be far behind. Three examples illustrate the basis for this fear.

In the early 1970s the government tried to respond to political concerns that government research contributed too little to social well-being by creating a program at NSF called Research Applied to National Needs (RANN).[15] This program addressed concerns such as fire research, and both social and natural scientists were expected to participate. As the name implies, this was NSF's attempt to induce scientists accustomed to opportunity-based research to redirect their attention to what the government viewed as need-driven. In point of fact, some the research conducted under RANN received generally high marks from independent evaluators. However, scientists remained concerned that NSF should be undertaking need-driven research at all. This was a legitimate concern. It is far from obvious that NSF is best equipped to set such priorities, but no other agency seemed to be available to do so.[16]

A second example is the "war on cancer," which threatened to divert biomedical research from a fundamental attack on molecular biology and immunology in the quest for a "quick fix" solution to cancer (a fear that only an extremely generous Congress and tenacious National Institutes of Health (NIH) management averted). Similar concerns emerged when AIDS research was given a special priority by the Congress.

The third example arose in 1992 when Walter Massey, then director of the NSF, requested that the National Science Board (NSB) establish a "Blue Ribbon Commission on the Future of NSF" to examine whether NSF should attempt to contribute to the government's effort to enhance the competitiveness of American industry. Pessimists jumped to the conclusion that such a mission priority would lead to the displacement of individual-investigator, opportunity-driven research by political perceptions of industrial need. A second fear was that this preference for need-driven research (in this case responding to industrial needs) at NSF might result in government officials selecting investigators without expert peer review, and evaluating both outputs and outcomes of the research. The Commission concluded, however, that scientific autonomy—based on peer review evaluation of competing, unsolicited proposals—can and should be preserved, even as NSF seeks to balance both intrinsic and extrinsic values by appropriate priority setting for its fields and areas of research.[17]

Neal Lane, director of the NSF, is careful to avoid this trap. In his 1995 testimony, he said:

NSF support of research focuses almost exclusively on answers to fundamental questions that defy our ability to predict the outcomes. Still, it is important to recognize that taxpayer-funded fundamental research can and should have a conscious relationship to the nation's priorities and societal needs. This does not mean a narrowly directed agenda of targeted research, but rather, a program of fundamental science and engineering [research] that clearly is in and for the national interest, in its most comprehensive interpretation.

In all of these cases it was research autonomy that was at stake. It was not an argument over the importance of the social goals to which research contributes so much. The concern of the researchers had been elevated by the tendency of politicians to imply that research of high public value should be managed differently from more conceptual or theoretical work. When the work might be of economic value, the concern escalates to the fear that politicians will conclude that such useful work could and should also be paid for from non-governmental sources. Where public goals are driving research investments, the agencies do feel accountable for the ultimate delivery of public benefits, but they must not let this lead them to micromanage the creative research on which they are depending.

Ensuring User Access to Research Results

The linkages between outputs from research and outcomes for society are often ill-defined (see Chapter 3 by Adam Jaffe on metrics) and operate outside the province of government control. This does not free government from the obligation to understand the processes that create public value from its research investments. When government is investing in research to build national capability, the extent of returns to public value is strongly influenced by the ease with which users can access the results and put them to effective use. Research environments that foster creativity also offer effective mechanisms of information and skill diffusion.

When basic technological research is performed in universities, students, project referees, academic visitors, and collaborating companies all contribute to the diffusion of new knowledge, adding greatly to the effectiveness of formal publication. The government provides special institutional mechanisms to foster information diffusion; among these are Cooperative Research and Development Agreements (CRADAs; see Chapter 9 by David Guston); government support for University-Industry Research Centers; and funding of post-doctoral research fellowships. When basic technology research is funded in industry, the use of consortia of firms, perhaps in collaboration with universities and state technology programs, provides an effective diffusion mechanism (see Chapter 18). Thus even where the most immediate public benefit from research might be the creation of jobs resulting from commercialization of the ideas, the employment of consortia is a way to increase the ratio of public to private benefits.

When Should Private Firms Be Funded to Perform Research?

The selection of performers of research should be based on competence, taking into account the productivity of the work, the skills and experience that will be developed, and the effectiveness of the diffusion of research outputs. If one is persuaded that government should fund technological as well as scientific research, the next question is, When, if ever, should private firms be funded to perform the work? Here policy-makers confront a dilemma. If one is to avoid politically sensitive choices among competing firms, the safe way out is to fund research only in government laboratories, universities, and other not-for-profit institutions. But avoiding this Scylla of choice delivers one to the Charybdis of needlessly isolating the research from its ultimate users in private industry. If new research is to be quickly and widely accessible, it should be conducted in industry laboratories or in institutions with effective links to industry. The most effective mechanism to foster commercialization of new ideas is to have the ideas arise inside industry itself. For these reasons we conclude it would be a serious mistake to categorically exclude industrial organizations from eligibility to perform basic scientific and technological research for the government. However, we support the NSF policy of giving its priority to universities, while the research programs of the "mission" agencies should cover the broader spectrum of research institutions, both public and private.

Allocating Resources to Publicly Funded Research

The growing budget pressure on public funding of scientific research exacerbates tensions that have accompanied the public funding of scientific research for a long time. Going all the way back to the writings of Francis Bacon, policy makers have struggled with the balance between resource allocation strategies supportive of scientific autonomy and those derived from identified public goals and values. This was the subject of major academic debates in the 1920s, with the protagonists represented by J.D. Bernal and Michael Polyani.[18] As Harvey Brooks has observed, research motivations fall generally into two categories: opportunity-driven research—pursuing the visions of scientists, and need-driven research—responding to the needs of society.[19] How should these two sources of motivation for the government research investor be balanced? To what extent can—or should—scientific research investments be based on government constructed plans, and to what extent should public investors rely on the intrinsic values of scientific research to ensure outcomes of maximum benefit to society?

Research Motivation: The Clinton-Gore Science Policy

In August of 1994 the Clinton-Gore administration issued its long-awaited "science policy," a companion to the technology policy declaration that appeared almost instantly after the 1993 inauguration.[20] The science policy was issued in a well-illustrated paper entitled *Science in the National Interest* (referred to as *SNI*).[21] *SNI* makes the case that there are two valid criteria that should be invoked in allocating resources for science, one involving centralized, goal-driven decisions, the other aimed at creating a strong scientific infrastructure on which all goal-oriented research can draw. Investments in this infrastructure, *SNI* says, should be based on the intrinsic values of science, reflecting the opportunities for conceptual progress identified by scientists.

SNI drives home the importance of opportunism in basic science. It says:

It has seldom proved possible to anticipate which areas of science will bring forward surprising and important breakthroughs at any given time. Therefore U.S. scientists must be among those working at the leading edge in all major fields in order for us to retain and improve our competitive position in the long term.... [N]ature yields her most precious secrets in surprising ways, to those who are well prepared and persistent, and with a schedule not often amenable to detailed planning. Thus although we can and must do more to identify and coordinate research thrusts aimed at strategic goals, we must not limit our future by restricting the range of our inquiry. Vibrant scientific disciplines are best guaranteed by the initiatives of talented investigators and in turn provide the strongest and most enduring foundation for science in the national interest.[22]

This very sensible vision correctly associates creation of a strong intellectual base for society's future use (policy for science) with the need to ensure that science serves the goals to which it can make decisive contributions (science for policy). It does not spell out, however, how the two criteria for choice—intrinsic scientific merit and extrinsic social utility—will be placed in balance. How much of each do we need, and who decides?

Need-Driven Research

The source of priority evaluation for need-driven exploratory research may be quite different from that for opportunity-oriented science, even when the motivations of the researchers are the same. Whereas opportunity-oriented research is proposed and evaluated in a competitive horizontal environment (peer review being the dominant mechanism), need-driven research derives its priority from vertical relationships. The need is typically expressed in terms of some capability to be realized through a technology, which in turn may derive its conceptual structure and future evolution from new science. The level of priority derives from the initial goal, but, as a practical matter, is derivative of the congressionally-authorized investment in the technology to which the science contributes. Thus, for example, the importance of new sources of energy and the likelihood that fusion can provide a welcome solution should determine the scale of investment in fusion. The technical agenda for fusion research will determine what fields of science are relevant, and will suggest where research might offer new options that can increase the likelihood of success.

DOE's criteria for deciding what kinds of plasma physics research to pursue are not the same as might be assigned to an opportunity-driven NSF project in, let us say, the plasma phenomena in formation of stars. Pertinence to fusion technology is clearly relevant for the DOE; not all forms of serendipity are equally welcome. Thus, equally competent investigators working on the same problem will find their work evaluated differently by DOE and by NSF—and, indeed, quite differently again if funded by a private commercial firm.

The fact that science is almost always embedded in a fabric of other technical activities—both in space and in time—means that allocation decisions also follow those chains of consequence and pertinence. A given research project in plasma physics might find itself justified by a commercial and public interest in new energy sources, by an academic curiosity about how stars form, or by the government's concern about the effects of atmospheric re-entry on space craft or military missiles. Which of these justifications dominates the public investment decision does say a lot about the amount of money to be invested and how the overall program of research is directed. But for this research to reveal the richness of potential options, it must be carried out in much the same style as one would pursue opportunity-oriented science. Thus the scientists performing it will describe their work as basic research, if their work environment is similar to that expected for opportunity-oriented science.

If all exploratory research, whether need-driven or opportunity driven, requires similar staffing skills and research environments, and if the sources of judgment about resource allocation are distinct but understood for each, why is it necessary to ask whether the research activities look more "scientific" or more "technological"? It is the motive of the investor that matters, not that of the investigator. The answer is that there remains one other dimension of policy to be addressed. How does government decide how to allocate its resources among the different kinds of scientific research goals?[23]

One answer to that question we have already given: government should sponsor a level of need-driven exploratory research appropriate to support the missions that created the need. It is time-honored U.S. policy that every federal agency should invest in basic scientific research in proportion to the agency's dependence on the skills and knowledge of the relevant scientific field.[24] This policy has provided a level of diversity of sources and perspectives in science that have greatly enriched the U.S. scientific enterprise.

Opportunity-Driven Research

But what about opportunity-driven research? How far does the scope of our conception of research driven by intrinsic scientific interest take us toward utility? The justification for government support of "basic research" may be at a maximum when the likelihood that basic concepts may be altered or extended is at a maximum: when the "laws" of science are created or repealed. But must its level of applicability to more practical matters also be at a minimum to satisfy the requirements for public support?

Is high energy physics "better" science than materials science and engineering? What about a project to characterize the properties of a new material, or research on a new idea for a scientific instrument, or measurements of the thermodynamic properties of a new polymer? This kind of research may be both opportunity-driven and need-driven. It may be very interesting science while also utilitarian. It usually requires the kinds of people and environments that are characteristic of "basic" research or exploratory science.

This is the kind of research the National Institute for Standards and Technology and its predecessor agency, the National Bureau of Standards, have done for decades to support the productivity growth of U.S. industry. Such research is deserving of public support for the same reason that other areas of need-driven research are supported, except that in this case the customers for the results are widely dispersed, like the customers for other "basic" research.

Such "basic and useful" work falls into the category that has been called "infrastructural," and has a counterpart in "infrastructural technology."[25] Unhappily for clean policy distinctions, but happily for the health of science, there is no discontinuity between intrinsic and extrinsic values in science. One cannot sort out the fields of science on a line, with the most prestigious at one end and the most utilitarian at the other. Quite often the best scientists working in a utilitarian field make a remarkable scientific discovery.[26] For example, work on the electrical properties of materials at low temperature, driven by the search for new electronics technologies for the computer industry, led to the discovery of high temperature superconductivity, one of the most startling events in physics in this century. It revitalized a field of physics that had become largely moribund because it had been prematurely assigned the "useful but not so interesting" label. Furthermore the most sophisticated science occasionally creates byproducts that are quite utilitarian; witness the evolution of the storage ring of high-energy physics into the x-ray lithography tool of the integrated circuit manufacturer.

How should decisions about investment in such work be made? Figure 5-1 suggests that research draws on both understanding and technology, and contributes both to understanding and to improved technology. Both outcomes are appropriate motivations for public investment in research. There must be two elements of

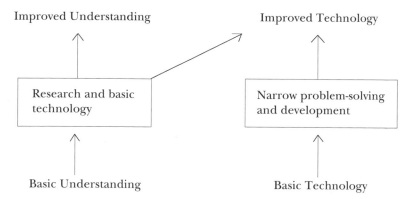

Figure 5-1   The relationship among the goals of public research investments and the nature of the technical endeavor. Adapted from a diagram presented by Stokes as "Pasteur's Quadrant."

motivation in research: the investor must be motivated to take financial risks, and the investigator must be motivate to take professional risks. These risks are generally higher in opportunity-driven research, but so too may be the rewards, both to the research and to society. A reasonable public policy involves a balance of risk and reward.

Conclusions and Recommendations

This leads us to our conclusions: First, the correct criterion for the appropriateness of federal investments in research is the expectation that the primary beneficiary will be the public, that is, the national interest. Where government makes the market (either through procurement, or in some cases through regulation), it may be appropriate for government to fund not only research but development as well, and to manage the projects to specific objectives, costs, and schedules. Where government is investing in the knowledge base, whether in response to learning and discovery opportunities or in response to identified public needs, government should invest in research performed under conditions appropriate for high productivity and creativity.

Second, research is not "pure" or "basic" because no uses for the results are expected. Instead, it is research because the knowledge gained is to a significant degree unpredictable and serendipitous and is expected to be widely diffused and therefore broadly beneficial. The primary distinction between research and narrow problem-solving is not found in the level of intellectual sophistication or in the level of utility of the work, but rather in the prior identification of the beneficiaries of the work.

Third, basic technology research is intimately related to basic scientific research and should receive resources and be assigned to performers using similar criteria to those used for basic science. Creative conditions of work are just as necessary for creating new technologies as for new science.

Fourth, resource allocation decisions for need-driven research must be made by the funding agencies based on their legislative mandates. Agencies authorized to address specific problem areas (such as energy, health, space, or defense) should further the nation's capabilities to address those problems by funding basic scientific and technological research in the relevant technical areas. The level of research investment should reflect the priority accorded to the mission objective by the political process and the opportunity that research offers for enabling mission success.

Fifth, resource allocation for opportunity-driven research should be based on professional assessment of the likelihood that success will create new and important intellectual as well as practical opportunities. The magnitude of investment should be proportionate to the need for research training in the universities and to the demand for research progress reflected in technological development commitments, both public and private.

Finally, the criteria for investing in basic technology research, like that for science, must be originality, intellectual rigor, and practical value. Like science, if technology research is to be creative, it must not be micromanaged by government.

If the consensus behind the federal support of basic scientific research is extended to basic technological research, and it is understood that the federal government subsidizes development of products and services only when these outputs are required to fulfill federal missions such as defense, health, and environment, then it should be relatively easy to come to a general understanding about federal support for basic research that is relevant to commercial as well as public purposes.

What is the practical effect of these conclusions? Before 1980 there were frequent complaints from the engineering professions that NSF treated engineering research (or technological research) as a lower-priority activity than the "hard" sciences. This debate even found expression in Congressman George Brown's threat (as chairman of the House Science and Technology Committee) to create a National Technology Foundation, which would have competed with NSF for funds and attention. This proposal was dropped and instead the Congress revised the NSF enabling statute to add the words "and engineering" everywhere the word "science" appeared. The National Science Board removed the words "applied research" from the Engineering and Applied Research Division, thus making it clear that NSF does not engage in narrow problem-solving research but does regard engineering research as parallel to chemistry and oceanography, and not simply a branch of applied research.[27] Today, it is fair to say that the Science Board's policy is to view research in its broad sweep, embracing fields as different as mathematics, chemical engineering, and econometrics, without intended intellectual prejudice.

What is required now is a more robust process for justifying budgets and allocating resources over the full range of opportunity-driven and need-driven criteria for investment. With this in mind, the NSB should consider reinstituting, perhaps in improved form, the "COSEPUP" studies chartered by the Council of the National Academy of Sciences and the Council of the Academy of Engineering and funded by the NSF. Performed by teams of research scientists within each discipline, they were intended to map out the most fruitful lines of research in the next five to ten years and to inform the research investments of federal agencies. These studies typically covered the full range of criteria for investment, and the experts themselves set priorities.[28] Two new features might be valuable. First, a stronger effort to engage the field sciences, engineering, and clinical communities in identifying need-driven priorities that might pay off in better balance in the overall NSF program.[29] Second, selected interdisciplinary subjects should be systematically studied.[30] Such studies might also explore the usefulness of technology roadmaps, as discussed in Chapter 18.

It is our hope that this discussion will prove most useful to the committees of the Congress that have struggled so long and hard to communicate their policy objectives to the public and to the agencies and—most important—to a nervous and sometimes defensive science and engineering community. If Congress can get comfortable with the support of research, without trying to deconstruct its intellectual content, while fulfilling the full Congressional responsibility to address the motives of its investments in research for the nation's future, most of the rancor can be eliminated and a bi-partisan research policy can be realized.

What the nation needs is not a science policy and a companion technology policy, but rather a research policy to support a research-based innovation policy.

Notes

1. The definition of research developed here is quite close to the scope of "federal science and technology" as defined by a panel of established by the National Academy of Sciences, the National Academy of Engineering, the Institute of Medicine and the National Research Council under the chairmanship of Frank Press. Committee on Criteria for Federal Support of Research and Development, *Allocating Federal Funds for Science and Technology* (Washington, D.C.: National Academy Press, 1995).

2. Research is also concerned with understanding human artifacts; see Herbert Simon, *Sciences of the Artificial* (Cambridge, Mass.: MIT Press, 1981).

3. Lewis M. Branscomb, "Public Funding of Scientific Research," *Sigma Xi Forum 1995: Vannevar Bush II: Science for the 21st Century* (Research Triangle Park, N.C.: The Scientific Research Society, 1995).

4. Susan Cozzens, "Derek Price and the Paradigm of Science Policy," *Science, Technology and Human Values,* Vol. 13 (1988), pp. 361–372.

5. These statistics are published annually in National Science Board, *Science and Engineering Indicators* (Washington, D.C.: National Science Foundation).

6. These examples are discussed in L.M. Branscomb, "Physics, Used and Unused," *Confessions of a Technophile* (Woodbury, N.Y.: American Institute of Physics, 1995), pp. 25–36.

7. A decade ago the National Science Foundation explored the wisdom of a change in the typology of research to address this problem. One approach, widely used in Europe, is to introduce a new category called "strategic research," meaning research without specific near-term outcomes to society, but nevertheless motivated by expectations of long-term capabilities for which uses can easily be imagined. This category essentially overlaps my usage of "basic technological research." I prefer the latter term, simply to help the reader understand that public policies for investment should be very similar for all kinds of research.

Ultimately, society should drop the "scientific" and "technological" qualifiers and simply deal with research, problem-solving, development, testing, systems engineering, and the like.

8. These categories refer to the primary purpose of the work. It must be understood, of course, that even in the most abstract scientific research, some need for narrow problem solving may arise. The mathematician may have to design new software to run a massively parallel computer; the scientist searching for new fundamental particles may face some very sophisticated engineering challenges.

9. Lewis M. Branscomb, "New Policies in Old Bottles: Adapting Federal Agencies to the New Economic Agenda," *Business and the Contemporary World,* Vol. 7, No. 2 (1995), pp. 28–43; Harvey Brooks, "The Relationship between Science and Technology," *Research Policy,* Vol. 23 (1994), pp. 477–486.

10. Neal Lane, Director, National Science Foundation, testimony before the Committee on Science, U.S. House of Representatives, January 6, 1995 (see text at <http://www2.whitehouse.gov/WH/EOP/OSTP/other/tsnsf.html>).

11. This quotation is from Neal Lane's address, ibid. Donald E. Stokes' manuscript entitled, *Pasteur's Quadrant,* widely circulated and often referred to, is to be published posthumously in the summer of 1997 by The Brookings Institution, but has no doubt been edited; the secondary quotes used may not be precisely as published.

12. Press statement from Congressman James Sensenbrenner accompanying the annual "Views and Estimates" report to the House Budget Committee on March 20, 1997.

13. The importance of academic autonomy for the research enterprise (in contrast to problem-solving, development, and testing) was given strong support by Vannevar Bush's dedication to the creative power of university research when driven by its own ethos. It is also strongly reinforced by three additional principles: a) privatization of government-funded science—a major Bush objective; b) academic scientists' distrust of micro-management of their work by sponsors; and c) the reservation of constitutional responsibility for higher education to states and private institutions. The federal government supports higher education in science through research project support rather than block grants to universities, as in other countries with a ministry responsible for higher education.

14. The ideas of pure mathematics find their uses in many areas of computer science; much of what chemists do today would have been found in a physics laboratory twenty years ago. Geophysics, oceanography, and other observational sciences draw on all the "core" disciplines.

15. Bruce L.R. Smith, *American Science Policy Since World War II* (Washington, D.C.: Brookings Institution, 1990), p. 79.

16. The obvious agency to conduct fire research was the Department of Commerce's National Bureau of Standards (NBS), which has a substantial and

sophisticated fire research program, but had no funds to support external research. Indeed in this instance NSF did turn to NBS for collaboration and assistance in managing the program.

17. William Danforth and Robert Galvin, co-chairs, National Science Board Commission on the Future of the National Science Foundation, *A Foundation for the 21st Century: A Progressive Framework for the National Science Foundation*, NSB 192–96 (Washington, D.C.: National Science Board, November 20, 1992).

18. Christopher Freeman, *The Economics of Hope: Essays on Technical Change, Economic Growth, and the Environment* (London and New York: Pinter Publishers, 1993), chapter 1.

19. Harvey Brooks, review of Christopher Freeman, *The Economics of Hope: Essays on Technical Change, Economic Growth, and the Environment*, published in *Minerva*, Vol. 33, No. 2, 1995.

20. President William J. Clinton and Vice President Albert Gore, Jr., "Technology for America's Economic Growth: A New Direction to Build Economic Strength," February 22, 1993.

21. President William J. Clinton and Vice President Albert Gore, Jr., *Science in the National Interest* (Washington, D.C.: Executive Office of the President, August 1994); this document is referred to below as *SNI*.

22. *SNI*, p. 9.

23. David H. Guston, "Principal-agent Theory and the Structure of Science Policy," *Science and Public Policy*, Vol. 23, No. 4, August 1996, pp. 229–240.

24. This policy, which derives logically from Vannevar Bush's report, was made explicit in the Steelman Report and implemented in an Executive Order from President Eisenhower. Vannevar Bush, *Science—The Endless Frontier* (Washington, D.C.: Office of Scientific Research and Development, July 1945; repr. National Science Foundation, 1960, 1980, 1990); John R. Steelman, Chairman, *Science and Public Policy: A Report to the President*, Vol. 1, *A Program for the Nation* (Washington, D.C.: U.S. Government Printing Office, August 27, 1947); Dwight David Eisenhower, Executive Order 10521, March 17, 1954.

25. John Alic, Lewis M. Branscomb, Harvey Brooks, Ashton Carter, and Gerald Epstein, *Beyond Spinoff: Military and Commercial Technologies in a Changing World* (Boston: Harvard Business School Press, 1992), chapter 12, p. 374.

26. A dramatic example is the discovery of the remnant microwave radiation from the "big bang" at the creation of the universe. Professor R.H. Dicke—who devoted his scientific life to testing Einstein's General Theory of Relativity—and his students were building instrumentation to search for this weak background radiation when Arno Penzias and Robert Wilson stumbled across it while calibrating an antenna at Bell Telephone Laboratories. It was Dicke who identified the unexplained noise source for them, but Penzias and Wilson received the Nobel Prize, which is given for discovery, not interpretations. See Jack Zirker, "A Radical in Tweeds: Robert H. Dicke and the General Theory of Relativity," *Mercury Magazine*, Vol. 23, No. 4 (1996), p. 23.

27. *American Science Policy Since World War II*, p. 95.

28. COSEPUP is the Committee on Science, Engineering and Public Policy; it is not a commission of the National Research Council, but works directly for the Councils of the National Academy of Sciences and the National Academy of Engineering.

29. I believe the advice given here is quite consistent with the intent of the NSB "Commission on the Future of the NSF" on which I served, discussed in Branscomb's *Confessions of a Technophile*, p. 216.

30. This is much more difficult than doing disciplinary studies, where the Academies can go to disciplinary professional societies to staff these very big, expensive projects. However, it has been done, for example in the series of studies made for the NSB on high-performance computing and networking.

II
Assessment of Technology Programs

6

The Advanced Technology Program: Opportunities for Enhancement

Christopher T. Hill

The Advanced Technology Program (ATP) in the National Institute of Standards and Technology (NIST) of the Department of Commerce was established under authority of the Omnibus Trade and Competitiveness Act of 1988 (the "Trade Act") signed by President Ronald Reagan. Implemented as a pilot program in 1990 by the Bush administration, ATP has become the flagship of the Clinton-Gore civilian technology policy, as well as the focal point of conservative critique of that policy. This chapter describes the evolution and implementation of ATP, as well as its strengths and weaknesses, and it proposes actions to improve ATP on which the Clinton administration and Congress should be able to find common ground.

Origins of ATP

The ATP is one of a series of modest steps in the evolution of U.S. civilian technology policy. ATP is the realization of a idea under development for more than a quarter of a century: that the federal government should financially support development and utilization of new and improved technology by industry. Its specific form, however, was a response by Congress to concerns about the competitiveness of U.S. industry in the 1980s.

In 1962, the Kennedy administration proposed, without success, to establish a Civilian Industrial Technology Program in the Department of Commerce (DOC) to fund research for lagging industries. Its State Technical Services Program, which funded state programs to disseminate existing technology to small firms, was adopted in 1965 and operated until 1969.

The Nixon administration considered a multi-billion dollar proposal for a New Technological Opportunities program to address the economic downturn of the late 1960s, as well as to respond to the threat to national technological resolve from the high profile defeat in Congress of the supersonic transport program.

President Jimmy Carter oversaw a domestic policy review of industrial innovation that recommended in 1979 an array of policies to help industry respond to the period's slow economic growth and high inflation. These same conditions, however, contributed to Carter's defeat by Ronald Reagan in 1980, and most of Carter's recommendations were not acted on.

The Stevenson-Wydler Technology Innovation Act of 1980 gave the DOC authority to assist Centers for Industrial Technology at universities or other non-profit organizations. These Centers would conduct research and development (R&D) on generic technologies cooperatively with industry, provide education and training about the innovation process, and offer technical assistance to industry. The Centers program was not adopted by the Reagan administration, although it did embrace the part of the Act making technology transfer a mission of all federal R&D agencies.

During the early 1980s, the U.S. economy experienced a sharp downturn; the U.S. balance of trade, especially with Japan, became highly unfavorable; and key industrial sectors such as autos, consumer electronics, machine tools, and semiconductor electronics lost both domestic and international market shares to Japanese firms. By the late 1980s, the debate over the declining "competitiveness" of U.S. industry was in full swing, and many proposals were made for programs and policies to improve U.S. industrial performance. Opponents argued vigorously on both ideological and practical grounds that such proposals would constitute unwarranted and ineffective intrusions into the private economy.

An early response to this challenge was the Engineering Research Centers program under which the National Science Foundation (NSF) funded interdisciplinary centers at leading universities to conduct research on technologies important to industry. Obtaining matching funds from industry was a condition of federal funding. NSF did not specify which technologies it would support, but depended instead on peer review of the quality of proposals to determine which technologies and centers to fund.

By 1987, Congress and the president were under considerable pressure to pass new trade legislation to reauthorize both the Export Administration Act and the president's authority for "fast-track" negotiation of trade agreements. However, the Reagan administration's draft trade legislation, presented in February 1987, soon became the legislative vehicle for a plethora of proposals to address the competitiveness problem. At passage, the Act had grown to include ten major titles with countless sections, subsections, and provisions addressing such matters as trade, export, and international financial policies; agricultural trade; foreign corrupt practices; education and training; small business assistance; patent policy; and ocean and air transportation, as well as technology policy.

A part of the Trade Act, entitled the Technology Competitiveness Act, established ATP and changed the name of the National Bureau of Standards (NBS) to the National Institute of Standards and Technology (NIST), to reflect its enhanced role in supporting the development and use of advanced technology in industry.

The National Institute of Standards and Technology Authorization Act for FY 1989, adopted a few weeks after the Trade Act, restructured the technology programs in the DOC. It created a new Technology Administration (TA), headed by a new Under Secretary of Commerce for Technology. Both the director of NIST and a new Assistant Secretary for Technology Policy, who oversees the Office of Technology Policy (OTP), report to the under secretary.

ATP might have been implemented directly by staff of the TA, an administrative agency, rather than through NIST, a federal laboratory. However, the arguments for assigning ATP to NIST were compelling. Only NIST had the technically skilled staff needed to act as reviewers of proposals and overseers of ATP projects, and it had a well-deserved reputation for integrity and fairness in dealing with complex technical matters, both in support of industrial performance and in the public interest. Furthermore, NIST had an "industrial technical services" office with an experienced staff, whereas the TA had a small staff with limited technical expertise. Neither NIST nor the other parts of the TA had much experience in running competitive research programs. Nevertheless, with its new responsibility for ATP, NIST would for the first time administer a large and visible program of external research.

ATP Implementation

In passing the ATP legislation, Congress and the president determined that the federal government should help U.S. industry by providing a limited amount of public funds on a competitive, cost-shared basis to firms and research consortia to help them develop new technologies that they and other firms could use to compete more effectively in world markets. In the words of Section 5131 of the Technology Competitiveness Act, ATP was established "for the purpose of assisting United States businesses in creating and applying the generic technology and research results necessary to (1) commercialize significant new scientific discoveries and technologies rapidly; and (2) refine manufacturing technologies."

To accomplish this purpose, the Act further states that the secretary of commerce, acting through the director of NIST, may:

aid [industry-led] United States joint research and development ventures...through (A) provision of organizational and technical advice and (B) participation in such joint ventures...which may include (i) partial start-up funding, (ii) provision of a minority share of the cost of such joint ventures for up to 5 years, and (iii) making available equipment, facilities, and personnel, provided that emphasis is placed on areas where the Institute has scientific or technological expertise, on solving generic problems of specific industries, and on making those industries more competitive in world markets.

Furthermore, the secretary, acting through the director, may:

[provide grants to and] enter into contracts and cooperative agreements with United States businesses, especially small businesses, and with independent research organizations, provided that emphasis is placed on applying the Institute's research, research techniques, and expertise to those organization's research programs.

The two inserts in brackets [ ] were added in 1992 by the American Technology Preeminence Act.

Implementation by the Bush Administration

The Reagan administration did not implement the Advanced Technology Program, in part because it was adopted near the end of his second term. This was not unexpected: the supporters of ATP were creating a framework within which future administrations of either party might implement a program to assist U.S. industry.

Senior members of the Bush administration, including the Deputy Secretary of Commerce, Thomas Murrin, and the Under Secretary for Technology, Robert M. White, were concerned about the competitive performance of U.S. industry and were generally supportive of ATP. The administration sought FY 1990 funds to implement the ATP, and $9 million was made available for the first round of ATP awards. ATP was assigned to a small group at NIST under the direction of George Uriano.[1] The program announced by NIST in July 1990 would "focus on supporting private sector development of precompetitive generic technologies and [would participate] in a number of industry initiatives." It would "avoid participation in development of specific products and processes by the private sector."[2]

Generic technology was defined by ATP in its first operating rule as "a concept, component, or process, or the further investigation of scientific phenomena, that has the potential to be applied to a broad range of products or processes."[3] Precompetitive technology was defined as "research and development activities up to the stage where technical uncertainties are sufficiently reduced to permit preliminary assessment of commercial potential and prior to development of application-specific commercial prototypes."[4] The rule also stated that "precompetitive generic technologies are 'enabling,' in that they offer wide breadth of potential application and form an important technical basis for the future product-specific applications; and 'high value,' in that, when applied, they offer significant benefits to the economy."

Projects to be funded were selected by two-stage competitive review of written proposals. The first stage examined scientific and technical merit; the second business and economic merit for those that survived stage one.[5] The technical reviewers were largely NIST staff, and the business review was done by consultants expert in business planning, finance, and technology transfer.

Projects could be supported by grants or cooperative agreements (NIST has used only the latter), and awards could be made either to individual firms or to joint research and development ventures ("consortia"). R&D consortia could include businesses, academic institutions, independent research organizations, and government entities. Since the amendments of 1992, eligible consortia must include two or more United States businesses. To receive ATP funds, R&D joint ventures must register with the Department of Justice pursuant to the National Cooperative Research Act of 1984.

Individual firms could receive awards of up to $2 million over three years. Such awards could be used to offset up to 100 percent of the direct costs of a project, but indirect costs had to be paid by the recipient. Consortia could receive awards for up to five years, the amount limited only by the availability of appropriated funds. ATP can pay for up to 50 percent of the costs of consortium projects (including a maximum of 50 percent of indirect costs). ATP does not provide any funds directly to other governmental entities or to academic institutions, even though both could participate in joint ventures and in subordinate roles to business or joint venture awardees.

The title to intellectual property resulting from an ATP-supported project is required to be held by businesses incorporated in the United States. A university, non-profit, or government agency partner cannot hold title to any invention resulting from ATP projects, (notwithstanding the Bayh-Dole Act of 1980 that gave universities, non-profits, and some private firms the rights to inventions made with federal funds). However, academic institutions and non-profit organizations may share in the royalties or licensing fees resulting from these inventions on whatever terms the participants agree to. In all events, the federal government retains the right to a royalty-free license to use ATP-based technologies for its own purposes.

In the first competition in 1990, eleven projects were funded from a total of 249 proposals; in the 1991 competition, 28 of 241 proposals were funded. The 1992 and 1993 competitions funded

21 and 29 projects respectively. Appropriations for ATP were 10, 36, 47 and 68 million dollars in fiscal years 1990 through 1993.

Some important changes in ATP were made by the American Technology Preeminence Act of 1992. The federal government would no longer receive a share of royalty payments and license fees resulting from ATP awards. Independent research institutions were no longer eligible to apply as single applicants for awards, but could participate in industry-led joint ventures. Furthermore, a new ATP rule issued by NIST under the revised authorization clarified that a research joint venture must include at least two United States businesses that would be eligible to apply to ATP individually, both of which must participate in the proposed R&D program and contribute to the cost-sharing requirement.[6] The 1992 Act also laid out a complicated set of conditions under which foreign firms could receive financial assistance from ATP.

Implementation by the Clinton Administration

ATP was a key element of the new Clinton administration's technology policy. In its February 22, 1993, statement on technology policy, the administration promised that ATP would be expanded "significantly."[7] Additional funds for ATP were included in the administration's supplemental FY1993 budget "stimulus package." These funds were not forthcoming, however, owing to defeat of the package in Congress in March 1993.

ATP has grown substantially during the Clinton years, despite fierce opposition to the program by the newly-ascendant Republican majority elected to Congress in November 1994. Appropriations in fiscal years 1994 through 1997 have been 199, 341, 221, and 225 million dollars respectively. The decline from 1995 to 1996 reflects congressional opposition. The administration has asked for $276 million for FY1998. In 1994, 88 new projects were funded. The number was 103 new projects in 1995, but it fell sharply to eight in 1996.

The Clinton administration published a revised rule in the Federal Register detailing procedures for the ATP in January 1994, incorporating several important changes.[8] First, in some competitions ATP now accepts pre-proposals to help proposers avoid investing in proposals that are unlikely to succeed. Successful pre-proposers then submit full proposals for review.

Second, ATP augmented its open competitions with "focused programs" in specific technology areas selected after consultation with industry. Firms and consortia are encouraged to submit white papers to ATP outlining technical needs and opportunities in specific technologies. ATP uses the number and quality of white papers to indicate industrial interest and builds focused programs around clusters of white papers on similar topics. Thus, the focused program areas are determined in response to industry initiative. Five focused competitions were announced in 1994. The number of focused programs has grown to twelve by 1997, and some have had more than one round of competition.

The revised proposal preparation kit released in May 1996 includes a list of the members of the Science and Technology Council of the States, a unit of the National Governors Association. The members are prepared to offer technical assistance to prospective and current ATP recipients.[9]

ATP awards have been made to a wide variety of industries and technologies, and they have gone to both small and large firms, as well as to a variety of consortia. Universities are active members of many of the funded consortia, as are other nonprofit organizations and some federal laboratories. NIST has characterized ATP awards as follows:[10]

- 288 total awards, involving 740 firms;
- 184 awards to single applicants, including 106 small businesses;
- 104 awards to joint ventures, including 28 led by small businesses;
- 262 known instances of university participation in the 288 awards, involving more than 100 institutions; and
- a total commitment of $989 million in ATP funds.

Although attribution of R&D projects to specific fields of technology is somewhat arbitrary, since many projects involve multiple technical fields, NIST reports that the ATP funds have been distributed as follows:[11]

- 32 percent to computing, information and communications;
- 15 percent to biotechnology;

- 16 percent to electronics;
- 14 percent to materials;
- 11 percent to manufacturing;
- 8 percent to chemicals and processing; and
- 4 percent to energy and environment.

The Debate over ATP's Existence

Despite the fact that ATP has been in place for more than seven years, its legitimacy and existence continue to be debated. The decision to try a pilot ATP program in 1990 was not universally popular in the Bush administration, especially among leading conservatives on the White House staff. ATP enjoyed a brief period of relative tranquillity during the first two years of the Clinton administration, but it came under attack in the congressional campaign in 1994. Since the change in political leadership in Congress in early 1995, the very existence of ATP has repeatedly been called into question by influential members in both Houses. Before turning to a discussion of how this long-standing debate might be satisfactorily resolved, it is useful to review the positions taken by ATP's supporters and opponents, especially during its establishment.

Arguments in Support of ATP

Supporters saw ATP as one way to address the challenge to American markets and the American standard of living from strong foreign competition. They were especially concerned that U.S. firms were facing competition from abroad from companies whose home governments were offering substantial financial assistance for developing and adopting new technology. Both Japan and the European Community were seen as subsidizing commercial industrial technology. In fact, ATP was, in part, a direct response to industrial R&D consortia organized or funded by the Japanese Ministry of International Trade and Industry (MITI).

In addition, the National Cooperative Research Act of 1984 had stimulated a new awareness of how industrial R&D consortia could help to both develop new technology and facilitate its diffusion among participating firms. U.S. consortia such as the Microelectronics and Computer Technology Corporation (MCC) and the Electric Power Research Institute (EPRI) were seen as models of what could be done on a broader scale if all industries were able to compete openly for federal assistance. Thus, the ATP can also be seen as an attempt to revive the Stevenson-Wydler Act's concept of Centers for Industrial Technology, which had never been implemented.

Furthermore, ATP was to be a means through which the federal government could help ensure that U.S. industry would take advantage of new technical opportunities, whether they are spin-offs from mission R&D programs, inventions made in universities or government laboratories, "orphan" discoveries made in industrial laboratories devoted to other technologies, or developments in other countries. In several high-profile cases during the 1980s, promising high-tech start-up companies had been unable to obtain domestic financing for their risky operations and were, as a result, sold to foreign interests. Furthermore, U.S. industry had lost its commanding positions in a number of industries. And, while the United States was among the world's best at discovering new science and making new inventions, it was lagging behind other countries in moving swiftly to commercialize these new discoveries and inventions. To address these problems, ATP was to identify promising new technologies in which U.S. industry was not investing adequately and to promote them with public investments.

ATP was also seen as a means of limiting the practice of direct congressional funding for specific technologies. Throughout the 1980s, various industries had sought federal help in developing new technologies to fend off tough or unfair foreign competition. Highly visible and expensive technology programs implemented through the Department of Defense, such as SEMATECH and the National Center for Manufacturing Sciences (NCMS), were prominent examples. Some of its supporters believed that ATP could subject such proposals to systematic scrutiny on their technical and financial merits and that this could relieve the Congress, which is ill-suited to making such determinations, from such tasks.

Finally, some supporters embraced a "market failure" rationale from modern economic theory as a basis for ATP. According to this theory, private firms tend to under-invest in high-risk, long-term, precompetitive research on enabling technologies, especially on manufacturing technologies that could be used by many firms, not just those undertaking the research. Several market failures are pertinent. For example, the high risks of uncertain future payoff from R&D cannot be reduced to acceptable levels by individual firms. Furthermore, the firms that pay for and perform R&D cannot always appropriate enough of its benefits to make the necessary investments worthwhile, because a significant part of the benefits, but not the costs, "spill over" to other firms and to society at large. Using the ideal free market as a touchstone, the theory argues that society is better off if public subsidies or other incentives are offered to firms to get them to spend more on R&D than they would spend acting in their own interests. Thus, by paying some of a firm's costs for R&D, ATP would act as a surrogate both for society as a whole and for other firms that would indirectly benefit from the R&D. By funding R&D consortia, ATP should help ensure that more than one firm would benefit and that the new technology would be disseminated broadly.

Arguments in Opposition to ATP

Opponents of ATP have also been diversely motivated. Opposition to ATP and its predecessors has centered on the view that U.S. industry does and should operate in a competitive free market arena, in which each firm is responsible for taking action—including the development and use of new technology—to maximize its chances of thriving and of contributing to the economic well-being of the nation. Any government engagement in the market economy is undesirable, and, from this perspective, when government must act, it should do so in the least intrusive manner possible. While many proponents of the unfettered market do recognize the existence of important imperfections in the market for new knowledge, they argue that these imperfections are largely limited to the realm of basic research, in which firms are unlikely to invest and for which government funding is appropriate, particularly at academic institutions. ATP opponents who do favor incentives for industrial R&D often prefer the Research and Experimentation Tax Credit, first adopted in 1981, as a superior alternative because it avoids having a government agency make determinations about which projects will be supported.

Other reasons for opposing ATP are more pragmatic and political in character. Opponents argue that even if ATP were a good idea in theory, government officials can not effectively "out-guess" the marketplace in practice; in fact, they are likely to be less well-informed about all aspects of market needs and opportunities, as well as about technology and production possibilities, than is the aggregate of industrial firms. Furthermore, government officials, it is argued, will be heavily influenced by non-market considerations in deciding which projects and performers to support, with the result that public funds will be spent less efficiently than those same funds would be if they were left in the hands of private parties.

Some oppose ATP-like programs because they can be seen as domestic-subsidy based impediments to efficiency-enhancing international trade. From this perspective, it would be better to work through international negotiations and world trade bodies to discourage other nations from subsidizing their domestic industries via technology support programs, than it would be to adopt our own in response.

Finally, some argue that U.S. industry annually spends nearly $100 billion of its own money on R&D and that ATP's budget of a few hundred million dollars is very unlikely to have a significant impact on industrial technology development in the United States.

Evaluation of ATP

Relative to its size and age, ATP has been the focus of an extraordinary level and quality of evaluation. In-house evaluations have been done by economists from ATP and other parts of NIST. In addition, ATP has contracted for evaluations by firms such as Solomon Associates and Silber and Associates,[12] as well as with the National Bureau of Economic Research and academic economists including Zvi Griliches, Edwin Mansfield,[13] Albert Link,[14] and Adam Jaffe.[15] The General Accounting Office (GAO) has conducted at least three ATP evaluations.[16]

Some ATP evaluations examine the administration of the program using data from its operations and surveys of program participants. These studies are concerned with ATP leadership and management and with effects on participants' organizations. They also look for early indications of project outcomes, impacts, and difficulties.

Other evaluations seek to determine whether ATP has achieved its goal of improving the performance of U.S. businesses. Some analysts have tried to estimate the private and social economic returns to ATP projects; however, such work remains largely at the conceptual level.[17] Others have developed case studies of the outcomes of successful and unsuccessful projects.[18]

ATP has supported research on analytical frameworks for evaluation that might help identify and characterize the spill-overs of knowledge created by ATP funded projects, as well as the benefits of the projects to participants and to others that flow through market transactions.[19]

Little effort has been addressed to assessment of other impacts of ATP on technology development and firm performance.[20] For example, ATP's operations may signal to industry that certain topics are ripe for technical effort, may overcome some of the reluctance of firms to join R&D consortia owing to their concerns about a loss of competitive advantage or the threat of antitrust action, may energize the formation of partnerships outside the ATP umbrella, and may facilitate communication among firms (and even within firms) about focused program topics. If these impacts are large, ATP's overall value will exceed the sum of the values of its individual projects. These areas seem ripe for further study, most likely outside the neoclassical economic paradigm that informs the current ATP evaluation effort.[21] (See the discussion of possible ATP contributions to social capital in Chapter 4.)

Thus, the value of the ATP program remains uncertain. The studies mentioned above include fragmentary data and suggestive analyses, but none of them attempts to make a summary statement of the social benefits of the program. Furthermore, as discussed below, it is not clear that it will ever be possible to do an evaluation of ATP that will satisfy those who hope to demonstrate conclusively that it is either a great success or a complete failure.

Limitations on ATP Evaluation

Analytical methods of evaluation have important limitations, whether used for project selection, project evaluation, or program evaluation. First, R&D projects are investments in the unknown, whose uncertainties are larger to the extent that projects are longer-term, higher-risk, or more generic in nature. Furthermore, the pay-off to research investments usually comes only after additional non-R&D investments are made to commercialize, produce, and market the resulting products and processes, so the "success" of an R&D project is contingent on the success of other activities over which R&D has no control. For these reasons, very few firms use formal, analytical processes for R&D project selection and assessment, even for the relatively simple case of development projects financed and conducted entirely within a single company.[22]

Second, some of the benefits of ATP projects are intended to "spill over" to firms other than those that receive ATP funds, but it is difficult, if not impossible, to identify and quantify the many spill-over pathways. For example, some benefits spill over to the project participants, others to their suppliers and customers, others to competitors that use the new knowledge (both with and without payment of royalties or fees), and still others to firms in other industries and markets. Thus, evaluation will almost certainly underestimate the total project benefits, but to an unknowable extent.

Third, the value of an ATP project should be assessed in comparison with what would have happened in the absence of the ATP support. However, determining the counter-factual circumstance for specific ATP projects is necessarily conjectural. There is no way to judge, for example, whether participants who are surveyed to find out what they would have done without ATP support respond accurately. One way to address this problem is to compare the performance of ATP awardees, not with their own counter-factual situation, but with the performance of a control group of firms that are not awardees, as has been done by GAO.[23]

Despite the serious barriers to satisfactory evaluation, ATP should continue to assess the program and its portfolio of projects. Each bit of intelligence and insight should help program staff make better funding decisions and help policy-makers decide whether ATP as a whole is well-managed and worthwhile. It is important that ATP be examined and evaluated by experts not financially supported by the program itself.

Issues Regarding ATP

A few of the most significant issues about ATP are discussed here, with a focus on how ATP might be modified to address them.

Can ATP Achieve Greater Political Support?

ATP is in the unenviable position of having become highly politicized, while its traditional political support is not strong. The strong endorsement of ATP by President Clinton made ATP a target of conservatives who sought to deny him political victories across a wide range of public policies. ATP has appeared on conservative "hit-lists," as well as on lists of "corporate welfare" programs targeted for elimination by both liberals and conservatives. Leading members of Congress have made strong statements opposing ATP. To be sure, not all the opposition has been politically motivated; indeed, much of the opposition has been on ideological grounds: it is said that the government has no business helping industry fund R&D for commercial purposes, because that funding is an unwarranted intrusion into the private sector.

ATP has not had widespread political appeal at any time in its existence. It was established originally owing to the determination of activist members and staff in Congress, supported by a few firms and some vocal commentators on the competitiveness of U.S. industry. It was not a response to pressure from the constituency it was intended to serve, although in recent years some industrial interests have become strong supporters. The ATP authorization passed by Congress was signed by President Reagan, not because he supported the bill, but because it was part of the much broader omnibus trade bill which the President was under great pressure to approve.

President Bush treated ATP as an experimental program and did not make it a priority. President Clinton has made ATP a priority in the recent budget battles with Congress, but congressional opposition and the balanced budget agreement have made it difficult for him to make a strong public case for additional ATP funding.

Unlike the Small Business Innovation Research (SBIR) and the Manufacturing Extension Partnerships (MEP) program (see Chapter 8 by Scott Wallsten and Chapter 10 by Philip Shapira in this volume), which help large numbers of firms in many states and congressional districts, ATP has made relatively few awards to relatively few firms. As a result, it has engendered little "hometown" support in Congress or in the general public.

Furthermore, ATP and its congressional overseers have assiduously avoided using it to support projects advanced by special interests through appropriations earmarks. This has earned good marks for ATP among those devoted to the cause of merit review in selection of federally supported R&D projects. However, its determination to avoid pork-barrel projects has denied ATP some of the devoted supporters enjoyed by many other programs.

Clearly, the political challenge is complex. One possible solution is to modify ATP so that it would attract more visible and committed constituencies that could overcome ideologically-based opposition by, for example, tying ATP funding to specific national goals or to state and regional economic development strategies. Another approach would be to more tightly limit the kinds of firm that can participate in ATP projects by, for example, funding only R&D consortia, or imposing strict prohibitions on the participation of foreign-owned firms. However, each of these approaches has its limitations and undesirable consequences.

Should ATP Fund Foreign-Owned Firms?

One of the most contentious issues surrounding ATP has been the question of how it should treat foreign-owned firms, especially those that are partners in research consortia that ATP might wish to support. Current law permits such participation but only pursuant to compliance by the firm and its home government with certain reciprocal privileges and certain protections of U.S. interests.

This issue highlights the question of whose interests ATP is intended to serve and how it can most effectively do so. In the case of "vertical" consortia, involving firms with differing capabilities, foreign firms may have unique technical strengths that would make important contributions to the outcome of an ATP project: in such cases their participation might be in the interests of the U.S. partners and of the United States as a whole, even if the foreign firm also benefited from its U.S. partners and ATP funding. However, foreign firms participating in "horizontal" consortia, in which all participants have similar technical capabilities, may stand to learn much more than they contribute.

Whether, in fact, foreign participation in any specific project yields benefits for U.S. corporations, shareholders, employees, or consumers probably depends on the facts of each project, making application of a blanket policy both difficult and not likely to be in the national interest. Thus, program officials need some latitude to judge whether foreign firms can participate in each case.

Complicating this issue is the fact that government support for ATP-like precompetitive industrial technology development programs has become an issue in international trade negotiations.[24] Current the domestic subsidy rules of the General Agreement on Tariffs and Trade (GATT) permit such programs only under limited conditions. There was an attempt during the recently completed GATT Uruguay Round to impose more stringent controls on programs like ATP, as well as on the European Community's "Framework" R&D program and similar activities in Japan and other countries. Additional challenges to such programs can be expected in future multilateral trade negotiations.

Should ATP Fund Large Firms?

Much has been made of the fact that large, well-known and profitable firms such as IBM, AT&T, Dupont, and a consortium that includes the Big-Three automobile manufacturers—Ford, Chrysler, and General Motors—have received ATP funds. The R&D budgets of some of these firms are greater than the budgets of ATP, NIST, or the entire Department of Commerce. Opponents of ATP have seized on ATP support of large firms to argue that ATP is simply corporate welfare to "big business." Proponents have argued, on the other hand, that the participation and support of leading firms is important to achieving the program's goals and essential to garnering effective political support for it.

Some of the concern about large-firm participation may result from a misunderstanding of ATP's goals and operations. ATP does not fund individual firms just to help them become more profitable. Instead, it funds firms and consortia to achieve broader goals: improvements in the technology-based performance of U.S. businesses generally. Thus, ATP tries to fund projects and performers that have the best chance of achieving high ratios of social to private returns. In doing so, ATP may find that the best route is to leverage the capabilities of large firms, small firms, or large firms in concert with smaller ones, to conduct projects. From this point of view, it would be conceptually as well as politically unwise to exclude large firms.

Furthermore, some ATP projects take advantage of new technical knowledge in large firms that may promise to be socially useful, but which the firm would not take advantage of itself. The new knowledge may not support the firm's current market strategy, the project may be too uncertain, or the project may not be expected to yield a defensible intellectual property position for the firm. These are exactly the kinds of circumstances for which ATP was established. In such cases ATP can help exploit new knowledge when a project would otherwise not meet the performer's own criteria for R&D investments.

Additionally, R&D is typically decentralized in large firms, and the divisions may operate more like independent small firms than as parts of a large one. ATP funds may help divisions finance projects at the divisional level for which corporate funds are not forthcoming. ATP can also support the entrepreneurial interests of individual researchers in large firms whose good ideas are not supported by their employers.

On balance, ATP funding of large firms is entirely consistent with the program's goals and should not be circumscribed. However, the political reality is that the program is under considerable pressure to change. If ATP is to survive and thrive, adjustments may be necessary. Furthermore, the Technology Competitiveness Act incorporates an explicit preference for funding small businesses over large ones. Thus, ATP should re-emphasize the roles of small firms as individual and consortium participants, but it should also maintain the option of funding large firms when it is in the public interest to do so.

Should ATP Fund Consortia Only?

It has been argued that ATP should fund only research consortia, typically on the political grounds that it is not appropriate for government to help one firm outperform its competitors by subsidizing technology improvements, or on the economic grounds that consortia provide a ready channel for knowledge to spill over to member firms.

The Technology Competitiveness Act can be read to give a mild preference to joint ventures for ATP funds, both because its provisions for funding joint ventures are more explicit and because joint ventures can be funded on terms more favorable to the participating firms than can individual firms.

On the other hand, if one keeps firmly in mind the public purpose of ATP—to fund the development of high-risk enabling technologies—then the selection of the vehicle for accomplishing this goal should be made on pragmatic grounds. One firm may have all the necessary capabilities to advance a technology that would offer significant benefits to other firms and to society, but it might not be able to capture enough profits to make the investment worthwhile, owing either to high risk or the inappropriability of the results. If the firm needs no technological help from other firms and institutions, and if no other firm is willing to enter into a joint venture, then the public interest may well be served by making an ATP award to one firm.

In the final analysis, ATP should be able to pursue a flexible strategy under which it may fund both individual firms and research consortia. At the same time, ATP should recognize that the public and key decision makers may better appreciate the arguments for public support of consortia.

Should Universities Be Eligible for ATP Awards?

The Technology Competitiveness Act, as amended, requires that ATP awards be made to single businesses or to consortia led by two

or more businesses. Academic institutions are welcome to participate as consortium partners and to receive federal funds indirectly
in that role, but they cannot be the lead partners in a joint venture
to obtain ATP funding.

The clear intent of the Act was to provide partial support to firms
and consortia to help realize the benefits of new technology in a
fairly direct way on behalf of the American people. Commercialization of new products and processes is not a core activity of academic
institutions, however, and it was thought to be essential that private
firms that are active in the marketplace play the lead role in ATP
projects to enhance the chances that new developments supported
by ATP would be effectively commercialized.

Undoubtedly, some academic institutions could organize consortia involving private firms to obtain ATP awards. Nevertheless,
in view of the multitude of alternative sources of federal funds
available to academic institutions and of the basic purposes of ATP,
the current policy is sound.

Should ATP Forego Cost-Sharing for Small Firms?

Some small firms, individually or in consortia, have complained
that they cannot afford to match ATP's funds with their own and
that this has kept them from participating in ATP. However, the
principle of cost sharing was embraced in the ATP legislation to
ensure that the participating firms put their own resources at risk
so that they will apply only for significant projects and will complete
ATP-supported projects successfully and in a timely manner. ATP
is not an "assistance" program; instead, it implements a strategy of
using private firms to accomplish public objectives. Furthermore,
the cost-sharing requirement also means that proposing firms must
diligently seek other private sources of funds if they have no
internal funds to invest. This helps to ensure that ATP will not
become the "source of first resort" for project funding.

Opportunities to Improve ATP

The ATP is in many ways the paradigm of a well-run and successful
government program. It is based on a rigorously competitive

process; it features an appropriate mix of incentives that encourage private participation and serves a broader national interest; and it engages in continuous self-examination and evaluation to ensure that its processes and strategies are effective. It is remarkably free of partisan and personal political influences and bases its decisions on the best available technical and business assessments. Nevertheless, ATP has become a focal point for continued political attack. Thus, one approaches the task of making recommendations to enhance ATP with some trepidation. The following sections offer a few specific ideas for changes in the program, not to repair its faults but to move it to the next level of success. Any changes in the program must preserve its professionalism and freedom from undue political influence, while also seeking a broader political consensus on which a stable program and budget can be sustained.

Stabilize the ATP Budget

The Clinton administration has promoted an aggressive growth path for ATP. Yet political battles over ATP's legitimacy, combined with the government-wide struggle to control federal deficit spending, have combined to create an air of uncertainty over ATP's future. Almost every year its budget has been in doubt, and for the past three years, the continued existence of the program has been threatened.

The ups and downs of ATP's budget and the continual challenges to the program's legitimacy have not contributed constructively to building a solid program with a sound fiscal administration and a secure image among its industrial constituency. Thus, the most important immediate goals of Congress and the administration should be to find a basis for ATP to continue and to focus the annual policy discussion on ATP's budget and on how its operations might be improved.

Despite its difficulties, the ATP budget has grown from $10 million to more than $200 million over the past seven years. On the one hand, this is an impressive rate of growth; on the other, even $200 million is a relatively small amount to invest in the nation's technological future. Taking other similar programs into account, a budget of the order of $0.5 to $1.5 billion annually would not be unreasonable for ATP.[25] An ATP budget of $1.5 billion would amount to only two percent of federal R&D funds. On the other hand, it would be equivalent to nearly 20 percent of industrial funds for basic research and could make a real difference to the technology base of the nation if properly leveraged with industry's own funds. Growth to this level should be proposed by the administration and appropriated by the Congress over the next decade, which would imply average growth of about $100 million annually.

Tie Some ATP Funds to Specific National Goals

ATP was not designed to be a "problem focused" program whose research agenda would be driven by high-profile national goals such as crime, terrorism, safety and environmental quality, affordable housing, infrastructure redevelopment, manufacturing quality, or national security. Instead, it was designed to be organized around domains of technology, such as bioprocessing, robotics, computers, semiconductor design, manufacturing processes, and the like. The tacit theory of this mode of organization is that societal ends will ultimately be served by the development of new technology and that the relationship of technology development to particular goals need not be an organizing principle for the program.

On the other hand, the present design has the unfortunate consequence of not appearing to focus in any direct and concrete way on important national needs that ordinary citizens and legislators can easily identify. Such relatively abstract goals as productivity, competitiveness, economic growth, and improved balance of trade have their supporters and enthusiasts, to be sure, but they seem unable to galvanize strong public support. The even more abstract goal of correcting "market failures" has essentially no constituency other than members of the economics profession and the community of "policy wonks."

The European Union's Framework Program for the support of industrial technology development suggests a useful alternative way to organize an ATP, keeping in mind that it has an order of magnitude greater funding than ATP to serve an industrial base of roughly the same size. Framework addresses abstract categories, such as growth and jobs; industrial technologies, such as materials; and specific national and multinational objectives such as better transportation systems and improved health care.[26] The contributions of ATP projects on automobile manufacturing to the goals of the Partnership for a New Generation of Vehicles (PNGV) suggests a similar model. While PNGV is a controversial program, it has the real virtue that ordinary citizens can understand its objectives.

Other federal R&D agencies with broad mandates structure their science and technology-driven programs around meeting national needs. For example, NIH is organized and funded around specific diseases, although it awards project funds along scientific lines. Similarly, the Department of Defense (DOD) awards its basic research (so-called "6.1") funds to fields of science and engineering, but specific program goals are already identified at that level.

A modest portion of ATP funds should be awarded through "focused programs" that reflect the kinds of national needs listed above. Devoting five to ten percent of next year's new funds to a pilot project of this type might be appropriate. A focus on environmentally sustainable manufacturing technologies, which would be compatible with the administration's Environmental Technology Initiative, would be an interesting choice. (See Chapter 11 by George Heaton and Darryl Banks in this volume).

Tie ATP Funds to State and Regional Development Strategies

During the past decade, the states have developed a new interest and competence in mobilizing technological change as a strategic approach to economic and social development (See Chapter 16 by Christopher Coburn and Duncan Brown in this volume). Every state has an array of programs and incentives intended to strengthen indigenous firms and to encourage new firms to initiate technology-based businesses to create jobs and wealth within the state. Many programs seek to focus state resources on strategic industrial goals that reflect the sectors and markets in which they have established strengths and inherent advantages. ATP now refers potential recipients of its funds to state science and technology program offices for technical assistance.

ATP could reinforce these state-based efforts by allocating a portion of its resources to work with regional consortia of firms, non-profits, local and state governments, and academic institutions to build technological strength in key sectors. It could conduct a competitive program that would make matching awards to consortia that take explicit account of the value of local and regional technology-based industrial agglomerations. Using existing authority, ATP should experiment with a "focused program" of awards to industry-led consortia organized on a regional or state basis in cooperation with nonprofit organizations and local governmental bodies. The major difference between this approach and the current focused program approach would be the addition of an additional criterion: a focus on a critical mass of regional or state-based firms structured around a particular technology or industry.

In addition to building on state and regional efforts, this approach would have the obvious political advantage of developing a higher profile for ATP in certain regions and would focus its limited funds in a way that further leverages the available state program and private funds. On the other hand, many research consortia form naturally among firms separated by long distances, so it would not be wise to limit ATP funds to state and regionally-based projects.

Beyond ATP: Strengthening the Role of the Department of Commerce

ATP is just one of many small steps taken during the last three decades to build a national civilian technology policy. ATP was not to be the final step; however, as the focus of sustained political debate, it has had to carry more of the load than it should. The Technology Administration (TA), established at nearly the same time as ATP, should be the institutional framework for a civilian technology policy that is broader than ATP's project-based R&D subsidies. This chapter concludes with a few suggestions to build on the ATP's success and the TA's charter to develop a more balanced and complete civilian technology policy.

A condition for building an effective TA is that it have a budget appropriate to an operating bureau, rather than the "policy shop" budget it now enjoys. The TA will also need a larger, technically rich staff. One way to accomplish that would be for it to employ temporary technical program staff, or "rotators," following the very successful practices of the Defense Advanced Research Projects Agency (DARPA) and NSF.

Move ATP to the Technology Administration

Putting ATP at NIST made great sense when ATP was a small, experimental program and when the TA was a new effort to rebuild its nearly moribund predecessor, the Office of Productivity, Technology, and Innovation. Today, however, ATP has grown to the point that its budget competes for funds with NIST's laboratory programs and that its direction and political defense absorb a substantial part of the attention of NIST's leadership.

Therefore, consideration should be given to relocating the responsibility for ATP from NIST in Gaithersburg, Maryland, to the TA in the main Commerce building in downtown Washington, D.C. Since NIST is overseen by the TA, the chain of responsibility for the ATP would continue to run through the under secretary for technology in DOC. Furthermore, the TA could continue to draw on the scientific and technical capabilities of the NIST staff to review ATP proposals and to help define new focus program topics. Only the program staff would be relocated; the NIST technical staff participants would continue to be located at NIST. Bringing ATP closer to the routine operations of DOC would also facilitate improved integration of all federal industrial programs concerned with technology, investment policy, labor-management relations, trade, training, regulation, and the like.

Supporting Large-Scale Research Consortia

Large-scale R&D consortia, such as SEMATECH and the National Center for Manufacturing Sciences (NCMS), and comprehensive integrated technology initiatives, such as PNGV and the American Textile consortium (AMTEX), involve federal funding that exceeds ATP's resources. They are also tied more closely to a national political agenda or to international trade policy than are the typical joint ventures supported by ATP. The TA should have the responsibility to ascertain the need for such large-scale consortia and should have a budget with which it would support them only if they pass rigorous merit review and after consultation with affected firms, industries, and other interests. This change may require new authorizing legislation.

Support for Technology-Related Graduate Research and Education

Nearly every federal agency that draws upon the nation's supply of scientists and engineers supports advanced education and research in relevant fields. While NSF is the agency most responsible for graduate education and training across the board, DOD, DOE, NASA, NIH, and the Department of Agriculture also support university-based graduate education and research tied to their missions. DOC is conspicuous by its failure to support advanced education in manufacturing engineering, applied sciences, the management of technology, and technology policy related to its industrial technology missions.

DOC should establish a program to support academic research and education in such areas, working in cooperation with the NSF Engineering Directorate and in consultation with leading educators. Section 6 of the Stevenson-Wydler Act seems to give DOC the authority for such a program; all that is needed are a budget, program rules, and staff.

Enhancing DOC's Analytical Capability

One of the purposes of TA is to do analysis for DOC in technology policy, technology strategy, and the management of technology. TA needs a larger budget and additional staff to fulfill this mission adequately. To ensure that the in-house studies are done objectively and to the highest standards, it should also give grants and offer contracts for such studies to academic researchers, analytical firms, and the Critical Technologies Institute at RAND. Support of graduate education and research would nicely complement this activity, as would management of ATP by the TA.

Strengthening Access to Foreign and Government Technical Information

The United States no longer dominates the world's scientific and technical development. Most new ideas come from other countries, increasingly from places where language, cultural differences, and long distances are significant barriers to awareness and understanding of what others are doing. The TA has a program to obtain and disseminate foreign scientific and technical information, building on the Office of Japanese Technical Information established under the Japanese Technical Literature Act of 1987. The National Technical Information Service aids in information distribution, and the NSF's World Technology Program at Loyola University does focused analyses of the state of the art of important technologies around the world, especially in Japan. Additional resources to support each of these efforts would be money well spent in avoiding duplication of effort by firms and universities and in ensuring that U.S. R&D organizations have effective access to the latest international developments.

Building U.S. Capability to Participate in International Technology Programs

International industrial R&D consortia initiatives, such as the Intelligent Manufacturing Systems (IMS) project initiated by Japan in the late 1980s, have been a problem for potential U.S. participants owing to the fact that no U.S. governmental agency has the authority and the budget to represent national interests and to support participation by universities and non-profit consortia. The TA should have the authority and budget to respond effectively to foreign R&D initiatives and to initiate such programs when they meet U.S. objectives. Other nations have used such programs to help them catch up to the United States in key technologies, and the TA should consider initiating international cooperative R&D as one approach to learning from the best around the world.

Establishing a Permanent High-Level Advisory Committee on Civilian Technology

The under secretary for technology should establish a permanent, high-level, external advisory committee to provide a direct means for continual advice and evaluation of the TA's programs and policy initiatives. Such a body could also advise the secretary of commerce on broader questions of industrial technology policy. It would be the counterpart for civilian technology of NSF's National Science Board and DOD's Defense Science Board. Members could be drawn from technology-based firms, labor, academia, the financial community, and consumer interests. Members should be experienced and skilled in such fields as industrial technology, analysis of the impact of technology on the workplace and society, the financing of technology-based enterprises, and public policy making.

Conclusion

The Advanced Technology Program was authorized by Congress nearly a decade ago to help U.S. businesses develop and improve commercial technology. It has succeeded admirably in building a substantial and well-managed program, despite the lack of consensus among political leaders regarding its appropriateness. Most of the criticism of ATP has focused, not on its operations or outcomes, but on its role and mission. While policy analysis and evaluation can contribute to improved management of ATP and may make a small difference in the views of its skeptics, resolving the question of its long-term stability is largely a matter of political will.

Opportunities exist to strengthen ATP substantively and politically. A few new experiments in ATP's operations could teach us a great deal about their potential to strengthen ATP. Similarly, a stronger Technology Administration could assume the responsibility for operating ATP, in cooperation with NIST staff, and could move further toward meeting the national need for an effective home for civilian technology policy and programs.

The rationales for government support of industrial technology were not universally accepted during the late 1980s when ATP was founded, nor are they now. Some would limit the government's role in technology development to actions clearly derivable from the economic theory of market failure. They are not convinced by the pragmatic, international, and political rationales for ATP. They should support ATP even on their own terms, however, because market failures abound in technology development. Furthermore, in a democracy, public policy should respond to political imperatives and to pressures resulting from other countries' actions, as well as to economic theory. The United States will be well-served if an enduring consensus can be reached on the need for and design of the ATP.

Notes

1. Department of Commerce, Technology Administration, "Advanced Technology Program Final Rule," 55 *Federal Register* (F.R.) 142, pp. 30150 et seq. (July 24, 1990).

2. Ibid.

3. Ibid.

4. Ibid.

5. The Act says, "No contract or award may be made until the research project in question has been subject to a merit review, and has, in the opinion of the reviewers...been shown to have scientific and technical merit." In recent years, proposals have gone through both stages of review to enable NIST to give unsuccessful applicants feedback on all aspects of their proposals.

6. Department of Commerce, Technology Administration, "Advanced Technology Program, Proposal Preparation Kit for Proposal Solicitations—ATP 92-01 and 93-01" (Gaithersburg, Md.: National Institute of Standards and Technology, 1992, pp. 2–4).

7. William J. Clinton and Albert Gore, Jr., "Technology for America's Economic Growth: A New Direction to Build Economic Strength" (Washington, D.C.: Executive Office of the President, February 22, 1993), p. 8.

8. Department of Commerce, Technology Administration, "Advanced Technology Program Proposal Preparation Kit" (Gaithersburg, MD: National Institute of Standards and Technology, February 1994), p. 2 and Appendix 2.

9. Department of Commerce, Technology Administration, "Advanced Technology Program Proposal Preparation Kit, Supplement" (Gaithersburg, Md.: National Institute of Standards and Technology, May 1996).

10. Susannah B. Schiller, personal communication from NIST staff, April 11, 1997.

11. Ibid.

12. Bohne Silber, "Survey of Advanced Technology Program 1990–1992 Awardees: Company Opinion About the ATP and Its Early Effects" (Clarksville, Md.: Silber and Associates, January 30, 1996).

13. Edwin Mansfield, "Estimating Social and Private Returns from Innovations Based on the Advanced Technology Program: Problems and Opportunities" (Philadelphia: University of Pennsylvania, January 1996).

14. Albert N. Link, "Advanced Technology Program: Economic Study of the Printed Wiring Board Joint Venture After Two Years," report prepared for the

Advanced Technology Program (Greensboro, N.C., April 1993); Albert N. Link, "Evaluating the Advanced Technology Program: A Preliminary Assessment of Economic Impacts," *International Journal of Technology Management*, Vol. 8, No. 6/7/8 (1993), pp.726–739.

15. Adam B. Jaffe, "Economic Analysis of Research Spillovers: Implications for the Advanced Technology Program" (Brandeis University and National Bureau of Economic Research, October, 1996).

16. General Accounting Office (GAO), "Federal Research: Advanced Technology Program's Indirect Cost Rates and Program Evaluation Status," Report GAO/RCED-93-221 (Washington, D.C.: U.S. General Accounting Office, September 1993); U.S. GAO, "Performance Measurement: Efforts to Evaluate the Advanced Technology Program," Report GAO/RCED-95-68 (Washington, D.C.: GAO, May 1995); U.S. GAO, "Measuring Performance: The Advanced Technology Program and Private Sector Funding," Report GAO/RCED-96-47 (Washington, D.C.: GAO, January 1996).

17. Mansfield, "Estimating Social and Private Returns."

18. Department of Commerce, Technology Administration, "NIST Industrial Impacts: A Sampling of Successful Partnerships" (Gaithersburg, Md.: National Institute of Standards and Technology, April 1995).

19. Under contract to ATP, Edwin Mansfield described how his path-breaking work on the private and social returns to R&D might be extended to ATP-supported projects, and Adam Jaffe proffered a complex and subtle analysis of the nature of project spill-overs and how they might be estimated and used by ATP, both in *ex ante* project selections and *ex post* project evaluations. See Mansfield, "Estimating Social and Private Returns," and Jaffe, "Economic Analysis of Research Spillovers."

20. Albert Link alludes to this kind of impact in his 1993 paper for ATP, but does not explicate how it might be assessed. See Link, "Advanced Technology Program: Economic Study."

21. See, for example, Rosalie Ruegg, "Guidelines for Economic Evaluation of the Advanced Technology Program" (Gaithersburg, Md.: National Institute of Standards and Technology, November 1996).

22. The Industrial Research Institute (IRI) has engaged for several years in a project to develop methods of valuing technology at the firm level. IRI's method of analysis, involving thirty-three metrics that firms might use to value technology, has recently been published. The methods are not intended to aid in project evaluation. See James W. Tipping, Eugene Zeffren, and Alan R. Fusfeld, "Assessing the Value of Your Technology," *Research-Technology Management*, September/October 1995, pp. 22–39.

23. GAO compared aspects of awardees with those of a set of "near winning" firms and consortia identified for GAO by ATP staff. See U.S. General Accounting Office, "Measuring Performance."

As another approach to dealing with the problem of the unknown counterfactual, it has been proposed to use a double-blind strategy similar to that used in clinical trials of new pharmaceuticals. (See Chapter 3 by Adam Jaffe in this volume.) ATP might first select a set of winning firms and consortia in the usual manner. Prior to award announcement, however, a lottery would be used to select only a fraction of the winners to receive awards. Those unsuccessful in the lottery would presumably be told only that their projects had not been selected; not that they had lost in the lottery. (If they were told they had lost the lottery, the double-blind character of the experiment would be compromised. This would, of course, cause major complications since ATP routinely briefs losing applicants on the reasons they were not selected.) Analysts would then compare the subsequent performance of the winning firms that were successful in the lottery with those that were not and would use this information to ascertain whether receiving ATP awards led to greater success than not.

For several reasons, however, this evaluation strategy cannot be satisfactorily analogized to drug testing. In clinical trials of drugs, neither the patient, the physician, nor the "public" knows who received the drug under test and who received an alternative or a placebo, so that no one can bias the outcome consciously or unwittingly. In the hypothetical ATP clinical trial, however, the identity of the winners would be known to ATP staff, winners, losers, competitors, and customers; and the identity of the losers would be known to almost as many groups, all of whom could influence the outcomes of both the winning and losing projects. Thus, this method offers no easy answer to the evaluation problem.

24. For an incisive description and comparison of such programs in several nations and the European Community, see George R. Heaton, Jr., "Advanced Technology Programs: Current Practices in the U.S., Japan and Europe," Report to the Division of Science, Technology and Industry of the Organization for Economic Cooperation and Development (November 1996).

25. By comparison, the National Aeronautics and Space Administration's budget is on the order of $860 million annually for research and technology development for the aeronautics industries alone; the National Institutes of Health (NIH) spends more than $11 billion on biomedical research, much of which directly aids the pharmaceutical and medical devices industries; the Department of Agriculture spends about $1.8 billion on research that supports agricultural industries; the Defense Advanced Research Projects Agency's budget is about $2.1 billion; and NSF spends more than $2.4 billion on research, largely at universities.

26. European Commission, "Community Research and Technological Development Policy," Report EWR 15637 EN (Luxembourg: European Commission DG XIII, 1994).

7

Dual-Use and the Technology Reinvestment Project

Linda R. Cohen

Between 1993 and 1996, the Technology Reinvestment Project (TRP) provided direct support for the development of dual-use technology. Like the other technology policy programs discussed in this volume, TRP was a cooperative industry-government program that emphasized industry management and project definition, cost sharing, consortia or team projects, and competitive solicitations. The program was administered by the Defense Advanced Research Projects Agency (DARPA) in the Department of Defense (DoD). To a substantially greater extent than the other new technology policy programs, TRP had a government mission orientation; it was intended to contribute to the defense mission of DoD as well as to strengthen commercial technology. At the start of the Clinton presidency, the program was the linchpin of Clinton's technology investment strategy. The program ended in 1996, although some related projects are underway at the new DoD Joint Dual Use Program Office.

The initial TRP program, which had a very broad scope, incorporated a coalition of interests bound together by budgetary politics. Once the budget situation shifted, however, the coalition unwound. The program subsequently focused on a narrower conception of dual-use technology, which led to two problems. First, the efficiency arguments in favor of using an industry-driven, cost-shared program became less compelling under the revised orientation. Second, the revised program aimed to integrate the defense and commercial technology bases so as to restructure the defense industry from a semi-oligopolistic to a competitive structure; this program orientation essentially required that project team members engage in activities that affected the core competition between them, rather than in precompetitive technology, and that they contribute to the costs of projects with dubious potential returns. Not surprisingly, in its final years the program was not strongly supported by the defense industry.

This chapter assesses whether it is useful to attempt to recreate the technology development component of the Technology Reinvestment Project at DARPA. I conclude that, independent of the technical merit of the TRP projects, not evaluated here, the TRP strategy has a number of serious difficulties. Specifically, institutional features of government and the defense industry suggest that the cooperative, cost-shared, competitive solicitation framework may not be the appropriate mechanism for promoting the development of a dual-use technology base.

The next section provides a brief history of TRP.[1] The subsequent section considers further the problems of using the technology policy strategy of TRP to promote a dual-use technology base. The final section provides recommendations for crafting policies that are better able to carry out the goals of TRP.

The Genesis of TRP

At the end of the 1980s, a series of influential reports focused attention on changes needed to maintain a technologically superior military force in the post–Cold War era.[2] These reports argued that changes in technology, economics, and domestic and foreign politics made it imperative to pursue and to broaden the scope of dual-use strategies in the defense sector. The reasoning started with the observation that the nation's technology base had become increasingly segregated into separate defense and civilian components. This divergence created problems for both sectors. On the civilian side, the substantial federal investment in defense R&D meant a neglect of potential economic benefits because application of defense R&D benefited only defense technology, rather than both defense and civilian. Spinoff technology from defense investments could improve the position of American industry. The spinoff argument was familiar; however, its importance was enhanced by the perceived problems with productivity and competitiveness for American industry during the 1980s.

On the military side, the argument for dual-use (civilian as well as military) technology rested on three legs. First, for some industries, the rate of technological advance had become so rapid in commercial applications that defense components lagged behind their commercial counterparts by a generation or more. Moreover, the reduction in defense procurement expenditures implied that defense applications would play an increasingly smaller role as the technology driver with the result that a segregated defense technology base was likely to fall even further behind commercial technology. Second, the commercial counterparts were not only in some cases better, but were in nearly all cases cheaper. Making greater use of commercial technology was a key factor in reducing the cost of defense procurement. Third, reduced procurement by the Department of Defense meant that existing firms would be unable to maintain operations based only on defense contracts, even if such a strategy were otherwise desirable. Maintaining a domestic supplier for critical defense technologies—or, preferably, multiple suppliers—would in many cases require that suppliers have commercial as well as military customers.

The dual-use umbrella includes policies ranging from changes in the way weapons systems are designed and how specifications of components are set, to reform of procurement and acquisition rules. All of these policies can affect the nature of the industrial technology base through the incentives given to firms to participate in defense procurement. The Technology Reinvestment Project was one component of the strategy, and aimed to provide direct support for technology development that would contribute to an integrated technology base.

Legislative authorization and appropriation for TRP came in the final year of the Bush administration. DARPA was a logical choice for housing a dual-use technology base effort, given the prior experience of DARPA (particularly prior to the 1970 Mansfield amendment, which effectively limited dual-use activities in the Department of Defense) and its technical reputation. During the 1980s, programs supporting the technology base—and in some

cases, the commercial competitiveness—of critical industries had
crept back into the DARPA budget. By 1992, DARPA was supporting several dual-use technology initiatives within its Advanced
Technology Development budget, including SEMATECH, and
other smaller "precompetitive technology" consortia. However,
these programs were modest compared to the 1992 Defense Appropriations Act, which appropriated to DARPA a billion dollars more
than the request for fiscal year 1993 submitted by President Bush.
The Act provided support for eight programs authorized by the
Defense Conversion, Reinvestment, and Transition Assistance Act
of 1992 that went well beyond DARPA's traditional activities.[3]
Indeed, of the eight TRP program areas, two were originally
intended for the National Science Foundation (they dealt with
manufacturing engineering education) and two for the National
Institutes of Standards and Technology (they dealt with regional
technology alliances and manufacturing extension).

The decision to authorize TRP entirely within DARPA, instead of
putting the logical components in NIST and NSF, has been blamed
on the Budget Enforcement Act of 1990, the successor to the
Gramm-Rudman Act. The Budget Enforcement Act established
spending caps for the five years subsequent to its passage. These
caps presumed higher levels of defense spending than were subsequently appropriated, so that in fiscal 1993 there was "slack" in the
defense budget not present on the civilian discretionary side.[4]
Whereas this asymmetry perhaps made it easier to justify a major
new program in the Defense Department than in the Department
of Commerce,[5] it masks a more critical feature of the budget
process: the relative bargaining positions of Congress and the
president over specific appropriation bills.

A key to ascertaining the relative power of the president and
Congress in budget negotiations is whether the president has a
credible veto threat.[6] The basic rule is that whichever arm of
government wants a smaller overall budget for a department is in
a stronger bargaining position over the budgetary details. Throughout the 1980s, Presidents Reagan and Bush could not credibly
threaten to veto the defense budget over relatively small increases
in the DARPA budget, since both wanted, in any event, higher
overall defense budgets than did Congress. A veto would have left

them without budgetary authority for other new or growing programs. Thus, Congress was able to sustain an appropriation for the program that it wanted and the president did not within the DARPA budget, whereas such a maneuver would have been more difficult in the Commerce Department budget.

This assignment of multiple responsibilities to DARPA, including some not within its traditional scope, was greeted with some concern by the policy community, especially by proponents of an active federal role in support of the technology base of commercial industries. These analysts worried that the Department of Defense would do a poor job at the education and technology deployment components of TRP. An additional concern was that DARPA was not a good technology agency in which to center technology activities (compared to the Commerce Department) because it might focus policies too narrowly and provide only case-by-case subsidies related to the defense base.[7] The Clinton administration, which came into office with a program to invest in both civilian and military technology, had plans for a much larger eventual role for the Commerce Department in these policies.[8] However, since a TRP appropriation already existed in DoD, it made sense for the president to go along with what was apparently the intent of Congress and attempt to shift DARPA's priorities and mission rather than the appropriation.[9] The program thus got underway with the joint, if somewhat worried, support of the proponents of its various components.

TRP: 1993–95

In 1993, DARPA—by then known as ARPA—organized the eight programs that initially comprised TRP into three broad areas: technology deployment, manufacturing education and training, and technology development. Of these, the last category is of interest here, as it was the part of the program that incorporated the "new" technology development strategy.[10] The program had similar requirements to most of the other technology policy programs discussed in this volume: awards were based on competitions, were open to teams of domestic companies, required at least fifty percent cost-sharing by participants, and encouraged the inclusion of small businesses, universities, and government laboratories. TRP required that projects be dual-use, but initially this requirement was broadly construed.

TRP initially appeared to industry to be a more attractive alternative than the Advanced Technology Program (ATP). TRP did not require the elaborate commercial development plans and review that the ATP program conducted. In addition, the private cost share was somewhat more loosely construed than for ATP, in that (after the first competition) small businesses could use awards that they received from the Small Business Innovation Research (SBIR) program as the private cost share. Any firm (with defense business) could use Independent Research and Development (IR&D) accounts toward its share.[11] In contrast, ATP is quite strict that the private share must come from private sources. In addition, a TRP award, together with the 50 percent private match required for the TRP award, could constitute part of the private share of a Cooperative Research and Development Agreement (CRADA) with a national laboratory. Thus, for a given project, the private share could in theory be quite small. A hypothetical project might include $50,000 from SBIR, $50,000 from private sources, a $100,000 TRP grant (matching the SBIR and industry funds), and a $200,000 match from a national lab under a CRADA (matching the SBIR, industry, and TRP money). Of the $400,000, the actual industry share is only 12 percent. This example is not, as far as I know, actually reflected in any TRP project, but the total public share of the activities conducted under TRP may have been rather larger than the official estimates.

The first competition was heavily oversubscribed. The value of proposed projects in all three categories amounted to $8.5 billion. Nearly 3,000 proposals were submitted, of which 212 were selected for support. The low rate of acceptance was perceived to be a problem in that firms were devoting considerable resources to preparing proposals, and the unsuccessful bidders were, of course, unhappy. For the fiscal 1994 competitions, ARPA instituted several changes designed to improve the success of applicants. ARPA defined certain technology areas that would be supported in the development category, encouraged potential proposers to submit pre-proposals, and held workshops explaining the nature of the programs and competition areas. Thus, the program focused more on certain technologies, and gave DoD a somewhat stronger hand in defining the relevant technologies. The importance of the shift is debatable; given the large number of proposals in the initial competition, ARPA could have restricted technical choices just as much there as it could by defining technology areas ex ante.

Tables 1, 2, and 3 contain summary data about the projects chosen during the three years of TRP competitions. Compared to the Advanced Technology Program, TRP supported larger projects: 15 percent of the TRP projects were valued at $20 million or more; 10 percent of the projects involved at least ten team members; and a substantial share included a university or government laboratory partner. Most of the projects included a "major defense contractor," i.e., one of the top sixty-five firms engaged in defense procurement contracting in the early 1990s.[12] Focus areas included information infrastructure, electronics design, shipbuilding, industrial infrastructure, materials/structures manufacturing; these are all areas where DARPA had long-standing interest as well as areas that contributed to some of the president's initiatives (e.g., advanced battery technology and vehicle technology).

1994–95: An Evolving Rationale for TRP

TRP became a target for criticism almost as soon as it began. Some of the dissatisfaction can be traced to confusion about the nature of the dual-use philosophy. ARPA's "conversion" goal did not aim to convert defense firms to civilian firms; rather, the idea was to convert the defense technology base (and some defense firms) to dual-use, as part of a much broader DoD strategy.[13] The confusion, however, is understandable. First, Pentagon officials characterized the initial competition as supporting civilian spinoffs, saying, for example, that: "The majority of funds will go to advanced development projects, most of them applying military technology to civilian applications."[14] Furthermore the manufacturing extension and education pieces of TRP did include programs that directly addressed the problems of displaced defense workers.

Nevertheless, the scope of TRP, whether derived from confusion or intent, was criticized both by those who expected ARPA to do

Table 7-1 Cost of TRP Development Projects

Range	Frequency	Cumulative %
$0–5M	48	36%
$5–10M	35	63%
$10–20M	31	86%
$20–30M	9	93%
$30–40M	3	95%
$40–50M	4	98%
$50–60M	0	98%
$60–71M	2	100%

Table 7-2 Number of Team Members in TRP Projects

Members	Frequency	Cumulative %
2	18	14%
3	25	33%
4	25	52%
6	24	70%
10	27	90%
More	13	100%

Table 7-3 TRP Development Project Characteristics: Annual Competitions

	1993	1994	1995	All Years
University member	46%	47%	38%	44%
Government lab. member	37%	37%	26%	34%
Major defense contractor	66%	67%	76%	69%
Average project cost ($1000s)*	$11,463	$13,387	$8,507	$11,139
Total cost per year ($1000s)*	$779,460	$401,620	$289,240	$1,470,320
Number of projects	68	30	34	132

* Private and federal contribution.

more for displaced workers and businesses, and by those who thought ARPA had no business outside traditionally defined military-preparedness goals.[15] Initially, however, the supporting coalition prevailed. ARPA's technology development plans, under TRP, addressed both military and commercial concerns. Some of the projects were genuine spinoff: military technology applied to civilian uses. The military rationale of such a project would center on its contribution to a stronger defense industry, rather than to any specific military project; its commercial, civilian benefits contributed to its attractiveness to ARPA under the original TRP program.

In 1994, the deployment and education components of the program were transferred to the Commerce Department, and the character of the TRP development program changed. Most visibly, the question of the military value of the program dominated the TRP debate. Underlying the shift in the debate was a change in the supporting coalition. No longer as concerned with TRP, some sponsors more concerned with subsidizing the civilian sector (the proponents of the deployment and education components) stopped defending the dual-use technology program. A reversion of ARPA to its pre-TRP role commenced.

The Clinton administration undertook a defense of TRP that culminated in the February 1995 publication of a document from the National Economic Council (NEC) that attempted to clarify the role of TRP in defense policy and provide an integrated justification of the dual-use strategy.[16] The strategy discussed in this report is consistent with the rationale developed three years before for TRP: it starts with the problems of segregated defense and commercial technology bases, and characterizes the dual-use strategy as composed of three major elements: supporting leading edge dual-use R&D, integrating commercial and military production, and developing policies to promote the use of commercial off-the-shelf products in defense systems. In cases where commercial uses drive technology, the report asserts, maintaining or establishing U.S. expertise at the leading edge "may require DoD to support leading-edge R&D that accelerates the development of emerging commercial technologies that are not currently in the repertory of U.S. firms."[17]

Important differences existed, however, between NEC's description of TRP and DARPA's program description two years earlier. The NEC report emphasizes the military benefits of the program rather than its role as part of a general technology and competitiveness strategy: "The mission of the TRP *is to give the Department of Defense greater access to affordable, leading-edge technology by leveraging commercial know-how, investments and markets for military benefit*" (emphasis in original). This theme became increasingly pronounced as the administration sought to save the program from being cut by the Republican Congress. Specifically, "spin-on" (the adaptation and use of civilian technology in military applications) and the cost-saving advantages of dealing with competitive commercial industry, rather than high-priced, concentrated defense firms, were emphasized in discussions.[18]

The 104th Congress threatened to rescind funds appropriated for TRP for fiscal 1995; ultimately enough were released for a competition to be held. These projects were jointly chosen by ARPA and the military services. Indeed, the press release announcing the results of the final competition does not refer to the other agencies that had previously joined DoD in running the program (Commerce, Transportation, Energy), and characterizes TRP as developing "militarily useful, commercially viable technology in order to improve the DOD's access to affordable advanced technology"; it emphasized that the supported technologies "can be kept affordable, accessible, and advanced through the dynamics of the commercial marketplace."[19]

Table 3 shows some differences between the fiscal 1995 awards and previous years' awards that appear to reflect the changing sentiments. Later awards are more likely to involve a major defense contractor, and are less likely to include government lab or university members. On average, financial awards and team sizes are smaller.

The fiscal 1995 competition was the final competition for TRP. The president initially requested an appropriation for further competitions in fiscal 1996, but Congress approved only sufficient funds to continue support for previously approved projects. In fiscal 1997 an appropriation was granted for the Dual-use Applications Program (DUAP), which is described as a successor to TRP. The program succeeds TRP in the sense that it attempts to accommodate some of the demonstrated institutional successes of the program (most importantly, not using the FARs, or federal acquisition regulations, in contracting; the involvement of civilian companies; and cost-sharing) in some components of defense acquisitions outside research and development. Of its $185 million budget for fiscal 1997, $100 million is appropriated to support demonstrations of the insertion of "commercial products and processes into fielded systems to reduce [operations and support] costs."[20] The remaining $85 million is for a dual-use "Science and Technology Initiative," intended to support a share of R&D projects of the three services that have dual-use characteristics. These projects are not subject to any special competitions or announcements, but rather are part of the routine R&D portfolio of the services.[21] Thus, DUAP departs in important ways from TRP. DARPA has far less control over coordination of technology choices; the perspective for the defense agencies has become paramount; and the budget for dual-use technology development has been reduced. As of spring 1997, information about competitions and awards under the DUAP Science and Technology program was not available. (The competitions were in progress, or had yet to be held.) However, it appears that the program will have only limited relevance to the goal emphasized in this chapter, which is to consider the possibility of the "new technology" strategy for dual-use technology development. Consequently, for the purpose of this chapter, the program effectively ended in 1996.

Evaluating TRP

The cancellation of TRP was not unexpected, given the criticism it had generated and the stated preferences of the 104th Congress. However, even leaving aside bipartisan politics, the program suffered from a separate problem serious enough that the program could not be renewed in its 1995 form. TRP violated what might be called the "precompetitive condition" of this sort of technology policy program. As a result, industrial participation in it is problematic.

In this section, I first discuss why the "politics" arguments are perhaps weaker than some observers have claimed, although they are not insignificant. I then review the precompetitive condition, which is discussed at length in Chapter 1 of this volume, and consider why TRP violates the condition. Briefly, the precompetitive condition can be characterized as follows. These technology programs depend on both competition and cooperation between firms. They require companies to cooperate at the development stage—to work in teams and, up to a point, to share results—and to compete in production. The final price of any product developed under the programs is not supposed to be monopolistic, and the firms are not supposed to leverage the development team into a production cartel. Rather, the initial development stage is intended to focus on activities that are, in some manner, "precompetitive."

"Precompetition" is not an entirely straightforward concept. In some cases, it applies to generic technology, such as the content of many of the cooperative activities undertaken by industry and the NIST laboratories under CRADAs. Sometimes, the activities might be more commercial, but upstream, as with the projects undertaken by SEMATECH to sponsor development of semiconductor manufacturing equipment. In this volume, the notion of "generic technology" is developed, which is potentially precompetitive. For purposes of this chapter, the concept I am interested in is simple: cooperative projects cannot include technological or other components that directly affect the competitive advantage of members of the consortium. Specific examples in the TRP context are provided below. I also suggest modifications that would be necessary to make a program like TRP consistent with the requirements of cooperative, cost-shared technology policy programs.

Politics and TRP

By the fiscal 1996 budgeting cycle in 1995, Republicans were in the majority in Congress, and made no secret of their opposition to TRP. First, they claimed the program was a "pork barrel" program, and that awards were made on the basis of political rather than technical considerations. Second, they argued that the program detracted from military needs, and was too involved with development of commercial technology.

The technical merit of new technology policy programs like TRP is very difficult to evaluate, for the projects are intended to be long-term. Indeed, the existence of many technical "success stories" (TRP has some) would raise the suspicion that, rather than supporting the sort of technology base activities that are the aim of these programs, they have instead targeted short-term investments that merely crowd out private sector support.

One measurable set of flaws would be the presence of politically motivated investments. The most obvious manifestation would be awards to undeserving projects in politically sensitive districts. However, it is particularly difficult to funnel TRP awards in this way. Indeed, because of the teaming characteristic of the projects, it is very difficult to characterize the geographic distribution of TRP awards. Consistent with the dual-use nature of the program, it is true that many of the lead firms are concentrated in states that otherwise have disproportionately large defense expenditures (e.g., Massachusetts, New Mexico, California); however, the awards in which major defense contractors participated were even more likely to have a large and geographically dispersed team than the those without large defense firms. Thus simple summations of awards to lead states substantially overstates the extent to which awards are concentrated, particularly in California.

As for whether TRP met military needs, the initial response of DARPA was to emphasize narrowly defined military benefits of the program. Obviously, any dual-use program must by definition have something to do with civilian industry, but an effort was made to show that awards could be entirely justified on the basis of cost savings or technological development of interest to the military. One could argue that the administration's claims about military value were inadequate, or that the commercial industrial policy component of the program was too unpopular to support it even if it had a military justification.

However, these are not sufficient to explain the fate of TRP, since the Advanced Technology Program, at the National Institutes of Standards and Technology, has continued to receive sufficient appropriations to maintain its program, albeit in smaller form than was planned a few years ago. TRP is substantially more mission-oriented than the Advanced Technology Program— so, on "unpopular commercial focus" grounds, ATP should have been canceled first. Furthermore, one might expect that President Clinton had relatively more control over aspects of the defense budget than the commerce budget, since the positions of the president and Congress had switched; since fiscal 1995, Congress has appropriated more money for the Department of Defense, and less for the Department of Commerce, than the president has requested.

In fact, the accounts of the final appropriation cycle for TRP suggest that the program was no longer a priority item for anyone.[22] This is not to say that dual use is no longer a priority; indeed, dual-use policy has many components in DoD, and is a key feature of defense policy. However, the problem with TRP is not merely budget politics or the unpopularity of commercial technology ventures. Instead, the program's requirements and industry's incentive to participate in it became incompatible.

Industrial Support for TRP

The coup de grace for TRP was the lack of support from the defense industry. Perhaps the most notable characteristic of the fiscal 1996 appropriation cycle was the absence of lobbying by the major defense contractors.[23] Their lack of enthusiasm reflects the industrial restructuring that TRP attempted to induce. The goals of TRP implied a revision of the structure of the defense contracting industry from one in which contractors had few competitors and could charge high prices to one with competitive pressures and rock-bottom, no-profit prices. This vision of the defense procurement industry was more clearly apparent in the later years of TRP, as it became (at least in the official descriptions) a program oriented towards "spin-on" rather than "spinoff" technology. As an industry restructuring program, it was, of course, in direct conflict with the profit incentives of military contractors.

This issue goes beyond whether the firms lobby for a program during the budgetary hearings—presumably their support for other DoD efforts to lower procurement costs and increase competition is similarly restrained. It would be surprising to see any cooperative industry effort (like lobbying) in support of a policy clearly to the aggregate disadvantage of the firms. But this is not to say that other DoD efforts to introduce more competition into procurement are doomed. A fundamental principle in economics is that often firms will individually pursue opportunities that undermine an oligopolistic industry structure, because doing so is in their short-term self-interest: they can make a bigger profit by undercutting monopolistic prices and expanding production than by abiding with a share of a cartelized market. Even if firms do not lobby for a procompetitive policy, they might choose to compete for it.

The critical problem with TRP was that, for some critical participants, the individual projects were also unattractive. By 1995, in its spin-on incarnation, TRP required defense contractors to team with "non-traditional firms" (i.e., civilian firms) in developing the wherewithal for civilian technology to be applied to defense purposes. If successful, DoD would then purchase the technology from a competitive industry, or, at least, from more firms than simply the defense contractor. The defense contractor, through its participation in the project, is enabling other firms to contract with, or sell to, the Department of Defense. This activity is not precompetitive; on the contrary, it presumes that the defense contractors give up a primary competitive advantage over the team participants: their expertise in dealing with DoD.

Among the other dual-use initiatives at DoD, and the more successful new technology programs, TRP is the only program that essentially targeted competitive parts of the team members' business. It is both undesirable and unfeasible for these collaborations to address competitive, as opposed to precompetitive technology. The undesirability ensues from potential antitrust problems. The unfeasibility comes from incentives of firms. Substantial evidence exists that firms are unlikely to participate in public-private consortia that address technology which forms a basis for the competition among the firms.[24]

Finally, TRP, in its spin-on form, not only asked firms to participate in consortia that would undermine the competitive advantage of some members, but also to pay half the cost of the project.

The logic of cost sharing is strained by the spin-on version of dual-use. Cost sharing in these programs is supposed to serve several purposes: it saves money for the government, and it gives some assurance that the private participants believe the project to be a worthwhile investment. The chief reason the beliefs of the private participants are relevant is that they have some particular expertise; usually, the reason given is that the technology is supposed to have commercial applications, and the commercial firms are more savvy about the private market than is the government.

If the project is mission-oriented to the extent of pure spin-on, only the first reason—saving public money—holds.[25] Furthermore, if DoD will be the only purchaser of the new technology, and if DoD plans to purchase it via a procurement competition (recall that the point of spin-on was procurement from a competitive industry), the private firms might decline the opportunity to contribute a significant share of the cost of the technology development project. Some return must accrue to a private investment, but if there is to be no civilian commercial product, and if DoD is to be a monopsonist purchaser of the new technology, the firms lack assurance of receiving an adequate return on their investment.[26]

Thus, politics aside, the version of TRP promoted during its final year is problematic as a matter of logic. These programs rely on the cooperation of private firms. TRP proposed that firms participate in placing themselves in a weak competitive position, and invest their own money in a project with poor prospects for subsequent profits. In sum, the goal of developing spin-on technology to further a dual-use technology base meshes poorly with the rationale and requirements of the technology policy strategy of TRP.

Recommendations

Assuming that further efforts to integrate the defense and commercial technology bases are desirable, the analysis of this chapter suggests several possible strategies. One is to restore TRP to the broader dual-use conception: spinoff as well as spin-on. The former should be a sufficiently large component that defense contractors have an incentive to participate. The carrot of civilian opportunities and potential commercial profits from spinoff technologies must compensate for the demand that they would give up their favored status as defense contractors. In fact, all that is needed is for some of the defense contractors to cooperate. If so, then the remainder are threatened by a competitive defense sector whether or not they participate in TRP. Participation, at a minimum, gives them a shot at the spinoffs.

The history presented above suggests that the original TRP program was, in fact, something of an anomaly. Specifically, the reason ARPA had so much flexibility in its technology development program in TRP was because of the bundling with the non-ARPA TRP components that were later switched to NIST and NSF. While this observation suggests that the politics of establishing a broader dual-use program are difficult, that does not detract from its potential efficiency.

A second possibility is to retain the current focus, but abandon significant cost-sharing or teaming requirements.[27] Such a program would be relatively expensive per project. DoD would need to pay the full R&D cost, and also the cost of familiarizing the civilian firms with DoD contracting practices. Procurement reforms would be a critical component of the strategy. This recommendation would merge TRP goals into traditional defense R&D activities; it essentially amounts to a recommendation that DARPA maintain or reestablish a dual-use focus.

A third strategy is to extend the science and technology (S&T) component of the Dual-use Applications Program to allow DARPA subsidies of dual-use ATP projects. The current S&T program allows DARPA to subsidize defense services projects that have dual-use components. Thus, it rewards projects that are defense-motivated and have a possible commercial application. Presumably, the logic of the strategy is to promote projects that might be marginal defense projects, but whose commercial prospects are sufficient to make the overall project desirable on efficiency grounds. (If the project is not marginal to begin with, no DARPA subsidy is necessary.) If DARPA could also participate in ATP awards, the reverse would hold: it could encourage support for projects that are marginal on commercial grounds but that have a defense component. Ideally, the projects would be those not sufficiently important to warrant a contract from one of the defense services, but which, combined with the commercial applications, would be in the interest of the country overall. A nice feature of this proposal is that in theory it builds on the relative strengths of DARPA. The additional expertise DARPA brings to ATP concerns potential defense applications. The current S&T program, alternatively, assumes DARPA contributes knowledge about civilian applications to the defense agency choices. It is not obvious why DARPA has an advantage in this respect as compared to alternative private venture capital sources.

To conclude: the new types of technology policy programs, with their emphasis on teaming, cost-sharing, and competitive solicitations, avoid some of the problems in previous government technology programs. They attempt to use the incentives of private firms to keep costs under control, investigate appropriate techniques, and avoid inappropriate, politically-motivated investments. But in order to work, the goals of the program must be aligned with the incentives of the target firms. Future dual-use technology programs should tailor program requirements to align with industry incentives.

Notes

1. This review is not comprehensive, and readers are urged to consult Jay Stowsky, *America's Technical Fix: The Pentagon's Dual Use Strategy, TRP, and the Political Economy of U.S. Technology Policy in the Clinton Era* (Berkeley, University of California: Berkeley Roundtable on the International Economy, 1996); and Richard H. White, et al., *A Survey of Dual-Use Issues*, IDA Paper P-3176 (Alexandria, Va.: Institute for Defense Analysis, 1996).

2. Influential reports include U. S. Department of Defense, *Final Report of the Defense Science Board 1988 Summer Study on the Defense Industrial and Technology Base* (Defense Science Board, October 1988); U. S. Department of Defense, *Report of the Defense Science Board Task Force on Use of Commercial Components in Military Equipment* (Defense Science Board, June 1989); U.S. Congress, Office of Technology Assessment (OTA), *After the Cold War: Living With Lower Defense Spending*, OTA-ITE-524 (Washington, D.C.: U.S. Government Printing Office [U.S. GPO], February, 1992); U.S. Congress, OTA, *Defense Conversion: Redirecting R&D*, OTA-ITE-552 (Washington, D.C.: U.S. GPO, May 1993); Carnegie Commission on Science, Technology and Government, *New Thinking and American Defense Technology* (New York: Carnegie Commission, August 1990); Carnegie Commission on Science, Technology and Government, *Technology and Economic Performance: Organizing the Executive Branch for a Stronger National Technology Base* (New York: Carnegie Commission, September 1991).

3. See ARPA, *Program Information Package for Defense Technology Conversion, Reinvestment, and Transition Assistance* (Washington, D.C.: ARPA, March 10, 1993), Appendix B; and White, et al., *A Survey of Dual-Use Issues*, p. III-3.

4. See, e.g., White et al., *A Survey of Dual-Use Issues*, p. III-11, fn. 24.

5. It is easier to blame Gramm Rudman et al. than to establish their direct influence on any program's budget or the deficit overall. See Marvin H. Kosters, editor, *Fiscal Politics and the Budget Enforcement Act* (Washington, D.C., AEI Press: 1992) for an enlightening discussion of the Budget Enforcement Act.

6. See D. Roderick Kiewiet and Mathew D. McCubbins, "Presidential Influence on Congressional Appropriations Decisions," *American Journal of Political Science*, Vol. 32, No. 3 (August, 1988) pp. 713–736.

7. John A. Alic, "The Dual Use of Technology: Concepts and Policies," *Technology in Society*, Vol. 16, No. 2 (1994), pp. 155–172.

8. See William J. Clinton and Albert Gore Jr., "Technology for American's Economic Growth: A New Direction to Build Economic Strength" (Washington, D.C.: White House, February 22, 1993).

9. This interpretation is discussed in Jay Stowsky, *America's Technical Fix*, p. 24. See also Lewis M. Branscomb and George Parker, "Funding Civilian and Dual-Use Industrial Technology," chapter 3 in Lewis M. Branscomb, ed., *Empowering Technology: Implementing A U.S. Strategy* (Cambridge, Mass.: MIT Press, 1993).

10. The deployment programs support Manufacturing Extension Centers, and were transferred to NIST in 1994. The education programs disappeared, although occasionally programs of a similar nature, not as generously supported, are authorized in other civilian agencies.

11. From the viewpoint of the firms, IR&D funds are real money, so that using them for TRP projects does not detract from the cost-sharing goal of proper industrial incentives. This was especially true in the final year of TRP, as firms were allowed to use IR&D for bid and proposal accounts as well as R&D.

12. See John A. Alic, Lewis M. Branscomb, Harvey Brooks, Ashton B. Carter, and Gerald L. Epstein, *Beyond Spinoff: Military and Commercial Technologies in a Changing World* (Boston: Harvard Business School Press, 1992), pp. 192–196.

13. See James Kitfield, "A New Partnership," in *National Journal*, Vol. 26, No. 32 (August 6, 1994), pp. 1840–1846.

14. Director of Defense Research and Engineering, quoted in *National Journal*, August 6, 1994, p. 1843.

15. Stowsky, *America's Technical Fix*, discusses these developments in detail.

16. National Economic Council (NEC), *Second to None: Preserving American's Military Advantage Through Dual-Use Technology* (Washington, D.C.: NEC, February 1995).

17. Ibid., p. 15.

18. See, e.g., David C. Morrison, "Technology Tussle," in *National Journal*, April 1, 1995, pp. 799–803.

19. Ken Jacobson, "Final TRP Competition," *New Technology Week*, January 8, 1996, p. 3.

20. *Fact Sheet: Dual-Use Applications Program*, February 5, 1997. Available on the joint Dual-Use Program Office web site, <www.jdupo.darpa.mil/jdupo/info/duap_fact.html>.

21. Paul Kaminski, *DOD News Briefing* (Washington, D.C.: Office of the Assistant Secretary of Defense, Public Affairs, January 14, 1997). See also the discussion in Ken Jacobson, "DOD Loyal To Dual Use, But Support Profile Falls," *New Technology Week*, January 21, 1997, p. 1.

22. See Jacobson, "DOD Loyal To Dual Use," p. 1; Jacobson, "Final TRP

Competition," p. 3; Morrison, "Technology Tussle," pp. 799–803.

23. Morrison, "Technology Tussle."

24. In addition to the discussion in Chapter 1, see E. Raymond Corey, *Technology Fountainheads: The Management Challenge of R&D Consortia* (Cambridge, Mass.: Harvard Business School Press, 1997).

25. If the firms conducting the project have technical expertise, or their effort can be monitored only with some cost to the government, a second reason for cost-sharing exists. Here, the sharing arrangement plays the role of an incentive contract for a principal-agent relationship.

26. For further development of the problems with private provision of mission research, see Linda R. Cohen and Roger G. Noll, "The Future of the National Labs," *Proceedings of the National Academy of Sciences,* Vol. 93 No. 23 (November 12, 1996), pp. 12678–12685.

27. The logic of the preceding section applies to acquisition programs at least as much as to technology development, so this recommendation also is relevant to the Operations and Support (O&S) component of the current Dual Use Applications Program.

8

Rethinking the Small Business Innovation Research Program

Scott J. Wallsten

While most federal science and technology programs attempt to advance specific types of research or to increase the overall amount of research conducted in the economy, the Small Business Innovation Research (SBIR) program changes the composition of who receives federal R&D support by mandating that small business receive a minimum share of federal R&D dollars. SBIR was created under the Small Business Innovation Development Act of 1982, and renewed most recently under the Small Business Innovation Research Program Reauthorization Act of 1992. The program is currently scheduled to end in October 2000.[1] Congress intended SBIR to stimulate technological innovation; use small business to meet federal research and development needs; foster and encourage participation by minority and disadvantaged persons in technological innovation; and increase private sector commercialization of innovations derived from federal research.

SBIR has no budget, per se. Instead, certain federal agencies are required to set aside a percentage of their extramural (contract and grants) R&D budgets for the program. This set-aside percentage increased in FY1997 by 25 percent to 2.5 percent of an agency's extramural budget, meaning that SBIR funding will exceed $1 billion per year, making it the largest federal technology program aimed at product commercialization. By comparison, the Advanced Technology Program (ATP)—the focus of intense debates in recent budget battles and often viewed as the Clinton administration's model technology program—has a budget less than one-fourth the size. Since its inception in 1983, SBIR has awarded nearly $6 billion to small business.

SBIR was controversial when first proposed. The federal agencies objected to losing control over a portion of their R&D budgets, and each congressional committee endorsed the idea of SBIR but wanted to exclude any agency over which it had jurisdiction.[2] The established research community—primarily academic groups and professional societies—also opposed the legislation. SBIR proponents, meanwhile, believed that small firms would never be included in federal R&D efforts without the set-aside.[3] Once the legislation became law, the controversy died down for more than a decade, largely because the program initially was fairly small. SBIR is again coming under scrutiny, however, as it passes the $1 billion mark while overall federal R&D support faces potential cuts in the name of balancing the federal budget.[4]

The first two sections of this chapter consider the R&D challenges and opportunities facing small firms, and describe SBIR. SBIR's official objectives seek to advance two broader goals; the third section evaluates both the justification for striving to achieve these goals and whether SBIR actually meets them. The first goal is redistribution: SBIR addresses a perceived *government failure* in federal R&D procurement policies (that small firms are unfairly excluded from the federal R&D procurement process) by transferring federal R&D funds to small firms. The second goal is innovation: SBIR addresses the *market failure* of R&D under-investment (discussed below) by providing funds to small firms.[5] I argue that it is not necessarily true that small firms are unfairly excluded from the federal R&D procurement process. And even if they are, a set-aside does not appropriately address that problem. Regarding innovation, it is difficult to say that SBIR stimulates research activity since its funding comes from existing R&D funds already allocated to federal agencies. In other words, the opportunity cost of R&D conducted under SBIR is R&D not conducted elsewhere.

The fourth section examines the incentives the program creates for firms and federal agencies, and concludes that SBIR probably crowds out industry R&D, and funds work that firms would undertake anyway. This section also reviews an empirical analysis that supports this conclusion. However, evaluating programs such as

SBIR is exceedingly difficult, in part because of a lack of data. To this end, I suggest using SBIR to implement the experiment Adam Jaffe proposes in Chapter 3, which would provide data necessary to conduct more thorough analyses.

Despite these criticisms of SBIR, it may still be true that small firms face specific problems in conducting R&D, and the federal government could play a useful role in mitigating these market failures. The conclusion presents two alternate policy proposals. The first proposal is intended to help SBIR promote research that would not be undertaken otherwise by requiring firms that apply for SBIR awards to provide more information about themselves to the awarding agencies than they currently do. Additional information would allow the agencies to determine more accurately if a project is likely to find non-SBIR funding. The second proposal is intended to promote small firm R&D more effectively by replacing SBIR with a partially refundable tax credit targeted at small firms.

Small Firms and R&D

Small firms play an important role in the U.S. economy, and particularly in technological innovation. This section briefly discusses the relative advantages in innovation enjoyed by small and large firms, and then notes potential obstacles small firms may face in conducting research.

Innovation in Small and Large Firms

According to some studies, small firms are responsible for a disproportionate share of innovations in terms of innovations per employee.[6] While small firms clearly are an important component of our R&D infrastructure, it is inaccurate to say that they are necessarily more "innovative" in general than are large firms. In some respects small firms enjoy advantages over large firms in innovation, while in other respects large firms have the advantage. The Small Business Administration (SBA) notes that for small firms "the incentives are greater: small firms may have the potential to create or capture an entire industry, while large firms are more often protecting a market position."[7] Small firms also can be more flexible than large firms, allowing them to change quickly the direction of their research when necessary. Large firms have other advantages in innovation: they can more easily overcome the fixed costs associated with conducting research; can more easily appropriate the returns to an innovation; and, in the case of a monopolist, may have an incentive to innovate to discourage new competitors.[8]

The relative advantages enjoyed by small and large firms suggest that small firms may be the more innovative group under some market structures, while large firms may be the more innovative group under other market structures. Indeed, empirical work confirms that in some industries small firms are responsible for a disproportionately large share of innovations, while in other industries they are responsible for almost none at all.[9]

Rationale for Government Support

Technological innovation is a key to economic growth, but economics suggests that firms of all sizes will invest less than the socially optimal amount in R&D. Two main factors are responsible for this under-investment. First, firms are unable to appropriate all of the returns to their investments as others use and extend research results. Second, firms may not have sufficient access to capital because they may be reluctant or unable to provide financiers with enough information to evaluate the potential success of a research project, and because R&D investments cannot be collateralized, unlike investments in machines or buildings. Many empirical studies have documented that these market failures are more than simply theoretical. Recent work confirms that cash flow is an important determinant of R&D investment, suggesting that capital markets are not perfect, while other studies commonly find that the social returns to innovations are far higher than their private returns, implying that market failures do lead to significant R&D under-investment.[10]

The market failures leading to R&D under-investment may be exacerbated for small firms. Small firms may have more trouble appropriating the returns to an innovation, and may have worse access to capital markets, in general, than do large firms. Since financiers have less information with which to evaluate the prospects of a small, new firm than they have about a large, established firm, they will demand a premium to provide capital to smaller firms. Capital market imperfections mean that the opportunity cost of internal funds may be lower than that of external funds, leading the firm to prefer cash flow for financing investment.[11]

While small firms can face difficulties obtaining funds, markets almost certainly do respond to investment opportunities afforded by small firms. In recent testimony to the House Committee on Small Business, Janet Yellen, then a member of the Federal Reserve Board of Governors, noted that small firms' access to credit markets has improved markedly in recent years, and that both large and small banks are increasingly willing to provide credit to small firms.[12] In addition, the venture capital market is an important source of finance for young firms, and its activity has increased dramatically since the early 1980s.[13]

Nonetheless, evidence of market failures specific to small firms suggests that government has a useful role to play with policies to help small firms perform a more socially optimal level of R&D.

SBIR Description and Institutional Details

SBIR's enabling legislation requires each of the eleven federal agencies with an extramural R&D budget of at least $100 million to set aside a specified percentage of that budget for SBIR grants. These agencies are the Departments of Defense (DoD); Health and Human Services (HHS); Energy (DOE); Agriculture (USDA); Commerce (DOC); Education (DOEd); Transportation (DOT); the National Aeronautics and Space Administration (NASA); National Science Foundation (NSF); Environmental Protection Agency (EPA); and the Nuclear Regulatory Commission (NRC).[14] DoD, NASA, HHS (particularly the National Institutes of Health (NIH) within HHS), DOE, and NSF together account for more than 90 percent of all SBIR awards, while DoD alone accounts for more than half of all awards.[15]

The set-aside was small at first, but has grown steadily over the years, leading to dramatic growth in the program's funding (see Figure 8-1). The 1982 enabling legislation phased in the set-aside, increasing it from 0.2 percent of the participating agency's extra-

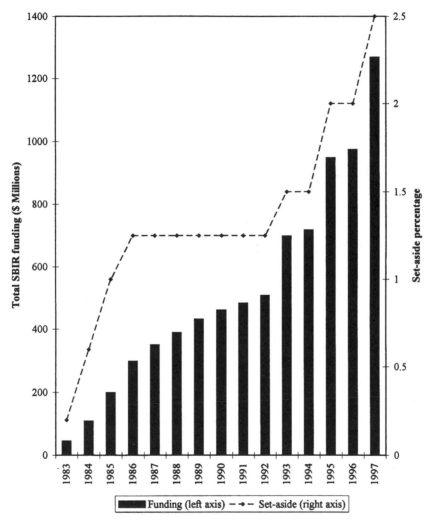

Figure 8-1 SBIR funding and set-aside level, 1983–97.

mural R&D budget in FY 1983 to 1.25 percent of that budget in FY 1986.[16] The 1992 Reauthorization Act increased the set-aside again to 1.5 percent in FY 1993 and 1994, 2.0 percent in FY 1995 and 1996, and finally to 2.5 percent in FY 1997 and each year thereafter. The most recent increase means that SBIR funding in FY 1997 will exceed $1 billion, making it one of the largest government-industry technology programs aimed at product commercialization.

A firm is eligible to apply for SBIR awards if it has no more than 500 employees, is for-profit, is American-owned and independently operated, and employs the principal researcher on the project.[17] SBIR is intended to move projects through three consecutive phases. Phase I determines "the scientific and technical merit and feasibility of ideas." Phase II is to "further develop the proposed ideas." Phase III is product commercialization. Firms apply first for Phase I and then for Phase II awards from the participating federal agencies, which use a competitive review process to make funding decisions. Each Phase I award can be as much as $100,000 and each Phase II award can be up to $750,000. SBIR funds are not to be used for Phase III.

Each participating agency runs its own SBIR program within broad guidelines established by the Act and further codified by regulatory directives.[18] Each agency independently determines the categories of projects it will fund; issues solicitations; evaluates proposals and selects awardees; and makes payments to the award recipients. The Small Business Administration (SBA) "directs the 11 agencies' implementation of SBIR, reviews their progress, and reports annually to Congress on its operation."[19]

Analyzing SBIR Objectives

SBIR has two basic goals: addressing a perceived government failure in federal R&D procurement by transferring funds to small firms, and addressing a market failure (stimulating innovation) by funding R&D in small firms. This section evaluates the rationale behind these goals, and whether SBIR is an effective way to meet them.

Government Failure?

One of SBIR's goals is to redress perceived government discrimination against small firms in federal R&D procurement. When SBIR was first proposed, the House Committee on Small Business stated that:

Capable small technological businesses are consistently overlooked and underutilized by research and development procuring agencies of the Federal government. And despite frequent assurances by these same agencies over the past few years that they will voluntarily improve their performance in making research and development awards to small business, the percentage of the R&D budget going to small firms remains virtually unchanged at less than four percent.[20]

However, while it is true that small firms received relatively few federal R&D dollars overall, it does not necessarily mean that a government failure exists.

The SBA suggests three reasons why small firms may be excluded: small firms face large fixed costs in learning about and responding to announcements of R&D procurement actions; procurement officials are wary of dealing with small firms; and most R&D contracts are too large for small firms.[21] The first two explanations imply that the procurement process in general is not friendly to small firms and that government agencies systematically discriminate against them. If so, these two conditions should be seen with procurement of all types, not only R&D procurement. In 1980, however, while small business received 6.7 percent of R&D contracts, they also received 42.2 percent of federal construction contracts, 13.2 percent of services contracts, and 14.0 percent of contracts for supplies and equipment.[22] Apparently, small firms are fairly successful at winning non-R&D procurement contracts, suggesting that the procurement process in general is not unfriendly to small business. (However, agencies must give preference to small business in many types of procurement, making it difficult to know what share of procurement small business would receive were it not for special treatment.)

Certain aspects of R&D procurement may differ from other procurement, which leads to the third suggested explanation for small business's low share of federal R&D—that many R&D contracts are too large. Some evidence seems to support this view. A study of federal procurement contracts from FY 1979 to 1982, for example, found that more than two-thirds of R&D funds for new contracts were worth more than $1 million. Meanwhile, small firms were eight times more likely to win contracts for less than $1 million than they were to win contracts for more than that amount.[23] These statistics do not necessarily imply that small firms are *unfairly* excluded. First, many R&D contracts are large because the projects they fund are large, not because that is a convenient way to exclude a group of firms. For example, about one-third of the total federal R&D budget goes to "special short-term projects for specific weapons systems."[24] The scale of much of this work may simply be too large for small firms, and it may not be feasible to divide these large contracts into several smaller contracts and still do the work efficiently. Second, the fact that small firms win a much larger share of contracts worth less than $1 million suggests that they do compete successfully for projects of a scale that they can perform.

Efficiency Considerations

If there is a procurement problem—for example, that the complexity of procurement regulations make small contracts infeasible—then it makes sense to eliminate these obstacles in contracting procedures since they entail real costs. Costs to firms are obvious—they must spend significant funds to learn about, understand, and comply with procurement rules. If the fixed costs of dealing with federal procurement rules costs are high enough, they could pose an insurmountable barrier to small firms. Overly complex procurement rules also impose real costs on the agencies. Direct costs incurred by the agencies include resources expended implementing procurement regulations and monitoring firms that receive contracts. A hidden, but real, cost to the agencies may be the impossibility of procuring technologies from firms that cannot overcome the fixed costs of dealing with procurement rules.

The SBIR solution to a possible procurement problem is to require agencies to set aside a certain part of their R&D budgets for small firms. This solution, too, is costly. In addition to the opportunity cost of the awards themselves (other R&D not undertaken), running the program imposes real costs on the agencies. These administrative costs include issuing proposal solicitations and reviewing the more than 20,000 proposals that they receive each year. Although the costs of a review process often are ignored because they are hidden, they can be quite high.[25] Moreover, while the set-aside guarantees small firms a minimum share of federal R&D dollars, by definition it changes the way agencies allocate extramural R&D funds, and thus affects the efficiency with which the agencies accomplish their missions.

Without the set-aside, an agency can attempt to maximize the efficiency with which it conducts its mission by using its entire extramural budget to fund proposals that best meet its needs.[26] Requiring an agency to set aside a percentage of that budget changes its decision process. The agency still will first fund the best proposals, but it can fund fewer because its unrestricted budget is now smaller (in the case of SBIR, it is 97.5 percent of its size absent the set-aside). Within the set-aside portion of the budget the agency also will fund the best proposals—but these proposals are restricted to a certain group of firms. The result of this altered decision process (absent discrimination in the procurement process) is an outcome that is less efficient (in terms of accomplishing mission-oriented work) than it would have been without the constraints imposed on the agencies.[27]

Although SBIR grants are intended to advance agency missions, it appears that the agencies do not find that the money they spend through the SBIR program contributes to their missions as much as money spent elsewhere. In 1992, NASA opposed the planned increase in SBIR funding, noting that "the scope of NASA's programs and its associated budget are determined through a very rigorous process in order to achieve a balanced set of objectives, programs, and missions. Recent years have imposed severe limitations on our budget and have forced the elimination of some major initiatives. . . . An increase in the magnitude of the SBIR program . . . would significantly modify the balance that has been created. NASA does not, therefore, support an increase in the program because it would require reductions in other areas."[28] In 1995, NASA stated that it "does not have the flexibility in terms of total resources to continue to balance the magnitude of resource demands of the SBIR program while maintaining the effectiveness and vitality of ongoing NASA programs."[29] NASA is not alone in its concerns. The Nuclear Regulatory Commission (NRC) petitioned to be exempted from SBIR when it first projected its extramural R&D budget to be below the $100 million threshold in 1989.[30] NRC is not issuing an SBIR solicitation in FY 1997 because of budget cuts.[31] If the agencies felt that SBIR was an effective and efficient way to complete their missions, they would be unlikely to protest increases or to stop issuing solicitations.

A better way to deal with a procurement problem is to reduce the original distortion in procurement policies rather than impose a second one. Already the Clinton administration and Congress have taken steps to reduce the regulatory burdens on contracting firms. The Federal Acquisition Streamlining Act (FASA) of 1994 was designed, in part, to streamline contracting procedures for small purchases. FASA was extended by the Federal Acquisition Reform Act (FARA) of 1995, which simplified procedures for contract purchases under $5 million by the Defense Department.[32] Procurement reform tends to be controversial, and FASA and FARA are no exception. Small business advocates claim that these new laws actually will harm small business. This view is not universal. Dr. Steven Kelman, administrator of the Office of Federal Procurement Policy, says that FARA is designed to "make the source selection process more common-sensical and less bureaucratic," and that the claim that FARA will hurt small business "has no merit whatsoever."[33] Regardless of the debate over this particular law, however, the point is that if small firms are excluded because of complicated procurement rules, then procurement reform is the proper way to address the problem.

Market Failure?

The SBIR seeks to "stimulate technological innovation," which implies that it addresses the under-investment problem. In general, federal R&D funding accomplishes this goal when it increases the amount of research conducted in the economy by supporting work that would not have been undertaken otherwise, and does not crowd out other industry spending. Ideally, funds should be targeted at areas of research with potentially large social returns but much smaller private returns, where a firm would have little incentive to invest on its own.

Because SBIR does not represent *additional* federal R&D funding, but instead simply takes funds from existing agency R&D budgets, it does not directly affect the net level of R&D spending in the economy.[34] That is, each dollar going to R&D under SBIR is a dollar not used for R&D elsewhere. Dr. Robert Rich of the American Association of Immunologists graphically highlighted this point in testimony before Congress, when he noted that the $162.2

million NIH was expected to spend on SBIR grants in FY1995 could instead have funded almost 500 other research projects.[35]

Although SBIR research is costly, the program may still partially address a market failure if it funds work that firms would be unlikely to undertake without federal support and does not crowd out other industry spending. This issue is discussed in the following section.

SBIR Evaluation

Does SBIR target areas in which the potential returns to society are high, but the expected returns to a firm may be too low to be considered a good investment from the firm's perspective? A rational profit-maximizing firm will invest first in projects with the highest expected payoff to the firm. An effective government program aimed at stimulating innovation should encourage the firm to undertake those additional projects (projects on the margin) where returns to society may be high—not simply subsidize those projects the firm already plans to pursue (inframarginal projects).

While it is likely that many firms would not be able to pursue their SBIR-funded projects without their awards, SBIR has no built-in mechanisms either to encourage firms to apply for funding for projects on the margin or to encourage agencies to select projects on the margin. In fact, SBIR is structured so that a rational firm may look to SBIR for funding *before* it looks to other potential sources of finance. The program is intentionally designed to make the application process simple, based on the notion that the complexity of the standard R&D procurement process effectively excludes small firms. But the ease of application, the limited oversight to which firms are subjected once they win an award, and the fact that the award is a grant rather than a loan can make SBIR much cheaper, from the firm's perspective, than other sources of finance.

The awarding agencies, meanwhile, use review processes that select the best technical proposals with the highest expected probability of commercial success, not necessarily the best among the group that could not receive funding elsewhere. That the proposed project is technically sound and has a high probability of commercial success may mean that private financiers would also be willing to fund the project if given the opportunity.

Analysis and Evidence

SBIR proponents generally point to the commercial success of SBIR-funded projects as proof that the program works. Indeed, the General Accounting Office (GAO) has found that SBIR firms show a good degree of Phase III—commercialization—success, and that the quality of SBIR projects tends to be high.[36] However, the fact that many SBIR projects find funds in later stages of development says nothing about whether those projects would have been funded without SBIR. If the review process does a good job identifying proposals with the greatest chance of commercial success, a reasonably large fraction of these projects should lead to Phase III activity. Simply because SBIR funded a commercially viable project does not mean that the program stimulated innovation or commercialization.

In addition, interpreting the results of the GAO studies is difficult since they rely on surveys of SBIR award recipients and make no attempt to identify a control group against which to compare results. Direct surveys of a program's beneficiaries are not the best way to analyze a program's effectiveness. A rational firm may not say that the funding it received (and, given the high incidence of winning multiple awards, hopes to receive more of in the future) was not important in continuing its project. Moreover, if the firm had not looked, it would not know if it could have received funding elsewhere.

In 1995, I reported the results of a study that relied on data from independent sources on SBIR award winners, firms that applied but were rejected, and eligible firms that did not apply.[37] Empirical analysis of this dataset revealed that firms appear to respond to the incentives described above, and suggests, not surprisingly, that SBIR funds primarily substitute for industry spending.[38] This conclusion is worrisome; because of its funding mechanism, any crowding out that SBIR causes actually reduces net R&D spending in the economy.

Some basic statistics show the result of an easy and inexpensive application process—many firms receive multiple awards from several agencies (see Table 8-1). The table shows, for example, that of the 513 winning firms in the sample (representing 3,511 awards),

Table 8-1 Multiple Award Winners, 1990–92

Number of firms winning at least x awards		Averages per firm			Total across firms	
x	# of firms	# of awards, phase I	# of awards, phase II	Total value ($millions)	# of awards, phase I	# of awards, phase II
1	513	5.1	1.8	$1.01	2610	901
5	152	12.6	4.2	$2.47	1919	644
10	67	20.4	6.5	$3.89	1369	438
20	25	33.7	10.4	$6.20	842	261

152 firms won at least five awards each from 1990 through 1992, averaging almost thirteen Phase I and more than four Phase II awards each, worth a total of $2.5 million per firm. Sixty-seven firms won at least ten awards over that three-year time period, averaging more than twenty Phase I and almost seven Phase II awards each, worth almost $6 million. The phenomenon of "SBIR mills"—firms whose main purpose seems to be to win SBIR awards—is well-known, and is an issue the awarding agencies have addressed. The key point here, however, is that the large number of awards some firms win suggests that once they are aware of the program, they do look to SBIR before looking elsewhere for funds. In addition, the observation that so many awards go to firms winning large numbers of awards casts doubt on the notion that the typical SBIR grant goes to a struggling entrepreneur who simply needs some cash to get an idea off the ground.

The data also suggest that these awards may primarily crowd out industry R&D spending. First, analysis of the sub-sample of publicly traded firms (the only firms for which R&D expenditure data are available) reveals that these firms, on average, reduce growth in their own R&D spending by the amount of the award they receive.[39] Second, analysis of the entire sample of firms reveals that awards are not correlated with changes in firm employment concurrent with winning either Phase I or Phase II awards—a finding that corroborates the R&D crowd-out result. Cash flow typically constrains R&D spending, especially in small, high-tech firms. Cash flow, however, consists of a transitory component and a more stable, permanent component. Since most R&D expenditures in small firms are on salaries of scientists and engineers, who cannot easily be hired and fired, these firms tend to smooth their R&D spending over time by basing it on the permanent component of cash flow. Changes in spending on other types of investment, meanwhile, more closely follow the transitory component.[40] If the firm undertakes a new project that it believes will yield a stream of profits and thus an increase in expected permanent cash flow, we would expect to see an increase in its employment. However, SBIR awards do not, on average, appear to bring about such increases.

Taken together, these findings suggest that the proposal review process does not select projects that would not be funded without federal support, but instead selects the "better" firms whose projects may be funded even absent federal support.

These conclusions do not imply that the program is mismanaged or that the federal agencies are incompetent. Indeed, the agencies try to implement congressionally mandated programs as best they can within the legislated framework and actively work to improve their SBIR programs. DoD, for example, now bases its Phase II awards decisions, in part, on how much the firm itself is willing to invest in commercialization activities, and how much additional non-SBIR funding the program has attracted. This move is consistent with principles underlying much of current technology policy, which increasingly emphasizes private-sector cost-sharing. The findings described here do not point to difficulties with SBIR implementation; they highlight the problems inherent in the program.

Data Issues

While these findings are interesting and revealing, the lack of available data, including the lack of a good control group of firms against which to compare the effectiveness of the federal funding, makes evaluating programs like SBIR extremely difficult. The large number of project proposals and awards granted each year would make SBIR ideal for conducting an experiment of the sort Adam Jaffe describes in his chapter. In essence, the experiment would involve randomly *not* funding a small number of proposals that were chosen as worthy of receiving public funding, and providing funding to a small number of proposal that were not. The performance of the worthy firms that receive no government funding, including whether or not they proceed with their proposed project, can be compared to the performance of firms that do receive funding. Such a comparison would allow us to determine whether or not the funding was important to the project and to give a better answer to one of the most important questions of R&D funding: did the program fund projects on the margin, or merely provide funding for projects the firm would have undertaken regardless of federal support?

The part of the experiment that funds some "rejected" projects could test the review process. As in many other programs such as ATP, SBIR proposals are reviewed for their technical and other merits, and awards are granted on the basis of these reviews. The government's ability to evaluate proposals for research intended to yield a commercializable product is a matter of intense debate. Comparing the outcomes of projects and performance of rejected firms that receive funding to the performance of rejected firms that do not would help determine whether the review process itself makes any difference.

Such experiments could be extremely useful in evaluating the importance of federal funding in bringing research to the market, as well as helping to identify strengths and weaknesses of the review processes used by the various agencies. The results could then be applied more generally to increase the efficiency and effectiveness of federal technology programs.

Policy Proposals

SBIR has two basic problems as a technology program: it probably funds inframarginal work, and it displaces other federal research. In this section I propose two alternative policies—one to make SBIR more consistent with the goals of technology policy, and one to replace SBIR with a partially refundable tax credit targeted at small firms.

Improving SBIR

SBIR is here at least until it expires on October 31, 2000, and perhaps much longer if it is renewed. It is thus important to make the program as effective as possible, and to attempt to make it consistent with other federal technology policies and goals.

In general, technology programs like SBIR should fund projects that, while close to yielding commercializable products, may be too risky for the private sector to fund on its own. Indeed, some agencies already note this as an important programmatic goal. The Ballistic Missile Defense Organization (BMDO), for example, states in its proposal solicitation that "BMDO SBIR will not further develop concepts already mature enough to compete for private capital or for government development funds."[41] Determining whether or not proposed projects can effectively compete for other funds is not a simple task. However, the agency could better make such an assessment by collecting certain additional information from applicants.

For example, agencies might ask whether the firm has already tried to obtain other sources of funding for the proposed project. A sound technical project for which the firm cannot find funding but which the agency thinks will yield high returns may be a good candidate for SBIR funding. An agency may also want to know other information such as the firm's employment and previous years' R&D spending and sales. The agencies have commented to GAO that they receive more worthy proposals than they are capable of funding.[42] If high-quality applications are not in short supply, then the agencies can use these firm-specific data to help pick projects that are less likely to receive other funding. For example, consider two firms that submit equally sound proposals from a technical point of view. One firm has several hundred employees, millions of dollars in annual sales, and a fairly substantial R&D budget. The other firm is a small start-up. Although their proposals may have identical probabilities of success, the larger firm can more easily find other sources of finance (from private financiers, government, or even its own cash flow) than can the smaller firm, which is more likely to face a liquidity constraint. In this case, SBIR funding is more likely to "make or break" the smaller firm's project than the larger firm's project.

Tax Credits: A Less Costly, More Effective Way to Aid Small Firm R&D

Improvements to the SBIR selection process may help encourage small firms to conduct research they could not conduct absent federal support, but would neither reduce SBIR's costs nor increase the efficiency with which agencies can accomplish their missions. To these latter ends, I propose a targeted tax credit as a replacement for SBIR.[43]

Tax credits are generally viewed as a relatively effective way to increase R&D investment at the margin. The United States has had some form of R&D tax credit since 1981, although the details have been changed several times.[44] In essence, the current allowed credit is 20 percent of qualified R&D expenditures above a base level. The effectiveness of the credit has been the subject of much research and debate. A credit lowers the firm's cost of conducting R&D. One way to measure the effectiveness of the credit is to estimate how much firms increase their R&D spending when their cost of performing R&D falls. Early studies in the 1980s tended to conclude that a dollar of tax credit stimulated less than a dollar increase in firm R&D. More recent analyses, however, commonly find that the R&D tax credit leads to at least one dollar in additional R&D for each dollar of lost tax revenue.[45]

The current R&D tax credit seems to benefit primarily large firms. In 1992, firms filed for a total of $1.6 billion in R&D tax credits.[46] Of that $1.6 billion, 30 percent was claimed by firms with assets of less than $250 million, 11 percent by firms with assets of less than $10 million, and 3 percent by firms with assets of less than $1 million.[47] Although the credit is somewhat more generous for start-up companies, small firms may face some obstacles to using the credit. One potential obstacle is the administrative cost to the firm of properly accounting for its research expenses. Another problem is that while current law allows a fifteen-year carryforward and three-year carryback, liquidity-constrained firms with no tax liabilities do not benefit immediately from this nonrefundable credit. However, a credit can be designed to benefit all firms, regardless of their current tax liabilities. Indeed, several industrialized countries—notably Canada, the Netherlands, and Italy—already have tax incentives to benefit small firms.

Canada offers small firms an "enhanced" 35 percent credit on the first $2 million of R&D expenditures, and it is fully refundable. (A 20 percent nonrefundable credit is available to all firms.) The Netherlands bases its tax incentive plan on wages, since most of a firm's R&D costs are for salaries. The plan allows a 25 percent deduction for R&D wage costs below Gld 100,000 (about $60,000), and a 12.5 percent deduction for costs above that amount. Firms can take the deduction monthly in order to benefit as the research is being done rather than waiting until the end of the tax year. In addition, self-employed people who spend more than 875 hours a year on R&D can claim an extra Gld 6,000. Italy allows a tax credit of 30 percent (up to a ceiling of L 500 million) for small firms in certain sectors, with an even further enhanced credit in certain regions of the country.[48]

A U.S. Small Business R&D Tax Credit

An effective tax credit for small firm R&D must contain three features. First, because small firms tend to smooth their R&D spending over time, a subsidy is more likely to be effective if it is a consistent flow over time rather than a one-shot cash infusion.[49] Second, it must be designed so that it also benefits firms with no tax liabilities. Finally, it should be relatively simple in order to keep down costs of compliance.

A tax credit that is partially refundable, with a carryforward of the nonrefundable portion, could meet those objectives. For example, such a law could follow the Canadian model and allow small firms an enhanced credit greater than the 20 percent currently allowed for all firms. The plan could then allow a firm a refund of that credit of up to, say, $500,000 a year, and allow the firm to carry forward the remainder of its credit (up to some level) for up to fifteen years, as the current law allows.

The refundable portion of the credit would provide liquidity-constrained firms with capital to conduct research whether or not they have tax liabilities. The nonrefundable portion of the credit means that firms would not receive some of the benefit until their work on this or other results in a stream of profits. This provision would help to provide the firm with proper incentives to commercialize new technologies—one of SBIR's goals. Since the firm must ultimately see a stream of profits in order to realize the benefits of the nonrefundable portion of the credit, the firm must truly believe that it is close to producing something marketable, but it would not require as high an expected return as it would without the credit.[50]

The tax credit outlined above is just a rough sketch of a plan that could aid small firms and, to some extent, work toward SBIR's goals. Designing and implementing such a plan is, of course, easier said than done. Any tax incentive must be designed to minimize the potential distortions it could cause in the market and in firms' investment decisions. Provisions designed to help target the credit better can have unintended consequences that reduce its effectiveness. For example, we may want the credit to apply to incremental R&D only, which would mean that the law should establish some base level of spending above which the firm receives the credit (as the existing law does). However, if the base were determined in part by the amount of R&D the firm performed in preceding years, then the firm would have an incentive to delay its R&D spending so as not to reduce its potential future credits. A fixed base would help eliminate this problem but would become less effective at rewarding only incremental R&D over the years. Moreover, each additional provision adds complexity (and thus costs) both to the firm and to the IRS, which must determine if claims are legitimate.

An additional important detail is determining exactly which firms should benefit from the credit. Indeed, a firm with 499 employees does not face the same obstacles as a firm with two employees simply because both fit the definition of "small." Differences among these firms may be important in capital markets. For example, 96 percent of all small firms in the Federal Reserve's 1993 National Survey of Small Business Finances used some type of financial service, and just over 55 percent used some type of credit line, loan, or capital lease. However, while only 42 percent of firms with not more than one employee used a credit line, loan, or capital lease, about 87 percent of small firms with at least 50 employees used these financial tools.[51] Under the plan outlined above, however, a larger "small" firm with significant tax liabilities would benefit more than would an especially small firm.

To address such concerns, the plan could have a "tiered" system or a sliding scale under which the size of the allowable credit is determined by firm size. The smallest firms (i.e., those that benefit the least from the existing credit) could receive the refundable credit for all of their R&D spending up to some reasonable limit. A baseline could be established for larger firms, who would receive the credit for R&D spending above that base. And, of course, at some size (perhaps well below the 500-employee definition of "small"), firms would be eligible only for the credit already in place.

The proposed tax credit would not be revenue-neutral, since current SBIR funds would revert to the agencies to be used in mission-oriented R&D. However, designing the credit to be most generous to the smallest firms and progressively less generous to larger firms not only provides increased government support where market failures may be greatest, but also limits the additional budgetary costs of the credit. In addition, targeting areas of greater market failure makes it more likely that the credit will stimulate additional firm R&D. Given the high social returns to R&D in general, the economic benefits from increasing firm R&D are likely to outweigh additional budgetary costs of the credit.

A plan involving tax credits for small firms would have several advantages over the current SBIR program. First, it would allow agencies to use their extramural R&D budgets more directly for their intended purposes. Second, it would allow the agencies to avoid the costs of running their SBIR programs. Third, the government could avoid having to make decisions about what technologies will be successful in the marketplace. Finally, the targeted tax credit could be an effective way to increase the amount of R&D conducted by small firms. Among potential disadvantages: the credit might subsidize some R&D firms would have conducted anyway; revenue consequences can be unpredictable;[52] and a credit may distort firm investment decisions.[53] However, if our goal is to increase innovation in small firms and in the economy overall, a tax credit is likely to be more effective than SBIR, and is likely to have much greater benefits at a lower cost.

Acknowledgments

I am grateful to Darin Boville, Richard Florida, Claude Reichard, and Greg Tassey for their thoughtful comments. I also thank Roger Noll for his comments and suggestions, as well as his continued support of my graduate work. Any errors are, of course, my own.

Notes

1. Public Law 97-219, July 22, 1982; Public Law 102-564, October 28, 1992.

2. House of Representatives, *Small Business Innovation Development Act of 1981, Report Together with Additional Views (to accompany H.R. 4326)*, House Report 97-349, Part IV.

3. House Report 97-349, Part IV.

4. See, for example, Jeffrey Mervis, "A $1 billion Tax on R&D," *Science*, Vol. 272 (May 17, 1996).

5. In this chapter I do not discuss SBIR's goal of supporting minority and disadvantaged firms; instead I discuss SBIR only as a technology program. The provision to aid minority firms is a relatively minor aspect of the program: it appeared to play little role in justifying the enabling legislation, and the agencies do not give special preference to minority firms in the proposal review process. Instead, the agencies use outreach programs to increase awareness of the program among minority firms. U.S. General Accounting Office (GAO), *Federal Research: Assessment of Small Business Innovation Research Programs*, GAO/RCED-89-39, (Washington, D.C.: U.S. Government Printing Office [U.S. GPO], January, 1989).

6. Small Business Administration (SBA), *The State of Small Business: A Report of the President* (Washington, D.C.: U.S. Government Printing Office [U.S. GPO], 1994), p. 114.

7. Ibid., p.111.

8. Linda Cohen and Roger Noll, *The Technology Pork Barrel* (Washington, D.C.: The Brookings Institution, 1991), Chapter 2; U.S. SBA, *The State of Small Business*, pp. 111–112.

9. Cohen and Noll, *The Technology Pork Barrel*, p. 25; Zoltan Acs and David Audretsch, *Innovation and Small Firms* (Cambridge, Mass.: The MIT Press, 1990), p. 57, find that "the relative innovative advantage of large firms tends to be promoted in industries that are capital-intensive, advertising-intensive, concentrated, and highly unionized. By contrast, in industries that are highly innovative and composed predominantly of large firms, the relative innovative advantage is held by small firms."

10. For a discussion of capital constraints and R&D investment, see Bronwyn Hall, "Investment and Research and Development at the Firm Level: Does the Source of Financing Matter?" *NBER Working Paper*, No. 4096 (Washington, D.C.: National Bureau of Economic Research, June 1992); and Charles Himmelberg and Bruce Petersen, "R&D and Internal Finance: A Panel Study of Small Firms in High-Tech Industries," *Review of Economics and Statistics*, Vol. 76, No. 1 (February 1994), pp. 38–51. For a discussion of R&D spillovers, see, for example, Zvi Griliches, "The Search for R&D Spillovers," *Scandinavian Journal of Economics*, Vol. 94, Supplement (1992), pp. 29–47. For overviews of the literature on this general topic, see Cohen and Noll, *The Technology Pork Barrel*, Chapter 2; Ishaq

Nadiri, "Innovations and Technological Spillovers," *NBER Working Paper*, No. 4423 (Washington, D.C.: National Bureau of Economic Research, August 1993); and Council of Economic Advisers, *Supporting Research and Development: The Federal Government's Role* (Washington, D.C.: CEA, October 1995).

11. Steven Fazzari, Glenn Hubbard, and Bruce Petersen, "Financing Constraints and Corporate Investment," *Brookings Papers on Economic Activity*, Vol. 1 (1988), pp. 141–206.

12. Janet Yellen, Statement to Congress, *Federal Reserve Bulletin*, Vol. 82, No. 7 (July 1996), pp. 652–655.

13. Joshua Lerner, "The Government as Venture Capitalist: The Long-Run Impact of the SBIR Program," *NBER Working Paper*, No. 5753 (September 1996)

14. The NRC is not participating in FY 1997 due to budget cuts, bringing the number of agencies involved to ten (at least temporarily).

15. GAO, *Federal Research: Assessment of the Small Business Innovation Research Program*, GAO/RCED-89-39 (Washington, D.C.: U.S. GPO, January 1989); U.S. GAO, *Federal Research: Interim Report on the Small Business Innovation Research Program*, GAO/RCED-95-59 (Washington, D.C.: U.S. GPO, March 1995).

16. Agencies with extramural R&D budgets exceeding $10 billion had to set aside only 0.1 percent of that budget in FY 1983, but they, too, had to set aside 1.25 percent for SBIR awards by FY 1986.

17. Small Business Administration (SBA) Web Site (1996): <http://www.sbaonline .sba.gov/Research_And_Development/sbir.html>.

18. "Small Business Innovation Research Policy Directive," 58 *Federal Register* 15 (January 26, 1993).

19. SBA web site.

20. House Report 97-349, Part I, p.7. Note that according to the SBA, small business actually received 6.7 percent of federal *contract* (rather than total) R&D funds in 1980; U.S. Small Business Administration, *State of Small Busines*s. SBIR proponents also sometimes state—as an extreme example of agency discrimination against small firms—that prior to SBIR the National Institutes of Health provided no funds to small business: see, for example, Terry Bibbens, "Innovation, Commercialization, and SBIR: It's Déjà Vu All Over Again," *The Small Business Advocate*, Vol. 15, No. 5 (July 1996), pp. 6–7. This observation, however, appears to be incorrect. According to the Federal Procurement Data System, the Department of Health and Human Services (HHS) (in which almost all R&D spending is through the NIH) provided almost $50 million to small firms in 1980—a substantial share of HHS funding to industry. Report S97-064, prepared by the Federal Data Procurement System for this author. These data also can be obtained from the Federal Procurement Data System, *Federal Procurement Report*, published annually.

21. Small Business Administration, *State of Small Business*, p. 125.

22. Ibid., Table C-7. In FY 1992, these statistics were 8.5 percent, 48.1 percent, 17.0 percent, and 12.1 percent, respectively.

23. Ibid., p. 125.

24. Executive Office of the President, U.S. National Science and Technology Council, *Technology in the National Interest* (Washington, D.C.:1996).

25. Barry Bozeman, "Peer Review and Evaluation of R&D Impacts," Barry Bozeman and Julia Melkers, eds., *Evaluating R&D Impacts: Methods and Practice* (Boston: Kluwer Academic Publishers, 1993).

26. See Cohen and Noll, *The Technology Pork Barrel*, Chapter 3, for a discussion of how the agencies try to manage their R&D budgets.

27. The inconsistency of SBIR's two goals—redistributing funds to small firms and promoting technological innovation and commercialization—exacerbates this problem. If the agency emphasizes the goal of using small firms to complete mission-oriented R&D, then the problem is precisely as described here. If the agency focuses, instead, on innovation and the potential commercial success of the projects it funds, then its mission-oriented work may further suffer.

28. *Testimony before the House Committee on Science, Space and Technology,* June 23, 1992.

29. *Testimony before the Subcommittee on Government Programs of the House Committee on Small Business*, April 8, 1995.

30. Congress, House of Representatives. "Nuclear Regulatory Commission [NRC] Proposal to Withdraw from the Small Business Innovation Research Program," *Hearing Before the Committee on Small Business*, Serial No. 100-39 (March 1, 1988).

31. NRC SBIR Web site: <http://www.dsu.edu:8000/nrc.html>.

32. National Science and Technology Council, *Technology in the National Interest*, p. 74.

33. "Group Asks Senate to Protect Competitive Range," *Set-Aside Alert*, Vol. 5, No. 3 (February 10, 1997).

34. The program may, however, *indirectly* affect the level of federal R&D expenditures. The existence of SBIR means that the small business community has an incentive to support increases in the overall level of federal R&D spending, since each dollar increase in extramural R&D spending means $0.025 to small business.

35. Robert Rich, *Testimony before the House Labor-HHS Appropriations Subcommittee*, January 27, 1995.

36. General Accounting Office (GAO), *Federal Research: Assessment of the Small Business Innovation Research Program*, GAO/RCED-89-39 (Washington, D.C.: U.S. GPO, January 1989); U.S. GAO, *Federal Research: Small Business Innovation Research Shows Success but Can Be Strengthened*, GAO/RCED-92-37 (Washington, D.C.: U.S. GPO, March 1992); GAO, *Federal Research: Interim Report on the Small Business Innovation Research Program*, GAO/RCED-95-59 (Washington, D.C.: U.S. GPO, March 1995).

37. Scott Wallsten, "The Small Business Innovation Research Program: Encouraging Technological Innovation and Commercialization in Small Firms?" Stanford University Working Paper, August 1995. Most financial data came from Dunn and Bradstreet financial reports. Data for public firms came also from Standard and Poor's Compustat database. SBIR award information came from SBA's annual *Listing of Award Winners for FY 1988–92.*

38. Lerner, "The Government as Venture Capitalist," studied firms that won awards in the first three years of SBIR's existence. He found no effect of awards on sales and employment overall, but found that firms that won Phase II awards and were located in geographic areas with a high degree of venture capital activity grew more than did a matched set of firms that did not win awards. SBIR was a much smaller program in its first years (awarding about $470 million from 1983 through 1985) than it is now (from 1990 through 1992, the time period included in the analysis discussed here, SBIR awarded more than $1.5 billion in awards). A young, small, program will function differently from an older, much larger program. In addition, Lerner did not control for selection criteria. Just as research investigating wage premiums to union membership or to holding a college degree must control for the possibility that people with greater wage-earning potential may be selected by (or self-select into) unions and colleges, so too must analyses of the effects of technology programs control for the possibility that firms that will succeed anyway are picked for awards.

39. Some have suggested that any results based on data from public firms will be biased because these firms may be older and larger than the typical SBIR awardee. This observation, however, is not a critique of the finding. Instead, if the result does indeed only apply to these larger "small" firms, then it suggests a modest policy proposal: limit SBIR awards to firms much smaller than the typical publicly-traded award winner. Indeed, as discussed in subsequent sections, there is no reason to believe that a firm with several hundred employees faces the same problems as a start-up company with one or two employees.

40. Charles Himmelberg and Bruce Petersen, "R&D and Internal Finance: A Panel Study of Small Firms in High-Tech Industries," *Review of Economics and Statistics*, Vol. 76, No. 1 (February 1994), pp. 38–51.

41. Department of Defense, *FY 1997 Small Business Innovation Research (SBIR) Program*, Program Solicitation 97.1 (1996), p. BMDO-1.

42. General Accounting Office, *Federal Research: Interim Report*, 1995, p.3.

43. In addition to the sources cited below, I gained useful knowledge from the following sources: Stephane Lhuillery, "Problems Involved in Designing and Implementing R&D Tax Incentive Schemes," *Fiscal Measures to Promote R&D and Innovation*, OCDE/GD(96)165 (Paris: Organisation for Economic Cooperation and Development, [OECD] 1996); Lawrence Meyer, Joel Varvares, and Chris Varvares, "Policy Watch: Designing an Effective Investment Tax Credit," *Journal of Economic Perspectives*, Vol. 7, No. 2 (Spring 1993), pp. 189–196; and Jacek

Warda, "Measuring the Value of R&D Tax Provisions," *Fiscal Measures to Promote R&D and Innovation*, OCDE/GD(96)165 (1996).

44. Officially this credit is called the "Research and Experimentation Tax Credit" (or R&E tax credit). For consistency, in this chapter it will simply be called an "R&D tax credit." See Bronwyn Hall, "R&D Tax Policy for the 1980s: Success or Failure," James Poterba, ed., *Tax Policy and the Economy*, Vol. 7 (Cambridge, Mass.: The MIT Press, 1993), pp. 1–35; U.S. Congress, Office of Technology Assessment, *The Effectiveness of the Research and Experimentation Tax Credits* (September 20, 1995) for an overview of the history of the credit and analyses of its effectiveness; and U.S. GAO, *Tax Policy and Administration: Review of Studies of the Effectiveness of the Research Tax Credit*, GAO/GGD-96-43 (May 1996) for a concise summary of many of the evaluations of the credit.

45. OTA, *The Effectiveness of the Research and Experimentation Tax Credits.*

46. Ibid. OTA notes that although firms *filed* for $1.6 billion in credits, "several complicating factors . . . in all likelihood, reduce[d] the actual tax subsidy provided to firms"; p.6.

47. Ibid.

48. See Revenue Canada, *Canada-U.S. Canada: North America's Choice Investment Location* (1996); and Revenue Canada, 1996, <http:/www.revcan.ca/menu/EmenuHUA.html>, <http://www.revcan.ca/E/pub/gd/405295et/405295e.txt.html> for information on the Canadian tax credit; Jeroen Nijland "The R&D Tax Scheme in the Netherlands," *Fiscal Measures to Promote R&D and Innovation*, OCED/GD(96)165 (Paris: OECD, 1996) for information on the Dutch credit; and Organization for Cooperation and Development, *Taxation and Small Business* (Paris: OECD, 1994) and Franco Malerba, "The National System of Innovation: Italy," in Richard Nelson, ed., *National Innovation Systems: A Comparative Analysis* (New York: Oxford University Press: 1993), for information on the Italian credit.

49. Hall, "R&D Tax Policy During the 1980s"; Himmelberg and Petersen, "R&D and Internal Finance."

50. The suggestion of using a tax credit as an alternative way to accomplish some of SBIR's goals should not be interpreted as implying that tax incentives can substitute for direct funding in general. Both tax incentives and direct funding are important components of our federal science and technology portfolio. Gregory Tassey, "Choosing Government R&D Policies: Tax Incentives vs. Direct Funding," *Review of Industrial Organization*, Vol. 11, No. 5 (October 1996), pp. 579–600, notes that tax incentives can increase the *level* of R&D performed, while direct funding can alter the *composition* of R&D performed. However, SBIR is intended to increase the amount of R&D performed by a particular type of firm—not to increase R&D in a particular technology area—and thus a tax credit targeted at small firms is a reasonable substitute in this case.

51. Rebel Cole and John Wolken, "Financial Services Used by Small Businesses: Evidence From the National Survey of Small Business Finances," *Federal Reserve Bulletin*, Vol. 81, No. 7 (July 1995), pp. 630–666, Table A.2.

52. Albert Link, "Fiscal Measures to Promote R&D and Innovation—Trends and Issues," *Fiscal Measures to Promote R&D and Innovation*, OCDE/GD(96)165 (Paris: OECD, 1996).

53. Just as SBIR contains hidden costs, a tax credit also contains real costs not reflected in the budgetary estimates of lost revenue, in terms of effort required by firms to file and by the IRS to monitor. This point underscores the need for simplicity. However, the *additional* costs of the credit on firms are likely to be small since it uses the existing tax infrastructure, with which firms already must comply.

Technology Transfer and the Use of CRADAs at the National Institutes of Health

David H. Guston

Technology transfer is the process by which expertise and its embodiment in people, processes and artifacts move from one organization, sector, or country, to another. Because the federal government makes large investments in research and development (R&D) in the pursuit of national goals—but often relies on organizations other than the research performers to pursue those goals more directly—the efficient transfer of technology from the research-performing organization to other organizations is of federal concern. For example, about 24 percent of federal R&D spending in fiscal year (FY) 1996 went to laboratories owned by the federal government.[1] But because the primary mission of these laboratories usually does not involve increasing employment or creating new commercial products, they must be able to transfer the technology they produce to firms responsible for these tasks. The more effectively these laboratories can transfer technology, and the faster the recipients can translate new knowledge into socially useful goals, the better an investment the original R&D spending will prove to be.

This chapter assesses one aspect of U.S. policy for technology transfer, the Cooperative Research and Development Agreement (CRADA). A CRADA is a novel form of contract that allows federal laboratories to conduct research in partnership with nonfederal organizations (firms, universities and other nonprofit organizations, and state and local government), in part by the prior settlement of disposition of any intellectual property created by the research in a way that is relatively favorable to the nonfederal partner.

All federal agencies that conduct R&D can participate in CRADAs, and the rules regarding their implementation are flexible enough that CRADA policy may represent well the principle that technology policy should not be "one size fits all." This chapter evaluates the implementation of CRADAs only at the intramural laboratories of the National Institutes of Health (NIH), although it makes some comparisons to experiences at the Department of Energy (DOE) and other agencies.[2] The chapter also offers a set of recommendations to improve the implementation of technology transfer policy; some are specific to NIH, but many are generalizable.

In this chapter, I argue that CRADA policy should not be conceived of as primarily for the development of commercial technology. Rather, CRADAs are primarily a mechanism that permits the sharing of expertise and the leveraging of R&D capacity in both the federal and nonfederal partners, allowing each to pursue goals that may or may not be directly related to commercial products. Because the R&D capacities of federal and nonfederal laboratories vary considerably among agencies and sectors, and because the intellectual property opportunities that CRADAs offer vary in commercial importance among sectors, the evaluation of technology transfer policy in general and CRADAs in particular must meet crucial criteria. They must not rely on broad comparisons among federal entities; must not rely solely on indicators derived from intellectual property for policy and program evaluation; and must begin to develop indicators related to the leveraging of R&D capacity and the specific missions of the federal partners. Congress and agencies must enable the development, collection, organization, and analysis of such data for the furtherance of policy. The government must also continue to clarify areas of uncertainty in the provision of intellectual property rights, and monitor the application of such rights and other incentives to assure the effective implementation of technology transfer policy.

The Making of Technology Transfer Policy

For most of the period since World War II, the United States did not have a national policy for technology transfer. Policy-makers as-

sumed that the flow of scientific research to technology development was a free and automatic process.[3] However, particular
agencies have had programs oriented at a narrow industrial clien-
tele, such as the long-standing and successful Agricultural Extension Service and the newer Technology Utilization Program of the
National Aeronautics and Space Administration (NASA).[4] In the
1970s, however, with the U.S. economy flagging even in high-
technology sectors, policy makers began to reconsider how best to
connect the federal investment in R&D to economic and other
goals. The United States then embarked on a tentative but bipartisan technology transfer policy that, although implemented slowly
by R&D agencies, has profoundly changed the way R&D laboratories in different sectors interact with one another.

The Bipartisan Mandate

Congress passed two important pieces of legislation in 1980 that
launched a national technology transfer policy. The first, the
Technology Innovation Act (P.L. 96-480), also known as Stevenson-
Wydler, made technology transfer a mission of all federal laboratories and required the major ones to establish Offices of Research
and Technology Applications (ORTAs) to perform this mission.[5]
The second, the Patent and Trademark Amendments Act (P.L. 96-
517), also known as Bayh-Dole, unified the checkerboard system of
patents that had evolved since World War II.[6] Bayh-Dole allowed
universities and other performers of federally sponsored research
to obtain title to inventions more easily, and it instructed them to
share royalties derived from licenses with individual inventors.[7]
Bayh-Dole also permitted federal agencies, including government-
owned, government-operated (GOGO) laboratories, to grant exclusive licenses on government-held patents.

   Bayh-Dole sparked more opposition in Congress than Stevenson-
Wydler, generally among populist Democrats who viewed the
private ownership of federally sponsored innovations as contrary to
the public interest. Indeed, Bayh-Dole "marked a major retreat
from the principle that knowledge subsidized by the government
should circulate freely."[8] But Congress passed both acts with a
broad bipartisan consensus.

During the Reagan administration, Congress amended both acts. In 1984, prompted in part by the report of the Federal Laboratory Review Panel of the Office of Science and Technology Policy (OSTP),[9] Congress passed the Trademark Clarification Act (P.L. 98-620) to amend Bayh-Dole and grant broader authorities to the directors of government-owned, contractor-operated (GOCO) laboratories to engage in technology transfer activities. In 1986, Congress passed the Federal Technology Transfer Act (FTTA, P.L. 99-502), which amended Stevenson-Wydler to allow GOGO labs to enter into CRADAs with nonfederal organizations, and to mandate that employees receive a share of any royalties from licenses of their inventions. Under the Act, the nonfederal partner may provide material, personnel, and funding to the CRADA, but the federal laboratory may provide only material and personnel (whose salary continues to be paid by the government).

Again, Congress passed both laws with broad bipartisan support. The National Governors' Association praised the effort, arguing that the United States "can no longer afford the luxury of isolating its government laboratories from university and industry."[10] President Reagan had threatened to veto FTTA, but the Republican leadership in Congress broke with the administration and supported FTTA. Reagan then endorsed FTTA in Executive Order 12591.[11] In the National Competitiveness Technology Transfer Act of 1989 (P.L. 101-189), Congress extended the authority to engage in cooperative research to GOCOs as well.

Congress refined the intellectual property rules governing CRADAs in the National Technology Transfer and Advancement Act of 1995 (NTTA, P.L. 104-113). Passed by voice vote in both chambers, NTTA was signed by President Clinton on March 7, 1996. It amended Stevenson-Wydler to allow the nonfederal partner the option to choose an exclusive or nonexclusive license for a negotiated field of use for a CRADA invention, but it also allowed the government to require a partner to grant third-party licenses to meet exceptional public health or safety needs, to meet federal requirements, or if the partner failed to comply with the terms of the agreement. It further provided that—in cases where a partner retains title to an invention made solely by its employees—the government may acquire a worldwide license to use the invention "for research or other Government purposes."

Implementing Technology Transfer

Agencies implemented FTTA sluggishly. A General Accounting Office (GAO) report in 1989 found that some agencies and laboratories had encountered barriers, including the desire by nonfederal partners for greater protection of proprietary information and less burdensome procedures, and government researchers' need for a clearer policy regarding conflicts of interest.[12] In 1990, GAO reported that, despite the FTTA mandate, nearly 80 percent of laboratories had not developed any guidelines for the use of technology transfer activity as a factor in promotion decisions.[13] Even in 1991, GAO reported that "the major provisions [of FTTA] still have not been fully implemented."[14]

The delays cited by GAO seem largely the product of the agencies' inexperience and the need for cultural as well as procedural changes.[15] For example, once the agencies established "boilerplate" or "model" CRADAs, the average time to process a CRADA dropped significantly. NIH has trimmed its time from 69 to 28 days since 1993, and DOE has cut its average time in half over the same period.[16] As shown in Table 9-1, the number of active CRADAs across all agencies increased as they gained experience in overcoming these barriers.[17]

In 1992, GAO concluded that the "royalty-sharing programs at federal laboratories have not increased scientists' interest in patenting."[18] Although the link between royalty-sharing and patenting is mediated by other factors—including the fact that few patents are ever licensed or bear royalties—the NTTA instructed agencies to pay inventors a minimum of the first $2000 of royalties from a licensed invention and then 15 percent of royalties thereafter (NIH pays inventors 25 percent of royalties).

The small number of empirical studies on the implementation of FTTA have documented a significant increase in technology transfer activities. David Roessner and Alden Bean found strong increases in research and licensing cooperation between national laboratories and large, high-tech firms from 1988 to 1992.[19] Likewise, in a survey of 276 federal and state government laboratories, Barry Bozeman and Michael Crow found an increase in the percentage of laboratories considering technology transfer a signifi-

Table 9-1 Increase in the Number of Active CRADAs, All Agencies (Except NASA and Social Security Administration), 1987– 94

	1987	1988	1989	1990	1991	1992	1993	1994
Total number of active CRADAs	34	98	271	460	731	1250	1847	2607

cant mission, from slightly more that 50 percent in 1988 to about 75 percent in 1990.[20] Bozeman and Crow also found that CRADAs were an increasing fraction of interactions between firms and federal laboratories, from 28 percent of all such interactions prior to 1992 to 56 percent in 1992–93.[21]

The most important findings of these studies involve what firms get out of cooperative R&D. More than 70 percent of Roessner and Bean's private sector respondents indicated that of ten specified ways of interacting with the federal laboratories, cooperative research held the most promise for their organization, up from 35 percent in 1988. Among the respondents who most favored cooperative research, more than one-half identified the primary benefit as access to expertise, and more than one-third identified it as leveraging in-house R&D, while fewer than 10 percent identified a business opportunity or the potential for profit. Bozeman and Crow similarly found that the most important motives for collaboration were access to the expertise of federal researchers and the unique facilities of federal laboratories, and the possibility of developing commercial products was less important.[22] These findings provide solid evidence for the view that CRADAs are not exclusively or even primarily a tool for the development of commercial products.

Despite the increase in company-initiated activity, Roessner and Bean found that levels of satisfaction with cooperative research were modest and not increasing for the period of 1988 to 1992.[23] Bozeman and Crow found a greater level of satisfaction, with 89 percent of their respondents reporting that "working with the federal lab proved to be a good use" of their company's time and resources.[24]

Technology Transfer and CRADAS at NIH

The intramural laboratories of NIH, located in Bethesda, Maryland, constitute the world's largest biomedical research facility. NIH received an appropriation for intramural R&D in FY 1997 of about $1.3 billion, or just over 20 percent of all federal funding for intramural civilian R&D.[25] NIH consists of more than two dozen separate institutes, centers, and divisions (ICDs), most dedicated to research related to specific disorders (e.g., the National Cancer Institute) or specific organs or systems (e.g., the National Heart, Lung, and Blood Institute).[26] Most ICDs maintain both an extramural (grant-making) program and a smaller intramural research program. Despite its size, NIH has been somewhat isolated from the mainstream of technology transfer policy discussions.

Technology Transfer before FTTA

Biomedical research received little attention in the preparation of Stevenson-Wydler, and a 1982 technical memorandum by the congressional Office of Technology Assessment (OTA) on *Technology Transfer at the National Institutes of Health* mentioned neither Stevenson-Wydler nor Bayh-Dole.[27] Instead, OTA identified two primary loci of technology transfer at NIH: the consensus development conferences and other activities managed by the Office of Medical Applications of Research (OMAR); and the clinical research programs at several ICDs. Despite its noncommercial orientation, OMAR became the designated Office of Research and Technology Application (ORTA) under Stevenson-Wydler and remained the focus of technology transfer until FTTA.

Following FTTA, this focus shifted markedly. The shift was not entirely attributable to the legislation, however, because biomedical research was then in the throes of a social revolution. The technical revolution had occurred in the early 1970s with the development of recombinant DNA. The social revolution followed the awarding of patents to the co-discoverors of the technique, Stanley Cohen of Stanford and Herbert Boyer of the University of California, San Francisco.[28] Prior to the Cohen-Boyer patents, NIH had a distant relationship with industry; but as the 1980s progressed, there was "a significant increase in NIH interactions with industry, owing in large part to the rise in biotechnology industries fostered by NIH-supported discoveries" in molecular biology.[29] The technology transfer legislation catalyzed this new interaction.

Implementing FTTA at NIH

In 1988, NIH established an Office of Invention Development, which then became the designated ORTA. From a three-person office, it grew into the Office of Technology Transfer (OTT), which directs all technology transfer activities of the Department of Health and Human Services (including the Centers for Disease Control and the Food and Drug Administration), employing the equivalent of 55 full-time staffers, some 40 of whom hold advanced degrees, including PhDs. Its FY1997 budget was about $4.1 million, derived from fees and the receipts of a service formula paid by the ICDs.

OTT is responsible for overseeing the prosecution of patents, marketing technologies, and negotiating licensing agreements, and overseeing and reviewing CRADAs. OTT also maintains close contact with Technology Development Coordinators (TDCs) in each of the ICDs, who work more directly with the researchers involved with technology transfer.[30]

Table 9-2 shows the growth of various kinds of technology transfer activities at NIH since 1985.[31] Researchers who believe that they may have a new invention file disclosures, or employee invention reports (EIRs). Most ICDs have a scientific review board to evaluate the invention reports and, with OTT's advice, decide whether or not to file a patent application.[32] OTT markets and attempts to license new technologies, with concurrence from the ICD.[33]

EIRs, patent applications, patents, licenses, and royalties are thus important output measures of technology transfer activities. The number of EIRs rose from 100 in FY1985 to 271 in FY1995, but declined to 196 in FY1996, perhaps because researchers are more often anticipating that patents will not be filed on their inventions and are therefore deciding not to submit EIRs. Patent applications rose from 62 in FY1985 to a high of 202 in FY1992, and fell back to

Table 9-2 Technology Transfer Activities at NIH, FY 1985–96

	Invention disclosures	Patent applications	Issued patents	Executed licenses	Royalties ($1000)
FY85	100	62	33	25	0
FY86	100	78	27	38	0
FY87	134	85	29	35	4,245
FY88	185	125	35	44	5,405
FY89	199	178	27	50	4,784
FY90	212	184	38	41	5,827
FY91	204	169	43	61	13,284
FY92	262	202	70	59	10,044
FY93	232	161	88	75	13,494
FY94	259	143	75	125	18,487
FY95	271	147	95	160	19,388
FY96	196	136	107	184	26,995
Total	**2354**	**1670**	**667**	**897**	**121,953**

136 in FY1996—the result of an intentional strategy to reduce time-consuming and costly "over-patenting." OTT maintains data about EIRs, patents, etc., only for the year of occurrence; it does not follow individual EIRs to determine what percentage become patent applications, or what percentage of applications become patents. Likewise, OTT cannot determine an indicator of what might be called "research patent productivity," that is, patents per research dollar expended (unit output per unit input), because patents are logged by the fiscal year in which they are awarded and not by the fiscal year in which the research leading to the patent was performed.

Although these measures of the production of intellectual property are important indicators, it does not follow that technology transfer policy should seek to maximize all or any of them. Maximizing royalties, which demonstrate the commercial success of a transferred technology, neglects contributions to public health that cannot be measured through sales. It might also bias negotiations in favor of granting exclusive licenses, which may bear greater royalties, than nonexclusive ones. Royalty payments also lag significantly, as many years may pass before commercialization because of the need for further development and, often, regulatory approval. Maximizing licenses means emphasizing outputs rather than actual market or other social outcomes; licenses signify only potential commercial success. Maximizing patents or patent applications creates questions of the quality of inventions and the internal allocation of staff and other resources for patent filings.

It might, however, be useful to seek to maximize the number of employee invention reports; this tactic would provide a reasonable performance measure of whether the idea of technology transfer had become a value for researchers rather than just a bureaucratic requirement. The quantity of EIRs seems a reasonable proxy for the commitment of researchers, and the ability of technology transfer organizations, to pursue the mission of technology transfer as established by Congress. In this view, the recent decline in EIRs is distressing.

Congress was explicit about its intention to create incentives for individual researchers by redistributing royalties to inventors and by directing agencies to include technology transfer activities in personnel decisions. The former incentive was re-emphasized by Congress in NTTA, but the status of the latter is unclear. There has been no specific follow-up to GAO's 1989 finding that most laboratories were not including technology transfer activities in personnel decisions, but neither is there any clear sense of how to include these activities positively in personnel review without penalizing researchers who do not engage in them (it was likewise Congress's intent to refrain from such penalties).

At NIH, promotion and tenure decisions for intramural researchers are managed at each ICD and judged by an external scientific panel, and therefore each ICD's policy may be different. The primary criterion remains, as it should, scientific quality. Because researchers are also judged for productivity according to their resources (CRADAs contribute considerable resources), the contribution of cooperative research is included in the review process in a partial way. But other technology transfer activities, such as filing EIRs, are seemingly unnoticed. The lack of clarity about the importance of technology transfer activities in personnel decisions puts NIH, and perhaps other agencies, in a politically vulnerable position.

CRADAs at NIH

One way in which the CRADA facilitates research collaborations between federal and nonfederal laboratories is through prior settlement of the disposition of intellectual property rights a way favorable to the nonfederal partner. These collaborations promote nonfederal access to the unique resources and expertise of federal laboratories, as well as federal access to the often-proprietary resources of nonfederal laboratories. For research in the public health mission of NIH, for example, nonfederal laboratories may gain access to novel gene therapy techniques refined by NIH researchers; federal researchers may gain access to proprietary reagents or to commercial-scale facilities for the production of potential new drugs.

Different agencies or laboratories may have different criteria for engaging in CRADAs. NIH articulates a general policy that asserts the primacy of its mission in biomedical research.[34] NIH maintains that any CRADA must be a highly focused research plan advancing a scientific purpose that could not be more appropriately achieved through any other mechanism. A majority of a lab's funding should not come from CRADAs, and CRADAs must not exist for the sole purpose of supporting fellows or technicians, obtaining supplies and equipment, or conducting research or tests for the collabora-tor. Other agencies may have more or less stringent general policies for establishing CRADAs—which may be appropriate for their specific missions—and the total number of CRADAs entered into may reflect these constraints.

NIH had executed 352 CRADAs through FY1996 and an addi-tional 17 in the first third of FY1997. Of these, 174 are still active for at least part of FY1997. Table 9-3 shows the distribution of the 352 CRADAs across the ICDs.[35] In FY1996, NIH introduced a new form of CRADA, the material transfer agreement CRADA (MTA-CRADA). The 40 new MTA-CRADAs account for the jump in FY1996. Re-searchers pursue MTA-CRADAs when they require a proprietary research material (e.g., a compound, reagent, cell line, etc.) from an outside source, but the scope of issues (e.g., the desire of the material's owner to maintain an interest in commercial products derived from it) goes beyond a simple material transfer agreement. The existence of MTA-CRADAs allows a finer assessment of CRADA

Table 9-3   Executed NIH CRADAs by ICD, FY85–96

ICD	FY85	FY86	FY87	FY88	FY89
Cancer Institute	1	2	8	6	16
Center for Human Genome Research	0	0	0	0	0
Center for Research Resources	0	0	0	2	0
Division of Computer Research and Technology	0	0	0	0	0
Eye Institute	0	0	0	0	0
Heart, Lung, and Blood Institute	0	0	0	0	1
Institute for Child Health and Human Development	0	0	0	3	0
Institute of Allergy and Infectious Diseases	0	0	0	0	4
Institute of Arthritis and Musculo-skelatal and Skin Diseases	0	0	0	0	1
Institute of Dental Research	0	1	1	0	2
Institute of Diabetes and Digestive and Kidney Diseases	0	0	1	1	3
Institute of Environmental Health Sciences	0	0	0	0	0
Institute of Mental Health	0	0	0	3	9
Institute of Neurological Disorders and Stroke	0	0	0	3	4
Institute on Aging	0	0	0	1	0
Institute on Drug Abuse	0	0	0	0	0
Institute on Deafness and other Communication Disorders	0	0	0	0	0
Warrren G. Magnuson Clinical Center	0	0	0	0	0
JOINT	0	1	0	1	2
Total	1	4	10	20	42

FY90	FY91	FY92	FY93	FY94	FY95	FY96	Total
9	10	7	10	8	9	20	106
0	0	0	0	0	3	10	13
1	0	0	0	0	0	0	3
1	0	0	0	0	0	0	1
3	0	1	1	1	1	0	7
0	2	3	2	1	4	4	17
0	1	1	1	0	0	3	9
4	4	9	7	7	6	15	56
0	0	0	0	0	0	2	3
3	0	2	3	1	0	3	16
4	4	2	4	5	2	5	31
0	0	0	1	1	2	4	8
3	0	2	6	1	1	1	26
3	2	0	3	2	2	9	28
0	0	0	0	1	0	2	4
0	2	1	0	1	1	0	5
0	0	0	0	0	0	2	2
1	0	1	2	1	1	0	6
0	1	1	1	1	0	3	11
32	26	30	41	31	32	83	352

activity because it allows collaborations that are essentially over materials to be separated from more interactive collaborations. MTA-CRADAs are also evidence that the availability of protections for proprietary technologies benefits intramural researchers in the normal course of their research, regardless of its commercial potential, for without them, the NIH researchers either could not pursue a line of research or would waste valuable time replicating an extant technology.

MTA-CRADAs are generally initiated by government researchers, as are many standard CRADAs at NIH. Although some research suggests that CRADAs initiated by the nonfederal partner are more commercially successful,[36] government-initiated CRADAs should not be discouraged, especially when there is a valid scientific objective for mission-oriented research.

NIH has executed thirteen licenses based on CRADAs. Because OTT does not keep track of the number of patent applications or patents from CRADAs specifically, and because of the difficulties attached to these kind of indicators, it is hard to use them to judge the efficacy of CRADAs themselves. GAO has taken a descriptive approach to the benefits of CRADAs, simply providing short case studies of CRADAs.[37] OTT is also looking to a more descriptive approach, particularly for CRADAs' public health impact.[38]

Other ways to assess CRADAs focus on their cooperative nature, rather than their less important commercial nature. Their leveraging impact can be measured by tracking the in-kind resources provided by both partners, as well as any direct financial support provided by the nonfederal partner.[39] NIH has gathered only the aggregate, direct financial contribution of nonfederal CRADA partners since FY1993. Those totals, by fiscal year, are: FY1993, $9.3 million; FY1994, $7.3 million; FY1995, $8.1 million; FY1996, $7.4 million.[40] More specific data of this type would be useful for evaluating the ability of CRADAs to leverage nonfederal investment. A second is to recognize that CRADAs may be good in themselves, as their ability to facilitate networks of researchers across sectoral boundaries may spur the formation of social capital and the ability to cope with complexity. Biomedical faculty, for example, who receive up to two-thirds of their research support from industry are more professionally active than their colleagues who did not receive industrial support.[41] This increased activity may hold true for federal participants in CRADAs as well.

Access

Access to CRADAs is generally first come, first served. The explicit intent of Congress in FTTA was to prevent the intricacies of procurement and competitive bidding from delaying or complicating cooperative research. Because CRADAs may have commercial potential, the possibility exists of creating "sore losers" who might cause political trouble. The degree of threat is likely to be related to the relative supply of and demand for CRADAs: if the demand outstrips supply, individual sore losers may attack the policy as unfair, and collective action is also possible.[42] NIH does see some examples of sore losers, particularly in the hottest technologies in its portfolio. But overall, the sense is that firms find the policy beneficial and understand that they would be worse off if NIH's $1.3 billion in-house R&D enterprise were inaccessible.

Another type of problem, seen with respect to DOE CRADAs, is that some firms view the collaborative activities as unfairly subsidizing or even creating competitors within an already mature product market. Such firms seem not to find the activities threatening—at least not yet—because they are skeptical of DOE's and the new partners' ability to develop and market new technologies. It therefore appears that the aggressive marketing of new technologies may be a sub-optimal strategy because it could spur opposition by established firms.[43] Nevertheless, "the risks of dealing with private firms on an exclusive basis may be overestimated," as Robert Carr has said, pointing to the forty years of experience at the National Institute of Standards and Technology with cooperative R&D—often in exclusive arrangements—without a single legal challenge.[44]

FTTA entitles small businesses to special consideration in licensing and CRADAs (and those that are located in the United States and agree to manufacture in the United States are entitled to preference). Through FY 1996, slightly more than 50 percent of NIH CRADAs have been executed with small businesses, slightly more than 40 percent with large businesses, and the remainder with organizations such as hospitals or universities (or jointly with other such organizations and businesses).[45] These numbers suggest that the expectation that larger companies would benefit more from cooperative research—because significant internal research capacity is required to make use of collaborations[46]—is misplaced, or at least corrected by the special consideration. Even small biotechnology companies tend to be research-intensive and may have the capacity to utilize CRADAs. The mix of small and large businesses will vary from agency to agency (and lab to lab), based on the nature of the associated industry, the presence of a local cluster of R&D-related activities, and other factors.[47]

Fair Pricing

The only important innovation during the Clinton administration with respect to technology transfer policy at NIH has been the elimination of the so-called fair pricing clause of CRADAs and licensing agreements, which stated that a licensee might be required to "submit documentation in confidence showing a reasonable relationship between the pricing of a Licensed Product, the public investment in that product and the health and safety needs of the public." The clause did not restrict the licensee's right to "obtain a reasonable profit."[48] The issue of fair pricing initially arose before the passage of FTTA during the dispute over the cost of the drug AZT which, when introduced exclusively by Burroughs-Wellcome after NIH researchers collaborated in its development, was the only drug available to treat AIDS. The fair pricing issue also arose with the collaboration between NIH and Bristol-Myers Squibb over another AIDS drug, called ddI. In neither case did the government actually invoke the clause to help set a price.

Some in the biotechnology industry feared that the clause would be expanded to extramural research, and Representative Ron Wyden (D-OR) had introduced a bill in 1993 that would have set prices for CRADA-developed drugs.[49] Others felt that NIH should not engage in regulation because of its lack of statutory authority and experience. Furthermore, the Clinton administration's rhetoric about the price of pharmaceuticals during the health care debate unsettled potential industrial research partners.[50] In July 1994, a special advisory panel recommended that NIH jettison the clause;[51] after a second meeting, NIH eliminated it in the spring of 1995.[52]

Nevertheless, under NTTA and as expressed in NIH's model CRADA, the government retains the right to a nonexclusive worldwide license to CRADA inventions made solely by the nonfederal partner "for research or other Government purposes."[53] For CRADA inventions made by a government researcher or jointly with the collaborator and licensed exclusively, the government retains the right to require third-party licensing "on terms that are reasonable under the circumstances," but only in "exceptional circumstances" where the government determines that health, safety, or regulatory needs require it; such determination is subject to administrative appeal and judicial review.[54]

Unresolved Issues

The broad outlines and many of the details of CRADA policy are clearly established, but a small number of unresolved issues remain. Some of them, such as questions of intellectual property and the availability of appropriate indicators, need to be resolved so the current policy can operate as efficiently as possible. Others, such as the role of CRADAs and technology transfer more generally, may affect the policy's intellectual coherence, as well as political support for technology policy generally.

Intellectual Property

The elimination of the fair pricing clause reduced a great deal of the uncertainty about the government role in CRADAs. However, other vague and difficult portions of the relevant statutes remain. The meaning of the government's rights to license technologies themselves or to compel third-party licensing—essential, given the commitment of public resources to CRADAs—must be clarified. Some uncertainty exists regarding the government's rights to inventions from collaborations for "Government purposes" beyond the narrower "research" purposes. Authoritative definition of these purposes would help quell some discomfort among potential collaborators and help provide a more predictable environment for investment. Another vague area is the FTTA mandate to give preference to companies that "substantially manufacture" CRADA inventions in the United States. FTTA does not define "substantially," and different agencies use different criteria.[55]

NTTA gave nonfederal partners the opportunity to choose an exclusive license for CRADA inventions; the Department of Commerce endorsed this proposal.[56] One perspective is that anything that can be done to help companies secure intellectual property rights for themselves from the beginning makes CRADAs more effective.[57] But the option for exclusive licenses might be an excessive inducement for at least two reasons. First, significant growth has unexpectedly occurred in nonexclusive licenses, which contradicts the "Bayh-Dole Act's assumption that exclusive licenses are needed to encourage the private sector to commercialize federal technology."[58] Furthermore, some technologies—like generic or platform technologies—are inappropriate for exclusive licenses because the private partner may not be technically or commercially competent to develop the technology into all its possible niches. The Cohen-Boyer recombinant DNA patents are an example of nonexclusive licensing and widespread commercialization.[59] Methods of performing ex-vivo gene therapy are a platform technology developed through CRADAs and exclusively licensed to Genetic Therapy, Inc., a firm created to commercialize the technology.[60] Any such arrangement with exclusive licenses should be monitored closely, and agencies should construe the field of application carefully to prevent exclusivity from giving firms control over technologies beyond their ability to commercialize them.

Although the ability of private partners to secure intellectual property rights is a key to unlocking the ability of federal laboratories to contribute to economic and other goals through collaborative research, it is still not clear whether such security decreases or increases technology transfer over the long term. Assigning the intellectual property rights to research materials, for example, runs counter to the norm of communalism within the scientific community,[61] but it also encourages the disclosure of materials which otherwise might be held as trade secrets. Although the normative guidance of communalism is romanticized,[62] it is possible that dense nexuses of licenses, materials transfer agreements, etc., may ultimately constrain commercialization by raising transaction costs for researchers to intolerable levels. A novel pharmaceutical, for example, may have been derived from a number of proprietary materials, and the claims of each proprietor on derivative products may render it unprofitable to pursue.

Some research on how publicly sponsored research supports private R&D in the pharmaceutical industry suggests that openness and other noncommercial norms of public sector R&D encourages the adoption of such norms in private R&D, to the benefit of the productivity of the latter. Thus, "policies [such as CRADAs] which weaken these [public sector] institutions, make public sector researchers more market-oriented, or redistribute rents through efforts to increase the appropriability of public research through restrictions on the ways in which public and private sectors work with each other may therefore be counterproductive in the long run."[63] The logic behind this argument is that firms that invest in basic research—whose laboratories have reward structures more similar to those of universities and government laboratories—have greater absorptive capacity than firms that do not make such investments, and that they can thus make better use of public investments. But with CRADAs, it is possible both that norms among federal researchers will not become more commercial (because many CRADAs do not involve commercial intentions) and that public norms could continue to influence commercial laboratories.

Implicit Goals

Technology transfer policy also has implicit goals, the achievement of which would not necessarily be socially optimal. One goal is to strengthen the labs politically in a time of fiscal stress and mission uncertainty by helping to link them to a broader economic and geographic constituency. Although CRADAs and other cooperative activities are important aspects of the laboratories' R&D programs and make real, if economically slight, contributions, the ability of labs to transfer technology seems a relatively thin rationale for maintaining the status quo at many of the laboratories.[64]

A second implicit goal is to prevent "brain drain" from the laboratories by giving intramural researchers the same opportunities to interact more closely with commercial interests and to profit from interactions that are enjoyed by extramural researchers. Assessing the achievement of this goal would take extremely detailed empirical work. Because knowledge flows among sectors are crucial to innovation, the prevention of brain drain may only be good if technology transfer more than substitutes for the knowledge flow that would have taken place. Moreover, the ability to cooperate with researchers in private firms may provide government scientists with greater exposure to different research environments and thus an inducement to leave, and the opportunity to engage in CRADAs may allow firms to retain their researchers, thus maintaining private research capacity. Of course, these flows of research personnel and knowledge will have different impacts on different industries based on, for example, the relative importance of new and established firms in innovation. The ambiguous effects of the assignment of intellectual property rights and of the implicit goals of technology transfer on innovation mean that developing more sophisticated indicators and other ways to evaluate the policy is essential.

Indicators

The creation of new intellectual property, with its licenses and royalty income, is not the essence of technology transfer, and technology transfer policy should not be evaluated along strictly economic criteria. David Roessner concludes that, "measures such as numbers of licenses and royalty payments attributable to federal research will substantially underestimate the full value of the labs to industry."[65] Productivity indicators could be useful for strategic planning purposes, and at the national level for informed portfolio management.[66] This combination of indicators and management style might help us better articulate what expectations of social and economic return we should have for cooperative research.

The ability of the laboratories and agencies to collect and organize appropriate indicators, let alone use them to evaluate programs and policy, is extremely limited. In 1994, the federal government's Interagency Committee on Federal Technology

Transfer issued a draft report on measures "for determining the impacts of federal technology transfer on the U.S. economy and U.S. competitiveness," but the draft was never followed up. (See also Adam Jaffe, "Measurement and Evaluation Issues," Chapter 3 in this volume.)[67] OTT has limited personnel resources and its database is not appropriately organized for such evaluation. DOE, which had maintained a more flexible and comprehensive database, suffered under a FY 1996 appropriation that eliminated the office maintaining this database. No current department-wide data are available from DOE, and data for FY 1996 are incomplete.

Small Business Technology Transfer Program

Congress was sensitive to the difficulty that CRADAs might cause in blending public and private interests. It therefore prohibited the use of federally appropriated money in CRADAs, even while it allowed federal employees and their laboratories and equipment to participate. The Small Business Technology Transfer (STTR) program seems to provide for an end run around the prohibition. Title II of the Small Business Research and Development Enhancement Act of 1992 (P.L. 102-564) amends the Small Business Innovation Act to establish STTR, a three-year pilot program under which a small fraction of a department's extramural R&D budget is set aside for awards to small businesses for collaborative R&D with nonprofit research institutions.[68] This pilot program counts GOCOs as nonprofit research institutions, and at DOE the mechanism of collaboration between a participating small business and the laboratory is the CRADA. STTR thus circumvents the prohibition by providing competitive grants to small businesses to collaborate. STTR also channels extramural grant money to GOCOs in a similar fashion. Other programs that stimulate government-industry partnerships may take advantage of this circuitous public funding of CRADAs, seemingly contrary to FTTA.[69]

CRADAs and Technology Policy

Linda Cohen and Roger Noll have argued that the economics of CRADAs are questionable. On the one hand, federal laboratories could not become "a significant factor in commercial R&D" because "the relevance of most work at national laboratories to commercial technology appears distant at best." On the other hand, broadening the ability of laboratories to make CRADAs more commercially relevant will drive the laboratories away from their missions.[70] The argument that R&D at the laboratories is commercially irrelevant, however, assumes the evidence. The output measures are at least suggestive of relevance, and the surveys conducted by Roessner and Bean and by Bozeman and Crow provide solid evidence of the desirability of cooperative R&D to firms.

Cohen and Noll further argue that "for a business to want to enter into a CRADA, it must expect to profit from its contribution to the joint R&D effort. The prospects for profitable exploitation of CRADA work depend on retaining property rights in the results of the research." If one infers that "the results of the research" are limited to inventions capable of being protected as intellectual property, then the claim is false; this is demonstrated by the surveys of potential and actual private sector partners, who acknowledge that access to expertise, research equipment, and other resources is a more important benefit to their firms than the potential of a commercial product. If one infers that companies must find positive value in the commercial potential, access to expertise, more learned and experienced research employees, etc., then no one is in a better position to judge than the companies themselves. If CRADAs leverage research capacity, educate a firm's researchers, and help that firm retain them, these outcomes can be as beneficial to the firm as new intellectual property.

Because CRADAs "require a high level of technical sophistication on the part of industry partners" to take advantage of the federal investment in R&D, as the National Academy of Sciences argues,[71] CRADAs and other technology transfer mechanisms are not a complete technology policy. Policies beyond technology transfer that help firms and other organizations build this capacity are also crucial to making the most of the direct federal investment in R&D. Indeed, this is one of the main messages of this book.

Recommendations

Technology transfer policy is a new way of doing business, elaborated by a complex of laws written over nearly two decades. There is broad political agreement on the outlines of this new way of doing business, with major pieces of legislation passed by both Republican and Democratic Congresses, and implemented and extended by administrations of both parties. Details of the policy are also subject to broad agreement, but some areas of uncertainty prevent the partnerships enabled by technology transfer policy from being as frequent and productive as possible.

CRADAs, a centerpiece of technology transfer policy, provide opportunities for federal and nonfederal laboratories to collaborate on research. Although the commercial potential of CRADAs is apparent to both parties, it is inappropriate to consider CRADAs primarily, or even substantially, as commercial development enterprises. Nonfederal participants in CRADAs say that they benefit more from the access to unique or less costly resources and expertise in the federal laboratories than they do from any specific commercial potential. Furthermore, as MTA-CRADAs at NIH demonstrate, federal researchers take advantage of the reciprocal access to private sector expertise and materials to accomplish their mission-related R&D as well.

Despite many indications of important collaborative and commercial activities enabled by technology transfer policy, it is not yet clear that strict intellectual property provisions in government R&D will be productive in the long run. Technology transfer policy has not only changed the technical dynamics of federal laboratories, but also their political dynamics. The implementation of technology transfer policy therefore continues to deserve the most informed scrutiny and oversight, based on sound and appropriate indicators of performance.

To inform and improve the implementation of technology transfer policy:

• Congress should enable all federal R&D agencies to develop, collect, organize, and analyze department-wide data on technology transfer activities;

• Agencies should make developing, collecting, organizing, and analyzing such data a priority; such data should include indicators of the productivity of research, the amount of private and public funds leveraged by CRADAs, and measures of mission-specific and other noncommercial outcomes;

• Agencies and laboratories should clarify and formalize, to the extent possible, the positive role in which researchers' technology transfer activities are considered in personnel decisions; specifically, they should consider providing additional incentives for the filing of invention reports;

• The Office of Science and Technology Policy or other appropriate offices should help agencies clarify areas of interpretation that continue to cause uncertainty, particularly the meaning of "substantially manufactured" under FTTA and "Government purposes" under NTTA;

• Congress and agencies should examine closely the experience with exclusive licenses to assure themselves and the public that nonfederal partners are not gaining control of technologies that they lack the technical or commercial skills to develop fully;

• Congress should examine closely the scope of participation of GOCO laboratories in the Small Business Technology Transfer program (STTR) and other partnerships in which federal extramural research funds may be used to fund CRADAs.

Adopting these recommendations will go a long way toward perfecting technology transfer policy. But because technology transfer is a capacity-leveraging and not a capacity-building policy, it should never be the entirety of federal technology policy.

Acknowledgments

The author gratefully acknowledges assistance from Donna Adderly, David Bellis, Bruce Bimber, Darin Boville, Kay Etzler, Paulette Goodman, Sonny Kreitman, Steven Lee, Barbara M. McGarey, James Raffel, David Roessner, Mark Rohrbaugh, Tyrone Taylor, and Christopher Tucker.

Notes

1. There are more than 700 federal laboratories, which are often separated into those that are both government-owned and government-operated (GOGOs) and those that are government-owned but contractor-operated (GOCOs). For the spending figure, see National Science Foundation, *Science and Engineering Indicators*, <http://www.nsf.gov/sbe/srs/seind96/start.htm>, table 100a.

2. For collaborative research involving university laboratories and private firms, see Harvey Brooks and Lucien Randazzese, "University-Industry Relations," Chapter 14 in this volume.

3. John A. Alic, Lewis M. Branscomb, Harvey Brooks, Ashton B. Carter, and Gerald L. Epstein, *Beyond Spinoff: Military and Commercial Technologies in a Changing World* (Boston: Harvard Business School Press, 1992).

4. See Samuel I. Doctors, *The Role of Federal Agencies in Technology Transfer*, with a foreword by Harvey Brooks (Cambridge: The MIT Press, 1969).

5. ORTAs largely replaced the licensing role of the National Technical Information Service.

6. In 1980, "at least 24 different patent policies were in effect in the federal agencies." Department of Commerce (DOC), Office of Technology Policy, *Effective Partnering: A Report to Congress on Federal Technology Partnerships* (Washington, D.C.: DOC, April 1996), p. 26.

7. By unifying and "liberalizing" federal patent policies, Bayh-Dole finally enacted the preferences that Vannevar Bush had espoused; see Vannevar Bush, *Science, The Endless Frontier* (Washington, D.C.: National Science Foundation, 1980 [orig. 1945]).

8. Richard E. Nelson and Paul M. Romer, "Science, Economic Growth and Public Policy," in Bruce L.R. Smith and Claude E. Barfield, eds., *Technology, R&D, and the Economy* (Washington, D.C.: Brookings Institution and American Enterprise Institute, 1996), pp. 49–74.

9. The so-called Packard Report found quality and productivity problems at the national laboratories and recommended that they be encouraged to interact more with both universities and industry. Office of Science and Technology Policy, *Report of the White House Science Council* (Washington, D.C.: Executive Office of the President, 1983).

10. See Senate Report 99-283: p. 2.

11. The order directed agencies to delegate CRADA authority to the laboratories themselves; FTTA had only authorized such delegation.

12. General Accounting Office (GAO), *Technology Transfer: Implementation Status of the Federal Technology Transfer Act of 1986*, RCED-89-154 (Washington, D.C.: GAO, 1989). FTTA had specified that agencies should review their conflicts of interest regulations; NIH needed to promulgate a new set of rules.

13. GAO, *Implementation of the Technology Transfer Act: A Preliminary Assessment*, T-PEMD-90-4 (Washington, D.C.: GAO, 1990).

14. GAO, *Diffusing Innovations: Implementing the Technology Transfer Act of 1986*, PEMD-91-23 (Washington, D.C.: GAO, 1991), p. 11.

15. Secretary of Commerce, *Technology Transfer Under the Stevenson-Wydler Technology Innovation Act: The Second Biennial Report*, Report to the President and Congress (Washington, D.C.: Department of Commerce, 1993).

16. DOC, *Effective Partnering*.

17. From DOC, *Effective Partnering*, figure 8. It is important to distinguish active CRADAs from executed CRADAs. CRADAs usually last for longer than one year, so a CRADA executed in 1990 may be active in 1990, 1991, and 1992.

18. GAO, *Technology Transfer: Barriers Limit Royalty Sharing's Effectiveness*, RCED-93-6 (Washington, D.C.: GAO, 1992).

19. David Roessner and Alden S. Bean, "Industry Interactions with Federal Labs Pays Off," *Research Technology Management*, September–October 1993, pp. 38–40.

20. Barry Bozeman and Michael Maurice Crow, "Red Tape and Technology Transfer in U.S. Government Laboratories," *Journal of Technology Transfer*, Spring 1991, pp. 29–37.

21. Barry Bozeman and Michael Crow, *Limited By Design: Federal Laboratories and the U.S. National Innovation System* (New York: Columbia University Press, forthcoming), chap. 5.

22. Roessner and Bean, "Industry Interactions with Federal Labs Pays Off"; Bozeman and Crow, *Limited By Design*, chap. 6.

23. Bozeman and Crow, *Limited By Design*, chap. 6; David Roessner and Alden Bean, "Patterns of Interaction with Federal Laboratories," *Journal of Technology Transfer*, December 1994, pp. 59–77.

24. Bozeman and Crow, *Limited By Design*, chap. 6.

25. Intersociety Working Group, *AAAS Report XXI: Research and Development, FY 1997* (Washington, D.C.: American Association for the Advancement of Science, 1996).

26. It is to the ICDs that the delegation of authority in E.O. 12591 applies.

27. Office of Technology Assessment, *Technology Transfer at the National Institutes of Health*, OTA-TM-H-10 (Washington, D.C.: U.S. Government Printing Office [U.S. GPO], 1982).

28. Stanford licenses the patents in a nonexclusive but royalty-bearing fashion.

29. Phillip S. Chen, Jr., "How the NIH forms linkages with participating companies," National Institutes of Health, November 4, 1987 (Bethesda). Also see Richard L. Chapman, "Implementing the 1986 Act: Signs of Progress," *Journal of Technology Transfer*, Winter 1989, pp. 5–13.

30. OTT web site, <http://www.nih.gov/od/ott/>.

31. Derived from data on NIH technology transfer activities, provided by NIH OTT.

32. Some ICDs also review papers prior to publication for technology transfer purposes.

33. ICDs with larger technology transfer operations may be more involved than those with smaller ones.

34. Public Health Service, "PHS Cooperative Research and Development Agreement Policy," *Technology Transfer Manual*, Chapter No. 400 (PHS Technology Transfer Policy Board, mimeo, January 25, 1996).

35. From data on executed CRADAs, FY1985–FY1996, provided by NIH OTT; ICDs with no executed CRADAs omitted.

36. Bozeman and Crow, *Limited By Design*.

37. GAO, *Technology Transfers: Benefits of Cooperative R&D Agreements* GAO/RCED-95-52 (Washington, D.C.: GAO, 1994).

38. See "The NIH 'Top Twenty' Inventions with Significant Current Commercial Product Sales," which provides brief case histories of important technology transfer products, from NIH OTT.

39. OMB has requested such data in the past from OTT, but I have yet to be able to obtain it. DOE provides aggregate financial data on the total contributions of federal and non-federal partners. The total contribution (funding plus in-kind) for fiscal years 1993 to 1996 for all DOE CRADAs was approximately $337 million, $397 million, $312 million, and $200 million, respectively. Data for FY 1996 are incomplete.

40. Data provided by NIH Office of Financial Management.

41. See David Blumenthal, Eric G. Campbell, Nancyanne Causino, and Karen Seashore Louis, "Participation of Life-Science Faculty in Research Relationships with Industry," *The New England Journal of Medicine*, Vol. 335 (December 5, 1996), pp. 1734–1739. For prescriptions for technology policies that face complexity, see Don E. Kash and Robert Rycroft, "Technology Policy in the 21st Century: How Will We Adapt to Complexity?" Annual Meeting of the American Association for the Advancement of Science, Seattle, February 1996. For more on research and social capital, see Jane Fountain, "Social Capital," Chapter 4 in this volume.

42. Linda Cohen and Roger G. Noll, "Feasibility of Effective Public-Private R&D Collaboration: The Case of Cooperative R&D Agreements," *International Journal of the Economics of Business*, Vol. 2, No. 2 (1995), pp. 223–240.

43. I am grateful to James Raffel for bringing this example to my attention.

44. Robert K. Carr, "Doing Technology Transfer in Federal Laboratories (Part 1)," *Journal of Technology Transfer*, Spring-Summer 1992, pp. 8–23.

45. From data on executed CRADAs, FY1985–FY1996, provided by NIH OTT.

46. David Roessner and Anne Wise, "Public Policy and Emerging Sources of Technology and Technical Information Available to Industry," *Policy Studies Journal*, Vol. 22, No. 2 (1994), pp. 349–358.

47. Through FY1996, approximately 42 percent of DOE CRADAs have been with small businesses, 20 percent with large businesses, and fewer than 5 percent with academic institutions, other nonprofit organizations, and state or local governments. From "Aggregated Data Summary, Non-Federal Partner Type" (as of November 27, 1996), provided by DOE Office of Scientific and Technical Information. These data may be more easily available from DOE because until recently, unlike other agencies, each DOE "laboratory receives a separate budget allocation for in-kind and project cost related to CRADAs. These annual CRADA

budgets may not be exceeded, nor may funds from other accounts be transferred into CRADA budgets." Evan Michael Berman, "Technology Transfer and the Federal Laboratories: A Midterm Assessment of Cooperative Research," *Policy Studies Journal*, Vol. 22, No. 2 (1994), pp. 338–348.

48. Office of Technology Transfer, "[Model] Patent License Agreement, Exclusive," *1991 PHS Technology Transfer Directory* (Bethesda, Md.: NIH, 1991), p. 191.

49. Telephone interview with Chuck Ludlam, Biotechnology Industry Organization, December 30, 1996; Christopher Anderson, "NIH panel rejects pricing clause," *Science* (Vol. 265), July 29, 1994, p. 598.

50. OTA found that of twenty-nine companies surveyed, fourteen found the fair pricing clause to be a major concern causing them to "forego or retreat from a CRADA," while eight found it only a minor concern and seven of no concern at all. Office of Technology Assessment, *Federal Technology Transfer and the Human Genome Project: Background Paper*, OTA-BP-EHR-162 (Washington, D.C.: U.S. GPO, 1995), p. 34; also see Berman, "Technology Transfer and the Federal Laboratories," p. 345.

51. Anderson, "NIH panel rejects pricing clause."

52. Despite NIH's elimination of the clause, Representative Bernie Sanders (I-VT) regularly introduces a rider to NIH's appropriation to reinstate a fair pricing requirement.

53. Model PHS CRADA (form 053096), Article 7.4.

54. Model PHS CRADA, Article 7.5.

55. Berman, "Technology Transfer and the Federal Laboratories," p. 343.

56. DOC, *Effective Partnering*, p. 72; p. 15.

57. Ludlam interview.

58. DOC, *Effective Partnering*, p. 49.

59. Carr, "Doing Technology Transfer."

60. GTI has agreed to sublicense the technology.

61. Rebecca S. Eisenberg, "Patents and the Progress of Science: Exclusive Rights and Experimental Use," *The University of Chicago Law Review*, Vol. 56, No. 3 (1989), pp. 1017–1086.

62. Michael J. Mulkay, "Norms and ideology in science," *Social Science Information*, No. 4-5 (1975), pp. 637–656.

63. Iain Cockburn and Rebecca Henderson, "Public-Private Interaction and the Productivity of Pharmaceutical Research," Micro-BPEA Conference, Washington, D.C., June 1996, p. 26.

64. The economic impact of laboratories may be slight at the national level but profound at a local or regional level. See Secretary of Commerce, *Technology Transfer Under Stevenson-Wydler*; and Ann Markusen, James Raffel, Michael Odin, and Marlen Llanes, *Coming in from the Cold: The Future of Los Alamos and Sandia National Laboratories*, Working Paper No. 91, Center for Urban Policy Research/

Project on Regional and Industrial Economics (New Brunswick, N.J.: Rutgers, The State University of New Jersey, 1995).

65. David Roessner, "What Companies Want from the Federal Labs," *Issues in Science and Technology*, Vol. 10, No. 1 (1993), pp. 37–42, p. 42. Also Roessner and Bean, "Industry Interactions with Federal Labs Pays Off."

66. Michael McGeary and Philip M. Smith, "The R&D Portfolio: A Concept for Allocating Science and Technology Funds," *Science*, Vol. 274 (November 29, 1996), pp. 1484–1485.

67. Interagency Committee on Federal Technology Transfer, *Collective Reporting and Common Measures (Draft for Comment)*, Working Group on Technology Transfer Measurement and Evaluation (November 1994).

68. The legislation authorized the Departments of Defense, Energy, and Health and Human Services, as well as NASA and NSF, to participate in STTR. The size of the set-aside was set at 0.05 percent in FY 1994, 0.10 percent in FY 1995, and 0.15 percent in FY 1996 and FY 1997. For more on SBIR generally, see Scott Wallsten, "Rethinking the Small Business Innovation Research Program," Chapter 8 in this volume.

69. However, NASA, whose authority to engage in collaborative research flows from the Space Act, may spend public money on collaborative research.

70. Cohen and Noll, "Feasibility of Effective Public-Private R&D Collaboration."

71. National Academy of Sciences, *The Government Role in Civilian Technology: Building a New Alliance* (Washington, D.C.: National Academy Press, 1992), p. 146.

10

Manufacturing Extension: Performance, Challenges, and Policy Issues

Philip Shapira

One of the major successes of federal technology policy in the 1990s has been the development of a comprehensive system to support the deployment of new technologies and improved business practices among small and mid-sized manufacturing enterprises across the United States. At the start of the decade, the nation's infrastructure for such manufacturing extension services was patchy, comprising a handful of individual state programs, a few embryonic federal manufacturing technology centers, and a series of other rather uncoordinated federal and state technology transfer efforts. However, by 1997, more than seventy manufacturing technology centers or programs were operational in all fifty states, under the aegis of a national network of technology and business service providers known as the Manufacturing Extension Partnership (MEP). The MEP is a collaborative initiative between federal and state governments that also involves non-profit organizations, academic institutions, and industry groups. The MEP's federal sponsor, the National Institute of Standards and Technology (NIST), within the U.S. Department of Commerce, has emerged as a focal point of federal initiatives to assist manufacturing technology deployment and industrial competitiveness.

During a period when support for federal technology policy has been uncertain, the MEP represents a remarkable exception. The program has garnered a rare degree of broad bipartisan support; it is one of the few new federal technology policy initiatives to see its budget increased between 1992 and 1997. The MEP has also pioneered a collaborative management style: a variety of technology and business assistance providers in the public and private sectors are brought together to offer comprehensive, locally managed, and demand-driven services to small and mid-sized manufacturers. This approach stands in contrast to the fragmented "technology-push" methods that characterized many previous federal technology transfer programs.

At the same time, a series of challenges and opportunities face the MEP program, its stakeholders and industry partners, and the federal technology policy-making community. Institutional, organizational, and funding issues must be addressed as the MEP evolves from its rapid start-up phase in the early to mid-1990s to one of slower growth and maturity over the balance of the decade. There are concerns about where and how the program should concentrate its resources to achieve maximum effectiveness during the next stage of its development and operation, as well as issues related to the integration of the MEP with other federal technology and business assistance policies. After reviewing the recent growth of the MEP and its performance, this chapter considers these strategic issues and how they might be addressed.

The Development of the Manufacturing Extension Partnership

In the United States, manufacturing extension services focus mainly on industrial companies with fewer than 500 employees. There are some 380,000 of these small and mid-sized manufacturers, forming an important and integral part of America's industrial base. Many of these smaller firms find it difficult to introduce modern manufacturing technologies and methods.[1] There are market failures on both the demand and supply side. Smaller firms frequently lack information, expertise, time, money, and confidence to upgrade their manufacturing operations, resulting in under-investment in more productive technologies and missed opportunities to improve product performance, workforce training, quality, and waste reduction. At the same time, private consultants, equipment vendors, universities, and other assistance sources often overlook or cannot economically serve the needs of smaller firms; potential suppliers of information and assistance also face learning costs, a lack of expertise, or other barriers in promoting the diffusion of rewarding technologies. System-level factors, such as the lack of standardization, regulatory impediments, weaknesses in financial mechanisms, and poorly organized inter-firm relationships, further constrain the pace of technological diffusion and investment.

The MEP aims to address these problems by organizing manufacturing extension services that promote the diffusion and deployment of new technologies and improved business practices among industrial firms and also by coordinating networks of public and private service providers to better meet the needs of smaller firms, regions, and industries. Manufacturing extension centers typically employ industrially experienced field personnel who work directly with firms to identify needs, broker resources, and develop appropriate assistance projects. Manufacturing extension centers also offer a variety of other services, including information provision, technology demonstration, training, and referrals. Given the economy-wide benefits of accelerating the deployment of technology (considered in Chapter 2 by Michael Borrus and Jay Stowsky) and the difficulties many companies and industries face in independently implementing technological upgrades, the MEP is a classic example of how collective public action in partnership with the private sector can make markets and the economic development process more effective.

The seeds for the development of the MEP were planted before the 1990s. A few states have operated manufacturing extension programs since the 1950s and 1960s, while several others established programs in the 1980s in response to regional industrial decline and to stem the loss of manufacturing jobs.[2] These state programs served as models for federal initiatives. Additionally, in 1988, the Omnibus Trade and Competitiveness Act was passed by Congress, under Democratic party leadership, and approved by a Republican administration. Driven by national concerns about the loss of American industrial and technological competitiveness, this Act gave the National Institute of Standards and Technology (created from the old National Bureau of Standards) the mission of strengthening the civilian industrial base and supporting the formation of regional manufacturing technology centers to accelerate the adoption of new technologies by industry.

While there was a small increase in federal support for manufacturing extension in the first few years following the 1988 Act, by far the biggest expansion came after 1992. The Clinton administration pledged to build a national system of manufacturing centers to help small and medium-sized manufacturers adopt new technology, production techniques, and business practices.[3] This promise formed part of the administration's plan to deal with defense downsizing and to strengthen the country's technological infrastructure. Initially, 170 U.S. manufacturing centers were proposed—the number of equivalent technology centers in Japan. Later, the administration pared back its goal to one of establishing "100 manufacturing centers nationwide by 1997."[4] The administration supported this revised commitment with funding from its defense conversion initiative, the Technology Reinvestment Project (TRP), supplemented by additional funds through the regular Department of Commerce appropriation.[5] Federal funds, allocated through a competitive process and managed by NIST, were made available to states through what became known as the Manufacturing Extension Partnership; the states had to provide matching funding. These resources were used to expand existing state manufacturing extension programs as well as to establish new centers and programs. From a base of seven federally sponsored centers in 1992, the system grew rapidly to include MEP centers in 32 states at the end of 1994, and by 1997 there were more than 70 MEP centers, with at least one in each of the fifty states. Regional and national support programs have also been sponsored in such areas as manufacturing extension staff training, methods for customer assessment and performance benchmarking, and evaluation. In FY 1997, about $95 million in federal funding for the MEP plus some additional TRP funds were matched by at least a further $100 million, including mostly state and some private funds. In FY 1998, NIST will assume the complete federal share of the expanded MEP network without Department of Defense appropriations. Congressional action is pending on the FY 1998 budget, with an appropriation of $114 million under consideration (compared to the president's MEP budget request of $123 million). If approved, the MEP's FY 1998 federal budget will be more than six times the $18 million 1993 federal appropriation.

The change in congressional leadership after the fall 1994 election initially raised fears about ongoing support for the MEP program, as members of the new Republican majority expressed skepticism about the Clinton administration's technology policy initiatives.[6] However, bipartisan support for the MEP has been maintained. States, MEP centers (through their trade association, the Modernization Forum), and several other associated industry groups have worked with Congress to highlight the MEP's customer-driven market orientation, the involvement of private sector groups, its leveraging of non-federal resources, the program's "quality control" methods of ensuring that affiliated centers are well managed, and even its possible "budget-positive" effect through additional tax revenues associated with the program's economic impacts on industrial firms.[7] These efforts have deflected the criticisms of ill-advised market interference, corporate subsidies, and general governmental ineffectiveness that have been levied against other federal technology programs. The significant state role in the MEP has also allowed the program to be rationalized on the basis of assistance to economic development and support for small business, which have long been accepted grounds for state government intervention. Finally, with numerous centers established around the country, legislators can associate the program with particular centers in their states and districts and have become amenable to supporting federal funding, regardless of party affiliation.

The Performance of the MEP

At the start of the 1990s, the U.S. public infrastructure for manufacturing technology deployment compared unfavorably in scale and scope with the systems found in other advanced industrialized economies.[8] However, rapid progress has been made: the MEP now offers comprehensive services with a level of market penetration that is not drastically out of line with efforts elsewhere. Around 56,000 firms have been assisted by the MEP since 1989, with current service loads beginning to exceed 30,000 firms a year.

The typical MEP center employs about thirty-five professional and technical staff and uses an additional ten consultants each quarter. The average number of targeted manufacturers in an MEP's service area is around 6,200; smaller MEPs, usually serving dispersed rural areas, target 1,300 to 1,500 enterprises; and a few larger centers in urbanized locations target more than 15,000 firms. Each quarter, an average MEP center assists about 120 firms through a combination of initial visits, assessments, technical assistance projects, and training events; some larger centers serve many more customers, other smaller centers serve fewer. More than two-thirds of the firms served have fewer than 100 employees. MEP technical assistance projects tend to focus on process techniques and "soft" business and manufacturing practices rather than "hard" new technologies such as factory automation: for MEP activities involving eight or more hours of staff time, the most common projects involve process improvement, quality and inspection, business systems and management, human resources, and market development.[9]

While the MEP has more resources and is serving more firms, the program's overall impact is harder to measure, for three reasons. First, since many centers are still in the early years of startup, evaluations of the program's performance must be regarded as preliminary. Second, different stakeholders in the system have varied perspectives on how the MEP's performance should be measured.[10] For example, federal goals emphasize industrial competitiveness and technology diffusion; states are most interested in local economic development and employment effects; individual firms seek such results as cost or time savings, increased sales, better quality, or improved profitability; for workers, employment security and higher wages may be the desired outcomes. Third, the important "soft" effects of MEP intervention are intrinsically hard to measure in strict economic terms; for example, strengthening long-term inter-firm relationships within industries and localities can improve knowledge flows that cannot easily be assigned a dollar value, yet which are critical for business success.[11]

With these caveats made, what is the evidence to date about the performance and impact of the MEP? Early studies of the original federal manufacturing technology centers found them helpful in assisting firms to modernize business and technological practices, although it was acknowledged that the small number of centers at that time and their separation from other federal and state programs limited their total effect.[12] Since then, the MEP has grown rapidly and has developed a more coordinated service delivery system. [13] Rather than duplicate services or provide assistance directly from the federal level, MEP awards are designed to get existing public and private service providers to coordinate their efforts and to develop local service networks that are accessible and responsive to manufacturers. The current network of MEP centers directly operates over 300 local offices (See Figure 10-1) and works with more than 2,500 affiliated public and private organizations. These organizations are quite varied; they include non-profit technology or business assistance centers, economic development groups, universities and community colleges, private consultants, utilities, federal laboratories, and industry associations. A cooperative relationship between the public and private sectors has been encouraged: MEP centers generally have governing or advisory boards that include representatives from industry, other private groups, and the public sector. In addition to better coordinating public service providers, MEP centers have integrated and leveraged private sources. For example, it has been found that the MEP, rather than competing with private consultants, helps companies use private consultants more effectively. Interaction with the MEP assists in the front-end assessment of problems, helps to match firms with qualified consultants, and encourages firms to implement consultants' recommendations.[14] Overall, the program is decentralized and flexible, and individual centers can develop strategies and services which are appropriate to state and local conditions.

A steadily growing body of evaluation studies using varied quantitative and qualitative methods shows that the MEP's impacts on businesses and the economy are also broadly positive. For example, in a recent congressional oversight study, 73 percent of 389 business respondents to a survey of manufacturing extension customers indicated that their overall business performance had been improved.[15] Evaluation studies of the Georgia Manufacturing Extension Alliance indicate that one year after service, 68 percent of assisted firms had taken action, with more than 40 percent reporting reduced costs, 32 percent reporting improved quality, and 28

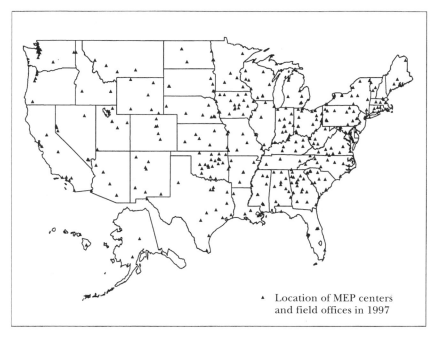

Figure 10-1 The U.S. Manufacturing Extension Partnership. Source: Mapped from data provided by the National Institute of Standards and Technology.

percent indicating a capital investment was made.[16] A benefit-cost study of projects completed in one year of the Georgia program finds combined net public and private economic benefits exceeding costs by a ratio of 1.2:1 to 2.7:1.[17] Structured case studies of MEP projects show that program services help smaller manufacturers to modernize their operations, improve quality, and increase profitability through such means as reducing waste, redesigning plant layouts, and improved inventory control and employee training.[18] A study in Michigan using seventeen key technology and business performance metrics finds that manufacturing technology center customers improve faster overall than comparable firms in a control group that did not receive assistance.[19] In this study, however, the assisted firms had smaller increases in computer-based technologies, raising some questions about the assistance strategies of the center, an issue considered below. Less ambiguously, studies in 1994 and 1996 of New York's Industrial Extension Service (an affiliate of the MEP) find that the business performance of assisted firms is improved when compared with non-assisted but similar companies.[20] Longitudinal controlled studies using census data also suggest that assistance by extension services improves productivity.[21]

Progress has also been made in identifying "best practices" for industrial modernization—processes, practices and systems recognized as improving the performance and efficiency of MEP programs and service offerings. [22] The early federal manufacturing technology centers were envisaged as transferring federally developed advanced technology to private industrial firms. It was soon realized, however, that small firms generally need assistance with commercially proven technologies. These firms also need assistance with workforce training, marketing, and overall business management so as to make best use of existing and newly introduced technologies. Most MEP centers now structure their services to address industrial customers' training and business needs, as well as promote technology deployment. The MEP has found that industrially experienced staff and consultants are better able than researchers to deliver services to firms, that services must be offered geographically close to industrial clusters, and that the quality of affiliated center operations and services can be maintained through merit-based competition for funding and regular management reviews (which often involve outside reviewers).

Challenges and Future Directions for the MEP

In many ways, the MEP is a model program. More than most other recent federal technology policy initiatives, it has gained bipartisan sponsorship in Washington and appreciable support and matching dollars from the states. Over the past four years, the program has ramped up quickly to achieve national coverage. Support systems, in terms of training, information sharing, and evaluation, have been put into place. Most importantly, the early evidence indicates that the services of MEP affiliates are leading to desired business and economic impacts. The MEP has also incorporated most of the principles of flexible operation, collaborative partnership, and quality control advanced by recent advocates of governmental reform and "reinvented government."[23] Nonetheless, four major categories of issues and challenges face the MEP in the next years: the program's strategic orientation, its operation as a partnership, the underlying funding framework, and its role within an overall technology policy framework.

The Strategic Orientation of the MEP

Like other public programs, the MEP pays considerable attention to issues of justification. The MEP has to address questions about the need for the program, its effectiveness, and the extent to which the program is subsidizing or substituting services that could be better provided by the private sector. In a dynamic political and economic environment that values accountability, desires to strengthen rather than replace market incentives, and has many other pressing demands for scarce public tax resources (including not raising those taxes), these are appropriate concerns. The growing body of evidence about the MEP's performance, impacts on customers, and linkages with industry and private service providers has allowed its proponents to argue that the program addresses clearly identified market failures and produces net economic and social benefits. The ability of a program, especially a young one, to marshal evidence about its effectiveness and to motivate a constituency of support is crucial to survival; yet, the focus on program justification has at times overshadowed equally important challenges for the MEP related to program improvement and strategic orientation. For example, can the program be more effective? What changes in MEP intervention methods and its service delivery mix would lead to further improvements in program outcomes?

To date, the services offered by MEP affiliates have tended to help firms become leaner, and more efficient, through assistance with solving production problems, improving quality and lowering costs, and encouraging firms to adopt modern manufacturing technologies and management techniques. These services are consistent with the design of the MEP as an incremental business improvement intervention. But reducing costs and improving efficiency is only one part of a strategic approach to manufacturing and technology-based economic development. Although the number of small and mid-sized manufacturing firms in the United States has grown in recent decades, the average wages paid by these smaller firms have increasingly lagged behind those of larger companies.[24] While the reasons for this are complex, at least part of the problem is that many U.S. small firms produce routine commodities that are now subject to intense worldwide competition. If they are to offer higher wages in the future, more smaller American manufacturers must find ways not only to reduce waste and improve productivity but also to command market premiums through distinctive products, processes, and business strategies.[25] To help small firms develop these capabilities, the MEP may need to offer a different service mix and approach—a change that would have implications for the system as a whole. There is some recognition of this point within the MEP, with several centers shifting to offer deeper and more long-term services. But more needs to be done.

For instance, the MEP could increase its product design and development assistance to help more small firms enter new high-value domestic and export markets. This would affect MEP staffing needs, and would require stronger links with research and development centers and with financing and marketing specialists. Similarly, the MEP could give greater emphasis to collaborative inter-firm and industry-level initiatives, for example in promoting local networks of small firms to accelerate the dissemination of information and to encourage collaborative problem solving, product development, and marketing. Already underway is a project to improve supplier development, with the MEP working as a service franchise to upgrade multiple suppliers of a firm or industry across state boundaries; such efforts ought to be expanded. Support might also be deepened to help clusters of small and mid-sized firms deploy those new technologies and methods that are likely to be critical for market leadership in coming years, such as environmentally conscious manufacturing, working with new materials, or exploiting new communications technologies in organizing production within related industries.

However, efforts that go beyond incremental short-term problem solving into a more strategic approach to intervention would require parallel changes in the MEP's underlying incentive framework. At present, many MEP centers strive to maximize the number of completed individual projects with firms. Center staff typically work "one-on-one" with specific firms, focusing on immediate needs. This approach can generate fee revenue from individual customers, but may also result in high marketing and service costs as well as many short-duration, low-contact, and probably low-impact projects. Longer-term initiatives to address structural industry problems, build stronger inter-firm relationships, or pursue riskier but potentially more rewarding product development outcomes tend to get postponed due to the day-to-day pressures of maintaining project counts or fee income. In part, this focus on the short term reflects funding uncertainty and weaknesses in the systems of incentives offered to centers and field staff. A longer-term federal funding commitment and changes in NIST management guidance and grant formulas would improve the climate for a more strategic approach. However, there is a limit to the effectiveness of "top-down" management directives given the MEP's decentralized partnership structure and the powerful engineering culture evident among many MEP field staff which leads them to focus on problems that are immediately "fixable." Also needed are parallel measures to strengthen learning and evaluation systems and to promote informed comparison and feedback at the local level: such efforts would help center managers, staff, governing boards, and state program sponsors better understand the impacts of different types of interventions, identify best practices, and work with industry stakeholders to determine strategic needs and opportunities.

The Operation of the MEP as a Partnership

The MEP's working partnership between the federal government, the states, and other public and private service providers has improved the coordination and flexibility of manufacturing extension services, integrated a wider range of service expertise, reduced inefficient overlaps, and helped new centers expand quickly by leveraging existing resources.[26] Yet partnerships have costs too. They can be expensive to maintain, in terms of administrative coordination and political capital. Some local MEP partnerships were put together hastily, for the purposes of grant application, leading to instability in the partnership; in other instances, technically competent but politically weak service providers have been subordinated. As the MEP shifts from rapid growth to maturity, it must address these deficiencies. MEP's ongoing review process allows it to deal with poorly organized or sub-par local affiliates. The issue now is to continue to ensure the integrity of the review process, to include external reviewers, and to avoid undue political interference when NIST has to make hard decisions about discontinuing funding or recommending organizational changes that affect local centers.

Other issues related to MEP structure and organization will also need fresh attention in the next few years. One such issue is the geographic coverage of the MEP. The program has grown in disjointed stages, reflecting separate rounds of federal funding as well as variations in state and local abilities to prepare winning proposals and find matching funds. While MEP affiliates have now been funded in all states, there is a mismatch between the allocation of federal resources and the geographic distribution of industry. For example, dense concentrations of manufacturers in California and the Northeast are relatively under-served, while several rural areas are relatively over-served. The targeting of competitions to expand MEP services to under-served major industrial clusters may be a useful next step, if additional federal funds for new centers are forthcoming. Otherwise, NIST may have to revisit how it distributes its federal funding and consider how it could allocate its existing resources to better match the clustering of industry.

Another key issue is the role that the states and private interests should play in the MEP. While states have put up money to match the federal commitment, they differ in their degree of participation. Some states play a minimal role: they let the federal government act as the dominant partner. Other states wish to be very active in setting directions for their MEP program, which has at times led to conflicts of policy. The management capabilities and experience of individual MEP centers also varies: some centers are brand new while others have been in operation for two or more decades. These differences raise the question of how NIST should relate to the states and individual centers: there is a wish to avoid seeing the states just as voiceless funders and the centers as mere operational arms; at the same time, a "hands-off" federal role would probably result in wide variations in local program performance and might actually diminish states' support. NIST has worked through organizations like the National Governors Association to create inter-governmental mechanisms to consider MEP policy issues, and there is a need to extend such discussions between federal and state policy-makers, particularly on the strategic orientation of the MEP and on how to make the partnership most effective. Similarly, what role should industry play? While there is local advisory participation, small and mid-sized manufacturers are not well organized to participate in the MEP. Industry associations may have to be convinced, and further strengthened, to be more fully engaged with the MEP, to diffuse knowledge about improved technologies and practices to association members more efficiently, and to serve as full partners in strategic efforts to upgrade particular industrial clusters. More vigorously involved industry, state, and local partners will help to minimize the risks of bureaucratization and micro-management that could affect NIST's administration of the MEP now that the rapid growth phase is over.

The Underlying Funding Framework

A major area of uncertainty for the MEP is its underlying funding framework; this issue is tied to questions about the program's objectives and to expectations about the longer-term commitment of its strategic partners, particularly the federal government. The 1988 Omnibus Trade and Competitiveness Act set a six-year limit on federal funding to a manufacturing technology center, with a "ramp-down" of federal dollars after the third year of NIST funding. The aim was to encourage centers to become "self-sustaining" without federal funds. In part, the "self-sustaining" clause reflected a necessary political compromise to avoid an open-ended commitment to a new government program; there was also the idea that if the centers were truly market-driven and customer-focused, they would be able to generate significant fee revenues from private firms, once established with initial public seed funding.

The original legislative design is admirable in that it motivates MEP centers to seek fee revenues, which helps to ensure that they provide services that firms want and for which they are willing to pay. But the idea that centers can completely replace federal funds with fee revenues has proven to be flawed, for several reasons. There are policy conflicts among MEP centers and sponsors—not so much on fee-generation per se, but on the aggressiveness with which fees should be sought. In several cases, the state partner has taken the view that industrial extension is a "public service" mission that should make assistance available to all small firms, even to those with only limited capabilities to pay. In other locations, MEP centers (often with less secure state funding) have aggressively sought fee revenue. However, these centers tend to narrow their scope of service to maximize fees by "selling" short-term projects (which may not be the projects of most strategic value to companies or industries) and serving larger firms (who can afford to pay more). Direct competition with private consultants is also increased. Additionally, as a practical matter, it seems that even the most aggressive centers cannot cover much more than one-third of their real costs through fee revenue. Indeed, most centers have found that the unit costs of marketing and servicing small firms are high relative to the fees that can be charged. (This is a reason why the private market for consulting services to small firms is weak and is one of the market failures that the MEP seeks to address with public subsidy.)

The issue of six-year self-sufficiency (also known as the "sunset" provision) has been a nagging problem within the MEP system and has hampered long-term planning. However, there are optimistic signs that this issue is now being addressed. There is an improved recognition in the policy-making community that maintaining an effective array of manufacturing extension services for small and mid-sized firms requires a core of public support. A clause in the federal 1997 appropriations language for the MEP allowed several centers that had exceeded the six-year limit to continue to obtain funds. However, this is a temporary and ungainly fix. There remains a need to revisit the legislative intent of the MEP program, to rescind the six-year sunset clause, and to legitimize an ongoing a continuing public role in manufacturing extension. Indeed, in mid-1997, Congressional committees are considering a legislative amendment (supported by a number of state governors, both Republican and Democrat) to remove the sunset provision and to allow continued federal funding after the sixth year of an MEP center's life at one-third of operating costs, subject to positive performance and reviews.

As yet, no final action has been taken on the sunset provision, but it does seem that the principle of an ongoing public commitment to manufacturing extension is being established. However, this still leaves plenty of room for debate about the size of the system, the appropriate level of funding, the precise nature of the federal role, and the methods and mix of support from other governmental and private stakeholders. Many practitioners advocate funding for the MEP over the long term in equal thirds by federal, state, and fee-generated revenues. This appears to be a workable formula to support the direct delivery of services to small and mid-sized firms, but there are circumstances where variations are warranted. For example, the possibilities for fee generation are likely to be greater in urban locations than in rural areas, and an allowance for this should be made.

The strategic and infrastructural investments necessary for an effective manufacturing extension framework also require different funding methods. For key technologies and industrial priorities, national or regional (rather than state) centers of excellence may appropriate to stimulate the sharing of expertise and tools, encourage information flows across state lines, and avoid the duplication of specialized services in several states. One example of a center of excellence is the Ohio-based Edison Welding Institute, which has worked with MEP affiliates in other states to provide its materials-joining expertise to manufacturers. Similarly, efforts to promote supply-chain improvement, inter-firm collaboration, worker training consortia, and program infrastructure services like staff training, resource networks, or evaluation are often most optimally implemented with regional or national (and, in some cases, international) coordination. "State-less" federal investments in these areas are important in integrating the MEP system, allowing strategic priorities to be emphasized, realizing spillovers from state investments, and promoting learning and the spread of best practices. State and private resources can be obtained in some instances for these activities, especially for industry-focused technology centers; in other areas, such as the development of new tools or the promotion of information exchange, it is harder to find matching funds and a greater federal contribution is usually required to start and maintain such initiatives. Currently, about $12 million is allocated by the MEP for such efforts, under the heading of "national programs." NIST has established initiatives in environmental, information, and printing technologies and in supply chain optimization, and has supported pilot projects to promote inter-firm networking. Further efforts to deploy advanced technologies are planned. As the MEP shifts from the phase of establishing new centers to one of optimizing an in-place system, increased federal funding to the level of about $30 million for national programs (matched in part with additional state and private funds) would allow a more extensive portfolio of strategic and infrastructural initiatives to be implemented.

Although the likely FY 1998 MEP budget will allow the current MEP system to be maintained, there is a case, in succeeding budget years, for enhancing the level of MEP services in selected key manufacturing clusters. An additional $30–40 million (matched by equivalent state, local, and private funds) could usefully increase market penetration in under-served large urban industrial areas such as New York or Los Angeles.[27] In total, adding together the costs of this system expansion with those of an increased budget for strategic and infrastructural initiatives, an annual federal investment of some $180 million to $190 million is implied. Matched with state funds and private fee revenues, this would result in a manufacturing extension system that more completely served U.S. industry; through intensive projects, it would aid about 10 percent of American small and mid-sized manufacturers each year and offer training, information, referral, and other forms of assistance. The system would also have the resources to introduce strategic new initiatives. With effective management, the potential productivity benefits from this investment should result in compensating net positive returns to the economy. One estimate suggests that if the average annual growth of productivity in U.S. small and mid-sized manufacturers could be increased by one-tenth of one percentage point and sustained for five years, about $6.7 billion in savings would be realized by firms and customers. Workers could also realize up to $3.8 billion in added payroll.[28] These returns significantly exceed MEP program expenditures.

The ability of the MEP system to generate these kinds of improvements requires stable, long-term core support from the states as well as the federal government. While funding for industrial extension is quite solid in several states, in many others it is not. As economic conditions and political priorities change among these states, some MEP centers may find it increasingly difficult to obtain their state matching funds. However, there does appear to be a relationship between the availability of federal funds and the continued commitment of state resources. An ongoing federal commitment will make state withdrawals less likely.

The Broader Technology Policy and Economic Development Framework

A final challenge for MEP is how the program can be better coordinated with other federal technology and business development initiatives for manufacturers. The federal government invests more than $3 billion annually in an array of cooperative technology programs, and sponsors at least thirty separate programs to help industrial enterprises.[29] Perhaps it is not surprising that one recent congressional task force reported "a deep sense of confusion about what federal initiatives are available to assist manufacturers."[30] Federal programs include support for numerous small business development and export centers, the Economic Development Administration's industry-university centers, the National Aeronautics and Space Administration's regional technology transfer centers, and a series of defense-related technology and trade assistance adjustment centers. There are also various financial assistance, training and workforce programs. Additionally, federal laboratories have been encouraged to establish their own systems of technology transfer to business. On paper, the federal lab transfer mission is different, but in practice there is an overlap with the MEP; for example, federal labs market and provide relatively simple technical assistance to many of the same small and mid-sized firms served by MEP centers.

How can we make better sense of this federal technology and business assistance system? Unfortunately, there are significant political and administrative barriers in Washington to more logically organizing the package of manufacturing services supported by the federal government. Agencies and constituencies frequently defend individual programs against cuts or reallocations of resources. Moreover, indicating that small firms are helped as part of an agency or laboratory mission provides an aura of relevance that assists in maintaining funding in tight budgetary times, even if those services are not entirely necessary and overlap with other federal and state programs. It is too much to expect that the MEP, by itself, can rationalize this system. This is a task for a broader review of technology and business support for manufacturers. Additionally, caution should be exercised before suggesting that the MEP can supersede some of these federal programs; if it did, it might become overloaded with too many missions and mandates.

However, the MEP can play a critical role in the selective integration and improvement of services offered to manufacturers by existing programs. The MEP, through NIST and the Department of Commerce, can help to broker agreements at the national level with other agencies to coordinate and deliver services. NIST has coordination agreements with the Labor and Agriculture Departments, a pilot collaboration with elements of the Small Business Development Centers program, and is working with the Environmental Protection Agency to use the MEP network to provide environmental services to small and mid-sized firms; there are likely to be further opportunities to use the MEP as an effective distribution network for other federal services targeted to small firms. Equally important, the MEP's flexible structure can be used to promote working relationships at the local level among different programs, seeking to bring together expert service providers who can add value to manufacturing firms. For example, MEP programs can develop agreements with federal laboratories in particular regions through which the MEP would focus on outreach and routine services to small manufacturers, but then join with experts from federal laboratories to address more sophisticated problems. Similarly, as is already beginning to happen, MEP programs can be encouraged to collocate their field offices with small business assistance centers to offer a full range of advice in technological, marketing, business planning, and financial areas to local firms.

The MEP's role in coordinating technology and business services to manufacturers is not restricted to federally sponsored programs.

MEP partnerships already help to integrate varied service providers at the local level, including colleges, state and local business development programs, and private groups. Encouraging the MEP to play an even greater role in coordinating assistance services to manufacturers can reduce confusing and wasteful overlaps, help share marketing and service tools, and lead to important improvements in the quality and comprehensiveness of services available to firms. However, the development and operation of effective local partnerships incurs economic and political costs, including transaction costs associated with information sharing, quality monitoring, and dealing with inter-organizational tensions. Although the benefits appear to outweigh the costs, these costs should not be ignored. Indeed, a more coordinated service framework is an externality that benefits industrial firms and regional economies more than any individual program. In most cases, local manufacturing service partnerships could not exist without the stimulus (and absorption of coordination costs) possible with the relatively small amount of flexible federal funding provided through the MEP.

While the MEP can help to improve the coordination of manufacturing assistance services within our rather fragmented federal system, there are limits to coordination and to the ability of any single initiative to effect substantive change within a complex and large political economy. The MEP must be complemented by supporting policies and reforms in such areas as workforce training, tax incentives and financing for research and technological investment, and regulatory compliance. Often, manufacturing extension agents help firms to overcome barriers that are caused by other failures in the policy system. A case in point: the use of MEP resources to assist firms in developing literacy and basic educational programs for their industrial workers—critical before new technology can be used effectively—demonstrates the glaring need to restructure public education and training, particularly in urban areas where many smaller manufacturers are located. Manufacturers in the United States will continue to be disadvantaged, to degrees that manufacturing extension cannot overcome, as long as such deficiencies in basic public services remain.

Conclusion: Charting a Strategic Future for the MEP

The MEP represents an important development in federal technology policy in at least three interrelated ways. First, it marks a fundamental additional policy thrust. For at least the past five decades, federal policy has stressed technological innovation (the development of new technologies, often in defense, space, and energy). More recently, the federal government has paid increased attention to technology transfer (shifting federally developed advanced technology into commercial use). Yet, while the federal government has long supported programs of agricultural extension, an explicit federal concern with civilian manufacturing technology deployment and best practice (promoting the widespread adoption of proven as well as new technologies and the improvement of manufacturing and business methods) is new. In the context of rapid international flows of information and capital and increased global competition, many have argued that strategic national and regional efforts to maintain industrial competitiveness depend not only on innovation but more than ever on the diffusion, effective application, and further improvement of proven technologies.[31] This is not a new concept, and earlier state programs recognized the importance of technology deployment. But only with the growth of the MEP has the United States begun to put in place a nationwide system to match industrial needs and opportunities with concrete technology deployment services.

Second, the MEP represents an important investment in the social infrastructure for diffusing technologies and improved business practices. Such factors as institutional arrangements, interorganizational relationships, trust, and the balance between competition and collaboration within regional and national economies are increasingly believed to affect technological and industrial success.[32] (The role of social infrastructure in facilitating technological development is discussed in Chapter 4 by Jane Fountain.) Through its emphasis on building local manufacturing service partnerships and public-private linkages, the MEP is starting to play an important role not just in aiding particular manufacturers but also in strengthening manufacturing communities. The MEP could and should do more along these lines, for example, through increased support for collaborative initiatives that get suppliers and buyers to talk more to one another, that promote inter-firm networks for business development, and that support local industrial associations.

Finally, the MEP is significant because, in a period of renewed debate about the effectiveness of government, it is a program that works. This is not to say there are no weaknesses and opportunities for strategic improvement. But, overall, the MEP has, in a remarkably short period, established a national presence and stimulated a series of state manufacturing service partnerships, each involving many other associated organizations. Centers are operational, staff are in place, working relationships have been forged between public and private service providers, assistance tools have been developed, and firms are being aided. The early evaluations of program performance are positive.

There is a temptation, in today's good economic (but poor budgetary) times, to suggest that the MEP may no longer be necessary, or at least that federal support might be reduced. This would be a misreading of both the present situation and future possibilities. At present, despite some short-term improvements, the long-run growth rate of American industrial productivity is still very modest, with small firms on average continuing to lag in technology use, productivity, and wages. In the future, the effective use of technology is likely to grow ever more important in influencing industrial competitiveness, regional development, jobs, and wages. Without federal investment, the infrastructure to support and stimulate the effective use of available and emerging technologies by small and mid-sized firms will be substantially weakened, and potentially very significant private and public benefits will be lost. Public investments in the MEP are complementary to, and stimulate the use of, private sources: there is little evidence that private sources will, by themselves, be able to profitably step in and profitably serve the range of firms currently assisted by the MEP. Moreover, while a number of states would probably continue to support manufacturing modernization at a reduced level, without a significant federal role there would be a reversion back to the incomplete patchwork of unconnected programs that existed before the MEP, and the interstate sharing of expertise, tools, and best practices would be stymied.

Thus, the importance of both the MEP and the federal role in structuring comprehensive manufacturing extension services must be recognized. There are cautiously optimistic signs here. Already, a base of support has been built for the MEP that crosses political, industrial, and geographic lines. As a minimum, this base of support needs to be drawn upon to ensure that the existing MEP network is stabilized. Federal funding for the MEP should at least maintain the scale of what has already been established, with commitments to individual centers based solely on performance. The MEP's underlying legislative framework should also be updated by removing the clause that generally limits ongoing federal support for MEP centers.

There is also an opportunity to move the MEP into an even more strategic role to build on the basic infrastructure already established. Even in an era of tight budgets, there is justification, as argued above, for increasing federal support of the MEP by perhaps a further $60–70 million. This additional investment, leveraged by further state and private funds, would deepen coverage in key urban manufacturing clusters and enhance shared infrastructural capabilities. Such an expansion should be linked to refining the strategic approach of the MEP; strengthening its activities at the level of manufacturing communities as well as individual firms; supporting the diffusion of emerging technologies; and further integrating MEP centers with other federal technology transfer, business development, and workforce training policies.

Whether an enlarged and more strategic future is possible for the MEP depends on a shared understanding about ends as well as means. A broader social accord needs to be fostered, one that not only promotes a high-wage, technologically capable sector of small and mid-sized manufacturing firms, but also values a collaborative public-private deployment strategy like the MEP as a means to achieve this, and supports policy measures to address associated concerns such as training, finance, and regulation. Industrial, workforce and community groups must be involved with federal policy-makers and the states in further building this consensus. It is a task that will require ongoing political and economic investments to ensure success: if it can be done, the payoffs to the nation's technological and economic development will be considerable.

Acknowledgments

Helpful comments and suggestions were provided by Kevin Carr, Marc Cummings, Ruth Haines, Hans Klein, Phil Nanzetta, Robert Springfield, David Roessner, Jack Russell, and Jan Youtie, for which the author is most grateful. The author alone remains responsible for the views expressed in this chapter.

Notes

1. See, for example, Office of Technology Assessment, *Making Things Better: Competing in Manufacturing* (Washington, D.C.: U.S. Congress, U.S. Government Printing Office [U.S. GPO], 1990); Stuart Rosenfeld, *Competitive Manufacturing: New Strategies for Regional Development* (New Brunswick, N.J.: Center for Urban Policy Research, 1992); and National Research Council, *Learning to Change: Opportunities to Improve the Performance of Smaller Manufacturers* (Washington, D.C.: Manufacturing Studies Board, National Academy Press, 1993).

2. David S. Clifton, Larry R. Edens, Harris T. Johnson, and Robert W. Springfield, "Elements of an Effective Technology Assistance Policy to Stimulate Economic Development," *Economic Development Quarterly*, Vol. 3, No. 1 (February 1989), pp. 52–57; Philip Shapira, "Modern Times: Learning from New State Initiatives in Industrial Extension and Technology Transfer," *Economic Development Quarterly*, Vol. 4, No. 3 (August 1990), pp. 186–202.

3. William J. Clinton and Albert Gore, Jr., *Manufacturing for the 21st Century: Turning Ideas Into Jobs* (Little Rock, Ark.: National Campaign Headquarters, September 8, 1992); William J. Clinton and Albert Gore, Jr., "Technology for America's Economic Growth: A New Direction to Build Economic Strength" (Washington, D.C.: Executive Office of the President, February 22, 1993).

4. National Science and Technology Council, *National Security Science and Technology Strategy* (Washington, D.C.: Executive Office of the President, 1995).

5. The TRP is described in Advanced Research Projects Agency, *Technology Reinvestment Project: Program Information Package* (Arlington, Va.: U.S. Department of Defense, 1993).

6. National Coalition for Advanced Manufacturing, "New Direction of the House Science Committee," *NACFAM Alert* (Washington, D.C.), December 15, 1994; E. Andrews, "Congress and White House Split on High Tech, *New York Times*, January 3, 1995, p. C19.

7. Modernization Forum, *The Role and Importance of the Manufacturing Extension Partnership Centers* (Dearborn, Mich.: The Modernization Forum, 1994).

8. Committee for Scientific and Technological Policy, *Diffusing Technology to Industry: Government Policies and Programmes*, OECD/GD(97)60 (Paris: Organization for Economic Cooperation and Development [OECD], 1996); Philip

Shapira, "Modernizing Small Manufacturers in the United States and Japan: Public Technology Infrastructures and Strategies," in Morris Teubal, Dominique Foray, Moshe Justman, and Ehud Zuscovitch, eds., *Technological Infrastructure Policy (TIP): An International Perspective* (Boston, Mass.: Kluwer Academic Publishers, 1996).

9. Lucy Richards, *The Manufacturing Extension Partnership: An Overview* (Washington, D.C.: Office of Technology Administration, U.S. Department of Commerce, 1996), Presentation at OECD Workshop on Technology Diffusion, Paris, December 13, 1996; Manufacturing Extension Partnership, *MEP National Data Highlights* (Gaithersburg, Md.: National Institute of Standards and Technology, April 18, 1997).

10. Philip Shapira, Jan Youtie, and J. David Roessner, "Current Practices in the Evaluation of U.S. Industrial Modernization Programs," *Research Policy*, Vol. 25, No. 2 (March 1996), pp. 185–214).

11. Maryellen R. Kelley and Ashish Arora, "The Role of Institution-Building in US. Industrial Modernization Programs," *Research Policy*, Vol. 25, No. 2 (March 1996), pp. 265–279.

12. U.S. General Accounting Office [GAO], *Technology Transfer: Federal Efforts to Enhance the Competitiveness of Small Manufacturers*, GAO/RCED-92-30 (Washington, D.C.: GAO, 1991); U.S. Department of Commerce, *Manufacturing Technology Centers: Broad Programmatic Issues*, Third Year External Review Panel (Gaithersburg, Md.: National Institute of Standards and Technologies, 1992).

13. Philip Shapira and Jan Youtie, *Coordinating Industrial Modernization Services: Impacts and Insights from the Manufacturing Extension Partnership* (Atlanta: School of Public Policy and Economic Development Institute, Georgia Institute of Technology, 1996).

14. Nexus Associates, *Manufacturing Extension Centers and Private Consultants: Collaboration or Competition* (Belmont, Mass.: Nexus Associates, Inc., 1995).

15. U.S. General Accounting Office, *Manufacturing Extension Programs: Manufacturers' Views of Services*, GAO/GGD-95-21-216BR (Washington, D.C.: U.S. GAO, 1995).

16. Jan Youtie, Alan Olisko, Philip Shapira, and Michael Lane, *GMEA Customer Progress: Results of a One Year Follow-up Survey*, GMEA Evaluation Working Paper E9505 (Atlanta: School of Public Policy and Economic Development Institute, Georgia Institute of Technology, 1995).

17. Philip Shapira and Jan Youtie, *Assessing GMEA's Economic Impacts: Towards a Benefit-Cost Methodology*, GMEA Evaluation Working Paper E9502 (Atlanta: School of Public Policy and Economic Development Institute, Georgia Institute of Technology, 1995).

18. Cosmos Corporation, *A Day in the Life of the Manufacturing Partnership: Case Studies of Exemplary Engagements with Clients by MEP Centers* (Gaithersburg, Md.: National Institute of Standards and Technologies, 1996).

19. Dan Luria and Edith Wiarda, "Performance Benchmarking and Measuring Program Impacts on Customers: Lessons from the Midwest Manufacturing Technology Center," *Research Policy*, Vol. 25, No. 2 (March 1996), pp. 233–246.

20. Eric Oldsman, "Does Manufacturing Extension Matter? An Evaluation of the Industrial Technology Extension Service in New York," *Research Policy*, Vol. 25, No. 2 (March 1996), pp. 215–232; Eric Oldsman, *Impact of the New York Manufacturing Extension Program: A Quasi-Experiment* (Belmont, Mass.: Nexus Associates, Inc., 1996).

21. Ron Jarmin, *Measuring the Impact of Manufacturing Extension*, Working Paper CES96-8 (Washington, D.C.: Center for Economic Studies, U.S. Bureau of the Census, 1996).

22. Philip Shapira, J. David Roessner, and Richard Barke, "New Public Infrastructures for Small Firm Industrial Modernization in the USA," *Entrepreneurship and Regional Development*, Vol. 7 (1995), pp. 63–84.

23. David Osborne and Ted Gaebler, *Reinventing Government: How the Entrepreneurial Spirit is Transforming the Public Sector* (New York: Plume, 1993).

24. Matt Kane with Dan Luria, Jack Russell, and Chris Heye, "The Value of Manufacturing Extension Programs in America." in Philip Shapira and Jan Youtie eds., *Manufacturing Modernization: Learning from Evaluation Practices and Results* (Atlanta: School of Public Policy and Economic Development Institute, Georgia Institute of Technology, 1997), pp. 21–28.

25. Dan Luria, "Toward Lean or Rich? What Performance Benchmarking Tells Us about SME Performance, and Some Implications for Extension Center Services and Mission," in Shapira and Youtie, *Manufacturing Modernization*, pp. 99–108.

26. Shapira and Youtie, *Coordinating Industrial Modernization Services*.

27. NIST staff note that enlarging the MEP's urban coverage has been difficult in some areas due to the difficulty of finding adequate state and local matching funds and to the rural influence often found in state legislatures.

28. Kane et al., "The Value of Manufacturing Extension Programs in America."

29. Chris Coburn and Dan Beglund, *Partnerships: A Compendium of State and Federal Cooperative Technology Programs* (Columbus, Ohio: Battelle Memorial Institute, 1995).

30. Charles Bartsch, Kerry Sutten, and Richard Purcell, *Advancing Manufacturing Competitiveness: A Practitioners' Guide to Federal Assistance* (Washington, D.C.: Northeast-Midwest Institute, 1995).

31. Organisation for Economic Cooperation and Development, *Technology, Productivity and Job Creation: The OECD Jobs Strategy* (Paris: OECD, 1996).

32. Rosenfeld, *Competitive Manufacturing*; AnnaLee Saxenian, *Regional Advantage: Culture and Competition in Silicon Valley and Route 128* (Cambridge, Mass.: Harvard University Press, 1994).

11

Toward a New Generation of Environmental Technology

George R. Heaton, Jr., and R. Darryl Banks

The close connection between technology and environmental policy has been consistently under-appreciated. Until recently, the communities concerned with these two areas of policy have remained separate and sometimes close to antagonistic.[1] Fortunately, these entrenched positions have begun to loosen. The pivotal role of new technology in solving environmental problems is almost conventional wisdom, and business leaders regularly issue eloquent statements of environmental commitment.[2] Remarkably, in an arena not noted for consensus, one sees virtual unanimity about the need for a new generation of technology—eco-efficient, clean, economically competitive—as well the imperative of policy reforms to encourage its creation.[3]

Some progress toward reform has been realized. During the Bush administration, for example, environmental technologies—pollution minimization, remediation, and waste management—were listed as "critical" to the nation. An appreciation of the connection between environmental and technology policy perhaps reached its high-water mark with the Clinton administration's early policy statement that linked "long-term economic growth" and "protection of the environment" as primary national objectives.[4] Within months, the Environmental Technology Initiative (ETI) was launched to promote the development of environmental technology via a wide range of policy instruments, ranging from regulatory reform to large-scale R&D projects.[5]

There is indeed some cause for comfort in the new focus on technological change that now pervades the regulatory and business community. Nevertheless, today's experiments can only go so far before running up against the wall of a legislative regulatory structure that is at best unconcerned with, and at worst inimical to, technological innovation. Nor has the government's technology promotion effort seen much success: witness the ETI's failure to garner the budgets, focus, or follow-through necessary to make it a viable initiative.

In this chapter we argue that a coherent, vigorous environmental technology policy is necessary for meaningful progress toward environmental sustainability, and is an appropriate element of a new consensus that is unfolding in technology policy. While renewed commitments in the administration and private sector will of course be required, the current legislative framework represents the biggest obstacle to its realization. After considering the nature of these legislative obstacles, we assess the degree to which administrative reforms have been able to mitigate them. Analysis of the ETI and the history of Congressional quiescence leads us to propose statutory reforms that would turn environmental law's pervasive bias against innovation into a "demand pull" for new technology, and a set of measures to revivify support for environmental technology in the context of industrial technology policy.

How the Legislative Framework Impedes Innovation

Environmental regulation was conceived as a force for technological change in industry, and throughout at least its early history, it was. Air and water pollution regulation compelled firms to upgrade their processes; bans on toxic chemicals called forth innovative substitutions; whole sectors—automobiles, notably—redesigned their products in response to regulation combined with market forces; and a new global industry—pollution control—came into being. Regulation fathered a new, environmental ethos among the designers of industrial technology.

Today, however, environmental innovation is in a frustrating, albeit fertile, period.[6] Environmental innovators uniformly lament their treatment in the regulatory process, with its problems of uncertainty, red tape, and skepticism about new compliance techniques.[7] It also appears that one of the most creative segments of the industrial community—new companies, small firms, entrepreneurs—is uniquely disadvantaged by an overall regulatory framework that erects high entry barriers against new ideas. No one wants these problems; they persist because regulators and business people are still using the policy tool kit assembled by statutes passed in the early 1970s. Because industrial structures and practices have changed so drastically since then, and because the technologies now needed are so different from those needed in the past, the perpetuation of this statutory framework is bound to impose perverse effects.

Many of the problems derive from a fragmented statutory structure: air, water, waste, pesticides, toxic substances, consumer products, and occupational health (to name only some of the statutes) all have different legal and administrative regimes. While there is some truth to the justification that each of these areas constitutes a distinct problem, and it made sense to attack them separately twenty-five years ago, with new perspectives and current analytical tools such as industrial ecology (which analyzes the firm as an integrated energy and materials system), firms often perceive environmental problems as a much more integrated set than the law effectively allows. This can lead to considerable frustration in the development of new technologies. In the petroleum industry, for example, closed systems, recycling loops, and industrial process changes could reduce air, water, and occupational exposures simultaneously; however, their adoption is impeded by the necessity for acceptance in at least three regulatory contexts. Thus, if regulatory policy is to encourage technological innovation by firms, it must attack environmental problems in a manner that is consistent with an innovating firm's vantage point.[8]

A second major problem is a pervasive implicit bias against new technology. For example, pollution controls that are stricter for new sources than for old undermine innovation. While the justification for this is that new plants can install superior technologies more easily than their older counterparts, the effect has been to set up a perverse incentive in favor of the technological status quo. The same pattern appears in product regulation. For example, under the Toxic Substances Control Act (TSCA) and the Federal Insecticide, Fungicide, and Rodenticide Act (FIFRA), new chemicals are subject to review and testing, while those on the market before regulation arose are not. The resources to scrutinize these existing products are scant. The combined effect is to prolong the life of old technologies which, ironically, are likely, on balance, to present worse environmental risks than new technologies.

"Best available technology" (BAT) standards create another widely felt bias against innovation. In essence, such standards endorse a technological status quo at the time of rulemaking, thus narrowing the range of compliance options. Were BAT determinations routinely upgraded to take account of technological advance, the system might work, but because the regulatory decision process is slow and discontinuous, the standards quickly become obsolete in the face of continuing technical advance. This means that the public is getting much less environmental quality than it could.

BAT standards also fail to create any incentive for individual firms to continue technological improvements. In theory, most companies are trying to find the best and cheapest ways to comply with environmental standards, and many would like to continually improve their performance, just as environmentalists or regulators would like them to in principle. But since most permits are based on the technological status quo and contain no provisions for performance upgrades, why should firms improve? In fact, the net effect may suppress innovation; firms often express the fear that any change—even an environmentally positive one—could result in legal problems if it departs from the standard technological fixes regulators are known to endorse. The situation of the many firms whose processes already attain BAT levels when the standards are set is particularly ironic: since BAT standards ask nothing of them, the resulting technological inertia may soon put them at the tail rather than the leading edge of best practice.

Perhaps the root of regulators' and regulations' lack of sympathy for innovation is the fact that they have never been directed to encourage it. Our governmental system puts Congress in ultimate charge of regulatory design, but in no statute has Congress explicitly given the regulatory agencies any mission to encourage technological change as a means toward environmental improvement. On the contrary, skepticism about new technology's impact on the environment, and a risk-averse posture toward its acceptance, are pervasive legislative themes. Until a new Congressional mandate emerges, reforms to encourage innovation will be difficult to craft.

What Has Administrative Reform Accomplished?

The need to make environmental regulation more hospitable to innovators and entrepreneurs has not escaped the attention of a large and concerned community, in both regulatory agencies and the business sector. Since Congress has taken almost no action in this arena, much of the reform has proceeded behind the scenes, within administrative practice. The tenor of these administrative reforms remained remarkably consistent from the mid-1970s, when the first initiatives arose. In spite of research and experience that showed a complex pattern of both positive and negative regulatory impacts on technology, the simplistic notion that regulation only impeded innovation seemed to persist throughout the Carter and Reagan administrations.[9]

The prevailing mindset began to change during the Bush administration, when the United States Environmental Protection Agency (EPA) mobilized a broad-based advisory process, the National Advisory Council for Environmental Policy and Technology (NACEPT), to examine how the EPA's administrative practices were affecting innovation and entrepreneurs.[10] (The NACEPT process was designed conservatively, deliberately avoiding comment on the legislative framework.) Many recommendations were made, of which some have been put into place.

Soon after coming into office, the Clinton-Gore administration announced a number of ambitious initiatives that revealed an entirely new conceptual framework toward the environment and technology. Its overall national technology strategy took the unprecedented stance of according equal importance to economic growth and environmental protection.[11] The ETI, unveiled soon after, acknowledged the multiplicity of relevant policy areas, and proposed an extraordinarily broad package of initiatives ranging from R&D, to trade incentives, to regulatory reform.[12] Vice President Gore's "Reinventing Government" initiative also fit in to the equation by instituting widespread efforts across the regulatory agencies to curb the rigidities that are particularly inhospitable to innovators.[13]

Two of the regulatory reforms are particularly noteworthy. Project XL (Excellence in Leadership was the official, but unused, name) provides a pathway by which innovative companies and those that exceed current requirements can be treated flexibly within the regulatory structure. The goals are to reduce frustration with "one size fits all" regulation and thereby speed the introduction of innovative compliance technologies.[14] The Common Sense Initiative (CSI) addressed sectoral issues by attempting to integrate regulatory requirements across statutory regimes, allowing firms in an industry to develop holistic compliance strategies.[15] These initiatives are important because each contains the germ of a potentially profound change: neither special consideration of innovators nor cross-cutting industry strategies had ever before been elements of the legislative framework.

The impetus toward regulatory reform is perhaps even stronger among the states. Two types of initiatives deserve particular mention: integrated permitting, in which a regulated facility is spared time and red tape through a single permitting process for modernizations or new technologies; and technology verification or certification, in which regulators confirm the performance of new technologies or indicate their willingness to accept them as compliance options. Integrated permitting is both a cost-saver and a more hospitable environment for process changes that cross environmental media. For example, New Jersey has received interim EPA approval to use its facility-wide environmental permits, which eliminate a multiplicity of separate requirements, in the Clean Air Act Title V program.

Technology verification and certification enjoy considerable support among providers of new compliance technology, since these procedures widen the range of acceptable compliance technologies, thus defining and solidifying new markets. About two dozen states, led by California, have developed such procedures, and EPA has recognized them.[16] State or local institutions have also provided the locus for technical assistance and cooperative strategies among regulated firms, universities, labs, and companies that have helped firms upgrade environmental and economic performance in tandem.

These reforms represent a significant accomplishment, but one that has come close to reaching its limits. Perhaps above all, they have effected a quiet transformation among regulatory officials, who are now acutely conscious of new technologies and entrepreneurs, and the business community, which now presents long-term strategies in environmentally and economically congruent terms. But good intentions go only so far. Programmatic initiatives require funding, staff, and consistent follow-through, and these have been insufficient. More profoundly, the regulatory agencies cannot undo the many structural aspects of the environmental laws that tend to work against technological innovation. Nor can state action effect fundamental reform in an area that is overwhelmingly federal. Without a top-down legislative statement to supplement the bottom-up momentum of progress to date, encouraging innovation will continue to be a rear-guard campaign.

An Assessment of the ETI

The ETI emerged as a program with many objectives—environmental, technology development, and international—as well as a style that epitomized "partnership" between government and industry. Over the course of some two years, the nonregulatory elements of the ETI quickly proceeded from a sophisticated conceptual framework, to widespread adherence throughout the administration, congressional rejection, fragmentation, and ultimately a relatively moribund steady state. While personalities and politics offer a significant part of the explanation, the difficulties of imposing a coherent agenda across existing environmental, technical, and commercially oriented programs, without a clearly articulated legal mandate, are at the root of the problems ETI experienced.

The ETI was more an overarching programmatic idea than a program chartered by Congress or Executive Order. The National Science and Technology Council (NSTC) document, *Technology for a Sustainable Future*, set out its four primary goals: to facilitate innovation (through R&D, demonstration and diffusion); to encourage new policy approaches (regulatory, fiscal, market); to promote international commerce in environmental technologies; and to adopt cooperative strategies (public-private partnerships, cross-agency, etc). Efforts to implement the ETI proliferated across many agencies, including the Environmental Protection Agency, the Department of Commerce (DOC), the National Aeronautics and Space Administration (NASA), the Department of Energy (DOE), the Department of Defense (DoD), the Department of Transportation (DOT), the National Science Foundation (NSF), and more.[17] Yet two organizational questions quickly surfaced: how to coordinate and fund initiatives across agencies; and where the mandate to stimulate new environmental technologies should be placed. EPA became the lead administrative agency of the ETI, which had already evolved into an interagency effort to support the development and use of new environmental technologies through projects and public-private partnerships. Funds to support such partnerships were made available to EPA, which would then redistribute them to other agencies in response to proposals.

Most R&D on environmental technologies within the ETI was concentrated in the EPA, and did not depart greatly from traditional regulatory objectives; examples include plastics recycling, advanced adsorption technologies, and pollution prevention materials cleaning. A second element of EPA's programs moved farther afield; it focused on the development of process changes ("clean technology") that would serve both environmental and competitiveness agendas, as well as diffusion to the small business community. The third element, TIES (Technology for International Environmental Solutions), represented perhaps the largest stretch for EPA; it involved trade, international development assistance, and export promotion.[18]

Among the participating agencies, DOC was particularly active in conceptualizing the overall vision of the ETI effort as well as in specific initiatives relating to the commercial marketplace.[19] The conceptual basis of ETI—combining economic, environmental, and technical agendas—fit well with DOC's existing industry-support programs. Within the international trade sector, environmental exports became an important focus, and an Environmental Export Technology Council was formed to reach into the business community and across agencies. Although the Manufacturing Extension Partnership (MEP) in NIST was the only DOC program to apply for and receive ETI funding, other programs appreciated ETI's congruence with their objectives. The National Oceanic and Atmospheric Administration (NOAA) was also a major force behind ETI, and although never explicitly included, the Advanced

Technology Program (ATP) also recognized the environmental relevance of its support for industrial R&D.

The DOE's efforts to enlist the national labs in technology transfer and cooperative R&D with industry, and the role of the DOC and DOT in the Clean Car program, also deserve mention for their potential relevance.[20] But it needs to be emphasized that all such programs continued their independent identities outside the ETI.

The ETI has suffered from budget, focus, and administrative difficulties. It was launched with an initial appropriation of $36 million for FY 1994; this was followed in FY 1995 by an increase in appropriation to $68 million. In both years, the EPA was directed by Congress to pass substantial funds through to other federal agencies in order to build innovation across the government. The 104th Congress slashed the FY 1996 appropriation to $10 million and directed EPA to use the funds solely for environmental technology verification projects. This level of funding and congressional stipulation continued in the FY 1997 appropriation, thus reducing the initiative to a mere shadow of its initial conception.

While EPA was designated as the lead agency, this was not an entirely comfortable choice. Especially early on, the claim of the DOC was often discussed, given its pre-existing technology mandates, and the other participating agencies tended to retain control over their own budgets and agendas. All this has made it hard to manage, focus, and sustain the initiative. For example, many of the R&D activities included in the ETI were pre-existing projects, characterized and publicized in a new context. Few of the staff were oriented toward a central ETI premise: that the government should support the development of industrial technology that is environmentally and economically beneficial. The kinds of research that should have been supported—long-range work to go beyond end-of-pipe compliance into fundamentally new, generically applicable approaches—had no real voice or home in which to flourish. Neither the Clinton administration nor Congress came to terms with the need for an explicit program mandate or the funds to support a new R&D mission. Although several pieces of legislation introduced during the 103rd Congress would have accomplished this, none enjoyed strong administration support.[21] With the change

of majority in the 104th Congress, the prospect of a secure mandate
or funding base for the ETI evaporated.

Why the Congressional Quiescence?

While the agencies and the business community increasingly see a
need to connect technological innovation and environmental
goals, Congress has remained quiescent. This represents a major
missed opportunity, given its remarkable activity in the creation of
a national civilian technology policy. New policies as diverse as
antitrust law reform, new intellectual property rights, technology
transfer incentives, technical extension services, cooperative research and development, and government funding of cutting-edge
technologies in industrial firms have all emerged from the Congress.[22] But almost none of the principles and practices implicit in
these initiatives have been applied to the regulatory context. Most
statutory changes have not been motivated by concern about
technology, and some may unwittingly make the situation worse.
(Increased analytical requirements, for example, generally tend to
slow the regulatory system, often to the detriment of innovators,
who want it speeded up.)

The few occasions on which Congress has addressed innovation
in a regulatory context show the extent to which a new, broader
approach is called for. The only statute to take direct aim is the
Toxic Substances Control Act, which in 1976 directed EPA to
ensure that its authority be administered so as not to "unduly
impede" the course of technological innovation. The implicit
negativity in this provision is only one of the factors that made
TSCA difficult to operationalize.[23] More recently, the Pollution
Prevention Act of 1990 was motivated partly by the realization that
a fundamentally new technological approach was called for—i.e,
source reduction, not clean-up technologies. While this act provided waivers for innovative compliance technologies, these can
only be seen as an "escape hatch" around regulatory requirements
in a limited set of circumstances, not any real inducement to
innovation. Shortly before its dissolution, the Congressional Office
of Technology Assessment analyzed various types of regulatory
mechanisms which pointed the way toward more legislative atten-

tion to regulatory design with a view toward promoting innovation, but its work has not had much impact.[24]

An implicit mindset may well explain Congress's failure to act affirmatively toward innovation in the regulatory context. Hardly anywhere in the statutes that comprise environmental policy is technological innovation appreciated as a primary policy tool; on the contrary, control of technology's adverse impacts is the more prevalent animus. Little thought was devoted to the subtleties of encouraging innovation. Indeed, an assumption that it would flow automatically from industry seems to underlie much of Congress's regulatory thinking, both its early "technology forcing" initiatives and the later enthusiasm for economic instruments during the 1980s.[25]

A corollary mindset also may undermine technology-support initiatives like the ETI: if encouragement of new technology was not envisioned to be within the realm of environmental regulatory policy, neither were environmental goals thought to be within the ambit of technology policy. Only one bill advancing such an agenda surfaced from the science and technology committees of Congress: HR 3870, the Environmental Technologies Act of 1994. Lukewarm administration support, plus adamant opposition from anti-industrial-policy members of the House Science Committee, contributed to its demise. In the Senate, a similar bill was introduced into the Environment Committee, but it also failed to gather the requisite support.

At bottom, however, the lack of legislative progress toward linking environmental policy and technology policy has reflected a fundamental lack of political consensus about how to deal with either arena; an initiative of the conceptual and programmatic scope of the ETI was unlikely to be sustained by a Congress embroiled in controversies about whether to shut down the ATP, the DOC, or the entire government. Even within the technology policy community, the conservative critique of public support for privatetechnology development was strongly voiced. And if proponents of deregulation can be accused of making unrealistic proposals, the environmental community can also be taken to task for adopting an essentially defensive posture rather than an active role in proposing reform. As a result, even consensus proposals—

notably in the Superfund area—have seen no legislative success.[26]
If reform is to come, these entrenched positions must be given up.

Making Regulation a Force for Innovation: A Legislative Proposal

Legislative reform should begin at the top with the addition of an overarching "technology mandate" to the current statutory framework. This mandate should recognize that technological innovation is the main avenue our society can pursue to move toward environmental sustainability, and it should commit the government to assist environmental entrepreneurs in the private sector and to undertake research, development, and other measures with its own resources. Three main goals would be immediately furthered: setting a new objective clearly before environmental policymakers and the technical community; balancing the promotion and the control of technology; and legitimizing the administrative reforms now in an experimental stage.

A set of operational provisions should legislatively specify an entirely new approach to setting regulatory standards. First, the distinction between new and existing sources should be abolished to eliminate the perverse incentive to perpetuate old plant and equipment; this would be a significant move toward making regulations an engine of technological change instead of a deterrent.

Second, the way technology figures in determining levels of environmental protection must be entirely revamped. The "alphabet soup" of current standard types for air and water pollution and waste—BAT, BACT (best available control technology), RACT (reasonably available control technology), etc.—should be replaced by the concept of "environmental agendas." These agendas should articulate industry-specific long-range environmental goals. They would envision a wide range of ambitious environmental improvements that could be achieved through continuing technological changes implemented over a fairly long time-frame of at least ten years. All relevant technological pathways should be considered: reductions or changes in materials inputs, energy efficiency, process controls to prevent or minimize pollution, toxics reduction, product redesign, land use controls, etc. The environmental agendas would be used by firms and regulators as a referent toward which each firm would commit itself in an enforceable environmental improvement plan (discussed below).

It is important to emphasize what the agendas would not do. First, they would not go backward: current pollution and health standards should be seen as a minimum upon which to improve. Second, they would enumerate and assess—not specify or require—technologies capable of producing significant environmental improvement.

The development of such environmental agendas would be a complicated process. It would need to be cooperative, involving EPA, the regulated sector, environmental and community groups, and independent technical experts. Without a doubt, it would be difficult to strike the right balance between a short-term and a long-term focus and between over-ambition and under-ambition. But we are optimistic that it could be done. Indeed, the analytical approach resembles that already practiced by industrial ecologists. Some countries—Holland most notably—are already experimenting with something similar.[27] Some institutions in this country— notably the President's Council on Sustainable Development (PCSD)—have begun the process of articulating a vision of a sustainable U.S. economy sector by sector. Furthermore, the consensus-building techniques developed in sector-specific regulatory approaches—for example, CSI and negotiated rulemakings—could be drawn on in creating the "environmental agendas."

To make the environmental agenda approach a real incentive for technological change, a new implementation mechanism must be devised so that it can be applied to individual firms. This could be achieved if each firm now subject to current water, air, or other environmental permits would instead be required to develop and implement its own "integrated environmental plan." Such plans should cover a reasonably extended period of time—ideally the ten-year time frame of the environmental agendas—and they should detail the milestones and trajectory for technological change the firm would undertake to move toward the environmental agenda envisioned for its industry. Like the current environmental permits it would replace, the plan would be enforceable. Unlike several of the permit programs, it would require only one basic filing with regulatory authorities, amendable as situations change. Each firm would shift to the integrated environmental plan when its existing permits expire.

This approach would shift the burden of initiative from EPA to the private sector, where the sense of technological possibilities is both deepest and most immediate. EPA's role would thus change from being the prescriber of solutions to industry's environmental problems to one of counselor and enforcer. It should actively assist, negotiate, and counsel the development of firm-level environmental agendas that go beyond the current status quo. The enforcement of the integrated environmental plans would be more analogous to tax returns than to permits needing government approval; filers would be responsible for complying with the plan, and EPA would conduct enforcement audits on a sampling basis.

Another advantage of the integrated plans is that they allow for holistic technological solutions, much in the manner of some states' experimental integrated permits. But perhaps the major virtue of this new approach is that it would establish a framework for continual environmental improvements by the firm, which is lacking in today's regulatory framework.

Are there adequate monitoring and enforcement resources to implement integrated environmental plans? While the development of an integrated holistic environmental improvement plan for every firm may seem like a large undertaking, it is important to look realistically at what administrative requirements it would replace. Much of the workload in today's regulatory system is hardly more than routine. In the context of water pollution, for example, state regulators estimate that about 85 percent of technical staff time is involved in permit renewals that change few if any performance parameters. For many approvals, the workload and delay are large. For example, hazardous waste permits required by the U.S. Resource Concentration and Recovery Act (RCRA) typically require 18 to 24 months for approval. If the demands on administrative resources were indeed to increase under our proposal—which need not occur—it would likely be an up-front increase that would not persist over time.

In fact, there is reason to be optimistic that such reforms could actually streamline environmental administration: integrated environmental planning is not a major departure from what many firms are already doing. ISO 14000, the recently adopted environmental management standards; integrated permitting and Project XL; and the movement toward industrial ecology are all based on the recognition that technology change is a key factor in environmental improvement.[28] Regulators, too, have adopted new attitudes and practices, which are likely to dissuade them from micromanaging under a new administrative approach.

Whether or not these far-reaching reforms are implemented, the way EPA is now organized needs to be changed. First, it should set up an "Office of Environmental Innovation" that would serve environmental innovators, both in the environmental industry and among regulated firms. Such an office would be a "one-stop shopping" advocate for innovators, assisting them through the regulatory maze and helping craft creative solutions such as integrated permits, fast-track approvals, or verification of the performance of their technologies. A number of states have already started down this route, and their experience should be considered, and relied on, in fashioning a national capability.[29]

Because the reforms we are suggesting imply a new point of view and balance of missions in the EPA, they will require new skills, new analysis, and new organizational approaches. Originally, EPA's mandates focused on the identification of environmental problems and the prescription of solutions that responded to environmental or health goals. Congress and the courts have made its analytical task ever more complicated through the addition of economic and risk-based analytical requirements. We do not mean to add another requirement; on the contrary, we believe that the current list has already succumbed to the law of diminishing returns. However, we do believe that if environmental regulation is to become an effective inducement to innovation, EPA must be much better equipped to understand and aid industry in crafting technological solutions. This means more engineers of all stripes on the staff, more expert consultants, more cooperative research with industry, and a shift of analytical resources toward issues pertaining to technology development.

One way to effect this would be to give the EPA—perhaps its Office of Environmental Innovation proposed above—responsibility for assembling a broad knowledge of industrial technology and for conducting studies that assess the potential for change in various sectors of the economy. These would form the analytical basis for the "clean standards" toward which firms would move. An outreach function—technical assistance to small businesses, cooperative research, information dissemination, etc.—could also be an important role.

Another, more sweeping approach is to consider reorganizing EPA altogether in order to make its internal structure more compatible with the external world. EPA's media-specific organization corresponds to the statutes it administers, not to the nature of environmental problems or the structure of industry. Reorganizing it according to the structure of the economy would put it on the right footing to work with industry as a facilitator of technological change.

Critical as they are, the reforms to facilitate innovation outlined above cover only half of the agenda. Deliberate action to phase out obsolescent, environmentally unsound technologies must also be a major element. One way to do this is to make the phasing out of old technologies a key element of firms' integrated environmental plans. In addition, regulators should focus much more attention on identifying and attacking environmental and economic technologies that are ripe for replacement with superior technologies. To some extent, this is reminiscent of traditional regulatory action—such as the bans on polychlorinated biphenyls (PCBs) and chlorofluorocarbons (CFCs)—but a more systematic and sophisticated approach would be required. It must rest on careful analysis of the entire range of industrial technology: what exists, what changes are in progress, and what is on the horizon. We do not mean that EPA should have broad new authority to reformulate industrial products and processes at will; however, we do believe that it could take a much more aggressive stance—through information, technical assistance and its regulatory powers—to level the playing field for innovators whose products and processes could replace the environmentally inferior ones now in use.

Revivifying the ETI

The case for a public initiative like the ETI is compelling. There is widespread recognition that a new generation of environmental technology is necessary—one that discards the inefficient end-of-pipe solutions that are still all too common, and moves toward new design concepts that are optimized across both the environmental and economic dimensions. Such technologies are within reach.[30] Current public R&D spending devoted to environmental technology falls far short of meeting national need. Even accepting the 1994 estimates that the federal government spent $3 billion on R&D relevant to environmental technology, this represented less than 5 percent of the total R&D budget. Moreover, the lion's share of this amount was consumed by agencies—DOE, NASA, DoD—whose missions are relatively remote from the environmental problems encountered by industry.[31] Allocations in the most recent budget do not significantly change the picture.

There are three reasons why we cannot depend upon the private sector to produce such technologies. First, the current regulatory system constitutes a significant impediment both to innovation and to the long-term predictability that R&D investments demand. At a minimum, until it is reoriented, technology support and regulation should coexist. Second, much of the environmental R&D that does occur in the private sector is overly concentrated in a group of large firms, and beyond the reach of small companies and others most in need of improvement.[32] Third, the kinds of research that may help most over the long term often produce results of such generic applicability that no firm wants to invest. In other contexts, these are precisely the types of market failures that justify public R&D.

Although the ETI addressed these market failures, and was indeed well-conceived, if it is to be successfully revived, a number of important modifications should occur. First, is the issue of mandate. The statutory change in regulatory authority proposed above includes an explicit mandate to regulators to encourage actively the generation and application of new technology to solve environmental problems. This mandate should be expanded to the traditional mechanisms of technology policy: R&D support, demonstration, technology transfer, technology partnerships, etc. In parallel, the mandates of the main technical agencies that provide support for industrial technology—the National Institute of Standards and Technology (NIST), Advanced Research Projects Agency

(ARPA), Manufacturing Extension Program (MEP), National Science Foundation (NSF), national labs—should be broadened to establish environmental technology as an explicit element of their technical portfolios.

Second, the ETI should pursue only two main activities: support for long-range R&D, and facilitating immediate technology development, adaptation, and diffusion. The R&D agenda should concentrate on research of generic applicability to meet both environmental and economic goals. We envision this research being carried out in firms, much in the manner of the ATP. The technology diffusion agenda should also occur in the private sector, through cooperative programs that focus on solving environmental and economic problems simultaneously. MEP programs such as the Cleveland Advanced Manufacturing Program (CAMP) are successful institutional models that could be turned much more strongly toward this purpose. The fiscal, regulatory, and trade promotion aspects of the ETI should be discarded.

Third, the issues of budget, leadership, and focus that have plagued the ETI to date must be solved. The ETI must have a significant, dedicated budget to guarantee that new technical work actually occurs, and to provide a lever for leadership. A capability such as ARPA's—staff with the resources to envision and empower the next generation of technology that will undergird the solutions to environmental problems—is an activist, but desirable policy alternative. The ATP approach—responding with funding to industrial proposals—offers a different pathway to the same result. Where this capability finds a home—whether in EPA as envisioned in HR 3870, as a component of NIST, or elsewhere—is less important than that it exist. At the moment, unfortunately, the country has hardly any such public capability in place. Whether it sets or responds to R&D targets, though important, is a second-order design question.

Since many agencies' activities will continue to bear on environmental technology, the designation of a "lead agency" for environmental technology promotion is particularly important. The coordination and leadership of a program as broad, diverse, and diffuse as the ETI is difficult. Narrowing and deepening the scope of ETI, as suggested above, would make an EPA leadership role more viable, but new capabilities and commitment would still be necessary. The EPA "Office of Innovation" proposed above offers one possible locus for such leadership. It would both provide a focal point for technology promotion and provide a coordinating link to the new regulatory regime.

The question of whether a regulatory agency like EPA can also support industry in technology development is a perennial—and valid—concern. Some countries—Japan most notably—have installed environmental technology promotion in their industrial ministries. On balance, however, the best solution for the United States is to attempt to harmonize the two approaches in EPA. Regulation itself, it bears repeating, can be an effective force for innovation, and EPA could make it even more so with a new technology mandate and resources. But certainly, it should engage other agencies as well.

Given the breadth of the mandate that we have envisioned across the public research and technology enterprise and regulatory activities, the White House policy apparatus must also play a vigorous role. One critical function—which it exhibited early in the ETI—is to conceptualize, initiate, and act as an advocate for program development. But top-down coordination and synthesis of environmental R&D and technology support must also be pursued. Although these activities were implicitly recognized at least since the beginning of the ETI, their realization proceeded fitfully. More attention and staff needs to be devoted to this issue.

The Moment Is Ripe

Twenty-five years of relatively static law represents a long time in a field that changes as fast as environmental policy. Though these years have brought significant environmental progress, no attempt has yet been made to reassess the overall statutory framework to incorporate technological innovation as a lever of environmental policy. Industry's posture is now fundamentally different; the technological base of solutions has expanded dramatically; research has confirmed how regulation and technological change interact; changes in administrative practice now provide useful models; and a comprehensive national technology has matured outside of the environmental field.

The incoming Congress faces a particularly opportune moment to reassess the statutory framework. Several of the bedrock environmental statutes—the Clean Air Act, the Clean Water Act, Superfund—are due for reauthorization. Outside of the Congress, there is a groundswell toward reform. An environmental entrepreneurial community has been established, and its policy aims move in surprising concert with initiatives from the regulatory agencies. A number of well-structured reform efforts are likely to generate major policy proposals in the coming months.[33]

Yet in the movement toward legislative change, so far little attention has focused on technology. The assumption seems to be that broad-brush strategies—for example, a unified environmental statute or sectoral approaches to sustainability—will automatically create a climate conducive to innovation. We believe that this is misguided. Technological innovation is a social process that can be encouraged, managed, and directed, but to do so requires activism.

The legislative cure outlined above represents the first essential steps to integrate technology into environmental policy. It could be expanded into a distinct piece of legislation or folded in to a larger integrated statute. Above all, it conveys the need for government to take the initiative on technological innovation as the pathway to an environmentally improved future. While this is occurring within the regulatory community in an *ad hoc* manner, the momentum for reform cannot build and be sustained against the tide of an inhospitable statutory framework. The old regulatory strategies—enacted sensibly twenty-five years ago as a quick dose of strong, simple medicine—have played themselves out. For all their virtues, they now appear to constrict the flow of environmentally beneficial technological innovation, which we can ill afford. While there may be certain risks to opening up that flow—innovation is, after all, inherently unpredictable—it is high time for environmental policy to accept these risks in a spirit of constructive experimentation.

Notes

1. By the late 1970s, an anti-regulatory attitude characterized those in the business and technical communities who saw regulation inhibiting technological innovation. See National Academy of Sciences, *The Impact of Regulation on Industrial Innovation* (Washington, D.C.: National Academy of Sciences, 1979).

2. On the role of new technology, see George Heaton, Robert Repetto, and Rodney Sobin, *Transforming Technology: An Agenda for Environmentally Sustainable Growth in the Twenty-first Century* (Washington, D.C.: World Resources Institute, 1991). For a discussion of business's growing commitment, see Stephen Schmidheiny, *Changing Course* (Cambridge, Mass.: The MIT Press, 1992).

3. PCSD, *Sustainable America: A New Consensus* (Washington, D.C.: The President's Council on Sustainable Development, 1996); OSTP, *Bridge to A Sustainable Future: National Environmental Technology Strategy* (Washington, D.C.: Office of Science and Technology Policy, 1995).

4. President William J. Clinton and Vice President Albert Gore, Jr., "Technology for America's Economic Growth," February 23, 1993.

5. Environmental Protection Agency (EPA), "Environmental Technology Initiative: FY 1994 Program Plan," EPA 543-K-93-003 (Washington, D.C.: U.S. EPA, January 1994).

6. Office of Technology Assessment, *Industry, Technology and the Environment: Competitive Challenges and Business Opportunities*, OTA-ENV-586 (Washington, D.C.: U.S. Congress, Office of Technology Assessment, 1994).

7. The White House, *Working Papers of White House Conference on Environmental Technology* (Washington, D.C.: The White House, 1994).

8. Amoco Oil Company and U.S. EPA, *Amoco-U.S. EPA Pollution Prevention Project Yorktown, Virginia* (Chicago: Amoco, 1992).

9. Christopher Hill, ed., *Federal Regulation and Chemical Innovation* (Washington, D.C.: American Chemical Society, 1979); Nicholas Ashford and George Heaton, "Regulation and Technological Innovation in the Chemical Industry," *Journal of Law and Contemporary Problems*, Vol. 46, No. 3 (Summer 1983); David Wallace, *Environmental Policy and Industrial Innovation: Strategies in Europe, the U.S. and Japan* (London: Earthscan Publications, 1995); United States Regulatory Council, *Regulatory Reform Highlights: An Inventory of Initiatives, 1978–1980* (Washington, D.C.: U.S. Regulatory Council, 1980).

10. Report of the Technology Innovation and Economics Committee, The National Advisory Council for Environmental Policy and Technology, *Permitting and Compliance Policy: Barriers to U.S. Environmental Technology Innovation* (Washington, D.C.: U.S. Environmental Protection Agency, 1991).

11. Clinton and Gore, "Technology for America's Economic Growth."

12. See remarks of Vice President Al Gore, Secretary of Commerce Ron Brown, EPA Administrator Carol Browner, and Science Advisor John Gibbons, *White House Conference on Environmental Technology*, December 11, 1994.

13. President William J. Clinton and Vice President Albert Gore, Jr., "Reinventing Environmental Regulation," The White House, March 16, 1995.

14. "Regulatory Reinvention (XL) Pilot Projects," 60 *Federal Register* 99, May 23, 1995.

15. Carol M. Browner, "The Common Sense Initiative: A New Generation of Environmental Protection" (Washington, D.C.: U.S. Environmental Protection Agency, July 29, 1994).

16. California Environmental Protection Agency, *Certification Program for Hazardous Waste Technologies* (Sacramento: California Environmental Protection Agency, 1994).

17. See Appendix 1, NSTC, *Technology for a Sustainable Future: A Framework for Action* (Washington, D.C.: National Science and Technology Council, 1994).

18. These programs are all described in EPA, "Environmental Technology Initiative: FY 1994 Program Plan," EPA 543-K-93-003 (Washington, D.C.: U.S. EPA, January 1994).

19. See remarks of Secretary of Commerce Ron Brown, *White House Conference on Environmental Technology*, December 11, 1994.

20. The idea of governmental support for automotive technology has a long history and has been advanced under various names at different times. The Clean Car program is known today as PNGV (Partnership for a New Generation of Vehicles).

21. See S. 978, *National Environmental Technology Act of 1993*; Senate Report 103-156; H.R. 3870, *Environmental Technologies Act of 1994*; House of Representatives Report 103-156.

22. NSTC, *Technology for a Sustainable Future*; George Heaton, "Commercial Technology Development: A New Paradigm of Public Private Cooperation," *Business in the Contemporary World* (Autumn 1989).

23. EPA, *Supporting Innovation: A Policy Study*, EPA-560/12-80-002 (Washington, D.C.: EPA Office of Toxic Substances, 1980).

24. OTA, *Environmental Policy Tools: A Users Guide*, OTA-ENV-634 (Washington, D.C.: U.S. Congress, Office of Technology Assessment, 1995).

25. Thomas McGarrity, "Radical Technology Forcing in Environmental Regulation," *Loyola Law Review*, Vol. 27, No. (1994), p. 943; and T. Wirth, *Project 88— Round II, Incentives for Action: Designing Market-Based Environmental Strategies* (Washington, D.C.: Project 88 1991).

26. The National Commission on Superfund's long-discussed bipartisan proposals were avoided by the partisan-gridlocked 103rd Congress.

27. The Dutch government's ambitious National Environmental Policy Plan is a strategic effort designed to link long-term environmental goals with sector-specific implementation plans. See Dutch Committee for Long-Term Environmental Policy, ed., *The Environment: Towards A Sustainable Future* (Boston: Kluwer Academic Publishers, 1994).

28. Graedel and B.R. Allenby, *Industrial Ecology* (Englewood Cliffs, N.J.: Prentice Hall, 1995).

29. NEPI, *Building Partnerships for a Sustainable Future: A Framework for Action* (Washington, D.C.: National Science and Technology Council, 1994).

30. See, for example, George Heaton, Robert Repetto, and Rodney Sobin, *Backs to the Future: U.S. Government Policy Toward Environmentally Critical Technology* (Washington, D.C.: World Resources Institute, June 1992); and OSTP, *Bridge to a Sustainable Future* (Washington, D.C.: Office of Science and Technology Council, 1994).

31. About 45 percent of this total is DOE, 22 percent NASA, and 11 percent DoD, while EPA and DOC each only had 1 percent of the pollution avoidance R&D spending.

32. OSTP, *Bridge to a Sustainable Future.*

33. These efforts include the President's Council on Sustainable Development; Enterprise for the Environment; Yale Center for Environmental Law and Policy's Environmental Reform: The Next Generation Project; and the National Environmental Policy Institute's Regulatory Reinvention Project.

12

Federal Energy Research and Development for the Challenges of the 21st Century

John P. Holdren

High on the list of the proper aims of national technology policy is nurturing technological innovations—and promotion of the transfer of these to the marketplace—of types that (1) are likely to be important in improving and sustaining economic prosperity, environmental quality, and national security for this country's citizens; and (2) are unlikely, without the federal government's participation, to be developed and applied to these ends in a timely fashion by other actors such as state and local governments, private firms and consortia, and other nongovernmental organizations. I argue in this chapter that innovations in energy technology resoundingly satisfy the first condition and that they often satisfy the second. I also address how and why it has happened, nonetheless, that energy research and development have received such scant attention in discussions of national technology policy (and such scanty shares of the federal science and technology budget) over the past fifteen years—a period in which the inadequacies of this country's energy system in relation to the likely energy challenges of the first part of the twenty-first century were becoming increasingly obvious. The chapter concludes with a discussion of the prospects for reviving the government's interest in and support for energy research and development during the second Clinton term.

Why the United States Needs a Coherent Energy R&D Strategy

The arguments for a coherent national energy R&D strategy reside in the connections between energy and the economic, environmental, and national-security dimensions of the well-being of our citizens; in the potential for serious difficulties early in the twenty-first century arising from inadequacies of the current mix of energy options in relation to these connections; and in the constellation of reasons that the private sector, on its own, will do only a part of the energy R&D needed to address those inadequacies. Developing these arguments requires some understanding of recent and possible future trajectories of U.S. and world energy supply and demand, to which I now turn.

U.S. and World Energy Supply and Demand

In 1995, the 5.7 billion people then on the planet were using inanimate energy forms at a rate of about 14 terawatts, which can also be expressed as 14 terawatt-years per year, or 420 quadrillion Btus per year, or 2.5 kilowatts per average person in the world population.[1] Of this total 1995 energy supply, about 53 percent was derived from oil and gas, 22 percent from coal, 13 percent from biomass fuels (i.e., fuelwood, charcoal, crop wastes, and dung), and 6 percent each from hydropower and from nuclear fission.[2] (The contributions from geothermal energy, windpower, and direct use of solar energy totaled less than half a percent.) About two thirds of the total supply went to the 1.2 billion people living in industrialized countries, and about one third went to the 4.5 billion people living in less developed countries (LDCs).[3] Approximately 30 percent of the 14-terawatt world primary-energy supply was used to make some 12.5 trillion kilowatt-hours of electricity, nearly 80 percent of it used in the industrialized countries.

The global demand for energy in 1995 was more than four times larger than in 1950 and ten times larger than in 1900; and between 1900 and 1995 the annual amount of energy supplied by fossil fuels grew by sixteen-fold.[4] Under "business as usual" assumptions about the energy future, world energy demand in 2025 would be about twice as large—and that in 2050 about three times as large—as the 1995 figure, and fossil-fuel use would increase over these periods by similar factors.[5] (The "business-as-usual" scenarios entail real rates of global economic growth averaging about 3 percent per year to 2025, falling gradually thereafter toward 2 percent per year, and rates of improvement of macroeconomic energy efficiency—i.e., real economic product per unit of energy use—averaging 1 percent per year indefinitely.)

The United States, which with 4.6 percent of the world's population in 1995 accounted for about 22 percent of the energy demand, is even more fossil-fuel-intensive than the world as a whole: 85 percent of U.S. energy in 1995 was supplied by fossil fuels (versus 75 percent for the world), 8 percent by nuclear energy, 4 percent by hydropower, and 3 percent by biomass fuels; 38 percent of the total was oil, half of it imported.[6] U.S. energy demand in 1995 was 2.6 times larger than in 1950 and eight times larger than in 1900; in the 1990s it has been growing at an average rate of 1.4 percent per year while real economic growth was about 1.9 percent per year, implying a rate of increase of macroeconomic energy efficiency of 0.5 percent per year. (For comparison, in the thirteen years from 1973 to 1986 U.S. macroeconomic energy efficiency increased at an average of 2.7 percent per year.)

Economic Challenges in Our Energy Future

The challenges posed by the energy future to the economic well-being of the United States are of at least three kinds: controlling consumer costs for energy and energy-intensive products; reducing oil-import bills; and building international markets for U.S. energy technologies and other products.

Expenditures for energy—electricity and fuels—by individuals and organizations in the United States amounted in the mid-1990s to approximately $500 billion per year or about 7.5 percent of GNP.[7] U.S. energy prices are low both by historical standards and in comparison with other countries, but there is no guarantee that they will remain so. They could be driven up by increasing competition for world oil output, by manipulation of the world oil market, by political instability in the Persian Gulf, by environmentally motivated requirements to reduce emissions from fossil-fuel combustion, and by other eventualities of both foreseeable and unforeseeable types. As the oil-price shocks of the 1970s abundantly demonstrated, large and sudden energy-price increases produce not only immediate adverse effects in the form of erosion of purchasing power but also can drive the global economy into recession, at immense economic cost. The challenge to energy research and development here is to provide additional energy-supply and energy-efficiency options that can reduce U.S. dependence on the imported oil supplies that are subject to sharp price increases, to develop options that can shrink the cost of reducing emissions from fossil fuels (which includes the possibility of replacing some fossil-fuel use with non-fossil-fuel options less costly than those that would be available for this purpose today), and more generally to develop options that can "backstop" existing energy-supply technologies—that is, provide the possibility of substituting for them if their costs escalate beyond the cost of the "backstop" option.

U.S. oil imports in 1995 were a $60 billion item on the deficit side of this country's balance-of-payments ledger. The U.S. Department of Energy's "reference" forecast shows the U.S. oil-import bill reaching $108 billion per year (1995 dollars) by 2015—at which time this country will be importing 50 percent more oil than in 1995.[8] (This forecast assumes that U.S. use of oil will increase from 18 million barrels per day in 1995 to 22 million in 2015, while domestic production falls from 9 million to 8 million barrels per day.) Clearly there is the possibility of a substantial economic benefit from energy R&D (or other measures) that could lead to reducing U.S. oil imports over the next twenty years to below the trajectory forecasted in the DOE's reference case.

The third major U.S. economic stake in the energy future has to do with this country's capacity to sell both energy equipment and other products in international markets. With respect to energy equipment, the value of the world's energy-supply system today—the power plants, oil refineries, pipelines, drilling rigs, transmission lines, and so on—is in the range of $10 trillion at replacement cost.[9] If the average lifetime of these facilities is thirty years, then mere replacement of attrition in a system of constant size would entail investments of some $300 billion per year. To meet the "business as usual" projection of a doubling in energy use by 2025, however, the global energy system would need to double in size in the next thirty years, entailing an additional $300 billion per year in investments (assuming that the cost of a given quantity of energy-supply capacity does not change, which of course may not be true). As a very rough estimate, in any case, the world market for energy equipment and energy-facility construction over the next thirty years is going to be in the range of several hundred billion dollars per year. The challenge for U.S. energy R&D in this connection is to develop energy technologies of sufficient attractiveness—in relation to those being offered by others—to maintain a substantial share of this immense market (including the market in the United States, where if we are not diligent we could lose market share to, e.g., Japan, Germany, South Korea, and who knows who else). Part of this challenge, of course, is to shape some of our R&D to the economic and environmental needs of the most rapidly growing parts of the international market, such as China and India, rather than just developing energy options tailored only for U.S. conditions.

With respect to the capacity of the United States to sell other products in international markets, the connection to energy R&D is through the links between suitable energy technologies and economic growth. Adequate supplies of economically affordable and environmentally tolerable energy are an essential ingredient of increased economic prosperity around the world. To the extent that U.S. energy R&D can contribute to this end, it will be building potential markets for all of the products that the United States might like to export.

Environmental Challenges in Our Energy Future

Energy is perhaps the most intractable part of the planet's environmental problems, both because the impacts of energy systems are the dominant drivers of many of the most dangerous and difficult environmental problems at every geographic scale from the local to the global, and because the energy-system characteristics that cause these problems are often costly and time-consuming to change.[10] Environmental concerns, similarly, may well prove to be the heart of the energy problem, in the sense that environmental constraints and the costs of coping with them, much more than resource scarcity or the monetary costs of energy technology other than those arising from environmental considerations, may turn out to dominate society's choices about how much energy should be supplied from what sources.[11]

At the local level, the most pervasive and troublesome environmental problems include acute air pollution both in the outdoor environment of the world's cities (to which problem the hydrocarbons and particulates emitted in burning fossil and biomass fuels are invariably major contributors, albeit not the only ones) and in the indoor environment of poorly ventilated dwellings in both the urban and rural sectors of developing countries (where coal, fuelwood, charcoal, cropwastes, and dung are burned for heating and cooking). The latter problem is, in light of the combination of extremely high pollutant concentrations and large numbers of women and children exposed to them during a high proportion of the hours of the day, quite clearly a much more consequential problem for global public health than is the outdoor air-pollution problem.[12] Among the world's many local water-pollution problems, those produced by coal-mine drainage, oil-refinery emissions, oil spills from pipelines and tankers, and leakage into groundwater from underground fuel-storage tanks (this last problem one of the most pervasive bad actors in putting toxic-waste sites on the Superfund list) are prominent contributions from the energy sector.[13]

At the regional level, air-basin-wide smogs from the interaction of hydrocarbons and nitrogen oxides share the top of the air-pollution-hazard list with acidic hazes and fogs fed by varying combinations of nitrogen and sulfur oxides. The dangers include damage to crops and forests as well as to public health; the culprits are overwhelmingly fossil fuels burned in vehicles and power plants. Emissions of oxides of nitrogen and sulfur are also the primary sources of acid precipitation, arguably the dominant form of regional water and soil pollution in areas where soils and surface waters are poorly buffered (a description that applies to tens of millions of square kilometers of the world's land area), with potential impacts on forest health, fish and amphibian populations, nutrient cycling, and mobilization and uptake of toxic trace metals.[14]

At the global level, the emissions of greenhouse gases from fossil-fuel use—carbon dioxide and nitrous oxide from combustion of all fossil fuels, and methane from fossil-fuel production and natural-gas transport—are the dominant contributors to the threat of greenhouse-gas-induced climate disruption. There is no scientific doubt that the global composition of the atmosphere with respect to these climate-shaping gases has been significantly altered by human activities, above all fossil-fuel use, and there is an increasingly robust scientific consensus that the consequences of this human impact on the atmosphere are already evident in global climatic patterns.[15] Nor is there any doubt that the world is committed, by virtue of the long lifetime of anthropogenic greenhouse gases in the atmosphere and the difficulty of restraining their emission, to substantial further growth in their concentrations; the scientific arguments are only about degree and detail—the timing, severity, and geographic pattern with which the resulting changes in climate will unfold.

Notwithstanding the uncertainties about these aspects, a good case can be made that fossil-fuel-driven climate change is the most dangerous and intractable environmental problem on the planet. It is the most dangerous because climate change could reduce the productivity of farming, forestry, and fisheries around the globe; increase the virulence and geographic scope of important human diseases; increase the frequency and intensity of destructive storms; raise sea level; and accelerate the loss of planetary biodiversity (among other impacts).[16] It is the most intractable because the human activity that drives it—the mobilization and combustion of the coal, oil, and natural gas that supply three-quarters of the energy used by civilization—is a crucial contributor to economic well-being worldwide and very difficult to modify to reduce the offending characteristic, and because the evolution of the problem responds only slowly to changes in the human input.

Ameliorating the environmental problems caused by energy supply is partly a matter of improving the management practices of energy industries and partly a matter of developing appropriate incentives and regulations (and institutions for implementing these) to guide the behavior of energy producers and consumers alike. Much progress has been made along these lines in the last twenty-five years, in the United States and elsewhere. But improvements in energy technology itself are also essential for addressing environmental problems, and can often alleviate the burdens and economic inefficiencies that would be associated with stringent environmental regulations in the absence of technological advances. This is the environmental challenge to energy R&D: to provide energy options that can substantially ameliorate the local, regional, and global environmental risks and impacts of today's energy-supply system, that can do so at affordable costs and without incurring new environmental (or political) risks as serious as those that have been ameliorated, and that are applicable to the needs and contexts of developing countries as well as industrialized ones—and the sooner the better. It is a big order.

National-Security Challenges in Our Energy Future

The most demanding national-security challenges associated with energy are three: minimizing the dangers of conflict over access to oil and gas resources; controlling the links between nuclear-energy technologies and nuclear-weapons capabilities; and avoiding failures of energy strategy with economic or environmental consequences capable of aggravating or generating large-scale political instabilities.

The proposition that states may go to war over access to resources is solidly rooted in history; and, while there are few instances in international affairs in which a single factor explains everything, it is clear that in this century access to energy resources has more than once been a significant motivator of major conflict.[17] Certainly this was a factor in the aspirations of Germany and Japan leading up to World War II; and few would doubt that control of Kuwaiti oil was one of Saddam Hussein's primary goals in invading Kuwait, or that denying him this was one of the U.S.-led coalition's primary goals in throwing him out. The Persian Gulf, which remains one of the world's more unstable regions politically, today accounts for half of all the world's oil exports, and according to the forecast of the U.S. Department of Energy, this figure is likely to reach 72–75 percent by 2015.[18] Although exact allocations of the purposes of military spending are not possible, the widely repeated estimates that a quarter or more of the $270 billion per year U.S. defense budget is attributable to the need to be prepared to intervene in the Middle East are probably not far wrong.

The complexity of the international-security dimensions of world oil is certain to increase with the rapid growth of China's presence in the oil market. China shifted from being a net exporter to a net importer of oil in late 1993, by late 1996 was importing some 600,000 barrels per day, and could easily be importing 3 million barrels per day by 2010 and 10 million barrels per day by 2025 (more than the United States is importing today).[19] To suppose that oil-import-dependency of these magnitudes will not affect Chinese foreign and military policy would be naive, just as it would be naive to suppose that the increasingly strident and politically problematic Chinese territorial claims extending to the southern rim of the South China Sea have nothing to do with the potential undersea energy resources of that region. Chinese military spending has been rising—by 1995 it exceeded that of Japan, South Korea, Taiwan, Indonesia, Maylaysia, the Philippines, and Thailand combined, and was equal to one-third that of the United States—and growing along with it is China's capacity to project military force at increasing distances from her boundaries.[20]

To say that growing tensions and potential problems for the national-security interests of the United States are likely to arise from intensifying competition for world oil and gas supplies is not to recommend that the United States and other nations pursue energy independence, which is neither feasible nor, in today's multiply interdependent world, even desirable. But it *is* desirable to try to limit the tension-producing potential of overdependence on imports (especially on imports from regions of precarious political stability), as well as the tension-producing potential of resources of disputed ownership, by working to diversify sources of supply of oil and gas (including domestic supplies in the major importing regions), to develop further the non-oil-and-gas sources of portable fuels and electricity, and to increase the efficiency of energy end-use. Clearly energy R&D has roles to play in all of these connections although, equally clearly, it is not the only leverage point.

Nuclear energy is a partial answer to the import-dependence, air-pollution, and climate-change liabilities of fossil fuels which has been embraced by a number of countries,[21] but it carries significant national-security liabilities of its own in the form of the difficult-to-manage linkages between nuclear-energy technology and nuclear weaponry. The key point is that while any major country determined to acquire nuclear weapons could choose to do so without resorting to civilian nuclear-energy facilities for help, nuclear energy does bring together skills and technologies that could ease the path to weaponry (and lower its cost), and approaches to nuclear energy that involve the use of highly enriched uranium or the separation and recycle of plutonium provide particularly direct routes to weapons—including by theft of these materials by agents of radical states lacking their own nuclear technology, by terrorists, or by middlemen feeding an international black market.[22]

The scale of the global nuclear-energy enterprise has grown much more slowly than was widely forecast a few decades ago, partly because of slower-than-expected growth in the electricity sector overall, partly because of nuclear energy's particular problems at the intersection of cost and reactor-safety concerns, and partly because of wider public worries about radioactive waste management and nuclear weapons proliferation. Growing concerns now about the climate-change liabilities of fossil fuels might help produce a new surge of growth in nuclear power, but it is likely to be very limited in magnitude and duration unless concerns about cost, safety, wastes, and proliferation are convincingly addressed. All of these issues are challenges not only to the management and regulation of nuclear energy, but also to R&D. In my view the biggest challenge of all of them will be achieving the high degree of decoupling that society should and probably will insist upon between nuclear-energy generation and the spread of nuclear weapons, and this will require not only better regulation and management but new technology.

Probably the most fundamental and enduring source of conflict in the world is material deprivation or the threat of it; accordingly, it may well be that the most fundamental and enduring links between energy and international security are those in which energy decisions (or the absence of them) either ameliorate or aggravate widespread economic or environmental impoverishment or the threat of these. Because affordable energy is an indispensable ingredient of material prosperity, it is not hard to see that this energy-economy-security connection must be taken seriously. In light of what is now known or suspected about the potential for large-scale and widespread damage to human well-being from energy-related environmental impacts—above all from greenhouse-gas-induced global climate change—the energy-environment-security connection increasingly must be taken seriously as well.[23]

On the basis of all of the energy-security linkages just described, one can make a decent argument that the security of the United States is considerably more likely to be imperiled in the first half of the next century by the consequences of inadequacies in the energy options available to the world than by inadequacies in the capabilities of U.S. weapons systems. This makes it all the more striking that the federal government spends about twenty times more R&D money on the latter problem than on the former.

Is "Business As Usual" Practical?

The energy-related economic, environmental, and national-security challenges just described are formidable separately and are even more so in combination. A "business as usual" energy future—entailing a world in 2050 with half again as many people as in 2000, using three times as much energy, deriving nearly the same fraction of it as today from fossil fuels, and using a mix of energy-conversion and end-use technologies only modestly different from today's—is not likely to be the solution. Indeed, it is so likely to be massively problematic economically, environmentally, and politically that it cannot be achieved even it is attempted. It would not provide enough affordable energy in the developing countries for them to realize their economic aspirations (while providing *more* energy in the industrialized nations than would be required there if they gave appropriate emphasis to improving end-use efficiency); it would generate immense environmental problems from expanded fossil fuel use (including, above all, potentially intolerable impacts on global climate from the associated greenhouse-gas emissions); it might, even so, also entail the expansion of nuclear energy generation more rapidly than the technologies, trained personnel, and institutional machinery needed to operate these systems safely and proliferation-free could be propagated; and it would entail sharply increased global dependence on oil from the Persian Gulf, with attendant vulnerabilities and multi-nation political and military maneuvering to try to protect access to these and the other richest remaining sources of oil and natural gas.

Of course, pursuit of business-as-usual until this approach collapses is not the only possible energy future. An alternative can be envisioned entailing lower energy growth rates in the industrialized countries (not from economic sacrifice but from faster increases in the efficiencies of energy-conversion and end-use), greater availability of affordable energy options matched to the needs of developing countries, reduced-emission fossil-fuel technologies, improved technology and management for nuclear energy, and more rapid improvement and deployment of renewable energy technologies. Attaining this alternative future will require a combination of leadership, management, and technical innovation. These ingredients can and will come partly from the private sector. But because the requirement for them is driven in substantial measure by "public goods" considerations (environment, security, and societal economic benefits beyond those that firms would pursue for themselves in an unregulated market), they must come from government as well. The remainder of this chapter looks in more detail at the energy R&D component of what is required, at recent patterns of energy R&D spending both in government and in the private sector, and at the reasons these patterns diverge from what one might expect in light of the evident challenges and opportunities facing the energy system.

What Energy R&D Is Needed?

I find it useful to divide the possible focuses for energy R&D into two categories: "low-risk" possibilities, meaning there is a high probability that at least parts of the effort will bear fruit in the form of innovations that find significant commercial application; and "high-risk" possibilities, where the probability of success (by the foregoing definition) is lower but the potential payoff is high enough to make the work worth pursuing in the context of a balanced energy R&D portfolio. These two categories are treated here in turn.[24]

Low-Risk Energy R&D

Energy efficiency. The cornerstone of an energy strategy aimed at holding down monetary costs, environmental impacts, and oil imports is achievement of more rapid increases in energy efficiency (i.e., reductions in the ratio of energy to economic product) than the 1 percent per year long-term historical average typically used in forecasting. Improvements in energy efficiency are the equivalent of new energy supply, in that the energy "saved" by increased efficiency in one application can be used in another; and expansion of this efficiency "supply" occurred in many countries in the 10–15 years following the 1973 oil shock at 2–3 percent per year.[25] A large literature indicates that the potential for further cost-effective improvements in energy end-use efficiency is large in all sectors—residential and commercial buildings, industrial processes, agriculture, and transportation—and in industrializing and developing countries alike.[26] Achieving this potential is a matter of overcoming barriers to the implementation of already extant and cost-effective energy-efficiency options (and how to do this is itself an appropriate focus of research),[27] as well as of private-sector and public-sector investment in energy-efficiency-technology R&D to bring new options to the point of cost-effectiveness. The rates of return to federal government investments in energy-efficiency R&D, including through various forms of government/industry/ national-laboratory partnerships, have been unusually well documented and appear to be very high.[28] In my judgment these high rates of return are likely to persist.

Improved fossil-fuel and biomass technologies. Harvesting, transport, processing, and combustion of fossil and biomass fuels are responsible, as indicated above, for many of the most damaging and dangerous environmental impacts of human activity. These damages and risks are amenable to reduction by improved technologies for dealing with these fuels, from harvesting through combustion, focused on increased extraction and conversion efficiencies and lower emissions.[29] Cleaner technologies for electricity generation from coal—perhaps most importantly integrated-gasification combined-cycle (IGCC) systems—will be of particularly critical importance in light of the continuing heavy reliance on coal in high-energy-growth regions in Asia as well as elsewhere. Another promising line of development likely to come to significant commercial fruition in the next two decades is fuel cells, which can extract energy from hydrogen (derivable from fossil and biomass fuels alike) at about twice the efficiencies typically attained in combustion-based systems.[30] Also productive to date and promising for the future are improvements in the technology for finding and harvesting conventional and unconventional deposits of natural gas, which is intrinsically the cleanest, lowest-CO_2 fossil fuel and the easiest to use at high efficiency.[31] Cooperative efforts with China to find more gas there could be especially important. The gas resources that have been discovered in China to date are exceptionally small in relation to that country's land area and geologic circumstances.[32] Finding more gas and using it with high-efficiency, low-emissions technologies would be one of the more promising ways to reduce the environmental and political impacts likely to result from the massive growth in coal use and oil imports currently expected to take place in China over the next twenty-five years.

Higher-efficiency and/or lower-cost photovoltaic, solar-thermal, and wind energy systems. The cost of delivered energy from photovoltaic, solar-thermal (electric and nonelectric), and wind-electric energy systems has fallen sharply over the past two decades.[33] Wind is the closest of these to being competitive commercially with fossil-fueled electricity generation today—indeed it is already competitive at good wind sites where cheap natural gas is not available—and the worldwide potential for wind-electricity generation is probably comparable to that of hydropower. Solar-thermal systems are the next closest to competitiveness and have larger ultimate potential. Photovoltaics have the largest potential of all, but also the largest distance still to travel in order to be competitive for large-scale electricity generation. The leverage against the energy challenges of the next century likely to be gained from additional R&D on all three of these classes of renewable energy sources is large.

High-Risk Energy R&D

Improved fission energy options. Energy from nuclear fission, having achieved by 1995 an 18 percent share of world electricity generation delivered by some 425 operating power reactors, is no longer growing appreciably anywhere in the world except Asia. (In the United States, no new nuclear plant has been ordered since 1978, and nuclear output will soon start to shrink as retirements of older plants accelerate.) Whether the growth of nuclear energy will be sustained even in Asia depends, like the prospects for a revival of growth elsewhere, on the evolving characteristics of competing fossil-fuel and renewable energy options, on the evolution of the climate-change issue and attendant incentives to reduce dependence on fossil fuels, and on the future performance of nuclear-energy systems with respect to cost, safety, waste management, and protection of nuclear-weapon materials. Many critics of nuclear energy's prospects have argued that the outcome is already clear: that fission's cost will remain too high and its safety, waste-management, and materials-protection problems too intractable for it to play a significantly expanded role in the global energy future, even if the climate-change issue develops in such a way as to increase sharply the incentives for deploying non-fossil-fuel options.[34] In my view, however, no one's crystal ball is clear enough to allow such a conclusion to be reached with confidence: it is possible that the combination of demand for non-fossil-fuel energy-supply options and capacities of renewable energy technologies to meet these demands on attractive terms will evolve in a way that leaves room for a considerably expanded contribution from a nuclear-energy system with characteristics that might, with effort, be attainable. Prudence dictates that this possibility should be pursued by exploring, through R&D on advanced nuclear-energy technologies and on improved approaches to nuclear-energy management, how and by how much the characteristics of nuclear-energy systems could be improved with respect to cost, safety, waste management, and nuclear-materials protection. These problems are difficult enough, in my judgment, to warrant characterizing such R&D as "high-risk" in terms of the probability of achieving results that could transform fission's prospects, but there is no shortage of ideas about directions that ought to be explored.[35]

Sequestration of carbon dioxide from fossil fuels. Combustion of fossil fuels produces carbon dioxide in such immense quantities as to raise considerable doubt about the practicality of evading the climatological impact of this effluent by capturing it and storing it away from the atmosphere: world CO_2 emissions from fossil-fuel combustion in the mid-1990s were about 22 billion metric tonnes, equivalent to 11,000 cubic kilometers of carbon dioxide gas at standard temperature and pressure. Nonetheless, it clearly is possible in principle to capture much of the CO_2 from the stack gases of large combustion facilities such as coal-fired power plants or, alternatively, to capture CO_2 in the course of converting fossil fuels to hydrogen for use in large and small combustion devices alike, and then to store this captured CO_2 underground or by dissolving it in the deep layer of the oceans; the issue is the cost. Increasingly serious attention to these possibilities in the past few years has led to cost estimates for electricity-generation options in the range of $20–40 per tonne of CO_2 for capture and $15–50 per tonne for disposal, translating to cost penalties ranging from 2–4 cents per kilowatt-hour for advanced natural-gas-fired, coal-gasification, and fuel-cell generation technologies to 7–12 cents per kilowatt-hour for traditional pulverized-coal-fired electricity generation.[36] Cost estimates for CO_2 sequestration as part of a fossil-fuel-to-hydrogen approach to dispersed fuel uses vary over an even wider range, depending on assumptions about various aspects of system performance.[37] It is far from clear that incentives for reducing CO_2 emissions and the options for doing so by means other than sequestering the CO_2 from fossil fuels will develop in ways that make sequestration attractive, but the possibility is great enough to warrant further R&D on sequestration options, including the environmental impacts of large-scale disposal of CO_2 in the oceans.

Fusion. Harnessing nuclear fusion (the process that powers the stars and produces most of the bang in thermonuclear bombs) as a practical terrestrial source of electricity and fuel has long been a sort of Holy Grail in energy research; in principle, fusion energy technology could unlock stores of energy in ordinary sea water adequate to power an energy-intensive civilization for millions to billions of years, and could do so with safety, waste-management, and proliferation risks much easier to manage than those of nuclear fission.[38] As is well known, however, fusion energy technology has proven extremely difficult to master. Cumulative U.S. expenditures on fusion-energy research from the inception of this activity in the early 1950s through 1995 amounted to about $15 billion (1995 dollars), and the worldwide total was perhaps $40

Cold Fusion

billion; yet no fusion-energy experiment has yet demonstrated an energy output exceeding the energy input needed to operate the device, let alone the considerably higher output that is a necessary (although still not sufficient) condition for making fusion a commercially attractive energy source.[39] In light of the magnitude of the scientific and technological challenges still to be overcome, it seems likely that at least another forty years and another $40–60 billion would be required to bring fusion to commercial application, and even then there is no absolute guarantee of success: fusion could prove even more difficult than we now think and, on this time scale, breakthroughs in other essentially inexhaustible energy options might make fusion uncompetitive. But that outcome is not assured, either; and if fusion should turn out to be even moderately superior, in its combination of economic, environmental, and political characteristics, to other large-scale energy options available after the mid-twenty-first century, its benefits would be immense in relation to the size of the R&D investments that had been needed to acquire it.

Some "long shots." A number of energy-supply possibilities that are in the embryonic stage of development have a chance of coming to fruition toward the middle of the next century and would seem to warrant at least a modest continuing effort to clarify their potential. Prominent in this category are "hot dry rock" geothermal energy (which unlike the isolated deposits of hot water and steam exploited by the world's few commercial geothermal energy operations today, is an energy source that is both widely distributed and considerably larger in magnitude than the fossil fuels) and systems for producing hydrogen directly from sunlight, either by catalyzed thermochemical processes or in abiotic systems that imitate photosynthesis.[40] In contrast, ocean thermal energy conversion (OTEC), while sometimes mentioned in the same context with these other "long shots," has been sufficiently investigated to reveal quite formidable and fundamental obstacles to its ever achieving competitiveness with other long-term energy options—above all the high cost of building and maintaining, in the hostile marine environment, equipment that because of the low energy-density of the resource must be of vast scale in relation to the useful energy extracted.

What Energy R&D Is Being Done?

U.S. Department of Energy budget authorizations for energy-technology R&D from 1978 to 1997 are shown in Figure 12-1 in constant 1997 dollars.[41] The "energy technology" category of R&D funding as defined here includes research, development, and demonstration activities dealing with energy end-use efficiency ("conservation"), fossil fuels, nuclear fission, nuclear fusion, and renewable energy; it does not include the Department of Energy's research in "Basic Energy Sciences," in "Biomedical and Environmental Research," and in "General Science."[42] Table 12-1 gives the actual numerical data and includes the "Basic Energy Sciences" and "Biomedical and Environmental" categories, facilitating comparisons with other studies that sometimes include these latter categories in "energy R&D."

The picture of energy-technology R&D over the past twenty years painted by these data is one of quite stunning decline, alleviated only by a modest bulge produced by the "clean coal" development and demonstration program—a joint venture of the Department of Energy and industry—between 1988 and 1994. Corrected for inflation, the DOE's total budget authority for energy-technology R&D in Fiscal Year 1997 was only 20.9 percent of the corresponding figure in FY 1978, a drop of nearly five-fold. As percentages of FY 1978 levels, DOE fission-energy R&D in FY 1997 was 2.8 percent, renewables R&D 18.5 percent, and fossil-energy R&D 21.0 percent. If Basic Energy Sciences R&D is included in the total, then the drop in inflation-corrected energy R&D was from $6.55 billion (1997 dollars) in FY 1978 to $1.93 billion (1997 dollars) in FY 1997, a 3.4-fold decrease.

In longer historical perspective, the high levels of federal energy R&D at the end of the 1970s are seen to be an anomaly that resulted from the upsurge of attention to energy produced by that decade's oil-price shocks: data shown here in Figure 12-2 indicate that U.S. government energy R&D funding fluctuated in the range of $1.5–2.0 billion (1997 dollars) per year from 1960 to 1974, when the sharp climb toward the 1978–80 peak of $6–7 billion (1997 dollars) per year began.[43] Of course, as a fraction of U.S. GDP, $2 billion (1997 dollars) was a much bigger number in 1962 than it is now—real GDP in this country nearly tripled 1962-97—so by this standard

Federal Energy Research and Development

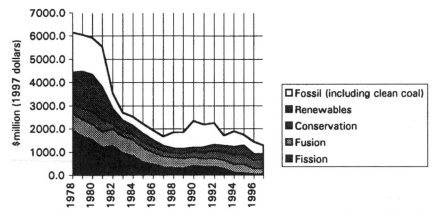

Figure 12-1 Budget authority for DOE energy-technology R&D, 1978–86.
Source: OMB, *Budget of the United States, Fiscal Year 1998.*

Table 12-1 DOE Energy R&D Budget Authority 1978–97 (million 1997 dollars)

Fiscal Year	Fission	Fusion	Cnsrve	Rnwbls	Fossil	Tech. total	BES	Bio/Env
1978	1946.1	744.2	387.6	1354.1	1713.7	6145.6	403.9	353.9
1979	1681.8	733.4	472.1	1590.1	1570.8	6048.2	422.8	327.3
1980	1534.0	665.1	559.7	1580.9	1585.8	5925.5	426.9	321.5
1981	1200.7	682.1	506.3	1424.3	1720.9	5534.2	393.6	286.8
1982	1262.5	729.4	245.6	648.1	675.4	3560.9	410.5	276.0
1983	975.4	709.2	208.2	470.3	335.9	2699.0	456.5	221.5
1984	832.3	696.3	223.1	380.3	388.8	2520.7	498.7	272.4
1985	578.7	618.0	252.5	345.3	415.7	2210.2	591.0	270.1
1986	487.5	505.5	242.6	278.3	432.7	1946.6	600.7	248.9
1987	357.6	464.0	217.9	233.6	398.2	1671.3	722.6	260.8
1988	332.8	434.8	203.5	191.9	683.9	1847.0	734.3	351.4
1989	303.1	436.7	206.9	185.8	711.5	1844.0	687.3	322.0
1990	412.2	383.1	229.0	168.3	1156.9	2349.4	682.3	369.4
1991	383.6	332.3	262.6	233.3	971.1	2183.0	818.4	465.0
1992	377.9	374.2	288.9	272.3	940.2	2253.5	856.5	410.8
1993	288.3	367.8	336.4	280.6	437.5	1710.6	935.0	400.0
1994	133.8	352.5	388.4	347.4	677.5	1899.6	812.9	601.3
1995	110.5	368.8	424.2	377.5	455.5	1736.6	747.0	581.8
1996	52.0	244.9	356.6	275.1	513.0	1441.5	793.6	552.2
1997	53.7	232.5	386.5	251.1	359.3	1283.0	649.7	389.1

Cnsrv: Conservation. Rnwbls: Renewables. Tech. total: Technology total.
BES: Basic energy sciences. Bio/Env: Biomedical/Environment.
Source: OMB, *Budget of the United States, Fiscal Year 1998.*

current federal energy R&D funding is, by a substantial margin, the lowest in the last thirty-five years.

The precipitous decline in U.S. government funding of energy R&D has not been without parallels in other industrialized nations. As indicated in Table 12-2, similar trends are evident in figures compiled by the International Energy Agency for the period 1984–94 for Germany, Italy, the United Kingdom, and Canada.[44] Data for 1984 were not available for France, but the trend from 1990 to 1994 was downward in that country. The only G-7 country not experiencing a decline in government energy-technology R&D in this period was Japan. It is worth noting that the 1994 figure for Japan is more than twice the corresponding figure for the United States and is more than four times the U.S. figure if expressed as a fraction of purchasing-power-parity-corrected GDP.

The sharpest decline in U.S. government spending on energy-technology R&D took place during the eight years of the Reagan administration (FY 1981–89), when President Reagan was expressing the view (and, on the government side, implementing it) that any energy R&D worth doing would be done by the private sector. But the expenditures of the U.S. private sector on energy-technology R&D also fell in this time period and thereafter, most sharply from 1985 to 1988 and then again from 1991 onward: the Department of Energy estimates that U.S. industry investments in energy R&D in 1993 were $3.9 billion (1997 dollars), down 33 percent in real terms from 1983's level;[45] a study at Battelle Pacific Northwest Laboratory shows U.S. private-sector energy R&D falling from $4.4 billion (1997 dollars) in 1985 to $2.6 billion in 1994, representing a drop of about 40 percent in this period.[46]

The differences in these figures for industry energy R&D spending arise from the difficulty of obtaining complete data on this subject and, presumably, from varying assumptions by different analysts about what categories of spending in what types of organizations should count as energy R&D. The trends appear to be consistent across all choices about what categories to include, however. Thus it is quite clear that the private sector did *not* pick up the energy R&D that the government dropped in this time period. It is also clear, whichever figure one chooses for mid-1990s industry spending on energy R&D in the United States, that the energy

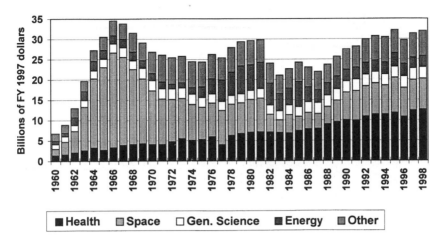

Figure 12-2 Trends in non-defense R&D by function, FY 1960–68: outlays for the conduct of R&D, in constant FY1997 $ billions. Source: AAAS, based on OMB historical tables; constant dollar conversion based on GDP deflators.

Table 12-2 Energy-Technology R&D in Other G-7 Countries, 1984 and 1994 (million 1997 dollars)

	Germany	Italy	UK	Canada	France	Japan
1984	1522	1241	695	493	NA	4130
1994	355	287	118	233	610	4479

Source: International Energy Agency, *Energy Policies of the IEA Countries* (1995)

business is one of the least research-intensive enterprises in the country measured as the percent of sales expended on R&D. Average industrial R&D expenditures for the whole U.S. economy in 1994 were about 3.5 percent of sales; for software the figure was about 14 percent, for pharmaceuticals about 12 percent, and for semiconductors about 8 percent. For energy, using the DOE's 1993 estimate of $3.5 billion (current dollars) for industrial R&D against energy sales of $493 billion in the same year indicates that energy R&D was 0.7 percent of sales; using the Battelle estimate of $2.4 billion for industrial energy R&D in 1993 makes it just 0.5 percent.

Consideration of the rationales for the government to undertake certain classes of R&D that are in the society's interest to get done, even though not in the private sector's interest to do, makes it plain that the private sector should not have been expected to compensate for much of the government's post-1980 decline in support for energy R&D. These rationales for government participation in R&D in general—and in energy R&D in particular—include the following:

First, some kinds of innovations that would lower costs for all consumers—hence are in society's interest—are not pursued by individual firms because the innovations are judged unlikely to be appropriable. That is, the firm that does the R&D to develop these innovations will get little advantage over competitors who can adopt the innovations nearly as fast as the firm originating them, but without paying for them. This "free rider" problem can be and is overcome to some extent within the private sector by research consortia, including industry-wide consortia such as the Gas Research Institute and the Electric Power Research Institute. But even in the context of such consortia, it remains an important reason that basic research and even much applied research tend to be eschewed by industry in favor of shorter-term product development.

Second, some kinds of innovations are not pursued by the private sector because they relate to production or preservation of public goods—national security, for example—that are not reflected in the profit-and-loss statements of firms. Still other kinds of innovations are not pursued by firms because they relate to reduction of externalities—above all, environmental externalities—which if not at least partly internalized by regulations, emissions charges, or other mechanisms do not generate economic incentives for energy producers.

Third, research that is costly and has a high chance of failure may exceed the risk aversion of the private sector, even though from a societal point of view a certain number of such projects in the national R&D portfolio is worthwhile because the occasional successes can bring very high gains. And research that will take a long time to complete is likely to fall short of the private sector's requirement for a rate of return attractive to investors, even if confidence of success is high. Fusion energy R&D provides an example where the chance of failure is substantial and the time scale would probably be too long for the private sector even if success were assured, but where the potential benefits of the technology are so large and the prospects of other very long-term energy options so uncertain that the government's investing in it is clearly in society's interest.

If it is not surprising that industry did not step in to compensate for diminishing government engagement in these roles in the period after 1980, however, one still may wonder why industry's R&D investments in industry's traditional domains actually *declined* in this time period. It is to the task of explaining that decline—as well as explaining why government funding for energy R&D did not strongly rebound after President Reagan and his ideological opposition to government activity in this area passed from the scene— that I turn in the next section.

Why Isn't There More Energy R&D?

Of course, expenditures on energy R&D—and ratios of expenditures divided by energy sales or by GDP—are not the only way to measure how much is going on, and knowing how much is spent is not the same thing as knowing how effectively it is spent. Spending is only an *input* measure of R&D, and ideally one should prefer *output* measures: papers published (or citations of these), patents granted, innovations finding application in the marketplace, or rates of return based on productivity gains or other cost savings from such innovations. Analyses looking at such output measures can be found in the literature, but they are incomplete and difficult to interpret, and attempting to summarize them is beyond the scope of this chapter.[47] Suffice it to say that I find it implausible (and I have not seen any analyses that assert) that the use of output measures would show an increase in the output of energy-technology R&D in this past twenty-year period when public and private investments in such R&D were falling so sharply. No doubt some ill-conceived and badly run projects were canceled, and probably the productivity of energy R&D (output per dollar of input) has increased overall. But these effects can hardly have been enough to compensate for the nearly five-fold decrease in public funding for energy-technology R&D in this period; and even the cited drop of

30–40 percent in private-sector energy R&D in a period of just a decade seems unlikely to have been wholly offset by productivity gains.

If it is accepted that the United States has been settling for declining investment in long-term energy-technology possibilities as well as, probably, a diminished stream of short-term energy-technology innovations, what are the possible explanations? Here are some factors that I think have been important.

Cheap Oil and Natural Gas

The average cost of domestic crude oil in the United States in 1995 was $14.65 per barrel, which compares to $13.30 per barrel in 1960 (in 1995 dollars); costs of imported oil in 1995 were $15–17 per barrel.[48] In 1981, when U.S. government energy R&D expenditures were near their peak, the cost of domestic oil in the United States averaged $52 per barrel and imported oil cost $57–62 per barrel (1995 dollars), about four times costlier than in 1995. Clearly, high oil prices encourage investments in R&D to develop alternatives to this costly oil, and low prices discourage such investments. Similarly, domestic natural gas in 1981 cost $2.72 per million Btu (1995 dollars) at the wellhead, compared to $1.44 per million Btu in 1995. This exceptionally low cost for the cleanest burning of the fossil fuels—which lends itself not only to direct use in industry and for space heating, water heating, and cooking in residential and commercial buildings, but also to low-emission, high-efficiency electricity generation in power plants much cheaper to construct than coal-burning or nuclear plants—will tend to discourage R&D investments in other energy options (including in energy end-use efficiency) wherever and whenever such cheap gas is available. Cheap oil and gas, which contributed 63 percent of U.S. energy supply in 1995, are probably the most important single reason for the decline in energy R&D in both the public and private sectors.

Deregulation of the Electricity Sector

There is abundant evidence that deregulation of the electricity business has caused sharp declines in energy R&D spending by the electric-utility industry in the European countries where deregulation has been underway for some time, and the same thing is now occurring in the United States.[49] The declines in overall R&D spending are being accompanied by shifts in the R&D portfolios of utilities toward short-term, low-risk projects. These shifts appear to be a result of deregulation's exposing the utilities to the day-to-day competitive pressures of "the bottom line," in contrast to the longer-term, public-interest orientation of many of the utility industry's former regulators.

Overall Budgetary Stringency in the Federal Government

The drive to constrain Federal spending in order to balance the budget and perhaps to cut taxes has apparently become so solidly entrenched in American politics that arguments for a substantial increase in any category of government expenditures face automatic and formidable opposition. General lack of confidence in government activities and programs, fueled in part by the propensity of national politicians in recent elections to run essentially "against the government," has contributed to maintaining the budget-cutting atmosphere. The pressure on so-called "discretionary" government spending—which of course includes government support for R&D of all kinds—has been especially intense, because until recently political leaders have been reluctant to go after the larger entitlements that are of direct benefit to so many voters.[50]

Budgetary Constraints on the Department of Energy

Within the atmosphere of reining in government overall, the Department of Energy has been singled out by opponents of "big government" as an example of a federal agency that is at least oversized and perhaps unnecessary, hence deserving of downsizing for certain and arguably a candidate for abolition. This position has been reinforced by vestiges of the Reagan view that any energy activities (including R&D) that are worth undertaking should and will be undertaken by the private sector, and by widely repeated ridicule of certain government energy initiatives of the energy R&D "boom" years of the late 1970s and early 1980s (such as the Synfuels corporation and DOE's development and demonstration projects on multi-megawatt windmills), which are easy to portray as failures. In my view, good counter-arguments can be made: (a) while certainly there were some badly run programs, much of what is now ridiculed in hindsight was the result of bad guesses about the persistence of high oil prices (a misjudgment in which the DOE had much good company in the private sector and in academia); (b) the overall record of effectiveness of DOE energy-technology R&D research is quite good and contains many striking success stories (well documented, for example, in the Secretary of Energy Advisory Board's 1995 report on energy R&D);[51] (c) abolition would generate sizable short-term costs (because most of the functions of the DOE, which by any reasonable conception of the responsibilities of government are necessary, would simply have to be relocated in other governmental departments) and little if any long-term benefits; and (d) abolition would send absolutely the wrong public signal at this particular moment about the importance of energy to national well-being. Nonetheless, bad-mouthing of the Department and threats to dismantle it have been taken seriously enough by the Clinton administration to motivate attempts to reduce the size of the target by shrinking the DOE's total budget.

Inability to Re-allocate DOE Funds within the Department

The problem of DOE's overall budgetary constraint is compounded by the circumstance that, within that total budget, energy R&D accounts for only a very modest share ($2.5 billion in FY 1995, with "Basic Energy Sciences" included, out of a total of $17.6. billion). This share cannot easily be increased at the expense of larger parts of the budget (such as the $6.6 billion in the FY 1995 budget for environmental cleanup in the nuclear-weapons production complex and $4.6 billion for nuclear-weapons research and "stockpile stewardship"), because these enjoy protection by statute and by high-level political bargains (as, for example, an administration commitment to protect "stockpile stewardship" that was made in pursuit of weapon-laboratory and Pentagon assent to the Comprehensive Test Ban Treaty).

"Eat Your Siblings" Energy Constituencies

Advocates of each class of energy options (e.g., nuclear fission, fossil fuels, renewables, energy end-use efficiency) tend to disparage the prospects of the other classes of options; these tendencies are aggravated, of course, by the zero-sum or declining-sum game characteristics of energy R&D funding. Thus the energy community itself formulates the arguments ("renewables are too costly," "fossil fuels are too dirty," "nuclear fission is too unforgiving," "fusion will never work," "efficiency means belt-tightening and sacrifice or is too much work for consumers") that the budget-cutters cheerfully employ to cut energy R&D programs one at a time. There is no coherent energy-community chorus calling for a responsible portfolio approach to energy R&D that seeks to address and ameliorate the shortcomings of all of the options.

"Allergies" to Nuclear Energy and to Energy Taxes

The prospects for such a portfolio approach have been further dimmed by two "allergies" afflicting contemporary American energy politics, namely an allergy to nuclear energy, which is judged so unpopular politically or so unpromising in terms of economics, safety, waste, and proliferation that few politicians have been willing to associate themselves publicly with providing funding to try to solve these problems; and an allergy to energy taxes, which although they are seen as sensible by virtually all energy economists and virtually all environmentalists are nonetheless seen as unspeakable if not unthinkable by contemporary politicians. As shown in Figure 12-1 and Table 12-1, R&D in nuclear fission has suffered deeper proportional cuts than any other class of energy options, having been nearly eradicated. But without nuclear fission in the portfolio, the chance of developing consensus on a portfolio approach to energy R&D seems next to nil in both the energy community and the Congress (some of the most informed and respected members of both of which are advocates of trying to fix nuclear fission, against the possibility that it will be badly needed, rather than forgetting it without further ado). A responsible portfolio approach to energy R&D would be easy to fund with very modest energy taxes: funding for a quadrupling of current U.S. federal support for energy-technology R&D could be garnered from a gasoline tax of less than five cents per gallon, for example.[52] The constraints upon and within the DOE make it unlikely that any substantial increase in energy R&D can be achieved without an earmarked increase in revenues of this sort.

Under-rated Links between Energy and Well-being

I return here to the rationales adduced for energy R&D in the first section of this chapter. Most citizens and most politicians do not care about Btus and kilowatt-hours *per se* (absent gasoline lines, blackouts, or high prices); and they do not understand, because no one has explained it to them persuasively, how inadequacies in the menu of energy options for the future are likely to influence the economic, environmental, and security values that they *do* care about. Until these connections are somehow made clearer—whether by articulate opinion leaders or by painful experience—inadequacies in the public investments devoted to energy R&D are likely to persist almost no matter what happens to the other R&D-inhibiting factors I have listed above.

The Challenge for the Second Clinton-Gore Term

As a result of the foregoing phenomena, the United States government does not have an energy R&D program remotely commensurate with the magnitude of the energy-linked challenges likely to emerge early in the next century to the economic, environmental, and international-security dimensions of our well-being. Neither does any other major government in the world have such a strategy (although Japan is closer than the others, at least in overall level of spending). While it is possible to hope that the private sector will do more in energy R&D than it is doing now, moreover, there are fundamental reasons (summarized above) that it will never do remotely as much as societal prudence requires. Without sensible incentives, regulatory guidance, and suitable partnerships with the government, the private sector will not even approach its potential.

A detailed treatment of how the obstacles to the creation of a responsible energy R&D strategy for the United States (not to mention other countries) might be overcome is well beyond the scope of this chapter, although some of the ingredients of an approach will be apparent to readers from the way I have described the problem. Certainly any such effort will require a considerable measure of political leadership, starting with the president and the vice president. Notwithstanding the current vice president's exceptionally sophisticated appreciation of the challenges posed nationally and globally by the intersection of problems of energy, economic well-being, environment, and security, and notwithstanding the exceptional background, as a world-class energy analyst, of the current incumbent in the position of special assistant to the president for science and technology,[53] it was difficult during the first Clinton-Gore term to get the energy issue onto the administration's policy agenda. The reasons for that are largely those adduced in the preceding section, compounded by the administration's first-term preoccupations with health-care policy, welfare policy, budget-balancing debates, nuclear-weapons-proliferation issues, and NATO expansion and, probably, by the view of the administration's political advisors that there would be little electoral mileage in pushing the energy issue at that time.

But there is reason not only to hope but to believe that this situation might change in the second Clinton-Gore term. Toward the end of the first term, the vice president conveyed to the President's Committee of Advisors on Science and Technology (PCAST) the president's request that PCAST set forth its views on the issues in science-and-technology policy that it deemed worthy of increased administration attention in a second term. On December 6, 1996, PCAST conveyed in a letter to the president its conviction that five such issues were particularly compelling, of which the first mentioned in the letter was "a national strategy for energy R&D."[54] (The other four were improved understanding and management of biological resources, research and technology to improve education and training, industry-government-university partnerships for technological innovation, and improved protection, management, and disposition of nuclear materials.) The text of the part of the PCAST letter dealing with energy was as follows:

Adequate and reliable supplies of affordable energy, obtained in environmentally sustainable ways, are essential to economic prosperity, environ-

new policy?

mental quality, and political stability around the world; and energy-supply and energy-efficiency technologies represent a multi-hundred-billion dollar per year global market. There is considerable doubt whether the world, which gets three-quarters of all its energy supply from oil, coal, and natural gas, can continue to rely on these fossil fuels to this degree through the expected economic growth of the next few decades without encountering intolerably disruptive climatic change caused by the resulting greenhouse-gas emissions. Yet the United States—which is the world's largest energy consumer, the largest greenhouse-gas emitter, is 85-percent dependent on fossil fuels, and imports nearly half of its oil at a cost of $50 billion per year—has allowed Federal spending on energy R&D to fall more than 3-fold in real terms in the past 15 years, a period in which private funding for energy R&D also was falling. Government spending on energy R&D is more than twice as high in Japan as in the United States in absolute terms, and about four times as much as a fraction of GNP.

We recommend a substantial and sustained increase in Federal expenditures on energy R&D, coupled with measures to encourage increased energy R&D in the private sector; this effort should include greatly increased work on renewable energy options and energy end-use efficiency; restoration of fusion R&D funding to the levels recommended by PCAST last year; exploration of whether and how an expanded contribution to world energy supply from nuclear fission can be achieved; and an expanded effort on clean-fossil-fuel technologies.

President Clinton responded to PCAST's "priorities" letter with a letter to PCAST Co-Chair John Young on January 14, 1997, in which the section treating the energy issue said:

In response to your recommendations, I have asked [Presidential Science Advisor] Jack Gibbons to work with the new Secretary of Energy, once he is confirmed by the Senate, to review the current national energy R&D portfolio, and make recommendations to me by October 1, 1997, on how to ensure that the United States has a program that addresses its energy and environmental needs for the next century. The analysis should be done in a global context, and the review should address both near- and long-term national needs including renewable and advanced fission and fusion energy supply options, and energy end-use efficiency.[55]

A twenty-one-member PCAST Panel on "Energy R&D for the Challenges of the 21st Century" has been formed to address the president's request, with representation from the energy-supply and energy-equipment industries, from academia, and from the public-interest sector, and with task forces on end-use efficiency, fossil-fuel technology, nuclear energy, and renewables. This Panel, which I have the privilege of chairing, is receiving the full cooperation of the Department of Energy in addressing the sweeping agenda proposed by the president. Its report, which will build on the solid foundation developed in the Secretary of Energy Advisory Board's 1995 report on energy R&D, will make recommendations concerning the federal government's portfolio of energy R&D investments, incentives for private-sector energy R&D, and U.S. commitments to international cooperation in energy R&D.

Of course, the commissioning of such a report is not the same thing as a commitment to lead a reshaping of public policy. But it could be a beginning. I hope that all those who understand the connection of adequate energy options to economic prosperity, environmental sustainability, and international security will join the effort to seize this opportunity by urging the administration and the Congress to push ahead.

Notes

1. These figures include all energy supplied as electricity, as heat, and as chemical fuel but exclude energy in the form of food for people and feed for domesticated animals.

2. British Petroleum, *BP Statistical Review of World Energy* (London: British Petroleum, 1996); Energy Information Administration, U.S. Department of Energy, *International Energy Annual 1995* (Washington, D.C.: U.S. Government Printing Office [U.S. GPO], 1996); Thomas B. Johansson, Henry Kelly, Amulya K.N. Reddy, and Robert H. Williams, eds., *Renewable Energy: Sources for Fuels and Electricity* (Washington, D.C.: Island Press, 1992); and author estimates.

3. Extrapolated from data in John P. Holdren and Patrick J. Gonzalez, "1993 World Population, Purchasing Power Parity GNP, and Commercial Energy" (Berkeley: Energy and Resources Group, University of California, December 1995).

4. The historical data are summarized in John P. Holdren, "Population and the Energy Problem," Population and Environment, Vol. 12, No. 3 (Spring 1991), pp. 231–255.

5. Intergovernmental Panel on Climate Change (IPCC), "Emissions Scenarios for IPCC: An Update," in *IPCC: Climate Change 1992* (Cambridge, UK: Cambridge University Press, 1992); World Energy Council, *Energy for Tomorrow's World* (New York: St. Martin's Press, 1993).

6. Economics and Statistics Administration, U.S. Department of Commerce, *Statistical Abstract of the United States 1996* (Washington, D.C.: U.S. GPO, 1996); Energy Information Administration, U.S. Department of Energy, *Monthly Energy Review* (Washington, D.C.: U.S. GPO, March 1997).

7. Based on data on energy quantities and prices (excluding taxes) and on GNP from Economics and Statistics Administration, *Statistical Abstract of the United States 1996.*

8. Energy Information Administration, U.S. Department of Energy, *Annual Energy Outlook 1997* (Washington, D.C.: U.S. GPO, 1997).

9. J. P. Holdren and R.K. Pachauri, "Energy," in International Council of Scientific Unions, *An Agenda of Science for Environment and Development into the 21st Century* (Cambridge, UK: Cambridge University Press, 1992), pp. 103–118.

10. Study of Critical Environmental Problems, *Man's Impact on the Global Environment* (Cambridge: The MIT Press, 1970); John P. Holdren, "Global Environmental Issues Related to Energy Supply," *Energy*, Vol. 12 (1987), pp. 975–992; B.L. Turner, W.C. Clark, R.W. Kates, J.F. Richards, J.T. Mathews, and W.B. Meyer, eds., *The Earth as Transformed by Human Action* (New York: Cambridge University Press, 1990).

11. John P. Holdren, "Energy Costs as Potential Limits to Growth," Chapter 3 in Denis C. Pirages, ed., *The Sustainable Society* (New York: Praeger, 1977), pp. 53–73; John P. Holdren, "Energy in Transition," *Scientific American*, September 1990, pp. 156–163; see also Holdren and Pachauri, "Energy."

12. Kirk R. Smith, *Biofuels, Air Pollution, and Health* (New York: Plenum, 1987); Kirk R. Smith, "Fuel Combustion, Air Pollution, and Health: The Situation in Developing Countries," *Annual Review of Energy and the Environment*, Vol. 18 (1993), pp. 529–566.

13. John Harte, Cheryl Holdren, Richard Schneider, and Christine Shirley, *Toxics A to Z: A Guide to Everyday Pollution Hazards* (Berkeley: University of California Press, 1991).

14. W.M. Stigliani and R.W. Shaw, "Energy Use and Acid Deposition: The View from Europe," *Annual Review of Energy and the Environment*, Vol. 15 (1990), pp. 201–216; James N. Galloway, "Anthropogenic Mobilization of Sulphur and Nitrogen: Immediate and Delayed Consequences," *Annual Review of Energy and the Environment*, Vol. 21 (1996); pp. 261–292.

15. Intergovernmental Panel on Climate Change (IPCC), *Climate Change 1995: Impacts, Adaptations and Mitigation of Climate Change: Scientific-Technical Analyses* (Cambridge, UK: Cambridge University Press, 1996).

16. The best introduction to this literature is the set of chapters on impacts in IPCC, *Climate Change 1995.*

17. For a guide to some of the considerable literature of this subject—and an argument against overly simplistic interpretation of it—see Ronnie D. Lipschutz, in *When Nations Clash: Raw Materials, Ideology, and Foreign Policy* (Cambridge, Mass.: Ballinger Publishers, 1989).

18. See Energy Information Administration, *Annual Energy Outlook 1997.*

19. See, e.g., Kent E. Calder, "Asia's Empty Gas Tank," *Foreign Affairs,* Vol. 75, No. 3 (March/April 1996), pp. 55–69.

20. International Institute of Strategic Studies, *The Military Balance 1996/97* (London: Brassey's, 1996).

21. Nuclear energy is only a partial answer in that, using currently available technologies, it can only serve as a source of electricity and (in a few instances) district heating and industrial-process heat in the power-plant's immediate vicinity; of particular importance, there is no currently economic way for nuclear energy to replace much of the oil used in transportation. While nuclear energy supplies nearly 20 percent of the world's electricity, electricity accounts for only 30 percent of total primary energy use (and a much smaller fraction of oil use).

22. D. Albright and H.A. Feiveson, "Plutonium Recycling and the Problem of Nuclear Proliferation," *Annual Review of Energy,* Vol. 13 (1988), pp. 239–265; John P. Holdren, "Civilian Nuclear Technologies and Nuclear Weapons Proliferation," in Carlo Schaerf, Brian Holden-Reid, and David Carlton, eds., *New Technologies and the Arms Race* (London: Macmillan, 1989), pp. 161–198; F. Berkhout and H.A. Feiveson, "Securing Nuclear Materials in a Changing World," *Annual Review of Energy and Environment,* Vol. 18 (1993), pp. 631–665.

23. See, e.g., Peter H. Gleick, "The Implications of Global Climatic Changes for International Security," *Climatic Change,* Vol. 15 (1989), pp. 309–325; T.H. Homer-Dixon, J.H. Boutwell, and G.W. Rathjens, "Environmental Change and Violent Conflict," *Scientific American,* February 1993, pp. 38–48.

24. This section draws heavily on Holdren and Pachauri, "Energy"; and on Robert H. Williams, "Making Energy R&D an Effective and Efficient Instrument for Meeting Long-Term Energy Policy Goals," Princeton University, Center for Energy and Environmental Studies, manuscript, June 19, 1995.

25. See, e.g., U.S. Department of Energy, Energy Information Administration, *Annual Energy Review 1990* (Washington, D.C.: U.S. GPO, 1991); L. Schipper, R.B. Howarth, and H. Geller, "United States Energy Use from 1973 to 1987: The Impacts of Improved Efficiency," *Annual Review of Energy and Environment,* Vol. 15 (1990), pp. 455–504; and S. Meyers and L. Schipper, "World Energy Use in the 1970s and 1980s: Exploring the Changes," *Annual Review of Energy and Environment,* Vol. 17 (1992), pp. 463–505.

26. See, e.g., R.H. Williams, E.D. Larson, and M.H. Ross, "Materials, Affluence, and Industrial Energy Use," *Annual Review of Energy,* Vol. 12 (1987), pp. 99–144; A. P. Fickett, C.W. Gellings, and A.B. Lovins, "Efficient Use of Electricity," in Scientific American, *Energy for Planet Earth* (New York: W.H. Freeman, 1991), pp. 11–23; R. Bevington and A.H. Rosenfeld, "Energy for Buildings and Homes," in Scientific American, *Energy for Planet Earth,* pp. 25–34; J. Goldemberg and A.K.N. Reddy, "Energy for the Developing World," *Scientific American,* September 1990, pp. 111–118; U.S. Congress, Office of Technology Assessment, *Energy Technology: Shaping Our Choices* (Washington, D.C.: U.S. GPO, 1991); U.S. Congress, Office

of Technology Assessment, *Advancing Automotive Technology: Visions of a Super-Efficient Family Car* (Washington, D.C.: U.S. GPO, 1995).

27. M.D. Levine, J.G. Koomey, J.E. McMahon, A.H. Sanstad, and E. Hirst, "Energy Efficiency and Market Failures," *Annual Review of Energy and the Environment*, Vol. 20 (1995), pp. 535–55.

28. U.S. Department of Energy, Secretary of Energy Advisory Board, *Energy R&D: Shaping Our Nation's Future in a Competitive World* (Washington, D.C.: U.S. GPO, 1995).

29. See, e.g., William Fulkerson, R.R. Judkins, and M.K. Sanghvi, "Energy from Fossil Fuels," in Scientific American, *Energy for Planet Earth*, pp. 83–94; Eric D. Larson, "Technology for Electricity and Fuels for Biomass," *Annual Review of Energy and the Environment*, Vol. 18 (1993), pp. 567–630; S.B. Alpert, "Clean Coal Technologies and Advanced Coal-Based Power Plants," *Annual Review of Energy and the Environment*, Vol. 16 (1991), pp. 567–630; and the "Technology Profiles" Annex in Secretary of Energy Advisory Board, Energy R & D.

30. S. Penner, "Commercialization of Fuel Cells: Report of the U.S. Department of Energy Advanced Fuel Cell Commercialization Working Group," *Energy—the International Journal*, Vol. 20 (May 1995 Special Issue); R.H. Williams, E.D. Larson, R.E. Katofsky, and R.H. Chen, "Methanol and Hydrogen from Biomass for Transportation," *Energy for Sustainable Development*, Vol. 1, No. 5 (January 1995), pp. 18–32.

31. Gordon J. MacDonald, "The Future of Methane as an Energy Resource," *Annual Review of Energy and Environment*, Vol. 15 (1990), pp. 53–83.

32. Department of Resources Conservation and Comprehensive Utilization, *China Energy Annual Review 1996*, State Economic and Trade Commission, People's Republic of China, 1996.

33. Carl J. Weinberg and Robert H. Williams, "Energy from the Sun," in Scientific American, *Energy for Planet Earth*, pp. 107–118; B. Sorensen, "History of and Recent Progress in Wind Energy Utilization," *Annual Review of Energy and the Environment*, Vol. 20 (1995), pp. 387–424; Raymond Dracker and Pasqual De Laquill III, "Progress Commercializing Solar-Electric Power Systems," *Annual Review of Energy and the Environment*, Vol. 21 (1996), pp. 371–402. See also Chapter 19 in the "Impacts, Adaptations, and Mitigation" volume of IPCC, *Climate Change 1995*.

34. See, e.g., A.B. Lovins and L.H. Lovins, "Least-Cost Climate Stabilization," *Annual Review of Energy and the Environment*, Vol. 16 (1991), pp. 433–531; Christopher Flavin, "Building a Bridge to Sustainable Energy," in Worldwatch Institute, *State of the World 1992* (New York: Norton, 1992), pp. 27–45.

35. C.W. Forsberg and A.M. Weinberg, "Advanced Reactors, Passive Safety, and Acceptance of Nuclear Energy," *Annual Review of Energy and the Environment*, Vol. 15 (1990), pp. 133–152; R.H. Williams and H.A. Feiveson, "Diversion-Resistance Criteria for Future Nuclear Power," *Energy Policy*, Vol. 18 (1990), pp. 543–549; Energy Engineering Board, National Research Council, *Nuclear Power: Technical*

and Institutional Options for the Future (Washington, D.C.: National Academy Press, 1992); Board on Radioactive Waste Management, National Research Council, *Nuclear Wastes: Technologies for Separations and Transmutations* (Washington, D.C.: National Academy Press, 1996).

36. H.J. Herzog and E.M. Drake, "Carbon Dioxide Recovery and Disposal from Large Energy Systems," *Annual Review of Energy and the Environment*, Vol. 21 (1996), pp. 145–166.

37. See Chapter 19 in IPCC, *Climate Change 1995.*

38. John P. Holdren, "Safety and Environmental Aspects of Fusion Energy," *Annual Review of Energy and the Environment*, Vol. 16 (1991), pp. 235–256.

39. President's Committee of Advisors on Science and Technology, Fusion Review Panel, *The U.S. Program of Fusion Energy Research and Development* (Washington, D.C.: Executive Office of the President of the United States, July 1995).

40. See Johansson et al., *Renewable Energy.*

41. The sources of these data are the annual federal budget documents of the Office of Management and Budget, Executive Office of the President of the President of the United States. See, most recently, Office of Management and Budget (OMB), *Budget of the United States Government, Fiscal Year 1998* (Washington, D.C.: U.S. GPO, 1997). Conventions for excluding certain non-R&D expenditures that are often tabulated together with R&D follow the DOE Task Force on Strategic Energy R&D; see Secretary of Energy Advisory Board (1995). "Budget authority," which is the same as "appropriations," is the term for the amounts that Congress authorizes an agency to spend. The other two measures of R&D funding in common use are "obligations" (commitments by the agency to provide the money to particular R&D performers) and "outlays" (actual expenditures in a given year). Budget authority figures are available with greater detail, consistency, and timeliness than figures for the other categories; in general, obligations and outlays track authority quite closely.

42. By U.S. Department of Energy accounting convention, the "renewable energy" category includes not only hydropower, wind, biomass, and solar energy technologies, but also geothermal energy (which is not entirely—or in the currently exploited forms even mostly—renewable), and energy storage, transmission, and distribution. The nuclear fission category, as tabulated here, does not include R&D on nuclear power sources for military and space applications. "Basic Energy Sciences" includes work in materials sciences, chemistry, applied math, biosciences, engineering, and geosciences that is not directed at development of a particular class of energy sources, as well as construction and operating support for such scientific facilities as the Advanced Photon Source at the Argonne National Laboratory and the Advanced Light Source at the Lawrence Livermore Laboratory. The "Biomedical and Environmental" category includes a wide range of topics in health, safety, and environment, including some not directly related to energy at all (such as the Human Genome project). "General Science" is mainly nuclear and high-energy physics. The Department of Energy

accounts for the great bulk of U.S. federal energy R&D. In 1993, for example, the sum of "Energy Technology" and "Basic Energy Sciences" R&D funded by the DOE was $2.38 billion in 1993 dollars while energy R&D funding by all other Federal agencies was $0.25 billion. See Secretary of Energy Advisory Board, *Energy R & D*.

43. Data taken from Table 9.8 of the "Historical Tables" in OMB, *Budget of the United States Government, FY 1998*. These data are for outlays, not budget authority, and they include the "basic energy sciences" and "biomedical and environmental" categories funded by the Department of Energy and its predecessor agencies.

44. International Energy Agency, (IEA), *Energy Policies of the IEA Countries* (Paris: IEA, 1995).

45. U.S. Department of Energy, Office of Policy, *Corporate R&D in Transition* (Washington, D.C.: U.S. DOE, March 1996).

46. J.J. Dooley, *Trends in U.S. Private-Sector Energy R&D Funding 1985–1994*, Report PNNL-11295 (Washington, D.C.: Battelle Pacific Northwest Laboratory for U.S. Department of Energy Office of Planning and Analysis, September 1996).

47. Ibid.; and Secretary of Energy Advisory Board, *Energy R&D*, and references cited on this point therein.

48. These and subsequent energy-price data are from U.S. Department of Energy, Energy Information Administration, *Annual Energy Review 1995* (Washington, D.C.: Department of Energy, July 1996); and U.S. Department of Energy, Energy Information Administration, *Monthly Energy Review* (Washington, D.C.: Department of Energy, April 1997).

49. See, e.g., J.J. Dooley, "Unintended Consequences: Energy R&D in a Deregulated Energy Market," manuscript, Pacific Northwest National Laboratory, February 1997.

50. Even Americans in the subset of the population that pays close attention to public affairs are often unaware of what a modest proportion of the federal budget is accounted for by the actual operations of government departments (where the R&D programs reside). Of the $1.7 trillion FY 1998 federal budget, for example, 50 percent will go to direct benefit payments to individuals, 15 percent will go to grants to states and localities, and 15 percent will go to net interest. Of the 20 percent that remains for government operations, three-fourths will go to defense, leaving altogether only 5 percent of the budget for the nondefense activities of the government. See, for example, OMB, *Budget of the United States Government, FY 1998*.

51. See Secretary of Energy Advisory Board, *Energy R&D*.

52. Americans currently burn 115 billion gallons of motor gasoline per year, so each penny per gallon in tax raises more than a billion dollars annually. See, e.g., Energy Information Administration, *International Energy Annual 1995*.

53. Dr. John H. Gibbons directed the Environmental Program at the Oak Ridge National Laboratory, was the founding Director of the Energy and Environment Program at the University of Tennessee, initiated and directed the Federal Office of Energy Conservation (with successive homes in the Department of Interior, Federal Energy Office, Federal Energy Administration, and Energy Research Administration), chaired the "Demand" Panel of the massive National of Academy of Sciences energy study in the late 1970s, and served as a guiding force of numerous major reviews of energy issues in his thirteen years as director of the Congressional Office of Technology Assessment.

54. Letter to President Clinton from John A. Young, Co-Chairman of the President's Committee of Advisors on Science and Technology, December 6, 1996 (available from the Office of Science and Technology Policy, Executive Office of the President).

55. Letter from President Clinton to John A. Young, Co-Chairman of the President's Committee of Advisors on Science and Technology, January 14, 1997 (available from the Office of Science and Technology Policy, Executive Office of the President).

III

Policy Tools and Institutions

13
Beyond the National Information Infrastructure Initiative

Brian Kahin

The National Information Infrastructure (NII) initiative was the most visible component of the first Clinton administration's technology policy. The administration primed the American public with expectations of an "information superhighway" to be delivered by the private sector with encouragement from government. It launched the initiative as a multifaceted assault on a panoply on issues that appeared as problems or opportunities.

The goal was to create an "advanced information infrastructure." What actually transpired over the first term of the administration was unexpected: instead of a bigger and faster "highway", there was a paradigm shift from circuits to tiny packets of information as the organizing unit of telecommunications. Instead of video on demand, there was the World Wide Web. Rather than another opportunity to recycle movies, there was something new: a networking of text and pictures.

The World Wide Web was not cutting-edge technology but the successful packaging of a limited set of functions for managing documents and other information objects. Unlike the proposed "superhighway," it did not require hundreds of billions dollars in centralized investment. Rather it has been driven by distributed private investment, hundreds of thousands of entrepreneurs, and the ability of millions of users to express themselves in new ways. Yet, ironically, it is built on an infrastructure that was the fruit of decades of investment by the U.S. government.

From that perspective, the success of the Internet and the Web appears to be an extraordinary validation of investment-based technology policy. The unique characteristics of information and communications technologies and markets make it difficult to generalize, but the success of the Internet seems to bolster the case for public investment where externalities are strong. On the other hand, the success of Microsoft during the same period also seems to bolster the case for private investment where externalities are strong. In the long run, part of the value of the public investment may be to limit the reach of private monopolies and to do so more productively and efficiently that antitrust enforcement.

Beyond that, the long-term significance of the Internet will be to extend and redirect "technology policy" to inform policy analysis and development for information policy, competition policy, trade policy, and other domains. One conspicuous success of the U.S. NII initiative was to inspire other nations to assess national strategy in terms of the long-term economic and social changes expected from information and communications technologies. The Internet will compel policymakers to address national policy and strategy in the shadow of globalized commerce and communications.

Background

Computing and networking technologies have long been favored areas for federal investment, and agencies have developed advanced networks as infrastructure for computing research. Thus, CSNET was created in 1979 to provide remote access to unique computing facilities for universities that were not on the DoD-funded ARPANET. Similarly, NSFNET was launched in 1986 by the National Science Foundation (NSF) to facilitate high-speed access to the new NSF-funded supercomputer centers by hundreds of research universities.

The importance of computing and networking technologies for a variety of mission-specific applications encouraged cooperation among federal agencies, so that by the late 1980s, the federal mission agencies were coordinating research on advanced technologies and the development of shared infrastructure. In early 1991, the interagency collaboration was endorsed by the Bush administration as a budget crosscut,[1] the High Performance Computing and Communications (HPCC) program. The High Performance Computing Act of 1991, authored by then-Senator Al Gore, was passed by Congress in November 1991, providing a legislative mandate for the program.

The networking research and infrastructure component of both the HPCC program and the Act was billed as the "National Research and Education Network (NREN)," suggesting a coherence and scale that was never actually planned or budgeted. The infrastructure piece became the "interagency interim NREN," in reality no more than the evolving NSFNET and the more limited and specialized networks of the other agencies. Nonetheless, the vision of a National Research and Education Network provided momentum for the broader and more ambitious vision of an advanced, commercialized National Information Infrastructure (NII) that became the Clinton administration's flagship technology policy initiative.

Design of the NII Initiative

As technology policy, the NII initiative was an anomaly in that it married strategic investment with a deregulatory approach to telecommunications policy that had been building a bipartisan head of steam since the court-ordered 1984 divestiture of AT&T. Putting the two together was a remarkable and unprecedented linking of classical investment-oriented technology policy with regulatory policy, possible only because of the leadership of Vice President Gore. Further rounding out the initiative, the administration ambitiously sought to address a set of critical information policy issues posed by the growth and convergence of information and communications technology. In effect, the dual-faceted technology policy behind the HPCC program, which promoted infrastructure as well as technology, was extended into a sprawling multifaceted initiative that offered not only a rationale for expanded investment but a vehicle for leveraging policy development in other domains.

However, the initiative lacked definition and resources. In contrast to the space race, with its well-defined goal of putting a man on the moon under the exclusive direction of a new agency, the NII initiative was a loosely formulated project embodied in a interagency task force with a laundry list of objectives and action items. (See Table 13-1.) Despite building on the momentum and bipartisan approbation of the HPCC program, and even though a new component anticipating the initiative, Information Infrastructure Technology and Applications (IITA), was added to the HPCC program in early 1993, the NII initiative did not incorporate the HPCC strategic investment activities.[2] The HPCC program retained its own National Coordinating Office,[3] located first at the National Library of Medicine and later at the National Science Foundation.

In some respects, the NII initiative complemented the HPCC program: the HPCC was a multi-agency program recognized by a crosscut in the federal budget, while the NII initiative was invisible in the budget. With no presence in the budget, the NII initiative remained exclusively an exercise of the Executive Branch. Unconstrained by legislation, it was able to cover a wide domain with a minimum of red tape. Its legitimacy derived from the interest and involvement of Vice President Gore and a high-profile private-sector advisory committee, which facilitated interaction among a diverse set of agencies with very different kinds of expertise and modes of operation.

Although many different agencies were involved, the Department of Commerce served as the principal home for the initiative outside of the White House. The chair of the Information Infrastructure Task Force was Commerce Secretary Ron Brown; of the three committees, two were chaired within Commerce. The Department's National Telecommunications and Information Administration served as secretariat for the IITF and chaired the Telecommunications Policy Committee, which was focused on the deregulatory legislation in Congress. The Commerce Department's National Institute for Standards and Technology (NIST), a research laboratory with a few funding programs attached, chaired the Committee on Applications and Technology (the "CAT"). The third committee, the Committee on Information Policy, was chaired by the Office of Information and Regulatory Affairs within the Office of Management and Budget, which is within the Executive Office of the President. However, it provided little more than an umbrella for three different working groups. The most visible of

Table 13-1   The National Information Infrastructure: Agenda for Action, September 15, 1993; Principles and Goals for Government Action (Section V)

1) Promote Private Sector Investment
   a) <u>Action</u>: Passage of communications reform legislation
   b) <u>Action</u>: Revision of tax policies

2) Extend the "Universal Service" Concept to Ensure that Information Resources Are Available to All at Affordable Prices
   a) <u>Action</u>: Develop a New Concept of Universal Service

3) Promote Technological Innovation and New Applications
   a) <u>Action</u>: Continue the High-Performance Computing and Communications Program
   b) <u>Action</u>: Implement the NII Pilot Projects Program
   c) <u>Action</u>: Inventory NII Applications Projects

4) Promote Seamless, Interactive, User-Driven Operation
   a) <u>Action</u>: Review and clarify the standards process to speed NII applications
   b) <u>Action</u>: Review and reform government regulations that impede development of Interactive services and applications

5) Ensure Information Security and Network Reliability
   a) <u>Action</u>: Review privacy concerns of the NII
   b) <u>Action</u>: Review of encryption technology
   c) <u>Action</u>: Work with industry to increase network reliability

6) Improve Management of the Radio Frequency Spectrum
   a) <u>Action</u>: Streamline allocation and use of spectrum
   b) <u>Action</u>: Promote market principles in spectrum distribution

7) Protect Intellectual Property Rights
   a) <u>Action</u>: Examine the adequacy of copyright laws
   b) <u>Action</u>: Explore ways to identify and reimburse copyright owners

8) Coordinate with Other Levels of Government and with Other Bodies
   Domestic
   a) <u>Action</u>: Seek ways to improve coordination with state and local officials
   International
   b) <u>Action</u>: Open up overseas markets
   c) <u>Action</u>: Eliminate barriers caused by incompatible standards
   d) <u>Action</u>: Examine international and U.S. trade regulations

9) Provide Access to Government Information and Improve Government Procurement
   a) <u>Action</u>: Improve the accessibility of government information
   b) <u>Action</u>: Upgrade the infrastructure for the delivery of government information
   c) <u>Action</u>: Enhance citizen access to government information
   d) <u>Action</u>: Strengthen interagency coordination through the use of electronic mail
   e) <u>Action</u>: Reform the Federal procurement process to make government a leading-edge technology adopter.

these, the Working Group on Intellectual Property Rights, was chaired by Assistant Secretary of Commerce and Commissioner of Patents and Trademarks Bruce Lehman.

Despite the key roles of these several Commerce agencies in the NII initiative, neither the department's Office of Technology Policy nor the Technology Administration above it were explicitly involved. The link with the HPCC agencies was made through the Technology Policy Working Group (TPWG) chaired by the Defense Advanced Research Projects Agency (DARPA). The TPWG was crucial to channeling technological insights to the initiative, as well as engaging industry in serious issues of research, standards, infrastructure architecture, and policy. But TPWG drew little attention from Commerce, other than from NIST, which chaired the parent Committee on Applications and Technology.

On paper NTIA, with its broad mandate for telecommunications and information, looked like a logical home for the NII initiative, but despite the "Information" in NTIA, the agency did not expand its policy agenda beyond its historical emphasis on spectrum management and facilities-based telecommunications. NTIA was designated to administer the only new funding program created under the NII rubric, the Telecommunications Infrastructure and Applications Assistance Program (TIAAP), but this very small program for funding cost-shared demonstration projects was embroiled in continual Congressional debate over funding.[4]

Both NTIA and NIST were targeted by the Republican Congress that took office in January of 1995. The Republicans did not take issue with the NII initiative as such, but TIAAP was attacked along with other funding programs under the two agencies. Even the HPCC was attacked, in part because it had come to be identified with Vice President Gore. Rooting the NII initiative within Commerce had been part of the administration's strategy for revitalizing Commerce, but the change in Congress brought forth calls for dismantling the Department altogether, indirectly jeopardizing the initiative.

With the Commerce Department and these key agencies on the defensive, the NII initiative lost momentum. In January 1996, the Telecommunications Reform Act was finally enacted, moving the action from Congress to the Federal Communications Commission (FCC), which as an independent regulatory agency was not part of the NII initiative. At the end of that month, the high-profile National Information Infrastructure Advisory Council terminated on schedule. Two months later, Secretary Brown's sudden death left the IITF without its chair. The secretariat was quietly transferred from NTIA to NIST, where it has remained little more than a Web site.[5]

Nonetheless, the Task Force has not been terminated officially, and a few working groups remained active in 1997. The Privacy Working Group issued a report, *Options for Promoting Privacy on the National Information Infrastructure*, in April 1997.[6] The Technology Policy Working Group continued to meet regularly, although in June 1997 it became the Technology Policy Subcommittee of the Committee on Computing, Information and Communications.[7] The Working Group on Government Information Technology also graduated out of the IITF to become the Government Information Technology and Services Board.

Beyond the IITF

Even in its heyday, the NII initiative was not an all-encompassing umbrella for the administration's interests in information infrastructure. The HPCC program, which laid important groundwork for the initiative, remained separate. The interagency team on cryptography policy operated entirely outside of the IITF. The Committee on Applications and Technology did not develop sector-specific working groups beyond health care and government services, and the administration's initiatives in education and technology were pursued independent of the IITF. The National Digital Library Initiative funded by NSF, DARPA, and NASA[8] was identified with HPCC/ITAA but not the NII initiative, even though digital libraries figured prominently in the rhetoric around the NII and the Global Information Infrastructure (GII). The Technology Reinvestment Program (aimed at defense industry conversion and involving four agencies in addition to DoD; see Chapter 7 by Linda Cohen) had a strong emphasis on information technology in its first year but had no direct relationship to the IITF.

In the spring of 1993, in the wake of its foundation technology policy document, *Technology for America's Economic Growth*, the administration planned a broader initiative in which the core HPCC, plus the new IITA component, plus the "on-ramps" program that would become TIAAP, would be the technology portion of the NII initiative.[9] But ultimately the NII initiative remained independent of all funding programs. IITA was added to the HPCC before the NII initiative was formalized. TIAAP, which was early identified with the administration's information infrastructure goals, was implemented entirely within NTIA. The initiative emerged as a policy development effort with links into the research agencies (mainly through the Technology Policy Working Group) but without any direct responsibility for R&D.

The NII initiative succeeded in the first instance as a shared vision of the transformative potential of information and communications technology. While it suffered from a lack of staff and resources, it demonstrated the power of the White House to serve as a "bully pulpit" and catalyst. The impact was perhaps most visible abroad, where the NII initiative and Gore's subsequent vision of the Global Information Infrastructure generated waves of studies, commissions, and conferences,[10] and eventually helped liberalize trade in the underlying technologies.[11]

Domestically, the evidence of its influence is less tangible. The public focus created by the initiative and Gore's special interest in "the information superhighway" contributed to the momentum behind the Telecommunications Act, although the increasing interest and clout of the computer industry also played a critical part in breaking the long-standing legislative impasse. In any case, even when the Democrats were in control in 1993 and 1994, the administration's strategy was to allow Congress to take the lead on telecommunications reform.

The NII initiative was instrumental in accelerating embrace of the Internet within the government. The White House set an example by unveiling its own Web site in mid-1994, including a page on Executive Branch agencies showing clearly which were linked and which were not. Most agencies implemented Internet-based electronic mail during the first two years of the Initiative, spurred as well by the vice president's parallel initiative on "reinventing government," the National Performance Review (NPR).[12] The synergy between the NPR and the IITF Working Group on

Government Information Technology lead to the formation of the Government Information Technology Services Board and its ongoing "Access America" project.[13]

The Technology Policy Working Group of the IITF[14] provided a critical link between the HPCC and the NII initiative, which enabled interaction among both program agencies and policy agencies. It was able to draw on the technological expertise and resources of key program agencies—DARPA (chair and host), NSF, and NIST—without laboring under an externally imposed agenda. It worked on digital television, NII architecture, government standards development processes, standards policy, interoperability, and security, as well as an overarching "roadmap" project. More than any other component of the NII initiative, the TPWG succeeded in constructively engaging the private sector.

The NII initiative was less successful in dealing with information policy issues. Although the IITF was not directly engaged on content control issues, the administration went on record as supporting the Communications Decency Act as part of the Telecommunications Act of 1996.[15] Policy on encryption, beginning with the unsuccessful Clipper Chip proposal, was developed under a separate interagency group but with links to the IITF through a National Security Issues Forum set up within IITF independent of the three committees. The administration's policies on copyright were explicitly the product of the IITF Working Group on Intellectual Property Rights. In that case, the very existence of the IITF helped overcome the lack of a clearly chartered office for developing domestic copyright policy within the Executive Branch.

The administration's positions on these three critical information policy issues compromised its standing within the rapidly growing community of Internet businesses and users. The Communications Decency Act was broadly reviled as a blow against free speech on the Internet. The encryption policy was seen as an unrealistic and futile attempt to bottle up a technology that was already widely disseminated. The copyright policy sided with the content industry against the communications industry, and the United States went to the World Intellectual Property Organization diplomatic conference in December 1996 domestically divided on key issues.

New Directions

The NII initiative was extremely successful at capturing the attention of industry and the public far beyond the public resources that went into it. In part a packaging of exploding technology and a growing market rather than a conventional government program, it rode the crest of a breaking wave. Ironically, it was ultimately overtaken by the phenomenal commercial success of the government's long-standing multifaceted investment in the Internet.

In 1993, the Web was unknown, the Internet was still viewed by industry as an academic toy, and it was widely assumed that the "information superhighway" would be some form of circuit-switched broadband, like the telephone system only with much greater bandwidth. The uncertainty as to how it would come about—in terms of technology, regulatory changes, and the huge investment assumed necessary to rewire every home in the country—left plenty of room for speculation and grandstanding.

Four years later, it is clear that the technological path to advanced information infrastructure is the Internet and that the upgrading of physical plant can proceed incrementally at far less cost than envisioned in 1993. The passage of the Telecommunications Act of 1996 has moved the primary arena for telecommunications policy reform to the FCC, but the process is subject to legal appeals which threaten to draw it out for years. The market seems likely to be shaped more by burgeoning demand for Internet access and services than by regulatory efforts to introduce competition in the local loop.[16]

The raging success of the Internet, including private intranets and extranets based on the same technology, makes it difficult, if not impossible, to develop coherent public policy. At one end of the spectrum, there is opportunity and desire to recreate the success of the Internet anew. At the other, there is growing awareness of the stresses that the Internet is placing on wide set of policy regimes, global as well as national level, raising inter-jurisdictional problems on top of substantive issues.

Next Generation Internet

Heralding the Internet as "the biggest change in human communications since the printing press," the administration announced the Next Generation Internet (NGI) initiative during the last month of the 1996 campaign.[17] The proposed budget would require approximately $50 million in new funding to be added to $50 million in redirected funding. Although in some respects the initiative would resurrect and revitalize the NREN program (refocused as Large Scale Networking in the recent reorganization of the HPCC[18]), it has a broader program with less emphasis on the deployment of production infrastructure.

There are three components: Experimental Research for Advanced Network Technologies; Next Generation Network Fabric; and Revolutionary Applications. The first addresses issues of scalability, resource reservation, quality of service, and security (including public key infrastructure). The second is a program to establish testbed networks with connections on the order of 150 Mbps (100 times conventional connections) at 100 universities, and 1500 Mbps (1000 times conventional connections) at ten universities. The third component would develop and test applications that depend on the technologies under the first component.

The Next Generation Internet initiative seeks to build on the monumental success of federal support for the Internet and to reinvigorate the federal investment strategy, much as the NREN component of the HPCC program sought to do in 1991. However, NGI is targeted at nearer-term problems in bolstering the functionality and capacity of the commercial Internet as general-purpose infrastructure by developing and testing generic technologies for commercial use. It is often confused with the "Internet 2" initiative recently launched by research universities with industry involvement.[19] Internet 2, by contrast, is focused on improving routine Internet connectivity among universities and other research centers.

Although NGI is a legitimate and important effort to build on the government's success in funding the technology of the Internet, it will be pushing the envelope in front of exploding commercial investment in Internet technologies. Work on higher-level services addressed in the first component will require careful engagement with industry, since many companies may complain that the government is skewing the playing field. This is a classic technology policy problem, but the commercial success of the Internet presents it under unprecedented and extreme conditions.

A Framework for Global Electronic Commerce

The globalization of the Internet and electronic commerce presents a different set of challenges about how science and technology can inform policy development, how to stimulate relevant expertise, how to diffuse knowledge to practitioners and policymakers, and how to make all this work on an international level.

As part of an effort to look at critical trade issues over a ten-year time frame, Ira Magaziner, senior advisor to the president for policy development, undertook a project in 1996 to examine the impact of the Internet on global electronic commerce and make recommendations. With the help of an ad hoc interagency task force, a draft report, *A Framework for Global Electronic Commerce*, was developed and posted for public comment at the end of December 1996. A final report was issued in July 1997.[20]

The report offers a set of five principles:

1. The private sector should lead.

2. Governments should avoid undue restrictions on electronic commerce.

3. Where governmental involvement is needed, its aim should be to support and enforce a predictable, minimalist, consistent and simple legal environment for commerce.

4. Governments should recognize the unique qualities of the Internet.

5. Electronic commerce over the Internet should be facilitated on an international basis.

The body of the report addresses a series of financial, legal, and market access issues: customs and taxation, electronic payment systems, application of the Uniform Commercial Code, intellectual property protection, privacy, security, telecommunications infrastructure and interoperability, content, and technical standards.

The report builds on earlier efforts to expand the vision and strategy of the NII initiative to a global level, beginning with Vice President Gore's speech to the International Telecommunication Union development conference in March 1994. Gore's speech and the subsequent *Agenda for Cooperation* (published just in time for the G-7 summit on the "Global Information Society" in February of 1995) had advanced the principles of the administration's domestic telecommunications policy as an agenda for telecommunications reform worldwide.[21] The applications that were important to the NII vision in the United States lacked a clear point of entry into international policy development. By contrast, *A Framework for Global Electronic Commerce* acknowledges the revolutionary impact of the Internet and focuses on facilitation of a global free market for commerce at the applications level.

The document is best known for the case it makes for maintaining the Internet as a tax-free zone, which helped forestall efforts to establish a "bit tax" on Internet commerce in Europe.[22] Other parts of the document are less newsworthy but provide a compendium of administration thinking on related issues. In fact, the principles seem to reflect a movement toward a more progressive posture on the most difficult information policy issues: encryption, content control (i.e., the Communications Decency Act), and intellectual property.

A Framework for Global Electronic Commerce attempts to assert principled leadership in the development of the Global Information Infrastructure and to forestall reactive policies towards the Internet by nations that are less familiar with the technology and more anxious about its impact on human behavior and information flows. Accordingly, Ira Magaziner and his colleagues consulted with counterparts in Europe and Japan in addition to publishing a preliminary draft on the Web.[23]

A Framework for Global Electronic Commerce is not technology policy in the conventional sense, but it does offer "technologically informed" policy. Indeed, the success of the Internet uniquely positions the United States for playing a leadership role in the evolution of Internet-enabled commerce worldwide. However, to succeed over the long run, this leadership effort must be as principled and transparent as the legal and regulatory environment it advocates, without lapsing conspicuously into strategies to advance particular domestic interests.

Together, the Next Generation Internet initiative and the Magaziner initiative on global electronic commerce effort represent a devolution of the NII initiative into its twin roots: coordinated federal investment in advanced technology and infrastructure in the HPCC tradition; and the evolution of market-oriented competition policy, not just for facilities-based telecommunications in the United States but for all levels of information infrastructure worldwide. The two-part vision (deregulation plus new applications) set forth in the NII and GII foundation documents has been superseded by the rise of the Internet as the practical embodiment of unregulated convergence and leveraged innovation.

Technology Policy for the Information Age

The difficulty of developing coherent public policy for a rapidly advancing commercial infrastructure requires caution in crafting quick solutions. However, there is an enduring, indeed expanding need to develop a deep understanding of the changing policy environment and a framework for mediating among competing interests and values. This environment is being transformed by changing technology, and the marketplace changes deriving from deregulation and technological change. Changes in the market, second and third-order effects, and the profusion of externalities create a situation without historical precedent that is difficult to assimilate. *A Framework for Global Electronic Commerce* argues rightly that this is a unique environment, and that traditional regulatory and legal models must not be uncritically applied. The principles underlying the old models may still be valid, but they are likely to operate in new ways in unaccustomed proximity to other policy domains.

If the principal goal of technology policy is to stimulate innovation in the economy, the exploding Internet demands a higher order of technology policy that comprehends the extraordinary interplay of cooperation and competition now underway. By spanning strategic public investment and telecommunications deregulation, the NII initiative was an unprecedented first effort in this direction. However, the initiative faced a number of competing and ultimately unsuccessful "superhighway" models, quite unlike the current common focus on the Internet and the Web. The initiative also lacked new resources for policy development (which could only be granted by Congress) and so remained unable to transcend traditional agency perspectives or assimilate a strategic understanding of the Internet as private companies have been able to do. The Information Infrastructure Task Force provided a vehicle for marshaling interagency expertise, but it often lacked the context and resources to do so consistently.

The white paper developed by the IITF Working Group on Intellectual Property Rights demonstrates this danger.[24] It argued for holding bulletin boards strictly liable for acts of their users that infringe copyright, claiming that the ability of the host services to police behavior of users and contract for indemnification puts such services in a better position than copyright owners to absorb losses from copyright infringement. The paper does not acknowledge the burden this policy would impose on another policy goal: making the Internet accessible to the largest number of users. However, the effect would be to induce providers to discriminate against impecunious users or to reduce expectations of privacy.

At this early point in Internet history it is difficult to assess just how different the technological and economic environment is or will be and how its characteristics—powerful network externalities, great economies of scale, and profound but hard-to-assess economies of scope—should inform competition policy. These characteristics combine to create path dependency and network tipping,[25] as evidenced in Microsoft's rise to dominance in operating systems and office suites. Exploitation of first-mover advantages and penetration pricing (even giving software away) to lock in a unique position in the market has become the classic Internet business strategy even for those who cannot hope to implement it on the scale of a Netscape or Microsoft.[26]

Transaction costs also play a critical role in this environment, especially as manufacturing and distribution costs associated with content and services diminish. Although the idea of friction-free capitalism gets good press, transaction costs remain diverse, complex, and highly contingent on the evolution and adoption of application-level infrastructure. Broadly speaking, transaction costs include costs associated with reducing or managing uncertainty, such as both uncertainty about market conditions and uncertainty about the application of laws or the likelihood of government regulation. Laws and policies may cloud the picture further by attempting to allocate the burdens of uncertainty. For example, the white paper of the IITF Working Group on Intellectual Property Rights argues for burdening service providers for the benefit of content owners. Such arguments make assumptions about technology, infrastructure, and business models, thereby prejudging the evolutionary path.

These economic characteristics vary greatly across the information infrastructure and are in constant flux. Information infrastructure is the product of converging industries, each with its own market structure, policy dynamics, and legal and regulatory traditions. Technological and market "convergence" does not lead to homogenization as is sometimes inferred from the blurring and breakdown of boundaries. Rather it breeds new forms of value, new business opportunities, and new market niches, where different policy domains interact in a variety of micro-climates.

Constructing a single regulatory framework that covers the whole of this increasingly seamless infrastructure, let alone developing it consistently, would be a hopeless task. Nevertheless, there are risks in allowing the legal and regulatory environment to develop without a coherent understanding of the underlying forces, especially since there is great disparity among stakeholders in their ability to assimilate and respond to rapid change. Inertia is a powerful force with many allies. Precedent-oriented legal arguments made in particular circumstances are likely to dominate policy development, because the long-term systemic impact is so difficult to capture and diagnose.

Microsoft's extraordinary success and its ability to leverage that success into adjacent markets presents the ultimate challenge for a competition policy informed by technology and economics. On the one hand, Microsoft is generating vast new wealth, including a large consumer surplus created by aggressively incorporating more and more functionality into its operating systems and applications software. It is relentlessly exploiting the economic characteristics of information infrastructure, which in turn give the company a market position that seems virtually unassailable. Remarkably, it has achieved this dominance without relying on stronger forms of intellectual property protection such as user-interface copyright and patents.

Microsoft's dominant market position arguably hurts the ability of other companies to compete on the basis of technological merit and innovation. Microsoft looks like the old AT&T, a natural monopoly because software, like other information, has virtually no marginal cost. Microsoft's users are locked in by externalities, habit, and the integration of functionality within and across product lines. Yet by providing a nearly ubiquitous operating system infrastructure, Microsoft provides a stable, standards-based environment for new applications.

Microsoft's dominance of the desktop has been mitigated to some degree by the emergence of the Internet as a driving force in the computer, communications, and content industries. The Internet presents a counter-paradigm to the Microsoft business model, not as a competitor but as a nonproprietary standards environment generating even more powerful and pervasive externalities. Of course, this Internet paradigm derives from the federal role in seeding Internet technology, infrastructure, and standards development. The Internet provided the opportunity for Netscape's Navigator to become the dominant web browser and for Sun's Java programming language to offer a new paradigm for software development that was network-oriented rather than bound to specific desktop operating systems.

Microsoft's reorientation to the Internet was not just to develop a competing browser or its variant of Java. Rather Microsoft was required to reestablish its position at the center of infrastructural innovation by visibly embracing a less proprietary standards strategy in the Internet/intranet arena. In some contexts, Microsoft now argues that Sun's or Netscape's strategy is too closed or proprietary.

The importance of Internet standards, combined with the difficulty of scoping and developing competition policy for the Internet, may urge further federal investment in Internet standards, not only for the value of the inherent externalities and spillover effects, but because open standards processes may help insure that the market itself remains open. Internet standards are not directly competitive with Microsoft's proprietary desktop, but the externalities they generate are so powerful that they limit Microsoft's ability to act on its own.

However, these arguments, like opposing arguments for proprietary incentives, are based largely on anecdotes. While there is a wealth of empirical data and analysis available to support policy-making in telecommunications, there is a conspicuous lack of quantitative research that might inform policy on standards and intellectual property. If, as is often supposed, telecommunications regulation will wither away and intellectual property rights emerge as the preeminent regulatory framework in the information economy, there must be a greater factual basis for assessing the limits of such rights, their proper application, and how they can be efficiently administered. Patent policy, colored by ideological views on how the system should work and enormous anxiety about transaction costs as experienced by small inventors, is especially in need of empirical grounding. Unlike copyright policy, which has always been about information, patent law and policy has been shaped and validated by experience in industrial-age technologies. If, as the *Framework for Global Electronic Commerce* posits, the Internet is unique, the application of patent law and practice to innovation in the Internet should be open to examination.[27]

This is not to argue for aggressive policy development but for a shared, documented understanding of how the technology and markets around the Internet work and the short and long-term implications for public policy. Toward this goal, appropriate funding agencies should support disinterested empirical research that produces results in the language of policy makers. In addition, the kind of interagency coordination attempted by the IITF should be institutionalized and strengthened by using interagency personnel agreements and fellowships to assign technology experts to policy development agencies and, conversely, policy experts to mission agencies.

Towards a Technology-Enabled Policy Environment

The *Framework for Global Electronic Commerce* emphasizes the importance of consensual or contract-based arrangements as an alternative to public regulation and new laws. The report suggests roles for technology in different contexts but does not elaborate on the relationship between contract and enabling technology. The preeminent example of such technology, PICS (the Platform for Internet Content Selection),[28] was developed as an industry response to the problem of children accessing pornography on the World Wide Web. PICS enables browsers to limit access to material in accordance with labels embedded in the material or provided by third-party servers using ratings of their choice. While PICS was initially concerned with sexual and violent content, it can also be used for managing intellectual property rights, privacy interests, and security. Offering a general distributed architecture for managing access to information through the use of metadata (information about information), PICS is policy-enabling infrastructure, whether the policy is that of individuals, companies, communities of interest, or national governments.

Metadata can constrain or enable. It can assist in the location, organization, and management of information. It can enable commerce by supporting authentication, validation, and certification and by facilitating exchange of contract terms and conditions. It can enable technology- and market-based mechanisms that serve as alternatives or supplements to legal controls. It can facilitate disclosure-and-consent approaches to privacy protection and consumer transactions; assert and waive rights (which could confirm or refine the public licenses implied by Web postings); set standards of reasonable behavior that trigger liability or establish a defense; or provide signals that establish presumptions as to jurisdiction and choice of law.

Metadata infrastructure is not advanced technology in the usual sense, but it requires thoughtful development in coordination with a wide variety of stakeholders. It provides an opportunity to rethink basic legal and policy problems at a higher level to arrive at uniform solutions premised on mutual consent. It addresses the breakdown of boundaries and the problems of jurisdiction and association inherent in the Internet environment by reconstructing boundaries at a finer level and by allowing choices to made efficiently. Properly implemented, it should do so without unnecessarily sacrificing simplicity and transparency.

The development of metadata infrastructure is, from one perspective, a strategic investment issue—and specifically an option for extending the NGI. At the same time, it offers a framework for addressing the policy problems of the global Internet and lessening the need for resolution totally within conventional legal and regulatory regimes. Designing this infrastructure is not so much a high-tech challenge as a packaging problem that must be informed by technology, law, and policy.

However, the use of contract and technology to address policy problems raises problems of its own. The interface between contract law and public law such as copyright is in itself controversial. Contract law works well to mediate relationships between businesses, but its application to mass-market consumer transactions is less clear-cut. Efforts to develop a new Article 2B for the Uniform Commercial Code that would deal with information contracts have slowed down in a ever-widening set of constituencies and in questions of how and when contracts may limit the application of copyright and consumer protection laws. Similarly, there is controversy over the extent to which U.S. law should limit efforts to defeat technology controls that may protect material under copyright.

Paradoxically, while contract and technology offer alternatives to law and regulation, they also complicate the policy picture. While they vastly increase the transaction options available in commerce, this heightens concern that consumers may not be able to make meaningful choices, especially in an environment in which they have come to value speed and quick "surfing" from site to site. New options introduce new questions that invite and demand the rebalancing of old values and old policies.

Notes

1. Budget crosscuts are identified as programs in the budget but with components identified with participating agencies and included in the separate budgets of those agencies.

2. < http://www.ccic.gov/blue94/section.3.4.html>.

3. The National Coordinating Office now reports to the Committee on Computing, Information, and Communications of the National Science and Technology Council.

4. Funding for TIAAP topped out at $36 million in FY 95.

5. < http://www.iitf.nist.gov>.

6. < http://www.iitf.nist.gov/ipc/privacy.htm>.

7. <http://www.ccic.gov/ccic/>.

8. See <http://www.cise.nsf.gov/iris/DLHome.html> and <http://dli.grainger.uiuc.edu/national.htm>.

9. Presentation by Mike Nelson, White House Office of Science and Technology Policy, "Forum on Information Infrastructure," convened by the Harvard Information Infrastructure Project, University Club, Washington, D.C., April 7, 1993.

10. See generally Brian Kahin and Ernest Wilson, eds., *National Information Infrastructure Initiatives: Vision and Policy Design* (Cambridge, Mass.: MIT Press, 1997).

11. See Ministerial Declaration on Trade in Information Technology Products, World Trade Organization, document WT/MIN(96)/16, December 13, 1996; and Report of the Group on Basic Telecommunications, World Trade Organization, document S/GBT/4 (97-0675), February 15, 1997.

12. <http://www.npr.gov/>.

13. < http://www.gits.fed.gov/>.

14. < http://nii.nist.gov/cat/tp/tp.html>.

15. P.L. 104-104, Title V.

16. This demand is already coloring debate over charges imposed for access to the local loop as local exchange carriers claim that Internet service providers and users are imposing a disproportionate, uncompensated burden on local telephone facilities. See "Report of Bell Atlantic on Internet Traffic," <http://www.ba.com/ea/fcc/report.htm>; summarized in Timothy K. Stevens and James E. Sylvester, "Superhighway Traffic Taxes Current LEC Networks," *Telephony,* July 19, 1996.

17. White House, Office of the Press Secretary, "Background on Clinton-Gore Administration's Next-Generation Internet Initiative," October 10, 1996, <http://www.iitf.nist.gov/documents/press/internet.htm>. A concept paper is posted at <http://www.ccic.gov/ngi/concept-Jul97/>.

18. Compare the FY 96 program at <http://www.hpcc.gov/blue96/program.org.html> with the FY 97 program at <http://www.hpcc.gov/blue97/future.html>.

19. <http://www.internet2.edu>.

20. < http://www.iitf.nist.gov/eleccomm/ecomm.htm>.

21. The frequently cited principles were five in number: encouraging private investment; promoting competition; providing open access; creating a flexible

regulatory environment; and ensuring universal service. See *The Global Information Infrastructure: Agenda For Cooperation*, posted at <http://www.iitf.nist.gov /documents/docs/gii/giiagend.html>.

22. See Luc Soete and Karin Kamp, "The 'BIT TAX': the case for further research," draft, August 12, 1996, <http://www.lovotax.nl/tax/onderwerp5 /15.html>.

23. The final version of the European counterpart was published in April 1997: European Commission, *A European Initiative in Electronic Commerce*, Communication to the European Parliament, the Council, the Economic and Social Committee and the Committee of the Regions, COM(97)157, <http://www.cordis.lu /esprit/src/ecomcom.htm>. A draft version of the Japanese counterpart, *Towards the Age of the Digital Economy*, was published by MITI in May 1997 (presently at <http://www.miti.go.jp/intro-e/a228101e.html>).

24. IITF Working Group on Intellectual Property Rights, *Intellectual Property and the National Information Infrastructure*, September 1995, <http://www.uspto.gov /web/offices/com/doc/ipnii/>.

25. "Path dependency" refers to the tendency of technology to evolve incrementally from the installed base of existing technology with the result that superior new technology may not be adopted. "Network tipping" is the tendency of product or service to end up with the entire market once it has reached a certain critical mass.

26. Netscape played a major role in advancing the model by disseminating its Navigator browser as shareware and allowing nonprofit institutions to use it without charge. Microsoft responded to Netscape's dominance in the browser market by making the Microsoft browser, Internet Explorer, available for free to all users.

27. Patents were barely mentioned in the 1995 white paper, *Intellectual Property and the National Information Infrastructure*, but are discussed as much as copyright in the 1997 *Framework for Global Electronic Commerce*.

28. <http://www.w3.org/PICS/>.

14

University-Industry Relations: The Next Four Years and Beyond

Harvey Brooks and Lucien P. Randazzese

Starting in the 1970s, and increasingly in the 1980s and 1990s, federal and state governments in the United States have established programs to stimulate formal university-industry relationships. In response to this increased interaction between universities and industry, and increasingly visible spin-offs from university research, especially in such areas as biotechnology, research ties between academia and industry have attracted growing attention from the academic, industrial, and public policy communities. Two related issues have been of particular importance.

First, while some have welcomed the closer ties between universities and industry, others have expressed apprehension that these ties and the resulting increased emphasis on commercially relevant research will come at the expense of more fundamental investigation, for which universities are more uniquely suited.[1] Of greater concern is that closer interaction with industry could lead universities to compromise their traditional commitment to the open disclosure of their results and equal access to their knowledge base for all qualified scholars. This commitment might also be compromised by increased academic efforts to derive revenue through aggressive assertion of intellectual property rights.[2] Indeed, several recent empirical studies of university-industry interaction provide evidence that university faculty who receive research support from industry conduct research that is more short-term and are more willing to accept restrictions on the free dissemination of their findings.[3]

The second issue concerns the role played by university-based research in technical advance in industry and economic development more generally. Recent work by Cohen, Nelson, and Walsh indicates that university research is more important to technical advance in industry than is generally acknowledged, and that the industrial impact of university research depends critically on a combination of public disclosure and informal channels of communication between industry and academia.[4] As Chapter 1 explains, the ability to create technological innovations, as well as new firms and even entire new industries based on these innovations, is a special American advantage. Ever since World War II, the United States has taken great pride in its research university system as a crucible for creativity. Thus, as U.S. industry faces stronger international competition, the question of the degree to which government incentives for closer university-industry ties can be an effective tool for accelerating innovation and increasing productivity in the American economy, without long-term adverse side effects for the universities, clearly becomes important.

In this chapter we review the history of university-industry relationships in the United States, highlight policy issues raised by these relationships, consider current university-industry relationships and the resulting policy debates, and suggest policy measures meant to protect the open character of the American university system while enhancing its contribution to technological innovation and economic development. We begin with a review of the history of university-industry relationships, since they have been a significant feature of the U.S. university system for a very long time.

History of University-Industry Relationships and Policy Issues

The history of university-industry relationships in the United States can be described as having four broad periods. The century before World War II was a time of pragmatic linkage of university research to general economic interests along with the gradual emergence of a relatively small but distinguished basic science capability. World War II and the challenge of the Cold War, followed by the coincidence of the shock of Sputnik and the arrival of the baby boom at college age ushered in a Golden Age of generous funding and rapid expansion of university research, freeing academic science of much of its prior dependence on industry and philanthropy. Beginning in about 1967, however, and continuing through the mid-1970s, was a period of declining financial, political and civic support for science, increased unemployment for scientists, especially young scientists, and general public disenchantment with the scientific enterprise. The decline in support was reversed in the early and mid-1970s with the rapid expansion of global competition. This fourth period was later characterized by the fading of the Cold War as a prime driver of public investment in scientific and technological research in fields other than health. A short summary of these four periods is instructive as we consider the problems, old and new, that surround the search for a long-term, stable relationship between university research and private innovation.

The Era of Pragmatic University Research, Linked to Emerging Industries

Historically, university research in the United States was modest in magnitude and generally quite applied in nature until the 1920s.[5] Although this began to change slowly in the 1920s, the practical emphasis persisted in most institutions for another two decades (notwithstanding the more fundamental orientation in some of the oldest east-coast universities). This earned American universities the condescension of their more science- and theory-based European counterparts.[6] In 1862, the Morrill Act furnished states with funds derived from the sale of federal lands, to "provide an endowment" for at least one college in each state for the promotion of education "related to agriculture and the mechanical arts." The Morrill Act left control over these schools to the states, leading to a decentralized system in which schools attempted to adapt their research to the specific economic needs of their regions. The agricultural research activities of the land grant schools were augmented by the creation of the federal system of agricultural experiment stations in 1887, and by the addition in 1914 of the cooperative extension service. Through this latter service the results of the research carried out in land-grant colleges and the experiment stations were adapted to local farming conditions. Contributing to this applied focus of American public universities in the later nineteenth and early twentieth centuries was their accessibility to a greater portion of the general population than the more class-sensitive European schools. This situation gradually provided a setting for the establishment of formal engineering departments during the early part of the twentieth century.

World War I also brought about stronger links between academic and industrial research, resulting in a rapid rise in the popularity and size of academic engineering programs following the war.[7] Throughout the early twentieth century (until World War II), science departments, and particularly engineering departments in U.S. universities continued to grow in size and number, and in their contributions to the scientific foundations of engineering practice and its codification, even during most of the Depression.[8]

It was also during this time that large-scale, multiproduct firms arose and began to develop separate internal R&D organizations. While these labs were at first rather empirical and product- and process-specific, they gradually became more "scientific" in focus. This also enhanced the importance of university departments as sources of new scientific knowledge and people with advanced training.[9] The best and most successful of the corporate research laboratories began encouraging their most creative people (often recruited from university faculties) to live in two worlds: the open world of academic science and engineering which gave them access to a world community of scholars, and the more restricted world of proprietary technological know-how required to protect the competitive advantage of their parent firm. At the same time, American research universities began to realize the financial benefits of embracing some industrially oriented research and became less resistant to industry research requests and increased limitations on disclosure and publication practices for industry-funded activities.[10] This receptivity to more immediately applicable research was often accompanied by a tendency to work more with teams in interdisciplinary centers. The coexistence of two distinct scientific cultures created a certain amount of tension and controversy within both.[11]

The Golden Age of American Science

By the time the United States entered World War II, American universities had not only experienced several decades of successful cooperation with industry but had also joined the ranks of the world's preeminent institutions of science. The scientific and technical resources of American university scientists were applied to war-related efforts with enormous success.[12] The first immediate effect was to advance the standing of American academic science greatly within the federal government. The second was to demonstrate that allowing scientists themselves to define problems and devise the best approaches to solving them frequently resulted in more effective and more generally applicable solutions than did task-oriented management by sponsors or ultimate users. This strategy—what came to be termed "the whole-problem" approach—was greatly facilitated by orders-of-magnitude increases in available financial resources, which encouraged more risk-taking and the parallel exploration of several technical approaches to the same broadly defined problem.[13]

The Soviet launch of Sputnik in October 1957 was widely (though somewhat incorrectly) interpreted as symptomatic of a dangerous U.S. lag in fundamental research, and resulted in a surge of federal support for basic academic research and institutional development in the 1960s, ushering in what has been called somewhat wistfully the "Golden Age of American Science." This expansion more than doubled the fraction of federal support for research in universities in the 1960s, and was accompanied by a rapid expansion of higher education nationally and a dramatic expansion of graduate school science enrollments (and graduate schools more generally).

By 1966, the budget of the National Science Foundation (NSF), which was $16 million in 1956, had grown to $480 million. The upsurge in federal support of both basic and applied biomedical research through the National Institutes of Health (NIH), also beginning in 1957, was even more dramatic, sometimes growing at 25 percent annually.[14] Thus, the 1960s saw the culmination of a process of intellectual redefinition of the academic research mission that had begun on American campuses in the years immediately prior to World War II. American universities became preeminent centers of scientific research and education in the world, benefiting both from generous support by the federal government, and from the employment of many top scientists who had migrated from Europe during and after the war. Even the engineering disciplines began to pursue more fundamental and generic research approaches, particularly stimulated by the rapid growth of solid state physics and materials science and the spread of these fields from pure physics into electrical engineering departments following the invention of the transistor in 1947. At the same time, many engineering schools dropped or curtailed their design courses and reduced their emphasis on process technology and traditional mechanical manufacturing based on machine tools, and took up device engineering, often derived from instrumentation and measurement techniques originally devised for pure physics research.

The Post–Cold War Era of Global Competition and Constrained Resources

The post-Sputnik research boom ended rather abruptly in 1967, primarily because of the escalating costs of the Vietnam War, but also because of a more generalized public disenchantment with technology, and a public belief that, with the spectacular success of the Apollo program, the primary rationale for the large U.S. public investment in science and technology (S&T) had disappeared because the United States had already "won" the race to demonstrate technological superiority in space. After 1967, university research support fell off rapidly through 1971. Federal R&D support to universities fell by 20 percent in four years.[15] The recession in total federal university support during this period, however, was actually much greater than in research support, bottoming out at about half the 1967 level as a result of the phasing out of several institutional development, support, and fellowship programs.[16] Between 1972 and 1975 support stagnated, but began to recover, at first only gradually, after 1975.

Beginning in the mid-1970s, and continuing strongly into the 1980s, a number of factors refocused policy attention on university research, including the relationship of universities with industry. Primary among these was competition from abroad, discussed in Chapter 1. Japanese and German firms began to capture a significant share of the market and profits in a variety of industries in which the U.S. had been a leader, such as automobiles, consumer electronics, and, somewhat later, semiconductors and other microelectronic components.[17] U.S. firms and government agencies began searching for ways to regain the nation's competitive edge. Among the strategies pursued by industry, with considerable policy encouragement from federal and state governments, was the re-establishment of industry's links with universities.[18] The Department of Defense (DoD) funding of academic research, which hit a low in the early 1970s, began to grow again during the late 1970s as part of the defense build-up begun in the second half of the Carter administration. This increase in funding, and the increasingly "top-down" programmatic nature of military support, partly stimulated a national reexamination of the university's role in commercial advance.

In 1978, an NSF pilot program that sponsored university-industry research centers (UIRCs) was expanded and formalized into the University-Industry Cooperative Research Centers program.[19] The NSF Engineering Research Centers (ERC) program was established in 1984, and the Science and Technology Centers (STC) program in 1987. Each of these programs was established to encourage closer cooperation among university researchers and industry or other organizations with operating responsibilities, and to make academic engineering research and education more immediately relevant to the long-term needs of industry and society. In addition to these federal efforts, state-supported programs (discussed by Christopher Coburn and Duncan Brown in Chapter 16) meant to establish UIRCs had been initiated in 26 of the 50 states by 1990. (Only three states had established such economic development programs prior to 1980).[20] At the same time, industry support of academic research became the fastest growing component of the university research economy, though it was still a minor component in the total and it varied a great deal across disciplines and across institutions. Individual companies increased their patronage while entire industries began to organize to make better use of university research.[21] These efforts were strengthened by trends in the character of academic R&D. Federal policy efforts a decade earlier yielded more engineering research than science research, measured in dollars of expenditure, for the first time in 1978, and by 1983, greater growth in the output of engineering relative to science PhDs.[22]

Along with these public and private programmatic initiatives, a number of legislative changes in intellectual property law, especially the Patent and Trademark Amendment Act of 1980 (Public Law 96-517, commonly referred to the Bayh-Dole Act), encouraged universities to look for commercial applications for their research by granting schools greater ownership rights to intellectual property developed with federal funding. Prior to this legislation, there had been great variation in patent policies across federal agencies as well as among universities. These legislative changes occurred at the same time as the development and maturation of several scientific fields with direct applications to commercial products, including biotechnology, microelectronics, materials and polymer science, software, computer-aided design (CAD), and robotics.[23]

Many universities responded to these changes in their environment with enthusiasm. As patentable inventions began to emerge from several areas of previously "pure" basic research, such as molecular biology, solid state physics, and computer science, some faculty began to pursue research agendas that were closer to developing final products for the market. Faculty doing research relevant to the newly emergent science-based industries started to form companies based on their academic research, and a few even left their faculty positions to become full-time entrepreneurs.[24] Corresponding changes were also made at the university administration level. By 1990, thirty-four of the top thirty-five NIH and NSF grant-receiving universities in the United States had established technology licensing offices that aggressively encouraged and administered faculty patenting.[25] Some universities even allowed venture capital firms to set up offices on campus, and experimented with investing university endowment funds in start-up firms, including those in which their own faculty had a predominant financial interest.[26]

Historically, then, university research has never been as "pure" as some of the ideology proclaimed during the basic research boom of the 1960s led the public to believe. Moreover, much fundamental academic research has always been stimulated by a quest for deeper conceptual understanding of scientific questions originating in practical problems, but pursued far more deeply than would appear to be strictly necessary for the solution of the specific problem at hand. Notwithstanding this historical association of academia with industry, however, the changing research climate has produced new strains in the American university system, leading to a good deal of soul-searching in academia and to a reevaluation of government polices that helps shape the industry-academy interface.

Current Situation

Academics now face a decline in the total research purchasing power available from the federal government, at least when measured on a per-researcher basis. On this measure, federal funding per full-time academic scientist active in R&D fell by 9.4 percent from 1979 to 1991.[27] At the same time, there has been a steady rise in the percentage of university research funded from sources other than the federal government. Industry funding has risen the most dramatically both as a proportion of the total and in real terms, though its share of academic support is still, on average, small compared to other sources. Between 1980 and 1995, private industry funding of university research grew from $236 million to an estimated $1.5 billion, a 249 percent real increase, and a 661 percent increase in real terms over the 1970 figure of $40 million.[28] Industry's share of R&D support to universities increased 166 percent, from 2.6 percent of the total in 1970 to an estimated 6.9 percent in 1995.[29] Most of this increase has been concentrated in a few disciplines and in more prestigious schools. Fully half of this support was provided through separately organized UIRCs.[30] Although industry in general has increased its contribution to university-based R&D, many firms, including those that have increased support to universities, have actually begun to cut back on their internal R&D expenditures. This phenomenon has been most visible among the large central R&D labs of such corporate giants as AT&T, General Electric, General Motors, DuPont, Xerox, Eastman Kodak, and IBM.[31]

Notwithstanding the growth in industry support for university R&D, anecdotal evidence suggests that industry is unlikely to make up for any appreciable share of cuts the federal government might make in R&D support to universities.[32] However, projections for federal support six years into the future are unreliable since they depend so heavily on uncertain forecasts regarding the growth of the U.S. economy, trends in labor productivity, and future reforms in entitlement programs such as Medicare and Social Security.[33] The most important agencies from the standpoint of academic research funding are NSF and NIH, which accounted for 68.1 percent of all academic R&D support in 1995, and which, based on current attitudes in Congress, are likely to fare better in future budget debates than the two other principal remaining potential funding sources, the Department of Energy (DOE) and the National Aeronautics and Space Administration (NASA). Given the unpredictability of these trends, then, we attempt to focus on the risks and benefits to both universities and the economy, and less on the sources of university funding, as we examine the policy issues associated with university-industry cooperation.

Policy Issues and Debates

In the following section we review what we believe to be the central policy issues of university involvement in industrial technology development. These issues arise from three interrelated problems that drive changes in the way universities cope with a rapidly growing world system of research: the likelihood of shrinking federal resources for research for some time to come, the resulting pressures on government agencies and investigators alike to become more conservative in their research investments and management styles, and the complexity and unpredictability of the search for financial resources for research at a time when the roles of government in the development of technology and the provision of incentives for innovation are in controversy. This discussion begins by considering the research support system, including the federal policy to encourage the emerging but still relatively small role for industrial funding, and goes on to discuss the effects on the universities of this growing industrial linkage. We then describe one institutional form that might serve to address the stresses that arise from conflicts between academic and industrial cultures, which we call "buffer institutions," and then briefly address the international dimensions of some of these issues.

The Level and Allocation of Federal Support for University
Research

Perhaps the most damaging result of a decline in federal funding
of university research would be the advent of increased conservatism in the distribution of funds and the concentration of funding
in well established fields where there are more likely to be diminishing but more certain returns to incremental effort.[34] Over time,
the peer-review process has tended to become more formalized
and bureaucratic and to emphasize fairness to all applicants at the
expense of support for novel but risky scientific opportunities, thus
locking in technical conservatism. The more research objectives
are precisely defined, results promised in advance, and outputs
measured against preconceived objectives and promises, the greater
will be the tendency to lock in current scientific thinking and
categories of R&D activity, for which outcomes are more predictable, and thus less likely to be either great discoveries or total
failure. For the same reason, in Chapter 5, Lewis Branscomb argues
that the federal research agenda should put more explicit emphasis on basic technology research and less on solving narrowly
defined problems in response to short-term industry needs. Whether
publicly funded research is undertaken for practical reasons or for
its inherent interest, the policies and conditions under which
research is conducted must be designed to maximize creativity,
especially when budgets are tight. There are institutional models
with which government has experience that illustrate the high
levels of creativity and value that can be created when block grants
are made available to interdisciplinary teams of researchers in first-
rate institutions. One example of such a model is the tri-service
electronics laboratories established at a number of universities
immediately after World War II which showed how excellent
research performed under wide discretionary authority can create
spillovers to quite practical interests, in this case affecting microelectronic devices, electromagnetic wave propagation, and many
other fields.[35]

Because both individual researchers and institutions tend to
become more conservative when resources are scarce, an ideal
policy would ensure growth in federal research support to academia

at rates slightly in excess of the rate of growth of the economy. Failing that, much more explicit and conscious effort needs to be devoted to reserving a proportion of total funding for risky ventures with high up-side potential but less assurance in advance of some valuable outcome.[36] In the so-called "mission" agencies, such as DoD, DOE and NASA, it may be necessary to segregate such funding in dedicated budget line items or to create special offices, like DARPA in the Department of Defense, specifically devoted to exploring new technologies of great potential value. More advanced, high-risk research by enterprises performing mission-oriented R&D under government contract can also be stimulated by an allocation for so-called "independent R&D." Here enterprises are given an extra overhead allocation for R&D of their own choice, essentially chargeable against future contracts for research to enhance their future capability. Some of this work may be performed in collaboration with universities.

It has occasionally been suggested that resource allocations should be made *within* research as a category, starting with a presidential decision on the total size of the federal science and technology (FS&T) budget.[37] This implies that trade-offs will not be made betwcen academic research and other nonresearch activities, including more applied development as well as other technical and non-technical follow-on activities external to academia or the R&D community. This would be an unnecessary and, indeed, potentially destructive constraint on policy since there are many situations in which research, both basic and applied, may be an attractive alternative to non-research or non-academic R&D expenditures. This can come about for a number of reasons, as indicated by the examples below.[38]

One of the prime reasons for the excellent performance of U.S. academic research is that budgeting has been able to accommodate the rapid exploitation of newly recognized technical opportunities without immediately threatening the stability of funding for existing subfields. This flexibility provides adequate time for evolutionary adaptation to new priorities in a sort of bottom-up fashion, as the most talented scientists gradually shift their priorities to take advantage of new and more promising scientific opportunities, not just new funding. For example, at the time the transistor was invented in 1947, only one or two universities were engaged in semiconductor research (Purdue being the principal one). Solid state physics was a very minor field in academic physics departments compared to such fields as nuclear physics. Solid state physics exploded in the universities only after the invention of the transistor and subsequently spread rapidly from physics into electrical engineering. If one had tried to plan academic research on a level of effort basis one would have had to practically wipe out all other subfields of physics in order to accommodate the level of effort required for solid state physics and related materials science and engineering disciplines to develop in academia. It was the ability to expand this effort rapidly in response to new opportunity that helped preserve the sizable early American lead in solid state electronics.

We also recommend that federal agencies that are major supporters of research should also consider setting aside some fraction of their support for academic science—even at the expense of existing programs—for regional multistate bodies or perhaps coalitions of professional organizations that would allocate these funds to projects by their own more localized peer-review process. These funds would be administered under general guidelines to ensure objectivity, and with an emphasis on addressing regional or other collective problems through exploiting particular regional or professional comparative strengths.[39] The purpose of this approach to funding would be both to encourage development of regional and institutional specialization and to conserve on the excessive use of scarce talent in the present wholly centralized national peer review process.

The Federal Role in Stimulating University-Industry Relationships

In the early 1980s, the National Science Board (NSB) began to explore ways to strengthen the NSF programs in engineering, recognizing that the downstream technical challenges in industry, which are so essential to a competitive position in manufacturing, can frequently be equally or even more intellectually challenging than the invention and perfection of very novel products. Processes, as well as products, were seen as the beneficiaries of creative, multidisciplinary research. In 1984 the NSF launched the Engineering Research Centers (ERCs), and subsequently the similarly constituted program of Science and Technology Centers (STCs).[40] Both of these programs involved research grants to universities that required academic partnerships with industry or other operating organizations such as government or non-profit organizations delivering public services. The large number of applications or inquiries received from universities tended to vindicate the philosophy underlying this new mechanism of support.

The center program proposals, which were considerably more involved than conventional grant requests, resulted in wholly new planning initiatives within universities. Many institutions benefited from the internal planning process that went into even the unsuccessful proposals, leading to new contacts with industry or other research organizations on a much wider scale than would have resulted from the successful proposals alone. Many initially unsuccessful proposals were later reworked and won subsequent support from NSF or other federal agencies. Thus, NSF in effect inaugurated a new piece of policy that was subsequently validated in a bottom-up process designed by and elaborated in negotiations with individual institutions or groups of researchers. In our opinion, this seems an ideal way to invent new science policy: a federal agency develops a rather generally stated idea that is then invented in detail, from the bottom up, within the scientific community itself through the winnowing out of many specific proposals. This is a pattern that has become well established and should provide a useful precedent for future initiatives. Not the least among its advantages is that it may divert less scarce talent into peer-review and other monitoring activities than the more conventional mechanisms of research support.[41]

The Effects of Industry Support on the Nature of University Research

Some recent empirical studies of university-industry research relationships suggest that ties with industry are associated with more applied research conducted by faculty.[42] Regression analyses of

UIRCs by Cohen and Randazzese do, indeed, show that higher percentages of industry support are correlated with the conduct of less basic research in such centers.[43] On the face of it, this seems quite plausible, since polymeric materials engineering, for example, is much more likely to attract industry attention than theoretical astrophysics. But the accommodation of the university and industrial cultures in a joint activity necessarily draws each somewhat toward the other. This effect does not seem to be pronounced, however. National Science Board data show that the overall share of university research that is classified as basic remained quite stable in the 1980s, despite a near doubling of the number of UIRCs formed in that period.[44]

While Cohen and Randazzese found an association between industry support and the conduct of more applied research, they also found an even stronger association between industry support and academic research reputation, and between academic reputation and the conduct of more basic (what they call "foundational") research. However, they find that when firms are more interested in specific applications, they appear to pay less attention to academic reputation in their selection of recipients.[45] Overall, the evidence is mixed on the effects of industry support on the nature of university research. There are clearly instances, both historically and recently, of links between industry needs and academic research that have resulted in benefit for both parties.

Two sector-wide initiatives within the semiconductor industry suggest more general lessons for public policy. The first was the formation in 1982 of the Semiconductor Research Corporation (SRC), through the efforts of the Semiconductor Industry Association (SIA). The SRC is a consortium made up of the principal U.S. semiconductor producers that supports university semiconductor research with funds it collects from its members. In an essay for a recent book on U.S. industrial research, Gordon Moore, co-founder of Intel, states that the "consortium's funds have been successful in keeping several major universities engaged in research that is immediately germane to the integrated circuit industry. Through faculty interest leading to proposals for government support as well, the industry has probably leveraged more than two to three times the money it has invested in the SRC, some $200 million over a ten-year period."[46] At the same time there is little evidence that SRC support has led academics to conduct research that is less "foundational" in character.[47] Thus, the SRC experience suggests that industry, acting through a consortium, has been able to help focus university research in areas more applicable to industrial technology development without adversely affecting its fundamental character and style.

In addition to establishing the SRC, in the early 1990s the SIA organized a group of researchers from across industry, government, and academia to put together a technology "roadmap" meant to coordinate long-range R&D projects within the industry and to identify key technology needs and the times at which those technologies would be needed in order to maintain the industry's historic annual 30 percent reduction in cost per function. This roadmap provides current guidance to academic researchers by identifying the most significant technology challenges in the field and thus encourages them to relate their research efforts to industry needs better without superseding their own best technical judgment. Moore remarks that while "there have been concerns that such a map may draw resources from existing work that may be more important, individual investigators seeking funding are likely to use it only as it makes sense and strike out on their own when they suspect they have better ideas. It is all in all more important not to dissipate resources through a failure to recognize problems and their relative importance."

This method of operation leaves the ultimate initiative and responsibility in the hands of the researcher, where it belongs. The most talented researchers will use their own best judgment, influenced but not dictated, by a centralized plan prepared by or in consultation with industry experts; the less original or less experienced scientists or engineers who require (and indeed may welcome) more guidance can rely on the roadmap to help them choose the most significant and relevant questions to investigate with more confidence in their practical value. Like the NSF's UIRC programs, the roadmap leads to a bottom-up process in the universities that leverages an amount of federal R&D money several times larger than the investment put up by the industry, but in a way that puts minimum restraint on the freedom of university investigators to exercise their own independent judgment. Funded proposals would be selected competitively by the usual peer review process, with participation by appropriate local industry and government experts as well as academics. This roadmap approach would allow government support to be leveraged by industry or public associations that could spend their own money to apply the results of the cooperatively supported R&D. We feel that the SRC and the technology roadmap constitute excellent models that could be followed by other R&D-intensive industries in leveraging government and academic research while still leaving the maximum freedom and intellectual initiative with individual academic researchers, thereby deriving maximum benefit from both academic and industrial cultures.

The Effects of Industry Support on the Disclosure of University Research Results

Industry often perceives an interest in limiting the disclosure of results from university research that it supports; this places its research style in conflict with the more open culture of universities.[48] Even though evidence regarding the influence of industry support on the nature of university research may be mixed, the available data are more certain on the effects of industry support on the disclosure of research results. In 1996 the *New York Times* reported that in "recent years, going against a long tradition of openness in science, many researchers have accepted secrecy as a common working practice. ... The trend toward secrecy ... has grown ... as competition for federal science grants has increased and more scientists have come to rely on grants or contracts from private companies."[49] In 1996 the *Wall Street Journal* reported on one drug company's attempt to suppress findings from research at the University of California at San Francisco that it had supported financially: the research had found that cheaper drugs available from other manufacturers could substitute therapeutically for its own thyroid drug.[50]

In addition to such anecdotal evidence, there is more broad-based quantitative evidence signaling an association between disclosure restrictions and industry support. In 1996, Blumenthal and his colleagues surveyed companies that support life science research within universities; they reported that 47 percent of such companies indicate that their agreements with universities occasionally require academic institutions to protect confidential proprietary information resulting from sponsored research for longer than is strictly necessary to file a patent application.[51] More recently, Blumenthal and his colleagues found that 19.8 percent of the life science faculty they surveyed had *themselves* delayed the publication of their work at least once for more than six months, and that 8.9 percent of faculty had refused to share research results or materials with other university scientists at least once in the previous three years.[52] Among the reasons for delaying publication or withholding information were to allow time for patent applications, to protect the proprietary or financial value of results, to protect the investigator's scientific lead or financial interest, and to delay the dissemination of results that might adversely affect the competitive status of the sponsor's product. This study further found that involvement with university-industry research relationships increased the likelihood of both a delay in publication and information-sharing restrictions.

In similar research, Dianne Rahm asked university technology managers and faculty at the hundred top R&D-performing universities in the United States about the extent of communication and publication restrictions sought or imposed by the firms they deal with.[53] Thirty-nine percent of technology managers indicated that in order to protect the secrecy of a potential commercial product, the firms they have dealt with have placed restrictions on how faculty may share with colleagues information regarding R&D breakthroughs. Seventy-nine percent of technology managers and 53 percent of faculty who have interacted with industry indicated that firms had asked that R&D results be delayed in their reporting or withheld from publication. A survey study of UIRCs by Cohen, Florida, and Goe found that for UIRCs nationwide, 53 percent permit firms to request publication delays and 35 percent of the centers allow information (of an unspecified kind) to be deleted from publication.[54] This survey also asked respondents whether center faculty and staff are ever restricted in sharing information about the projects they work on with others. Twenty-one percent of centers report restrictions on communication with other faculty and staff within their own university, 29 percent with faculty or staff at other universities, and 42 percent with the general public.[55] However, neither survey reveals how frequently the delays or excisions reported were inappropriate or unreasonable. For example, some deleted information may be proprietary to a partner company because it was developed entirely within the company, with company personnel and resources.

The restrictions reported in the surveys by Rahm and by Cohen, Florida, and Goe are generally more restrictive than what is recommended in the Government-University-Industry Roundtable and Industrial Research Institute's 1988 model agreements for university-industry cooperative research.[56] In examining academic disclosure, Cohen and Randazzese found that the academic researchers with greater academic reputation who attract more industry support are also less likely to suppress the disclosure of their results. However, when firms are less interested in basic research they tend to ignore faculty reputation in making university funding decisions. Thus, it appears that in the spectrum of research universities and firms, the best seem quite capable of protecting their traditional values of openness, with only modest concessions to the practical needs of industry, while other institutions are quite willing to undertake more proprietary work which calls for more traditional industrial restraints on disclosure. This situation needs to be carefully monitored, as increased competition for industrial and other non-government funding may eventually erode the determination of even the most prestigious institutions and investigators to resist pressures to restrict information flow.

Since there are clearly many benefits that derive from closer university-industry ties, these ties should not be regulated in any strong sense. It would be unfortunate if Congress were to overreact to a few well-publicized examples and attempt to restrict abuses by generalized legislation. It would be equally unfortunate if the research universities acceded to more restrictive policies than necessary because of increasing competition for industrial funding. Their bargaining power would be strengthened if, during their negotiations with firms, they were in a position to invoke strong institutional or other collectively agreed-upon and widely publicized guidelines bearing on research disclosure. A joint registry of disclosure restrictions acceptable to research universities would help institutions set and enforce their policies on individual faculty and researchers.

Intellectual Property

Closely related to the issue of disclosure restrictions are issues associated with intellectual property. As reported by Philip Abelson, a former editor of *Science*, corporate members of the Industrial Research Institute (IRI) consider difficulties over intellectual property to be a principal barrier to effective university-industry collaboration.[57] This is so, despite the fact that relatively few patentable inventions are expected from or produced by most industry-funded university research. There are, however, major exceptions, especially in the fields of molecular biology and in computer software. Universities are keenly interested in the option of exploiting patents derived from research performed by their faculty, employees, and students. Assigning rights (and financial responsibilities) for intellectual property within the university can also be quite complex. Deciding how the faculty members, their staff and students, the department and the university should share in any benefits that flow from patents and copyrights can create tensions within the institution. Firms, on the other hand, are anxious not to lose their proprietary rights in intellectual property that may be of commercial benefit to them.

Most firms are quite willing to allow the university partner to own patents arising from joint work, provided they are granted an exclusive license for a sufficient period of time to bring the invention to market. Universities are interested not only in possible revenues from their intellectual property but in the social goal of ensuring that useful university research results are not suppressed. Thus many agreements provide that if the firm fails to exploit an exclusive right after a stated period of time, the university is free to license it to others. Constraints on licensing were addressed in legislation and court actions in the 1920s and 1930s, when some large companies used their patent positions to slow the pace of technological change that could make their products or operations obsolete, or to reduce competition from new firms.[58] This issue may need to be revisited to make sure that intellectual property policy maximally promotes rather than retards the rapid commercialization of technological innovation and promotes competition on the basis of superiority of technical and marketing skills rather than cost cutting through wage and benefit restrictions, lax environmental performance, or export of production to low-wage countries.

Conflicts of Interest

Thus far, we have assumed that university researchers conform to the traditional model of academic behavior, that of disinterested pursuit of knowledge. However, the policy changes of the early 1980s with respect to intellectual property resulting from academic research have combined with the increased potential for commercial application in such areas as bio and information technology to create entirely new profit incentives for many university researchers. In addition, the increased use of fundamental research results to justify costly regulation or legal disputes raises the economic stakes in an increasingly broad range of science normally performed by academic researchers. Fundamentally oriented academic scientists have suddenly found themselves with potential or actual short-term financial interests in the results of their research, and may face a choice between pursuing those interests instead of unrestricted "open" science. A recent study conducted jointly at Tufts University and UCLA examined the financial interests of a group of authors from nonprofit or academic research institutions who had published a total of 789 articles in 14 leading scientific and medical journals in 1992.[59] The study found that for 267 of the 789 articles, at least one lead author had a financial interest in the results that were reported.[60] Yet none of these interests were actually reported either in the articles or elsewhere in the journals in which they appeared.

While such cases of potential conflict of interest have been most common in the biological sciences, they can also occur in other fields. Some journals, such as *Science*, have begun requiring financial interest disclosure from authors, but other journals, such as the

British journal *Nature*, have so far resisted the imposition of such requirements.[61] Similar requirements for disclosure are also specified by the NSF and NIH when researchers apply for grant support.[62] The argument can be made that in the short run, a failure by researchers to disclose potential financial interests in the outcome of their research might not only diminish the credibility of their own findings, but also to raise (possibly unjustified) suspicions of related findings in a whole field, thereby diminishing the value and usefulness of the science to both the government and the general public. The disclosure (or lack thereof) of financial or other interests by researchers can present a problem for nongovernmental and other organizations as well as individuals. The credibility of researchers can come under attack, for example, if their close affiliation with a particular organization is disclosed after they have been funded by government to conduct research or have published research whose results are strongly supportive of the organization's policy agenda.

Researchers are very likely to resist pressures to make such disclosures when their publications deal only with technical issues and do not address or have obvious implications for public policy, or legal or ethical questions. They may well feel that pressures for disclosure represent an unreasonable concession to those who believe that science is socially constructed and results cannot be evaluated without delving into the motives, ethical values, or political commitments of the investigator. How this matter of perceived conflicts is handled, especially when corporate or some types of foundation funds are involved, will be important in sustaining the strong public and political support and respect that science has enjoyed for most of this century. Society can ill afford to jeopardize scientific progress at the very time in history when good science is needed more than ever to help humanity with its transition to a sustainable world society. While these guidelines provide a good starting point for addressing the problems connected with conflict-of-interest disclosure, the issue is, unfortunately, not that easily solved. The basic problem here is that conflict of interest and commitment (not just self-interest) does not lend itself to generic bureaucratic regulation or legislation, both of which tend to cover too broad a field while missing more serious special cases which will arise in practice but can seldom be imagined in advance. The effort to cover all conceivable situations by general rules leads to unnecessary coverage of a great many trivial situations, while neglecting more serious possibilities because they are so subtle and indirect that they are unlikely to be imagined in advance.

One of the pitfalls of attempting general regulations regarding conflict of interest is the temptation to require complete exclusion of all individuals with alleged potential bias from receiving or evaluating research grants or from serving on policy advisory committees. Such exclusion might result in research or evaluation lacking important knowledge and experience. Instead, disclosure of potential bias should be used to ensure a proper balance between conflicting views. The diversity and the subtlety of the problems that may arise out of the conflict-of-interest issue are so complicated that we believe a more systematic effort rooted in a series of "bottom up" efforts within the technical community is required to resolve the problems. We think this effort should begin with a few major professional societies setting up their own study committees, including representatives of the nonprofessional interests most likely to be affected by the professional field in question. An outline of a common broad study agenda for each professional society that wished to participate might be established by an umbrella organization such as the American Association for the Advancement of Science (AAAS). It might also be best if some of the individual society studies were conducted in series rather than in parallel so that successive studies could learn from each other, leading ultimately to a series of proposed guidelines that could ultimately be integrated by a high-level commission of some sort.

Buffer Institutions: Linking Universities to Industry and Government

The incompatibilities between industry and the academy—those of research style, objectives, disclosure policies, intellectual property, and conflicting financial interest—threaten to undermine the basic purpose of universities and frustrate the expectations of the economic benefit that comes from closer university cooperation with industry. An institutional mechanism designed to bridge these inherent cultural gaps might be able to serve the interests of all. Such an institution, referred to as a "buffer institution," was proposed more than 24 years ago in a somewhat different context by Brooks.[63] In testimony to Congress, he described buffer institutions as:

institutions with both operational and research responsibilities which translate knowledge into application, especially in areas of public responsibility and in relation to local and state problems. These buffer institutions should be closely connected to universities but independently organized and managed. They should be placed where students and faculty could participate in real world problem-solving, but they should have their own permanent core staff, with a separate career line and reward structure.

There are already several such institutions bridging the needs and cultures of universities and operational government interests, such as the DoD's Johns Hopkins Applied Physics Laboratory, and the Charles Stark Draper Laboratory with its close links to MIT, as well as NASA's Jet Propulsion Laboratory, operated by the California Institute of Technology. However, such laboratories are often too close financially and managerially to their parent universities, while having too little regular intellectual interchange with them.

On the commercial side, examples of not-for-profit buffer institutions linking industrial research to universities are somewhat harder to find, but they exist. Many of the teaching hospitals clustered around the most research-intensive medical schools play the buffer institution role quite well. Even though their collaborating firms have commercial rather than public service purposes, the relationship is fostered by governments in the interest of delivering health benefits from the university research. Agricultural experiment stations located near state university campuses and linked to the food industry provide another example of how public goals can be furthered by commercial relationships.

The increased demand for community participation in decision-making means that researchers and other operating staff at buffer institutions will have to be much more concerned than scientists in the past with the societal acceptability of the technical solutions which they develop and often deliver to clients. This is an area in which universities, for good reasons, tend to be weakest, and is one of the key reasons that buffer institutions need to be organized separately from universities. In addition to providing a link between universities and large firms and industry consortia, buffer institutions might afford an especially useful way to connect universities with small and medium-sized enterprises that do not have formally organized R&D labs. Before they are likely to commercialize academic research findings, small firms will often require that academic research findings be pursued further downstream than is typical for university departments. This would require dedicated personnel who might not fit comfortably into the normal academic culture, where they might tend to be regarded as second-class citizens and be evaluated by criteria inappropriate for their real responsibilities.

Many communities, often with state government assistance, have created incubator institutions next to universities to encourage the formation of new firms based on university research. The core employees of the buffer institutions could carry out the necessary translation of academic research results to the point where they could be more readily adopted by small and medium companies. This core staff would have to receive its satisfactions and rewards on a different basis than university faculty members and the buffer institution would need to be somewhat insulated from the university so as not to create some of the cultural tensions that now frequently exist between universities and industry.

Buffer institutions should be deliberately organized so as to provide internship opportunities for students in various social problem areas, and are needed especially in areas related to the social sciences and in aspects of engineering related to problems in the public sector such as transportation, public education, environmental management, etc. State governments, which have strong interests in using their great investments in higher education to support economic prosperity, are in a good position to help initiate these buffer institutions and to foster the relationships between the state university and the smaller firms through such a mechanism. A number of such experiments are well known, in Michigan, Pennsylvania, Colorado, and other states. As suggested in the discussions of the federal Advanced Technology Program (ATP) in

Chapters 6 and 18, such a relationship might not only make the ATP program more effective, but create a more effective role for universities and for state innovation programs in a shared objective of rapid technological progress.

It must be noted that an inherent tradeoff exists with buffer institutions. In order for them to be able to translate university science, be it natural, engineering, or social science, into application, they need close physical and especially intellectual ties with their associated universities. The closer they get to the universities, however, the less of a "buffer" they provide between the university and the potentially damaging influences and pressures of the outside world. Accordingly, the implementation of such arrangements will require much experimentation and debate in order to become practical. However, if the right balance can be struck for these institutions between independence from and association with the universities, they may offer a means of keeping open academic and closed proprietary or politically sensitive norms separated while permitting those students and faculty so inclined to participate in both these cultures.

The Internationalization of University Science and Technology

One of the motivating factors behind the reinvigoration of university-industry relationships in the early 1980s was the advent of stiff international economic competition. Not only did this competition encourage U.S. firms to seek collaboration with American universities, but it also had the same effect on firms based internationally. In addition to the more recent rise in actual foreign support of U.S. universities, the more long-standing tradition of graduate education of foreign students continues to provide American research universities access to a pool of talent not available from the United States alone. Closer recent attention to the large numbers of foreign graduate students on American campuses, together with the advent of greater foreign sponsorship of American university research, has resulted in an unfortunate and economically ill-advised political backlash that threatens to limit prospective foreign students' and firms' access to American universities. Executive Order 12989, meant to address the problem of illegal aliens working in the United States, has resulted in burden-some visa obligations on foreign scholars and their academic host institutions when such scholars are invited to the United States for purposes of scientific exchange and are meant to receive travel reimbursement and honoraria.[64] Such pettiness, whether intended or inadvertent, will, if not corrected, reduce the flow of interna-tional scientific information into the United States and engender considerable resentment and possible retaliation by foreign scien-tists and nations that do not currently have such myopic policies. It is also, unfortunately, likely that there will be further attempts in the United States at such xenophobic policies.

General Accounting Office Data from 1988 suggest that foreign sources of all types accounted for only about 1 percent of all academic R&D spending at U.S. universities, with about one-third of that from foreign firms.[65] This foreign-sourced one third of 1 percent represents only about 5 percent of total industry support for academic R&D. Furthermore, five schools alone received more than 50 percent of all foreign support, so that the amount of funds received by the typical school from foreign sources, industrial or otherwise, is zero to negligible. Furthermore, while there are generally few differences between the kinds of university R&D sponsored by domestic and foreign firms, when there are differ-ences, foreign firms tend to focus on research that is longer-term.[66] In other words, foreign firms are less likely than domestic firms to apply pressure on U.S. academics to do work they would not otherwise want to do. Added to the general concern over foreign support of U.S. academic R&D have been recent congressional reactions to universities' industrial liaison programs and the rather implausible contention that these programs provide an incentive for faculty to interact more with foreign industry sponsors than domestic ones.[67] Not only are such specific claims largely baseless, but so are the more general fears regarding foreign involvement in domestic university research, even if such involvement were ever to reach much higher levels than at present.

It is increasingly unrealistic and unwise to attempt to nationalize science as an economic activity. The American university science system has been a tremendous source of innovation and economic growth. Accordingly, it would be misguided to place many restrictions on the worldwide free flow of information among university researchers, or on participation of foreign scientists and foreign students in unclassified university research programs sponsored by the U.S. government, for doing so would certainly retard the benefits of U.S. academic science to the *domestic* economy. While it seems superficially reasonable to require other countries to offer reciprocal access to their personnel and facilities as a condition for access to U.S. scientists and engineers (as well as other scholars), the routes of information flow are usually so indirect and complex that it becomes impractical to negotiate such access, let alone enforce it, on a bilateral country-by-country basis. Given the current state of comparative national development, there is no reason to expect the flow of information and people to be balanced between every pair of countries. Agreements on mutual access should be negotiated and enforced multilaterally, with the threat of withdrawal of reciprocity being used only as a last resort in cases of flagrant and repeated violation of well-established international norms.

Conclusions

The academic technical community faces a crisis in financial support which it has not experienced since the crisis of 1967–75, and the current crisis is much less likely to be mitigated in the foreseeable future by an external event such as the revival of the Cold War. It is much more related to long-term socioeconomic trends arising from aging populations in all the developed countries and the rapidly growing ratio of the population projected to become dependent on government entitlements to the working population that must support them on the present pay-as-you-go basis. Two developments could contribute to the alleviation of this crisis: a return to a rate of growth of labor productivity equal to or in excess of that which existed in the first two decades after World War II (a supply side development), and reform of the entitlements system, especially the government-funded part of the national health care system, which would greatly increase its cost-effectiveness (a demand side development). Science and technology taken in the broadest sense to include the social and economic as well as the natural sciences and engineering have the potential to contribute greatly to both the supply and demand developments. Thus the technical and scholarly community taken as a whole has a tremendous amount at stake to the extent that it can contribute to these possible positive developments, which are prerequisite to its own long term sources of support.

Of course, science and technology, even considered in its most expansive definition to include the social sciences and such disciplines as systems analysis and game theory as well as economics and management, cannot do it alone. In the words of Vannevar Bush in his famous report, "Science can be effective in the national welfare only as a member of a team, whether the conditions be peace or war." Further, academic science represents only a small fraction of the science and technology which is necessary. But academic science has the greatest potential to provide the conceptual foundations on which the role of the other members of the team, including its science and technology members, can be planned. Just as in Bush's day, the leaders of the scientific and engineering communities had the vision to plan for the crisis that erupted in World War II, the intellectual community must take the lead in planning for how to deal with the new "creeping" crisis that we face only the beginnings of today. We are possibly further along in dealing with the supply part of the solution, which is the main theme of this book, than with the demand part, which is the reorganization of the entitlements system. But dealing with the supply part is more immediately urgent because it will determine the resources we will be able dig up to deal with the demand part a decade or so hence.

Thus the heightened need for basic science and basic technology research to support the new forms of industrial innovation described in Chapter 1 is occurring at a time of budgetary stringency which will only grow worse if these new forms do not generate the required increase in labor productivity before the demand crisis hits in 2015. This calls for new roles for universities that allow them to deploy their creativity in ways that help industry to compete more effectively without compromising the values of academia. Universities can make important contributions not only in science but in technology as well, if government policies recognize that the universities must have the freedom to take intellectual risks and the resources to be highly productive. With relatively modest incentives from government to expand their ties to industry, most research universities have experimented with a broad variety of such relationships. Industry, accustomed to being sought after by the universities, is increasingly convinced that it must look outside for new ideas and technical support and is basing its university contacts more concretely on well-defined self-interest and less on its sense of corporate image and social responsibility. These are all favorable trends, and suggest that the universities will continue to be an important element in the national system of innovation for a long time.

We have identified a number of problems that make firms hesitate to make too great a commitment of their most valuable technical assets to a university relationship; at the same time, universities are uncertain how far they can or should go in exploiting their own intellectual assets without compromising the values that are most essential for fulfilling their primary role. There are still significant gaps in the picture. Many middle-sized and smaller firms, even many technically innovative ones, have difficulty extracting value from a university relationship without much more "translation" than the typical university researcher is willing or able to provide or absorb from his or her industrial client. This happens in part because the culture of the university does not reward its people for time spent in thoroughly learning and understanding the problems of the small business client. Here there are opportunities for state government to lend a hand and to utilize the buffer institution model to link a number of smaller firms with one or more research universities, with support coming from both state and federal sources.

The last few decades have been characterized by growing contributions of academic research to the foundations of industrial innovation and to the informing of regulatory decisions and legislation relating to resources, environment, health and safety. This positive development, however, has had certain side-effects that create problems for academic researchers and research institutions. One of these is the erosion of the traditional openness of the academic research system through restraints on the disclosure of, and free access of all qualified scholars to the results of academic research. A second is public concern about possible undisclosed conflicts-of-interest or strong ideological affiliations of university researchers and their effects on the objectivity and public credibility of the research results emanating from academic R&D. In the absence of widely agreed ground rules and guidelines there is increased danger of "government regulation-by anecdote"—fragmented and uncoordinated attempts to formulate or legislate very broad rules to prevent the repetition of a few especially bad examples. This is more likely to occur if the academic community, and the technical community more broadly, fails to take the problems seriously and to itself take the initiative in debating the problems and disseminating collectively agreed-upon norms of behavior that are widely understood and accepted both in the community itself and among the external organizations or groups potentially affected by their research findings. It is suggested that relevant professional societies and academic associations organize to study these matters and to debate and finally publish and disseminate their conclusions. It is to be hoped that these collective consensus judgments can help by means of peer pressure to enforce these norms on individual researchers and to strengthen the hands of individual researchers in dealing with external organizations, publishers, and others outside the technical community.

A somewhat similar set of problems arises from the growing internationalization of the science and technology system and inappropriate attempts of governments to constrain the international flow of unclassified and non-proprietary technical information and communications and the international visits of qualified scholars. Here again, a collective, multinational determination of consensus norms that can be invoked to support consistent behavior of both governments and researchers is much better than attempts to negotiate and enforce reciprocity on a country-by-country basis. In academic research at least, the Earth is quickly becoming one country, and academics its citizens.

Acknowledgments

The authors gratefully acknowledge the research assistance and insightful comments of Darin Boville.

Notes

1. Roger L. Geiger, *Research and Relevant Knowledge: American Research Universities Since World War II* (New York: Oxford University Press, 1993); Partha S. Dasgupta and Paul A. David, "Toward a New Economics of Science," *Research Policy*, Vol. 23 (1994), pp. 487–521; Nathan Rosenberg and Richard R. Nelson, "American Universities and Technical Advance in Industry," *Research Policy*, Vol. 23, No. 3 (1994), pp. 323–348.

2. Henry Etzkowitz, "Entrepreneurial Science in the Academy: A Case of the Transformation of Norms," *Social Problems*, Vol. 36, No. 1 (February 1989), pp. 14–29; David C. Mowery and Nathan Rosenberg, *Technology and the Pursuit of Economic Growth* (New York: Cambridge University Press, 1989); United States Congress, "Is Science for Sale? Transferring Technology from Universities to Foreign Corporations," 102nd Cong., 2nd Sess., House Report 102-1052 (Washington, D.C.: U.S. Government Printing Office [U.S. GPO], 1992); Dasgupta and David, "Toward a New Economics of Science."

3. David Blumenthal, Michael Gluck, Karen Seashore Louis, Michael A. Stoto, and David Wise, "University-Industry Research Relationships in Biotechnology: Implications for the University," *Science*, Vol. 232 (1986), pp. 1361–1366; Robert P. Morgan, Donald E. Strickland, Nirmala Kannankutty, and Carol Spelman, "Engineering Research in U.S. Universities: How Engineering Faculty View It," paper presented at IEEE-ASEE "Frontiers in Education" Conference, November 7, 1993; Robert P. Morgan, Donald E. Strickland, Nirmala Kannankutty, and Joy Grillon, "Engineering Research in U.S. Universities: How University-Based Research Directors See It," paper presented at ASEE Annual Conference, June 28, 1994; Wesley M. Cohen and Richard Florida with Richard W. Goe, *University-Industry Research Centers in the United States* (Pittsburgh: Carnegie Mellon University Press, August 1994); David Blumenthal, Eric G. Campbell, Melissa S. Anderson, Nancyanne Causino, and Karen Seashore Louis, "Withholding Research Results in Academic Life Sciences: Evidence from a National Survey of Faculty," *Journal of the American Medical Association*, Vol. 227, No. 15 (1996), pp. 1224–1228.

4. Wesley M. Cohen, Richard Nelson, and John Walsh, "Appropriability Conditions and Why Firms Patent and Why They Do Not in the American Manufacturing Sector," paper presented at the OECD, June, 1996. See also Francis Narin, Kimberly S. Hamilton, and Dominic Olivastro, "The Increasing Linkage between U.S. Technology and Public Science," *Research Policy* (forthcoming). The latter research involved an analysis of the citations of industrial patents and was supported by the National Science Foundation.

5. Government-University-Industry Research Roundtable, Industrial Research Institute, *New Alliances and Partnerships in Academic Science and Engineering* (Washington, D.C.: National Academy Press, 1986); Rosenberg and Nelson, "American Universities and Technical Advance in Industry."

6. Geiger, *Research and Relevant Knowledge.*

7. Much of this history section was drawn from ibid. and from Roger L. Geiger, *To Advance Knowledge: The Growth of American Research Universities 1900–1940* (New York: Oxford University Press, 1986. It should be noted that the decade following the first World War witnessed an extraordinary expansion in U.S. college enrollment in all fields.

8. There were several outstanding exceptions to this largely pragmatic emphasis of U.S. academic research. One may note, for some examples, the pioneering work of Josiah Willard Gibbs of Yale on the foundations of thermodynamics, the creation of John Hopkins University as an advanced graduate school devoted to fundamental research, the early lead of the United States in the construction and use of large optical telescopes, the pioneering Michelson-Morley experiments at Western Reserve University in Cleveland which helped establish the basis for Einstein's special theory of relativity, and the Rockefeller Institute for Medical Research. It is, however, symptomatic of the primarily pragmatic orientation of American science that the work of these pioneers was often more appreciated in Europe than in the United States.

9. National Science Foundation, *University-Industry Research Relationships: Myths, Realities and Potentials*, 14th Annual Report to the National Science Board (Washington, D.C.: U.S. GPO, 1982); David C. Mowery and Nathan Rosenberg, "The U.S. National Innovation System," in Richard R. Nelson, ed., *National Innovation Systems* (New York: Oxford University Press, 1993).

10. John W. Servos, "The Industrial Relations of Science: Chemical Engineering at MIT, 1900-1939," *ISIS*, Vol. 71, No. 259 (December 1980), pp. 531–549.

11. Servos, "The Industrial Relations of Science"; Geiger, *To Advance Knowledge*.

12. Rosenberg and Nelson, "American Universities and Technical Advance in Industry."

13. Warner Schilling, "Scientists, Foreign Policy and Politics" in R. Gilpin and C. Wright, eds., *Scientists in National Policy Making* (New York: Columbia University Press, 1964), p. 155.

14. On the NSF budget see J. Merton England, *A Patron for Pure Science: The National Science Foundation's Formative Years, 1945–1957* (Washington, D.C.: National Science Foundation, 1982); and Geiger, *To Advance Knowledge*. On the NIH budget, see Harvey Brooks, "The Physical Sciences: Bellwether of Science Policy," in James Shannon, ed., *Science and the Evolution of Public Policy* (New York: Rockefeller University Press, 1973).

15. The exception was biomedical research, whose federal support leveled, but declined very little in real terms if at all.

16. Harvey Brooks, "The Problem of Research Priorities," in Gerald S. Holton and Robert S. Morison, eds., *Limits of Scientific Inquiry* (New York: W.W. Norton Company, 1979). For further discussion, see B.L.R. Smith and J.J. Karlesky, *The State of Academic Science: The Universities and the Research Effort* (New York: Change Magazine Press, 1977).

17. Large fluctuations in exchange rates during the period from 1979 to the early 1990s make it very difficult to sort out the macroeconomic and microeconomic factors in comparative advantage across different industries.

18. Denis J. Prager and Gilbert S. Omenn, "Research, Innovation, and University-Industry Linkages," *Science*, Vol. 207 (January 1980), pp. 379–384; Erich Bloch and Carlos E. Kruytbosch, "The NSF Role in Fostering University-Industry Research Relationships," *IEEE Transactions on Education*, Vol. E-29, No. 2 (May 1989), pp. 51–57; Government-University-Industry Research Roundtable, Industrial Research Institute, *New Alliances and Partnerships in Academic Science and Engineering*; Government-University-Industry Research Roundtable, *Science and Technology in the Academic Enterprise: Status, Trends, and Issues* (Washington, D.C.: National Academy Press, 1989); Richard L. Florida and Martin Kenney, *The Breakthrough Illusion: Corporate America's Failure to Move from Innovation to Mass Production* (New York: BasicBooks, 1990); United States Congress, "Is Science for Sale?" Geiger, *Research and Relevant Knowledge.*

19. Denis Gray, Elmima C. Johnson, and Teresa R. Gidley, "Industry-University Projects and Centers: An Empirical Comparison of Two Federally Funded Models of Cooperative Science," *Evaluation Review*, Vol. 10, No. 6 (1986), pp. 175–193.

20. National Science Board, *Science and Engineering Indicators—1991* (Washington, D.C.: U.S. GPO, 1991). Irwin Feller, "The University as an Instrument of State and Regional Economic Development: The Rhetoric and Reality of the U.S. Experience," paper presented at the "CERP/AAAS Conference on University Goals, Institutional Mechanisms, and the "Industrial Transferability of Research"", March 18–20, 1994. Feller writes that by 1987, 43 states had created economic development programs meant to accelerate the establishment of partnerships between universities and industry. The 26-state figure reported above refers specifically to state-sponsored UIRCs.

21. National Science Foundation, *University-Industry Research Relationships.*

22. On research expenditures, see E. R. Krueger and Robert M. Hexter, "Perspectives on a New Paradigm for Cooperative Research," *IEEE Transactions on Education*, Vol. E-29, No. 2 (May 1989), pp. 78–84. On PhD production see National Science Board, *Science and Engineering Indicators—1996* (Washington, D.C.: U.S. GPO, 1996), Appendix Table 2-28.

23. It should be noted also that a good deal of the research and instruction carried out in engineering departments during this period began to include subjects that would have been considered the exclusive province of "pure science" departments a decade or so earlier. In engineering departments, however, the work carried a more applied flavor and was pursued further downstream to study the properties of actual devices and fabrication processes, often using adaptations of instrumentation originally developed for pure research.

24. Etzkowitz, "Entrepreneurial Science in the Academy."

25. United States Congress, "Is Science for Sale?" Geiger, *Research and Relevant Knowledge.*

26. Florida and Kenney, *The Breakthrough Illusion*; Etzkowitz, "Entrepreneurial Science in the Academy."

27. These figures are calculated from National Science Board, *Science and Engineering Indicators—1996*, Appendix Table 5-2 (support for academic R&D), and Appendix Table 5-26 (academic employment and R&D activity of doctoral scientists and engineers). It should be noted that the price deflator used to calculate these real decreases is the consumer price index (CPI), and not an R&D cost index; R&D costs are generally more inflationary than the CPI, and thus the 9.4 percent figure is probably an underestimate of the actual decline.

28. National Science Board, *Science and Engineering Indicators—1996.*

29. Ibid. The price deflator used to calculate these real increases is the CPI and not an R&D cost index.

30. Wesley M. Cohen, Richard Florida, and Lucien P. Randazzese, *For Knowledge and Profit: University-Industry Research Centers, Technical Advance and the Research University* (working title) (Oxford University Press, forthcoming).

31. Cutbacks in R&D by these and other large industrial American corporations have been well documented in the popular press. On the firms mentioned above, see, for example, the *Wall Street Journal*, December 18, 1992; May 7, 1993; October 17, 1994; September 22, 1995.

32. Cohen, Florida, and Randazzese, *For Knowledge and Profit.*

33. The real crunch arising from the growth of future entitlements, resulting from the aging of the U.S. population, does not begin until at least 2015. Moreover, the cost of these entitlements, particularly publicly funded medical care, could actually provide a powerful rationale, especially in the case of biomedical science, for more public support of R&D, though it might imply a considerable change from present priorities.

34. It can be argued that the marginal returns to R&D effort tend to decline as fields of science mature.

35. The Joint Services Electronics Program of the U.S. military services was established right after the end of World War II in 1946. This program supported groups of faculty members mainly in electrical engineering and atomic and molecular physics, most of whom had been associated either with the Radiation Laboratory at MIT or the Radio Research Laboratory (Radar Countermeasures) at Harvard during the war. The idea was to keep some of these people interested and engaged in military-related science after they returned to their home universities. Such programs were established at MIT, Harvard, U.C. Berkeley, Columbia, Stanford, UCLA, Purdue, the University of Pennsylvania and several other places. Faculty were supported as a group, projects were decided on locally by the group, and the money was used largely for preliminary exploratory work, with the idea that if it showed promise, the investigator would then go out and seek supplementary funding from other sources, usually also military. The first

work on nuclear magnetic resonance (Purcell, Pound, and Bloembergen), the first work on lasers (Townes), the first work on atomic beams (Rabi, Ramsey, and Zacharias), and the early work of many other scientists, were all supported in this way as was much of the early work on germanium and silicon semiconductors at Purdue and Penn that eventually contributed to the invention of the transistor at Bell Labs. A similar pattern was followed later in the establishment of the Advanced Research Projects Agency (ARPA) Materials Research Laboratories at several universities which fostered collaboration between physicists and metallurgists. (On and off throughout its history ARPA has also been known as DARPA, for Defense Advanced Research Projects Agency).

36. For one proposal along these lines, see Philip M. Smith and Michael Mcgeary, "Don't Look Back: Science Funding for the Future," *Issues in Science and Technology Policy*, Vol. 13, No. 3 (Spring 1997).

37. National Research Council Committee on Criteria for Federal Support of Research and Development, *Allocating Federal Funds for Science and Technology* (Washington, D.C.: National Academy Press, 1995), pp. 10. The report suggests that "at the beginning of the budget cycle, the President...decides on the aggregate level of funding for federal science and technology (FS&T) across the government."

38. In Chapter 17 in this volume, "Managing Technology Policy in the White House," David Hart asserts that the National Science and Technology Council (NSTC) structure misconceives the nature of federal technology policy decision-making by assuming that the decisions that need to be addressed trade one science or technology program off against another. In fact, R&D programs are traded off against other programs within the same agency or appropriations cluster, some of which may be R&D programs, but many of which are not.

39. There is in fact an extensive literature that highlights the persistently regional character of much economic activity, especially in the high-technology sectors. Cf. AnnaLee Saxenian, "The Origins and Dynamics of Production Networks in Silicon Valley," *Research Policy*, Vol. 20, No. 5 (1991), pp. 423–437.

40. At the time, the chairman of the NSB, a vice president of IBM, had been responsible for investing $48 million of IBM's money in a competitive (declining rate) grant program for masters degrees in manufacturing systems engineering. With this precedent, the NSF, over the objections of some in the academic community who would have preferred a simple increase in conventional grants to individual investigators, proposed a new mechanism of support modeled on the IBM program.

41. This approach is not by any means applicable to all research support, but only to research that benefits substantially from downstream coupling to some form of public or private service delivery.

42. David Blumenthal, Nancyanne Causino, Eric Campbell and Karen Seashore Louis. "Relationships Between Academic Institutions and Industry in the Life Sciences—An Industry Survey," *The New England Journal of Medicine*, Vol. 334, No.

6 (1996), pp. 368–373; Morgan et al., "Engineering Research in U.S. Universities: How Engineering Faculty View It"; Morgan et al., "Engineering Research in U.S. Universities: How University-Based Researcher Directors See It"; Rahm, "University-Firm Linkages for Industrial Innovation," Department of Government and International Affairs, University of South Florida, 1995; Cohen et al., *University-Industry Research Centers in the United States.*

43. Wesley M. Cohen and Lucien P. Randazzese, "Eminence and Enterprise: The Impact of Industry Support on the Conduct of Academic Research in Science and Engineering," working paper, Belfer Center for Science and International Affairs, John F. Kennedy School of Government, Harvard University, 1997.

44. National Science Board, *Science and Engineering Indicators—1996.*

45. It is not necessarily harmful to the university with a higher academic reputation if its faculty takes an interest in problems inspired by industrial applications, provided they retain sufficient autonomy in regard to their detailed research strategy and publication policy. The best universities insist on preserving that autonomy, as they have so far generally been able to do.

46. The information in this paragraph and the next two is derived from Richard S. Rosenbloom and William J. Spencer, eds., *Engines of Innovation: U.S. Industrial Research at the End of an Era* (Boston: Harvard Business School Press, 1996). Most of the information and all of the quotations are taken from Gordon E. Moore's chapter, "Some personal perspective on research in the microelectronics industry." Some paraphrasing and elaboration on Moore's ideas, however, are the responsibility of the authors. See also Donald G. Rea, Harvey Brooks, Robert M. Burger, and Richard LaScala, "The Semiconductor Industry—Model for Industry/University/Government Cooperation," *Research Technology Management,* Vol. 40, No. 4 (1997).

47. Case studies of the SRC support of university CAD research are reported in Lucien P. Randazzese, "Exploring University-Industry Technology Transfer of CAD Technology," *IEEE Transactions on Engineering Management,* Vol. 43, No. 4 (November 1996), pp. 393–401; they suggest that there is some pressure by SRC member firms on academic researchers to conduct more applied research, but that this pressure is easily resisted by faculty. This subject is discussed in more detail below.

48. Partha S. Dasgupta and Paul A. David, "Information Disclosure and the Economics of Science and Technology," in George R. Feiwel, ed., *Arrow and the Ascent of Modern Economic Theory* (Washington Square: New York University Press, 1987); Dasgupta and David, "Toward a New Economics of Science." To be realistic, even in the most open style of research, researchers have some incentive not to disclose preliminary results until they are sufficiently certain of them and the correctness of their interpretation from a theoretical standpoint, since the adverse effects on reputation of premature disclosure of results not confirmed by later work can be severe.

49. *New York Times,* February 10, 1996.

50. *Wall Street Journal,* April 25, 1996. More recently, after six years of delay, this matter has been resolved by the company's agreement to publication of the data. See the *New York Times,* April 15, 1997, for coverage of recent events for this story.

The published paper is Betty J. Dong et al., "Bioequivalence of Generic Brand-name Levothyroxine Products in the Treatment of Hypothyroidism," *Journal of the American Medical Association*, Vol. 227, No. 15 (April 16), pp. 1205–1213.

51. Blumenthal et al., "Relationships Between Academic Institutions and Industry in the Life Sciences—An Industry Survey."

52. Blumenthal et al., "Withholding Research Results in Academic Life Sciences: Evidence from a National Survey of Faculty."

53. Rahm, "University-Firm Linkages for Industrial Innovation." The 1013 faculty and 121 technology managers were from the disciplines of biology, chemistry, computer science, electrical engineering and physics.

54. Cohen et al., *University-Industry Research Centers in the United States.*

55. These figures refer to policy only; they shed no light on the frequency with which industry actually exercises its restriction rights.

56. Government-University-Industry Research Roundtable, Industrial Research Institute, *Simplified and Standardized Model Agreements for University-Industry Cooperative Research* (Washington, D.C.: National Academy Press, 1988). For background to these findings concerning disclosure restrictions see Cohen et al., "Appropriability Conditions," reporting that between 1983 and 1994 firms have come to rely much more heavily on secrecy to protect their profits from innovation than they had previously.

57. Philip H. Abelson, "Evolution in Industrial Research," *Science*, Vol. 265, No. 299 (1994).

58. David M. Hart, *Forging the Postwar Consensus: Science, Technology and Economic Policy in the United States, 1921–1953* (Princeton University Press, forthcoming).

59. Krimsky, L.S. Rothenberg, P. Stott, and G. Kyle, "Financial Interests of Authors in Scientific Journals: A Pilot Study of 14 Publications," *Science and Engineering Ethics*, Vol. 2, No. 4 (1996), pp. 395–410.

60. Authors were considered to have a financial interest in the results being reported if they are listed as inventors in a patent or patent application closely related to their published work; serve on a scientific advisory board of a biotechnology company; or are officers, directors, or major shareholders (beneficial owner of 10 percent or more of stock issued) in a firm that has commercial interests related to their research. There are, of course, political biases to be considered as well, which may result in research that is less than objective even in the absence of financial reward.

61. Sheldon Krimsky, "Impure Science: The Public is Ill-Served When Researchers can Secretly Profit from Their Work," *Boston Globe*, March 23, 1997.

62. In 1995, the Public Health Service issued regulations that require universities to establish review procedures to evaluate whether information provided under mandatory disclosure of financial interest by grant applicants indicates a significant conflict of interest. The National Science Foundation has established a similar practice, and a number of scientific journals, reacting to concerns over

the appearance or allegation of bias in their journals, have established interest disclosure policies for their publications. See Krimsky et al., "Financial Interests of Authors in Scientific Journals."

63. Statement of Dr. Harvey Brooks, Dean of Engineering and Applied Physics, Harvard University, in "National Science Policy," H. Con. Res. #666, Hearings before the Subcommittee on Science, Research, and Development of the Committee on Science and Astronautics, U.S. House of Representatives, 91st Cong., 2nd Sess., printed for the use of the Committee on Science and Astronautics (Washington, D.C.: U.S. GPO, 1970), pp. 136–154. A very similar proposal, oriented more towards technology transfer to industry rather than to public sector agencies like the Brooks proposal, has been put forward in Richard R. Nelson, Richard Rosenbloom, and William J Spencer, "Conclusion: Shaping a New Era," in Rosenbloom and Spencer, *Engines of Innovation*.

64. The White House, Office of the Press Secretary, "Economy And Efficiency In Government Procurement Through Compliance With Certain Immigration And Naturalization Act Provisions," Executive Order 12989, February 13, 1996.

65. General Accounting Office of the United States (GAO), *R&D Funding: Foreign Sponsorship of U.S. University Research*, GAO/RCED-88-89BR (Washington, D.C.: U.S. GAO, 1988).

66. Ibid. Data from a more recent survey of UIRCs indicates that centers with foreign company sponsors devote a greater share of their total effort to basic research than do centers with corporate sponsors from the United States only. Cohen et al., *University-Industry Research Centers in the United States*).

67. General Accounting Office of the United States, *University Research: Controlling Inappropriate Access to Federally Funded Research Results*, GAO/RCED-92-104 (Washington, D.C.: U.S. GAO, 1992); and especially United States Congress, "Is Science for Sale?"

15

Industry Consortia

Daniel Roos, Frank Field, and James Neely

Today's industries must confront a complex series of issues when developing their technology strategies. There is a growing realization that research and development (R&D) are central to the viability of any industry, whatever its level of maturity. However, increases in the number, scope, and deployment rate of new technological opportunities are making it difficult for individual organizations to commit the financial resources necessary to pursue every possible avenue. Compounding the riskiness of such investments is the increasing globalization of the markets within which these industries compete.

Consequently, industries are turning to new research and development approaches which help maximize R&D investment value while limiting exposure. A particularly promising alternative is the research consortium. Most research consortia consist of private sector members. However, several industry-government consortia have also been implemented. These consortia have yielded some impressive results for domestic U.S. industry, while affording the government an active role that does not overly limit industry's flexibility or imagination.

These consortia are not easy to devise, manage, or bring to fruition. Since no two industries are the same, a "one size fits all" approach to constructing consortia is unlikely to work. Rather, the process must be informed by a detailed and subtle appreciation of the structure and dynamics of the specific industry, and the implications of the technological challenges it faces.

This chapter describes the forces which are driving industry and government to become partners on major technology initiatives, reviews successes and struggles encountered in two high-profile government-industry consortia, and introduces the industry study as a potentially powerful precursor to developing well structured and focused consortia. First, the changing landscape of technology and industry is discussed. We explain why cooperative efforts are becoming increasingly important, why no single approach to structuring these programs is sufficient, and why government interaction with industry partnerships is inevitable. Next, SEMATECH and the Partnership for a New Generation of Vehicles (PNGV), are reviewed. The role of government, problems encountered, and key differences in their objectives are noted, as well as the importance and difficulty of properly setting up these programs. Finally, we describe how industry studies can provide a policy formation basis and serve as potential precursors to government-industry partnerships. The success of the Lean Aircraft Initiative at the Massachusetts Institute of Technology is cited as an example of a model industry study, where private and public representatives are working together to achieve a broad understanding of technology-policy issues critical to the future of the aerospace industry. Overall, the objective of this chapter is to detail lessons learned from existing industry consortia and industry studies, and to demonstrate how these experiences can be applied to better structure similar initiatives.

Drivers for Cooperation

Worldwide, industry is facing increasing pressures for collaboration on technology and product development. The rapid pace, breadth, and cost of innovation; the decrease in product development times; the globalization of markets; and social and environmental objectives are all factors that have collided to change the shape of competition radically. Recognizing that going-it-alone is often not a feasible strategy, firms in most major industries have reacted to these pressures by pursuing both formal and informal cooperative relationships.[1]

Companies are struggling to keep up with the increasing breadth, tempo, and scale of technology. Often, single firms are no longer capable of maintaining competencies in all relevant technology fields, especially when the technology scope spans many industrial sectors and can be more efficiently treated by specialized organizations. Although technology is routinely viewed as central to young, dynamic industries, it is also a crucial factor in more established sectors. For example, the "mature" automobile industry is grappling with the implications of a wide range of new technologies, including advanced materials and materials processing technologies, electronics, and alternative propulsion systems. Further, the level of investment required for technology development and deployment is also increasing, and firms are frequently hesitant to take on all of the risk. Consequently, the role of suppliers, both as sources of new technology and as development partners, has become increasingly important as product complexity has grown.

Additional pressures for cooperation stem from decreasing product life and design time, globalization considerations, and increasing complexity of product requirements. The shortening of product development cycles encourages more involvement with suppliers; they may provide a means to improve design process efficiency and minimize cost pressures. Globalization raises multiple issues for product development. Sometimes foreign content is required for market access. Often the perspective of a foreign partner is critical to product success. Participation in multiple locales also requires an appreciation of regional differences both in consumer demands and regulatory requirements. Finally, products must satisfy a more complex and changing set of criteria. Some criteria, such as increasing affordability and quality, are pressures that can be predominantly managed by industry. Other issues, especially those related to the environment and sustainability, seek to achieve social objectives rather than to satisfy consumer needs, and are likely to require government interaction. To be effective, government and industry interactions aimed at specific policy objectives must be sensitive to all of these concerns.

Changes in the U.S. automotive industry illustrate the magnitude of change in the industrial and technical environment. At the time of Henry Ford and Alfred Sloan, full vertical integration was considered highly desirable. Commonly, most major components of a car were researched, designed, manufactured, and assembled by monolithic firms, often under the same roof. When outside suppliers were utilized, the decision was typically a sole matter of make-versus-buy economics. Distribution was primarily on a national basis. Overall, the individual automotive producers behaved almost autonomously.

Today the linear model of a vertically integrated industry no longer fits. Rather, technology and product development occur in a complex, international network of suppliers and original equipment manufacturers (OEMs) such as Ford, Chrysler and General Motors. These "Big Three" U.S. auto producers maintain a focus on assembly, but many of the major systems and subsystems are developed and designed by outside suppliers. Although each OEM has adopted this approach to a different degree, all make greater use of the technical capabilities of their suppliers than they did even a decade ago.

The increasing prevalence of cooperation among companies is well documented and spans many industries. For example, the burgeoning telecommunications and computing industries almost daily announce joint ventures, mergers, and partnerships. Whether cooperation occurs as formal ventures or as simple working agreements, these efforts are considered a mechanism for gaining access to otherwise unavailable expertise, sharing risk, spreading costs, learning, and minimizing transaction costs.[2,3]

While incentives to pursue cooperative ventures are gaining strength, the success of even simple two-party efforts can be problematic. Much can be learned from studies of cooperative efforts and the partnering firms. Strict attention must be paid to apportioning responsibilities, distributing authority, and assuring the participants of mutual protection from opportunistic actions. Cooperation is most likely to succeed if the firms have common strategic interests, but very different competitive bases; are not dominant industry leaders; and can learn from each other while simultaneously protecting proprietary interests.[4]

The history of the Micro-Electronics and Computer Technology Corporation (MCC), America's first major, private, for-profit R&D consortium, points out typical problems. MCC was chartered in 1983 to work on high-risk, precompetitive technology for the purpose of enhancing the competitive position of U.S. companies.

As the effort progressed, it became clear that member companies were hesitant to dedicate their best staff to the project; reaching consensus on research planning was difficult; and no clear technology transfer mechanisms were established.[5] Many of these initial shortcomings have been overcome and MCC still draws support from its member companies. However, MCC clearly demonstrated that cooperative efforts must be carefully engineered.

Since cooperation is becoming a standard approach for industry to address complex problems, government must be prepared to engage the private sector on this level if it expects to have an effective, coordinated, technology policy. Familiar mechanisms, such as funding projects at individual companies or sponsoring generic technology development, will not provide the targeted, systemic results required to address major policy concerns in specific industries. Further, government is not isolated from the pressures for cooperation; it stands to gain in many of the same ways as industry, if the relationships are well managed.

When government takes an active role in industry-level cooperative efforts, additional complexities can arise. In particular, government and industry objectives may conflict. The role of government in these cases is to push industry to pursue goals that would otherwise have lower priorities, for the benefit of stakeholders with less immediate interest.

For example, the government-industry consortium mechanism was recently selected as a basis for addressing conflicting social and market pressures in the automotive industry. The Partnership for a New Generation of Vehicles (PNGV) aims to dramatically reduce the environmental impact of automobiles, especially as related to oil consumption, while simultaneously maintaining current levels of affordability, quality, and consumer satisfaction. A government-industry consortium approach may be ideal in this case because it is unlikely that a single firm could develop and combine the full set of required technologies, which range from lightweight materials to alternative power sources and energy storage devices, and the objectives of the effort are not entirely congruent with what industry would pursue on its own. Further, the complexity of PNGV's goals virtually assures that a simple mandate to produce high fuel-economy or low emissions vehicles, similar to that attempted by the State of California, would be inappropriate. The consortia approach affords government and industry much more flexibility to adjust efforts based on what it learns from actively pursuing technology development. A more nearly optimal solution is almost guaranteed.

However, industry and government objectives do not always need to be at odds for the consortia mechanism to be a useful technology policy instrument. Topics of national concern might drive the initiation of these alliances. For example, national competitiveness was the major driver for the formation of SEMATECH, which helped revitalize the semiconductor manufacturing industry in the United States.

Regardless of objectives, government-industry consortia are not immune from the problems encountered by private cooperative efforts, and conflicts between the public and private sector can make these ventures even more difficult to manage. Thus, from a public policy perspective, government-industry consortia must be approached with great care to improve the likelihood that a favorable outcome will be reached. These issues are highlighted in the next section through a more detailed comparison of SEMATECH and PNGV.

Experience with the Consortia Approach

This section evaluates two high-profile industry consortia, SEMATECH and PNGV. SEMATECH is a consortium that has drawn upon government funding to help revitalize semiconductor manufacturing in the United States. PNGV (Partnership for a New Generation of Vehicles) is a cooperative effort between the government, academia, and the United States Council for Automotive Research (USCAR), an industry partnership of the Big Three U.S. automotive producers that conducts precompetitive research. SEMATECH was established by an ailing but essential industrial sector as a means of self-preservation; PNGV represents a more complex interaction of government and industry primarily to address social objectives. Together, they illustrate the range over which government may choose to interact with industry, and the level of understanding required to develop successful policies.

SEMATECH

Over the past decade, the U.S. government has spent $800 million on the SEMATECH consortium, which was established in 1987 to improve domestic competency in chip-manufacturing processes.[6] This industry sector is now again a world-class competitor, and while the turnaround cannot be attributed solely to SEMATECH, it has received significant praise for convincing competitors to cooperate for mutual benefit. Now in its tenth year, the consortium plans to continue, without further government support.

From its formation, SEMATECH enjoyed strong industry support. Leading executives spent time championing the effort and prominent figures headed the organization. SEMATECH's current leader, William Spencer, began his career at Bell Labs and held senior positions at Sandia National Laboratory and Xerox before he was appointed to run SEMATECH. Other renowned scientists and the CEO of National Semiconductor took strong public positions in favor of the consortium.[7]

SEMATECH had a clear, industry-focused mission: improve the competitiveness of the U.S. chip manufacturers. This focus helped participants overcome their hesitations about working together. As work proceeded, concerns over revealing sensitive problems were alleviated when it became apparent that many parties were facing the same issues. Eventually, the recognition that equipment suppliers could play a key role in addressing manufacturing problems resulted in close interaction with these industry participants as well.

A hands-off approach by the government, with regard to program direction, gave SEMATECH the flexibility and autonomy it needed for effective management. Industry was in the best position to judge what efforts should be pursued to address the critical competitiveness problems. Minimal government restrictions on the use of funds allowed rapid changes in program direction in response to findings. For example, the increased interaction with processing equipment manufacturers was one midstream, programmatic decision that was eased by the minimization of bureaucracy. A lack of flexibility to change program emphasis has been a noted problem in other consortia; thus, it seems SEMATECH avoided a key pitfall of cooperative interaction.

Perhaps the strongest criticism of SEMATECH is that it is not possible to link definitively the resurgence in the U.S. chip-making industry to the creation of the consortium.[8] Other U.S. industries made appreciable recoveries during the same period without the aid of a consortium, and the economic conditions faced by the United States and Japan have leveled over the past decade. Further, American manufacturers have learned the importance of producing high-quality products. Whether these trends were necessary or sufficient to produce the semiconductor industry's turnaround is a subject of debate.

A second criticism is that the consortium was predominantly founded by large companies that had already lost the game, and shut out smaller, more innovative firms. Combined with the turning economic tide, these smaller companies might have forged the industry turnaround SEMATECH was founded to achieve. A drawback in the consortium's design was its emphasis on picking technologies and promoting domestic exclusivity. In several instances, companies with unique and critical technologies which absorbed millions of SEMATECH funding dollars either were nearly acquired by foreign firms or filed for bankruptcy. Replacing the lost technology was either impossible or excessively expensive. More recently, highly advanced manufacturing technology was licensed to a Japanese firm, to keep another SEMATECH member from failing. Thus, while the strengthening of domestic industry is a key goal of the consortium, the degree to which this means limiting technology diffusion has been problematic.

The lesson to learn from SEMATECH is that appropriately structured industry consortia can successfully address nationally important technology policy issues. In the case of SEMATECH, where the major goals were aligned with industry needs and strong sector support existed, the government wisely minimized its role in day-to-day oversight of the program.

The Partnership for a New Generation of Vehicles

The Partnership for a New Generation of Vehicles was formed in 1993 to meet three goals: improve national competitiveness in manufacturing by upgrading U.S. manufacturing technology; implement commercially viable research innovations in conventional vehicles (particularly those which improve fuel economy and reduce emissions); and develop vehicles that can achieve up to three times the fuel efficiency of 1994 family sedans, with equivalent performance and costs.[9]

The goal of fuel efficiency (known as Goal 3) has become the centerpiece of the partnership, at least in the public eye. This widely heralded objective would dramatically improve the fuel economy of passenger vehicles by the early years of the coming millennium, while maintaining affordability, safety, size, and functionality. Goal 3 is tied to key social and national security concerns, especially environmental improvement and reducing U.S. dependence on both foreign and domestic fossil fuels. Without government encouragement, the auto industry most likely would not pursue this goal. This explicit blending of social and technological objectives gives PNGV a different flavor from the competitiveness-focused SEMATECH. It is not surprising that government is more directly involved and that program management difficulties have been encountered.

Compounding the complexity of PNGV is the involvement of the federal national laboratories, which have been active in pursuing opportunities to work with industry and to transfer technological expertise. The efficacy of this policy is debated, but much of the funding for PNGV flows from agencies such as the Department of Energy (DOE), which oversee these facilities.[10] As a result, there is significant pressure on industry to partner with one of the national labs. This means that funding decisions can be influenced by the degree to which the broader agendas of specific government laboratories may be leveraged. In fact, although there are some funds specifically earmarked for PNGV, a large fraction of the budget for this program is comprised of funding for current and ongoing national lab research projects with potential relevance in the transportation area.

Fragmentation of responsibilities and authority is another problem with the structure of PNGV. The program is largely funded from DOE sources, but is directed by the Department of Commerce. PNGV focuses on social goals that have not traditionally been the core mission of either of these agencies.

Further, PNGV initially consisted of a series of programs without an overall systematic perspective and framework. To correct this deficiency, the National Research Council (NRC) was asked to form a committee to review the PNGV's progress.[11] The oversight function of the NRC committee has been a positive influence on PNGV.

The industry partners have also had their share of difficulties. Cooperation has been a particular problem, with the degree of participation almost inversely related to each firm's perception of its relative technical strength in many of the areas under consideration. In addition, at first the partnership focused entirely upon Chrysler, Ford, and General Motors, in an effort to retain the results for indigenous firms; unfortunately, this also kept the automobile supplier firms on the sidelines. This critical limitation has since been rectified. However, universities, a major source of innovation, remain largely absent from the partnership.

Another criticism of PNGV arises from the possibly over-ambitious nature of its goals. Programs with narrowly focused, easy-to-understand challenges can be promoted and evaluated more easily. A classic example is President Kennedy's challenge to place a man on the moon within a decade. SEMATECH's goal of saving an industry had the advantage that a variety of outcomes would potentially serve to demonstrate the success of the program. On the other hand, what has become the centerpiece of PNGV's research effort, Goal 3, requires the simultaneous achievement of three technological goals: a trebling of automobile fuel efficiency, while retaining equivalent vehicle performance in terms of handling, cargo capacity, safety, etc., with vehicles costing no more than today's automobile. Although any two of the three goals are within the grasp of the industry today, achieving all three will be a major feat, definitely one worth attempting. However, because the program was initially presented as an all-or-nothing effort emphasizing Goal 3, the ability of the PNGV to demonstrate results to either Congress or the public has been weakened.

While that limitation has been ameliorated somewhat with the introduction of program review cycles that disclose results and future plans, it remains difficult to ascertain the reception that would be given to a vehicle that "only" doubles fuel efficiency while meeting the economic and performance targets. Although such a vehicle would be a major technological feat, the wider audience may be far less enthusiastic given the expectations that have been raised. Thus, a critical lesson to remember from PNGV is that a balanced presentation of program goals is necessary to protect a program's credibility and support.

Many of the difficulties associated with PNGV are related to how the partnership was initiated. In the face of increased political interest in reexamining the current government Corporate Average Fuel Economy (CAFE) standards policy, the decision to move forward was "top-down," based on an agreement between the executive branch (largely through the efforts of Vice President Al Gore) and the presidents of Ford, Chrysler, and General Motors.[12] There was little staff consultation on either side nor much planning of the overall effort, which was unfortunate given the eventual "bottom-up" implementation of the program. This lack of coordination between means and ends is reflected in the number and scope of the partnership objectives, which are broader than those of other programs. While it can be argued that the PNGV effort requires an ambitious program, the blend of the detailed technological and industrial goals with the broader social and environmental ones is unprecedented, and managing the inevitable conflicts among these disparate objectives has been difficult. With better coordination of the objectives some of the management difficulties might have been avoided.

While PNGV clearly faces some difficult issues, it is important to point out several positive results. The effort has brought together the major participants in the automotive industry in a forum that improves communications both between companies and, most importantly, between government and industry. Fostering these types of interactions long-term is an important part of establishing a basis for developing a coordinated, industry-focused technology policy. Further, many of the problems discussed are being addressed, or have been resolved. The Technology Administration of the Department of Commerce deserves credit for putting together a program that works as well as PNGV does, having been handed from the top a minimally thought-out "done deal." From this perspective, PNGV in its current form can be thought of as a start of cooperation, but not necessarily the final product. The program and others like it are likely to evolve over time.

Overall, PNGV demonstrates the complexities that can arise in assembling consortia. A key question is, "Are the proper structures and incentives in place to assure that the government will see the fruition of the policy goal to demonstrate and eventually commercialize high fuel-economy, family-size passenger vehicles?" PNGV represents an important step away from command and control legislation, which is proving increasingly problematic as the constraints on auto-making have become more confining. However, there is no guarantee that the policy objectives will be completely reached.

Although industrial R&D programs are designed assuming that only a fraction will succeed, the failure of a government-funded research program is politically unacceptable. By explicitly accounting for the realities of both the risks of R&D and the need for certain success in government programs, the framers of the PNGV might have found a more modest set of goals that would not expose the program participants to the kind of second-guessing that accompanies any perception of failure of government-funded programs.

Learning from Past Experiences and Shaping Future Efforts

A number of other consortia could also be examined in industries ranging from computers to textiles. In particular, the textiles example (Textile/Clothing Technology Corporation; known as TC2) is noteworthy for both its longevity and its successes. It will be instructive to see what emerges from the more recent American Textile Partnership (AMTEX), which brings the national laboratories into partnership with the textile industry. Lessons from the experiences of other nations and even smaller-scale, private cooperative efforts can also go a long way to assisting in the design of effective government-industry consortia.[13]

But each consortium must be grounded in a unique, industry-specific context, and approaches to government-industry interaction must be tailored to fit. Since many cooperative efforts are just getting underway in the United States and the general trend toward collaboration has only really gained momentum over the last decade, a great opportunity exists to inform and shape these initiatives.

Industry Studies

Regardless of the potential drawbacks, cooperative efforts between government and industry demonstrate the potential to be powerful policy development mechanisms, especially when combined with complementary policy tools, including regulation and incentives. Rather than simplistically mandating that a problem be solved, cooperation places government in a position to understand the limitations and opportunities faced by industry.

No single approach to initiating cooperative efforts is likely to work. Industries differ in such critical factors as capital requirements for product and process development, the importance of technology, the degree of vertical integration, etc. Any effective technology policy program must reflect these differences and focus on the most important needs. Stakeholders, objectives, products, processes, technology needs, and relationships all have significant implications for policy. To develop a successful industry-focused cooperative venture, these factors must be understood up front. Therefore, public and private participants need to have access to basic data on industrial performance to assess competitiveness and industry needs.

Unfortunately, this sort of knowledge base is lacking for many basic U.S. industries. Macro-economic indications are available, but data relating to industrial performance is largely absent, particularly in a global context. Similarly, benchmarking studies of industrial performance are generally quite closely held.

Conducting a series of industry studies aimed at establishing an objective knowledge base of industrial performance in basic industries could help to fill the void. The longest running industry study is the International Motor Vehicle Program (IMVP), coordinated by the Massachusetts Institute of Technology. The IMVP established a research network of more than fifty scholars from twenty universities around the world to conduct comparative research on the auto industry. Experience with several such studies, including the IMVP, demonstrates that the necessary information can be developed through comparative research studies and benchmarking of various production processes on the value chain. This knowledge base can be used to identify the principal factors influencing competitiveness in each industry and to assess relative competitiveness by country and company. The data can also provide the basis to assess industry needs and determine how they may best be met. Such information can be used by individual companies to establish where each stands relative to its competitors. The knowledge base arising from industry studies could also become a primary input in the development of more rational and effective public policies.

The absence of such an information base can lead to misconceptions and counterproductive public policies. For example, in the 1980s the U.S. auto companies incorrectly believed that the Japanese auto companies could only build small "econobox" cars for their home market. The U.S. producers convinced the U.S. government to pressure Japan to accept voluntary restraints on the number of cars that could be exported to the United States. This policy hurt the U.S. industry in several ways. First, because supply was limited, the price for the cars increased and the Japanese companies made record profits, while U.S. companies were shielded from the very competitive pressures necessary to force needed technological and organizational improvements. Second, since the limitation was on the number of cars sold, the Japanese manufactures chose to produce larger, more luxurious vehicles that competed successfully with mainstream U.S. models. Third, the Japanese moved their production facilities offshore and established "transplant" manufacturing facilities in the United States which employed U.S. workers and were able to achieve productivity and quality comparable to production in Japan.

IMVP research demonstrated that the U.S. auto industry misunderstood the reasons for the success of the Japanese and that the policies were counterproductive. Six years ago the IMVP published *The Machine That Changed The World*, which revealed dramatic differences between companies in manufacturing quality, productivity, and the time and engineering effort to develop a new car.[14]

The findings presented in *The Machine That Changed The World* further demonstrated that the Japanese companies with superior performance were utilizing a new "lean production" system that was fundamentally superior to the mass production system utilized by Western firms.[15] Robert Lutz, president of Chrysler, said the book was a "wake-up call" to U.S. firms in general, and Chrysler in particular. Today, each of the Big Three U.S. producers has adopted the principles of lean production identified through the IMVP. Overall industry performance has increased dramatically due to improvements in manufacturing, supplier relations, and product development.

Another benefit of conducting an industry study derives from the study process itself, which involves all the principal stakeholders: industry, government, labor, and the investment community. The stakeholders meet periodically to determine the research agenda, critique the research results and discuss the implications of the findings. The process is coordinated by an objective third party, typically a university, which serves as a facilitator or "honest broker." The unique aspect of the industry study context is the integration of the meeting process into the research program. The discussions are guided by the research issues, rather than merely war stories and unconstructive advocacy. Too often, industries operate in an adversarial environment, where the various stakeholders compete with each other or have different objectives. Public policy makers who lack technical expertise are often presented with conflicting claims by different stakeholders or interest groups and do not know whom to believe. A principal objective of the industry studies is to normalize the data base of conflicting claims, so that data can be presented to policy makers in a more consistent format and against a broader industry perspective.

Beyond impartiality, another benefit of centering industry studies at major universities is the development of a knowledgeable corps of faculty and an emerging group of students who are intimately familiar with a particular industry. The downside is industry's lack of confidence in universities to deal realistically with issues in a timely manner. However, current experience with these studies suggests that this is not the case and there are workable models which have yielded substantial benefits to participants, both in industry and government.

To be most effective, industry studies should be implemented on a long-term basis. The data base can then be updated periodically

Table 15-1   Sloan Foundation Industry Studies

Industrial Sector	University
Apparel and Textile	Harvard University
Steel	Carnegie Mellon University and The University of Pittsburgh
Pharmaceuticals	Massachusetts Institute of Technology
Financial Institutions	Wharton School, University of Pennsylvania
Semiconductor Manufacturing	University of California, Berkeley
Computer Industry	Stanford University
Motor Vehicles (IMVP)	Massachusetts Institute of Technology
Powder Metallurgy	Worcester Polytechnic Institute
Retail Food Industry	University of Minnesota
Trucking Service	University of Michigan
Managed Healthcare	Harvard University
Construction	University of Texas, Austin

so that changes in performance can be observed and new issues of importance to the industry can be examined. Faculty can make long-term commitments to become experts in particular industries.

An Example Set of Industry Studies

The Alfred P. Sloan Foundation, acting on a belief in the fundamental importance of industry studies, has provided seed money to establish several Centers of Excellence at universities around the United States. Table 15-1 provides a list of the ongoing efforts. The IMVP has served as a model for the various Sloan sponsored industry studies.

Semiconductors are the subject of an another industry study. They are manufactured in many countries by many companies. All use the same raw materials and, for the most part, the same processing machines. However, the benchmark tests conducted over the past six years by the Semiconductor Manufacturing Center at Berkeley show that there is a large variation in both productivity and quality from company to company and even plant to plant. For example, when full production of a new chip design begins, the initial yield (the number of good circuits per chip per run) may be more than twice as high in some companies as in others. Yields rise at the same rate in most plants. This means that those with initial high quality can offer good chips in higher quantity earlier, and thus corner and hold the market.

The Sloan Center at Carnegie Mellon University and the University of Pittsburgh has considered a number of issues of current interest to steel companies, including how certain changes in work organization and human resource management such as teams, incentive pay, and cross-training affect performance. A very detailed study of steel finishing mills has shown that the systematic use of a large number of these changes yields considerable performance increase, whereas the use of only one or two does not. The result holds true as well for integrated mills and mini-mills. Researchers have also found that new technology in a steel mill generally produces higher output and quality, but that mills with older technology can perform as well if they make effective use of their work organization and human resource systems.

The Sloan Financial Services Industry Center at the Wharton School has studied retail banking, including internal banking processing and service marketing efforts. The study compared the contributions of technology, human resources, and management in creating efficient banking functions. It has shown, for example, that a large investment in computer and communication technology must be accompanied by large efforts in human resource preparation—such training, incentives, career ladders—and work organization to have an effective payoff. Some small banks can provide effective, quality services with low technology and minimal attention from workers.

Despite the uniqueness of each sector, industry studies have revealed a central theme: in spite of equal inputs and processes, there are large variations in firms' productivity and the quality of their products and services. For example, the Sloan Food Industry Center at the University of Minnesota examined supermarkets in one part of the state and found that some stores have twice the sales per square foot of others. In the Trucking Industry Center at the University of Michigan, competitors in the relatively profitable, less-than truckload business have vastly different turnover rates for drivers. Similar findings are being obtained in the pharmaceutical (MIT) and computer industry (Stanford) centers.

The Role of Government

Such analyses are valuable to federal, state and local government. Several Sloan Centers have already been called upon by the U.S. Department of Commerce for benchmark studies, by the Federal Trade Commission to understand the bases for competition in each industry, and by the Department of Energy for a special vision study of the steel industry. The IMVP influenced European automotive policy enacted by the European Economic Community. As the prevalence of government-industry partnerships increases, these and similar industry studies could play a valuable precursor and supportive role.

The Sloan Foundation provided seed funding for the industry studies described. Over time as this support diminishes, industry and government would benefit from supporting the studies on an ongoing basis. Industry funding has been forthcoming, but government funding has not. This represents a major missed opportunity for the federal government.

For example, the IMVP is funded by every major auto company in the world, many principal suppliers, and numerous governments including Canada, the European Economic Community, the United Kingdom, and Australia. However, there is no funding from the U.S. government. This was not always the case. In the early years of the program both the Departments of Commerce and of Transportation were active participants, and senior officials from those agencies benefited greatly from interactions with industry and labor representatives at IMVP Policy Forum discussions.

Government should also actively participate in these industry study programs. As a stakeholder in many of these industries, the government should be a part of the process. The industry study provides a potential framework for launching important cooperative programs. But if the government is not an active participant in the process, then the ability to leverage industry studies in shaping technology industry-government cooperative initiatives is more limited. Government participation is necessary to ensure that the data generated is useful, credible, and sufficient for making public policy.

A Model Industry Study

The Lean Aircraft Initiative (LAI) is an industry study that focuses on the defense aircraft industry. The LAI represents a model partnership among industry, government, labor, and academe to address a significant national need for fundamental change in a key industry through teamwork-based research and implementation. It further serves as an example of how an effective industry study might lay the groundwork for future consortia initiatives by having key stakeholders, including government, work together to identify and address critical industry needs.

Launched in May 1993 as a three-year implementation-oriented industry study at MIT, LAI is sponsored jointly by the U.S. Air Force and a group of major aerospace companies. In 1996, the program entered a second three-year phase with expanded government sponsorship, and now includes three military services, the U.S. Coast Guard, NASA, DARPA, and an expanded set of industry participants. Stakeholders also include national labor organizations and industry associations. The LAI is a cost-shared program, with the government and non-governmental stakeholders each contributing fifty percent of the total program cost.

The Lean Aircraft Initiative strives to define and help implement fundamental changes in both industry and government operations over the next decade. The program seeks to develop a knowledge base to significantly reduce cost and cycle time for military aircraft throughout the entire value chain while continuing to improve product performance. Specific objectives include greater affordability of systems, increased efficiency, higher quality, enhanced technological superiority, and increased international competitiveness.

The LAI has already led to significant changes in the defense aircraft industry. One company completely redesigned its factory operations after it learned about lean factory flow optimization methods. Others have adopted lean supply chain management practices based on documented benefits identified by research focusing on supplier partnerships and early supplier integration into design and development. One participant reduced its product development cycle time by thirty percent, another cut its composite part fabrication cycle time in half, and another member company reduced its production lead time by sixty-five percent. Other companies embracing lean concepts have realized significant productivity gains, with one company achieving as much as a 48 percent increase in productivity. There is tangible evidence that the senior leaders of many companies are personally involved in setting goals, priorities, rewards, and metrics intended to diffuse lean principles throughout their companies.

Conclusions

Establishing a national commitment to developing an improved basis for scoping, initiating and guiding government-industry interaction through consortia would be a timely endeavor. Many of the critical technology policy concerns of the future will require a detailed response at an industry or sector level. From the perspective of government support, generic or firm-level responses do not sufficiently address the specific issues of wide-scale and coordinated implementation that will be crucial to assuring the effectiveness of these policies. Further, the complex landscape faced by industry today virtually assures that simple policy tools, such as tax incentives and regulations, will be less effective or even counterproductive. Instead, a systematic, tailored approach to technology policy, at the level of a specific industry, must be crafted. Unfortunately, the basic industrial data needed to effectively shape such efforts is often unavailable.

Industry studies are a potentially promising mechanism for launching sound government-industry consortia. Typically centered at academic institutions, these studies can provide an information base that is useful for understanding complex technology problems from the perspectives of industry participants, and private and public institutions external to the industry. They can serve as an effective mechanism to "take the pulse" of the nation's critical industries and provide a basis for government to formulate effective policies in areas such as R&D, social regulation, trade and standard setting. Further, industry studies can provide an environment within which all of these participants can come together in a non-threatening environment that is conducive to discussing long-range issues, under a broad research agenda that has been constructed to illuminate these concerns.

Presently, such studies are largely underwritten by industrial and private foundations, with only irregular participation of governments. In light of their potential to shape and launch promising government-industry projects aimed at critical technological issues, government should consider providing national support for ongoing industry studies.

Acknowledgments

The authors wish to thank Hirsch Cohen of the Sloan Foundation and Kirkor Bozdogan of MIT's Center for Technology, Policy and Industrial Development for their contributions to this chapter.

Notes

1. *Endless Frontier, Limited Resources: U.S. R&D Policy for Competitiveness* (Washington, D.C.: Council on Competitiveness, 1996).

2. Bruce Kogut, "Joint Ventures: Theoretical and Empirical Perspectives," *Strategic Management Journal,* Vol. 9 (1988), pp. 319–332.

3. Klaus Brockhoff and Thorsten Teichert, "Cooperative R&D and Partners' Measures of Success," *International Journal of Technology Management,* Vol. 10, No. 1 (1995), pp. 111–123.

4. Gary Hamel, Yves Doz, and C.K. Prahalad, "Collaborate with Your Competitors and Win," *Harvard Business Review,* January-February 1989, pp. 133–139.

5. George Champine, "Did We Get Our $500 Million Worth?" *IEEE Spectrum,* January 1995, pp. 15–18.

6. John Horrigan, "Cooperation Among Competitors in Research Consortia: The Evolution of MCC and SEMATECH," unpublished Ph.D. dissertation, The University of Texas at Austin, December, 1996.

7. "Winning Through Cooperation: An Interview with William Spencer," *Technology Review,* January 1997, pp. 22–27.

8. "Uncle Sam's Helping Hand," *The Economist,* April 2, 1994, pp. 77–79.

9. National Academy of Science, *Review of the Research Program of the Partnership for*

a New Generation of Vehicles Second Report, (Washington, D.C.: National Academy Press, 1996).

10. GAO, *National Laboratories: Are Their R&D Activities Related to Commercial Product Development? Report to Congressional Requesters*, GAO/PEMD-95-2 (Washington D.C.: United States General Accounting Office [GAO], November 1994); Secretary of Energy Advisory Board, Task Force on Alternative Futures for the Department of Energy National Laboratories, *Alternative Futures for the Department of Energy National Laboratories* (Washington, D.C.: U.S. Department of Energy, February 1995).

11. Some observers have suggested that the oversight role was a part of the original intent of the partnership. However, the text of the Declaration of Intent suggests a peer review role, rather than the more active role that is currently being taken.

12. The Corporate Average Fuel Economy (CAFE) standard was established in the Energy Policy and Conservation Act of 1975. It establishes a fuel economy target, averaged over fleet sales, that each automaker must achieve.

13. Park, "Questioning Japan's Miracle," *Technology Review*, January 1997, pp. 61–63.

14. James Womack, Daniel Jones, and Daniel Roos, *The Machine That Changed the World* (New York: Rawson Associates/Macmillan, 1990).

15. Ibid.

16

State Governments: Partners in Innovation

Christopher M. Coburn and Duncan M. Brown

State involvement in forming and executing national policy for science and technology is vital. States are natural channels of technology deployment and commercialization, because they are attuned to the needs and structure of local and regional industry and have strong and direct political incentives to produce tangible economic results in the form of new wealth and employment gains. The private sector has begun to move toward collaborative innovation through its growing reliance on strategic alliances and networks of companies.[1] The federal government increasingly recognizes the need to work more flexibly and creatively with industry, nonprofit organizations, and other levels of government to reinforce these healthy tendencies. But it is the states that have the expertise and originality to best respond to this challenge. In recent decades states have pioneered partnerships with industry and the federal government that can form an important part of a more powerful innovation system that lets the nation efficiently develop and use commercial technology.[2]

State governments nationwide, under governors and legislators of both parties, have built a variety of technology-based programs to strengthen their economies over the past few decades. These programs are today found in every state, and they spend more than $400 million annually.[3] State cooperative technology programs involve various combinations of initiatives, generally including new relationships between industry and universities and between industry and other sources of technical assistance, with state government as catalyst and industry as a major source of funds and priorities.[4] The network-based approach is consistent with the modern collaborative innovation techniques that have emerged in industry. Most state cooperative technology initiatives are guided by the following strategies:

• The use of direct investments as catalysts for far larger private and federal commitments;

• The use of existing public facilities for the benefit of companies;

• Requirements that state investments be matched by private or other (often federal) sources;

• Precise identification of "gaps" in the innovation system, where state dollars can be most effectively spent; and sometimes

• Requirements that recipients pay back selected state investments, to ensure the state's capacity to make further investments.[5]

The states should also redirect some of the billions of dollars they spend in subsidies to influence business location decisions (which burden the national economy as well as state and local budgets) toward helping companies develop and deploy new technology. Unlike the location subsidies, the half billion dollars states spend on technology plays to the market's strengths. Turning even a fraction of the location subsidies toward technology-based innovation would increase productivity growth.

The Clinton administration sees the wisdom of cooperation with the states. The White House has entered into an agreement with the National Governors' Association (NGA) to launch a new "U.S. Innovation Partnership" (USIP), in which the White House and federal agencies will work with states to generate economic growth, improve education and health care, and protect the environment through joint use of science and technology.[6] On June 24, 1997, a memorandum of understanding establishing the USIP as federal and state policy was signed by the two governors who represent the National Governors' Association in technology matters, the U.S. Secretary of Commerce, and the president's advisor on science and technology. The agreement sets out principles and procedures for cooperation in forming and executing policy, including the establishment of state liaisons in federal agencies with science and technology responsibilities. In implementing this agreement, federal and state officials will need to build new partnerships with business and academic institutions to meet government needs and catalyze private investments in cases of market failure.

States have made progress already in building such relationships. Each of the fifty states has a set of programs to help businesses develop and deploy technology. Most have made concomitant improvements in their economic infrastructures of training, education, and academic research in the past decade. But they must continue to improve their policy assessment capabilities, developing tools to serve their increasingly important economic functions. At present the states vary dramatically in the sophistication and stability of their technology programs;[7] states will need to work together to improve their practices in each area of endeavor.

The next section describes the new collaborative innovation system and outlines how the states can identify and fill the gaps that are occurring. The third section provides examples of successful state technology programs, and the one that follows it evaluates the practice of offering subsidies to firms to induce them to locate in a state or locality. The final section offers recommendations for enhancing the role of states in designing and implementing technology policy.

Gaps in the Collaborative Innovation System

The innovation system is growing more complex, as firms begin to manage their portfolios of technology through partnerships. By looking beyond corporate boundaries for technology, they can form networks of relationships among organizations—large and small, private and public—to maximize their exposure to innovation at minimal cost. Strategic alliances of various types (from mergers to special-purpose R&D consortia to supplier contracts that demand innovation) are replacing industry's traditional approach, which centered on in-house labs.[8] Large U.S. corporations in many industries are spending less on fundamental research in-house, and funding more of it at universities.[9] Federal laboratories are also joining industry in cooperative research and technology transfer relationships such as the U.S. Advanced Battery Consortium and the Partnership for a New Generation of Vehicles (PNGV).

While the move toward collaborative research has great benefits, there are gaps that must be filled if the system is to function optimally. First, for shorter term research, aimed at improving processes and products, industry increasingly relies on small to medium-sized firms, often suppliers. Many of these firms are less well equipped than larger ones to choose and adopt appropriate new technology and less able to secure investment capital. This problem is complicated by today's shorter and more demanding product cycles.

Second, the growing emphasis on shorter term, product-related research in industry, the decline in defense-related R&D, and the shift of long-term industry R&D funds to academic institutions have led to concerns that important mid-term research, which in the past has been the source of much innovation, is not being adequately supported.[10]

Third, the barriers blocking collaboration can be substantial. Effective collaboration demands a special set of skills. These include the ability to identify and screen technology opportunities, to negotiate balanced relationships, and to work in what can be an ambiguous organizational environment, taking risks and managing the shifting priorities of partners. Effective internal and external communication is vital; otherwise the network loses sight of the market into which the innovation will flow.[11]

Fourth, firms retain an organizational bias toward doing strategic development in-house, which creates obvious barriers to collaboration. A final problem in the emerging collaborative innovation system is the distribution of capital, especially to early-stage ventures that have outgrown their initial informal investors.

In all of these cases there is an important role, albeit a narrow one, for the public sector. Government, acting principally through state technology initiatives, can create small but compelling incentives to further collaboration and ensure that early-stage capital is widely available. Some companies have discovered state and federal cooperative technology initiatives as they search for technology partners. They recognize that these initiatives can, at low cost, expose them to new partners, and to the vocabulary, the metrics, and the incentives of partnership. Public sector resources can be used to shift the traditional risk-return ratio in favor of experimenting with a collaborative development. These changes in the nature of private sector innovation are creating new roles for state technology programs in catalyzing the formation of networks and alliances of industry, government, and academic institutions to develop and apply technology. Such networks parallel those that pervade the private sector today. They depend on flexibility, local decision making, and the efficient flow of information. State-sponsored cooperative technology programs have in many ways anticipated these industrial trends, by building such networks for the benefit of local industry, and offer ready-made institutions.

For a variety of reasons discussed elsewhere in this book, the federal government is moving into the role of partner of private industry even in areas of technology that have traditionally been federal missions. The federal government share of national R&D spending is declining, from more than half in the 1970s to just over one-third today, largely owing to cuts in defense spending.[12] The private sector is recognized increasingly as the source of most important technology-based innovation. The federal government sponsors industry-government consortia, for example, as vehicles for advancing technology for both commercial and government benefits.[13]

In this context, state-sponsored technology programs dovetail with the complementary strengths of federal programs, and provide a tool for getting the most economic benefit from government's declining investments. State initiatives engage industry in cooperative arrangements in which both the costs and the benefits of technology development and technology diffusion are shared. Sources of technology (such as universities, federal laboratories, and companies) are linked in partnership with users of technology in the private sector. These arrangements, whether they be university-based technology centers or manufacturing extension programs, generally require the private sector partners to share the cost of each project; that way the investments are directed at problems of high priority to both the public and private sectors.

Examples of Successful State and State-Federal Programs

State cooperative technology programs are beginning to demonstrate significant and measurable economic benefits. Several of the older and better established ones, in particular, have been evaluated by outside experts:

• New York State has realized an estimated return of 3 to 1 on its investment in Centers for Advanced Technology. The state invested $61 million in these centers between 1982 and 1991. The resulting benefits to the state economy were estimated at $190–360 million (including external income brought to the state, increased or retained employment, and improvements in the quality of the technical work force.)[14]

• Virginia's Center for Innovative Technology (CIT) invested $72.9 million of taxpayers' money between 1988 and 1994, and received $266 million in direct benefits between 1988 and 1995.[15]

• New York's $12.9 million investment in the New York Manufacturing Extension Partnership (April 1993 to December 1994) had returned an estimated $30–100 million in value-added income to the state from 1992 to 1994.[16]

• Ohio's Edison Technology Centers spent $70 million in 1992–95, returning an estimated $738 million in direct economic impact.[17]

State government is particularly well suited to the task of partnership with industry to help deploy and commercialize technology developed in the public sector. By immersing themselves in local markets, state governments stimulate bonds among the vital elements of state economies: businesses of all sizes, academic institutions, entrepreneurs, and investors. They are natural channels of information flow and technology diffusion.

States offer especially valuable support for federal programs that must be tailored to local conditions. The Manufacturing Extension Partnership (MEP), a system of NIST-sponsored centers to help manufacturers adopt new methods that will help them stay ahead of their competition, is an example. States bid competitively for federal funds to support these centers (there are seventy to date), and have substantial flexibility in arranging their operations, subject to federal guidelines. In many states MEP centers are tied to existing state-sponsored extension centers. Centers' sponsors may include nonprofit organizations, academic institutions, and industry groups, as well as state and local government. Federal funding of MEP (about $95 million in fiscal year 1997) is matched by state and local funds (about $100 million in 1997); the president has requested $123 million in federal spending for 1998.[18] The White House-NGA agreement establishing the U.S. Innovation Partnership calls for increasing the capacity of the MEP.[19]

Research grants to small business under the multi-agency federal Small Business Innovation Research (SBIR) program also have strong state support and show promise of benefits from further cooperation.[20] While the program is intended to serve the research and development needs of federal agencies, it effectively makes available more than $1 billion in "risk capital" each year to small firms throughout the nation.[21] Most state governments help companies apply for SBIR funding, and many offer bridge grants to assist recipients between phases of the two-phase federal grant program and into commercialization. In these ways states help cement the links between small high-tech firms and the federal agencies that require research services. The SBIR program is strictly a federal program, with no direct participation by states. States' ability to exploit the opportunities presented by SBIR grants, however, suggests that there is great promise in additional collaboration between federal and state government.

These instances of *ad hoc* state-federal cooperation, which had to overcome many barriers to implementation, suggest that there is scope for much wider federal-state collaboration in applying science and technology in areas of joint interest, including education, environmental protection, health care, and other areas of domestic policy. In these partnerships, states offer flexibility, responsiveness, and direct access to local and regional institutions, including business of all kinds.

State Industrial Recruitment Subsidies

In the name of priming the economic pump, almost all states pursue economic development by industrial recruitment; they offer various subsidies—tax abatements, grants, tax-exempt bonds, free land and infrastructure improvements, job training support, and other inducements—to firms that agree to locate within their borders. Similarly, local government subsidy programs often reward companies for moving a few miles to cross a jurisdictional boundary.

Such incentives do little more than subsidize the cost of production. They do not support the creation of wealth, and they tend to skew market decisions. This problem is generally considered to be escalating, with states and localities competing to offer larger and larger subsidies that frequently defy economic or fiscal logic. Lawrence Reed, director of the Mackinac Center for Public Policy in Michigan, has called this heated competition "the economic war between the states."[22] The problem has gone unaddressed in part because of the difficulty of quantifying it. Most states, for example, do not include "tax expenditures" (revenues foregone for purposes of policy, such as attracting business) in their budgets.[23]

Those that do, however, present a telling picture. For example, in 1992 Massachusetts listed $2.5 billion in lost revenues for tax expenditures "in furtherance of commerce." Michigan listed $4.9 billion in tax expenditures in support of commerce in fiscal 1996–97, which dwarfs the state's $210 million of direct expenditures for that purpose. In 1993 New York listed more than $500 million in tax expenditures for specific investment and jobs incentives. Minnesota attributes $268.5 million in lost revenues to a program offering property tax exemptions to developers. California estimated that a new credit for manufacturing equipment would cost more than $400 million in fiscal year 1995–96.[24] Pennsylvania, after largely avoiding industrial location subsidies in the 1980s, has aggressively entered the competition, including a program of location grants and tax abatements totaling $52 million annually.[25] State Senator Chuck Horn of Ohio has found double-digit annual increases in Ohio's state and local spending for industrial recruitment (including tax abatements), reaching several hundred million dollars in 1995.[26] The Ohio General Assembly, accordingly, has mounted a study to quantify both the costs and the benefits of these subsidies. On a national basis, the annual budgetary cost to states and localities may be as high as $10 billion. State cooperative technology programs spend only about $400 million each year.[27]

The sizes of individual deals seem to be mushrooming. Tennessee paid $33 million in 1980 to attract a Nissan plan offering 1900 jobs. Five years later it took $150 million in state and local tax incentives for Tennessee to lure the Saturn plant, with 6,000 jobs. It cost Indianapolis $294 million a few years later to win the national competition for the 6,300 jobs involved in a new United Airlines maintenance facility. In 1993 Alabama delivered more than $300 million in incentives for the 1,500 jobs in a Mercedes-Benz plant.[28]

These subsidies are attempts to oppose the workings of the market. Even when the gain in state or local revenue is enough to cover the cost to taxpayers (and many recruitment deals cannot meet this test), the cost to the national economy is high.[29] These subsidies force companies that are already in place to compete against new, subsidized rivals, leading established firms in some states to demand the same subsidies as recruited firms. They encourage corporate inefficiencies, as companies reshape their operations to meet the terms of the subsidy deals. Once attracted, companies often fail to live up to their agreements to create a certain number of jobs or make the specified investments.[30] Moreover, the incentives draw business and jobs away from America's central cities.[31]

Remedies have been suggested. Economists Melvin Burstein and Arthur Rolnick of the Federal Reserve Bank of Minneapolis have proposed federal legislation prohibiting subsidies and preferential tax treatment for recruiting industry, on the grounds that recruitment subsidies interfere with interstate commerce. "To implement a legislative prohibition," they write, "Congress could impose sanctions such as taxing imputed income, denying tax-exempt status to public debt used to compete for businesses and impounding federal funds payable to states engaging in such competition."[32] Peter Enrich of the Northeastern University School of Law proposes that the U.S. Supreme Court could prohibit the use of such subsidies if a suit were brought under the Commerce Clause of the U.S. Constitution, since these subsidies are discriminatory with respect to interstate commerce.[33] Ohio State Senator Horn has introduced a resolution calling on Ohio's congressional delegation to support efforts to "identify and eliminate federally funded programs that are used by the states" in recruitment programs.

At the state level the problem has defied solution, as various regional cease-fire proposals have come and gone. In 1993 Illinois Governor Jim Edgar proposed guidelines to limit subsidies and tax breaks for industry. His proposal followed a 1983 joint initiative by the Council of Great Lakes Governors (including Edgar's predecessor) to forego such incentives, which collapsed when Indiana would not agree to its provisions. Little real action has resulted, except for growing use of "clawback" measures (notably by Louisiana, Ohio, and Texas), which reclaim subsidies from firms that do not live up to their agreements. Challenges to such moves have been upheld by state courts in some cases.

The problem of recruitment subsidies for industry is politically and legally challenging. Collaboration of the White House, Congress, and the states offers the best opportunity to bring it under control. States and localities must resist such short-term political gains at such high long-term costs. If instead they increased their spending on developing and deploying technology, they would create wealth and enhance competitiveness in ways that are more effective and more lasting.

Recommendations

U.S. prosperity in the twenty-first century will require a national effort to optimize the innovation system—an effort that requires vigorous leadership by the president, and Congress, and the full partnership of the states with the federal government in designing and implementing policy. Yet, no matter how compelling the need, cooperation with the states will not occur spontaneously throughout the federal government. This section provides recommendations that would position states and the federal government to make the most effective use of their current technology investments.

The U.S. Innovation Partnership

The U.S. Innovation Partnership is an important step toward forging a strong partnership of state and federal government to use science and technology for the public good. It establishes a new cooperative working relationship between the nation's governors and the White House, aimed at promoting innovation by removing barriers between sources of technology and the users of technology. In this, it follows the networking tradition of the state coopera-tive technology programs. It is intended to be "an interactive partnership among the states, industry, universities, and the fed-eral government to develop a national innovation system that can sustain long-term economic growth and rising living standards for all Americans."[34] It seeks to strengthen the national (not simply federal) science and technology system; clearly establish the role of the states in the national system; catalyze private sector investments in technology; and build national excellence in manufacturing.

Among the joint state-federal projects USIP plans to undertake are improving the capacity to commercialize technology in the various states; resolving regulatory issues in telecommunications; making technology available to small companies via the Internet; establishing reciprocal agreements among states for testing the compliance of environmental technologies to state certification requirements; streamlining building regulations; matching wealthy investors with entrepreneurial companies; expanding the Manu-facturing Extension Partnership; and revising the federal SBIR program of research grants so that states may compete for blocks of SBIR funding in return for commitments to additional support for grant recipients (using the established SBIR selection crite-ria).[35]

The Partnership traces its roots to a 1992 report by the Carnegie Commission on Science, Technology, and Government, entitled *Science, Technology, and the States in America's Third Century.* That report, by a broad group of experts in government, academic research, and industry, explored the broad implications of coordi-nation between federal and state government in science and technology. In response, the Clinton administration requested a study by an *ad hoc* State-Federal Technology Partnership Task Force, chaired jointly in 1995 by former governors Richard Celeste of Ohio and Dick Thornburgh of Pennsylvania, focusing more tightly on state-federal cooperation in technology for the sake of economic growth.

The administration has begun to advocate the USIP in Congress. The initial response seems to be positive. Staff-level activity in the White House, Congress, and the states is defining an agenda for action. If effectively implemented it will have broad economic benefits for the nation.

Presidential Leadership

The president should make strengthening the innovation system a central national priority. Far more is needed than simply supporting the funding of programs; the president is in a unique position to give the vitality and direction of the innovation system a prominent place in the nation's public life. The national discourse needs to be shifted from a debate over existing programs, involving a very small number of policy makers and analysts, to a dialogue that involves the broader population and that addresses national needs and opportunities. In the past the nation has given serious attention to science and technology when they were the focus of international competition. In fact, they are the focus of international competition today, and the private sector innovation system is likely to become ever more important to U.S. leadership as military priorities are reduced. Widespread public appreciation of the importance of innovation can be achieved only through a clearly articulated vision of the new collaborative innovation system and its importance to the U.S. economy. The consistent, active involvement of the president can engage CEOs, university presidents, governors, members of Congress, state legislators, bankers, venture capitalists, entrepreneurs, editors, and news anchors. Four years of advocacy by the president, based on an objective and timely assessment of the innovation system, can rekindle the passion for innovation that has long been an American tradition. A century and a half ago de Tocqueville observed that "America is a land of wonders, in which everything is in constant motion and every change seems an improvement . . . No natural boundary seems to be set to the efforts of man; and in his eyes what is not yet done is only what he has not yet attempted to do."[36]

The White House should implement and support the U.S. Innovation Partnership. In collaboration with the National Economic Council, the director of the Office of Science and Technology Policy should create a stable joint policy development mechanism with state governments. Among the highest priorities initially should be bringing state technology programs up to uniformly high standards by promoting the use of performance metrics; disseminating information about the best practices of state programs; and improving information sharing among the more than seventy federal cooperative technology programs and hundreds of federal laboratories. USIP, as a policy development mechanism, should also be the source of novel ideas and approaches for discussion, such as privatizing technology commercialization functions of federal laboratories; revising federal tax and other policies that directly or indirectly reward states and localities for industrial recruitment subsidies; creating incentives for federal research performers to reduce indirect expenses; or giving states a more active role in federal R&D programs such as the Small Business Innovation Research grant program.

State Governments

State governments should orient their economic development activities toward reinforcing the market's strengths, with substantially more emphasis on building healthy technology-based economies and dramatically less on industrial recruitment subsidies. The long-term goal is a dense network of market-oriented technology opportunities in each state that would tangibly improve the nation's ability to innovate. This new level of activity would result in greatly increased numbers of innovations, investment opportunities, companies, and entrepreneurs, and greatly reduced time to market.

To achieve this goal, the states need to work collaboratively with Congress and the White House to halt the spiral of industrial recruitment incentives. The recent remarkable cooperation of state attorneys general offers a precedent for such far-reaching collaboration. In an economic sense the stakes may be just as high.

States also need to work toward better understanding the innovation system as it operates in each state. This understanding should take in the role of the public sector in taxes, regulation, support of education, and direct investments in transportation, environmental protection, and health care. This understanding will clearly detail the role of technology in each state's economy.

Characterizing the National Innovation System

These recommendations can be given greater force by a national effort to characterize the workings of the national innovation system. The administration and Congress should sponsor a comprehensive assessment to describe the national innovation system objectively and quantitatively, and to recommend ways that the public sector can most efficiently contribute to economic growth based on technology. This study should characterize the role of each element of the public sector (the federal government, states, localities, universities, nonprofits, and foundations) in the changing innovation system; and characterize the economic development activities of federal, state, and local governments: How do they relate to one another? What are their costs and benefits? What are government's legitimate roles? What roles are illegitimate ?

Fundamental change is sweeping the national innovation system. Getting the most from scarce science and technology resources in the coming decades will require leadership and vision from the Executive Branch, beginning with the president, from Congress, and from the states. Government at all levels must attune itself to the needs of the market, working more flexibly and creatively with industry, universities, and nonprofit organizations to harness the private-sector sources of economic growth. States in particular are a valuable source of expertise and originality in responding to this challenge, through new kinds of partnerships with industry and the federal government. Every element of the system requires fresh approaches, based on a clear understanding of how the system works and how it is developing.

Notes

1. David C. Mowery and Richard R. Nelson, "The U.S. Corporation and Technical Progress," in Carl Kaysen, ed., *The American Corporation Today* (New York: Oxford University Press, 1996); Niren M. Vyas, William L. Shelburn, and Dennis C. Rogers, "An Analysis of Strategic Alliances: Forms, Functions and Framework," *Journal of Business and Industrial Marketing*, Vol. 10, No. 3 (1995), pp. 47–60.

2. Carnegie Commission on Science, Technology, and Government, *Science, Technology, and the States in America's Third Century* (New York: Carnegie Corporation, September 1992); Christopher Coburn and Dan Berglund, eds., *Partnerships: A Compendium of State and Federal Cooperative Technology Programs* (Columbus, Ohio: Battelle Memorial Institute, 1995).

3. State Science and Technology Institute, *State Funding for Cooperative Technology Programs* (Columbus, Ohio: State Science and Technology Institute, 1996).

4. Carnegie Commission, *Science, Technology, and the States*; Coburn and Berglund, *Partnerships*.

5. Coburn and Berglund, *Partnerships*.

6. Bill Clinton, Letter to Hon. Bob Miller, Chair, National Governor's Association (Washington, D.C.: The White House, February 3, 1997); National Governors' Association, *United States Innovation Partnership*, draft manuscript, February 6, 1997.

7. Carnegie Commission, *Science, Technology, and the States*.

8. Roy Rothwell, "Successful Industrial Innovation: Critical Factors for the 1990s," *R&D Management*, Vol. 22, No. 3 (July 1992), pp. 221–239.

9. Mowery and Nelson, "The U.S. Corporation and Technical Progress"; Richard S. Rosenbloom and William J. Spencer, "The Transformation of Industrial Research," *Issues in Science and Technology*, Vol. 12, No. 3 (Spring 1996), pp. 68–74.

10. See, for example, Charles M. Vest, "The Transformation of U.S. R&D," in *Competitiveness Index 1996* (Washington, D.C.: Council on Competitiveness, 1996).

11. Rothwell, "Successful Industrial Innovation."

12. National Science Board, *Science and Engineering Indicators 1996* (Arlington, Virginia: National Science Foundation, 1996), p. A-8; NSF Report 96-1.

13. Rosenbloom and Spencer, "The Transformation of Industrial Research."

14. Gary Anderson and Irwin Feller, *New York State Centers for Advanced Technology Program: Evaluating Past Performance and Preparing for the Future* (Washington, D.C.: SRI International, Center for Economic Competitiveness, April 6, 1992).

15. Battelle Memorial Institute, *Virginia's Center for Innovative Technology: An Economic Impact Assessment* (Columbus, Ohio: Battelle Memorial Institute, December 5, 1995).

16. Nexus Associates, *Evaluation of the New York Manufacturing Extension Partnership* (Belmont, Mass.: Nexus Associates, March 18, 1992).

17. Battelle Memorial Institute, *The Edison Technology Centers: An Economic Impact Study* (Columbus, Ohio: Battelle Memorial Institute, December 1996).

18. Kei Koizumi, "President Proposes $75.5 Billion for R&D in the FY 1988 Budget," *Science and Technology in Congress* (Washington, D.C.: American Association for the Advancement of Science, March 1997).

19. Clinton, Letter to Hon. Bob Miller; National Governor's Association, *United States Innovation Partnership*.

20. State-Federal Technology Partnership Task Force, *The State-Federal Technology Partnership Task Force, Final Report* (Washington D.C., 1995).

21. Coburn and Berglund, *Partnerships*.

22. Lawrence Reed, "Time to End the Economic War Between the States," unpublished manuscript, Mackinac Center, Michigan, 1996; available on World

Wide Web at <http://www.geocities.com/CapitolHill/2817/mackin2.html>.

23. Personal communication, Don Haider, Kellogg School of Management, Northwestern University, February 21, 1997.)

24. Peter D. Enrich, "Saving the States from Themselves: Commerce Clause Constraints on State Tax Incentives for Business," *Harvard Law Review*, Vol. 110, No. 2 (December 1996), pp. 377–468.

25. Personal communication, Timothy McNulty, Policy Director, Pennsylvania Department of Community and Economic Development, July 2, 1997.

26. Personal communication, Ohio State Senator Chuck Horn, April 9, 1997.

27. Coburn and Berglund, *Partnerships*.

28. Enrich, "Saving the States."

29. Melvin L. Burstein and Arthur J. Rolnick, "Congress Should End the Economic War Among the States," *NE-MW Economic Review* (Minneapolis: Federal Reserve Bank of Minneapolis, July 1995); Reed, "Time to End the Economic War."

30. Burstein and Rolnick, "Congress Should End the Economic War."

31. See, for example, Ken Zapinski, "Older Suburbs Unite for Survival," *Cleveland Plain Dealer*, March 16, 1997, p. 1-B.

32. Burstein and Rolnick, "Congress Should End the Economic War."

33. Enrich, "Saving the States."

34. National Governor's Association, *United States Innovation Partnership*.

35. National Governor's Association, *United States Innovation Partnership*.

36. Alexis de Tocqueville, *Democracy in America* (New York: Vintage Books, 1990), Vol. 1, p. 425.

17

Managing Technology Policy at the White House

David M. Hart

The Clinton administration came into office with ambitious plans to restructure the nation's technology policy. Its goals included the reallocation of R&D funds among federal agencies and missions; the transformation of the relationships among public, private, and non-profit institutions involved in the innovation process; and the rapid development of programs that were supposed to enhance the contribution of these institutions to economic growth. The Clinton-Gore technology policy was an integral part of the administration's larger economic "investment" program, whose success or failure was expected to be a central determinant of the American people's judgment of the administration at the polls.[1]

These ambitions inevitably placed new demands on the White House for development and oversight of technology policy. This chapter's purpose is to review how these functions have been handled during the first Clinton administration and to offer some suggestions for the future. The first section considers the broad motivations and pressures that have impelled presidents to expand their involvement in technology policy-making as the economy and the role of technology in it have evolved. The next section briefly describes the emergence over the past few decades of institutional capacities for managing technology policy in the Executive Office of the President, which set the stage for the Clinton administration's efforts, discussed in the following section. It describes the initiatives of President Clinton and Vice President Gore and assesses their effects on the ability of the administration to meet the expectations it established during the 1992 campaign. The chapter concludes with recommendations that aim to refine the technology policy-making process, with particular focus on the National Economic Council, the National Science and Technology Council, and the Office of Science and Technology Policy.

The President and the Challenge of Managing Technology Policy

The administration's vision of technology policy reflected economic facts, political calculations, and managerial necessities. Technological innovation plays an important role in economic growth, as Michael Borrus and Jay Stowsky show in Chapter 2 of this volume; this role is expanding as the international economy becomes more closely integrated. However, the innovation process is not uniform over time or across economic sectors. The market provides powerful incentives for innovation at some times and in some sectors, but it can also fail to provide such incentives in a variety of different ways. A centralized "one size fits all" technology policy would constitute a poor response to the challenge posed by these economic facts.

However, designing and calibrating policies that can address each type of market failure in industrial innovation is no mean task. The pluralistic American system of government is to some extent well-suited to the job, since it encompasses a variety of federal and state agencies that have diverse competencies stemming from their various missions. Each agency's skills and expertise might be drawn upon to address market failures specific to innovation processes in the particular industries or regions with which it is most familiar. The U.S. government has recorded quite a few technology policy successes in the past, allowing economically valuable ideas that might have otherwise been stifled to be reduced to practice and diffused. On the other hand, there have also been many occasions in which the public sector has wasted resources, misaligned incentives, or locked the national technical effort into "the hot pursuit of dead ends," as Harvey Brooks puts it.[2] The Clinton administration judged that the risk of market failure in technological innovation outweighed the risk of government failure. This judgment was, by necessity, largely political, since the conditions that determine each type of failure have not been (and perhaps cannot be) definitively established. The Clinton-Gore policy reflected a hope widely shared in the Democratic Party that technology might be an area in which faith in government economic activism could be restored.

This hope could not be fulfilled without careful management, as the administration recognized. The same pluralism that promises tailored policy solutions to particular barriers to innovation can also contribute to a variety of policy pathologies, including jurisdictional confusion, agency capture, and excessive bureaucratic autonomy. To be effective, the federal government must have a coordinated approach to the assessment of promising opportunities, the formulation of technology policy options, and decision-making. Once a policy has been authorized, responsibility for its implementation must be clearly assigned to the appropriate agency or agencies, multi-agency tasks allocated, and the policy evaluated in practice. These management tasks are the responsibility of the president. Congress plays an enormous role in technology policy and performs all of these functions to some extent but, because of its committee structure, it cannot do so as systematically nor take into account as broad a range of considerations as the president. The president has a longer time horizon than most members of Congress, and the office has the entire nation as its constituency. The incumbent is held responsible for the nation's economic performance and has taken the lead role in economic policy formulation through most of the twentieth century.

The President and Technology Policy: A Brief History

Herbert Hoover was the first president to take a deep interest in the impact of technological innovation on economic growth and to explore the potential for a constructive federal role in the innovation process. As secretary of commerce from 1921 to 1928, Hoover began to build what he sometimes called an economic "general staff" that could, among other things, identify technologically backward industries and assist them in organizing cooperative research programs. As president, Hoover sponsored two expert committees that considered this set of issues, but their reports yielded little in the way of concrete policy recommendations, much less a framework for implementation.

President Franklin D. Roosevelt established a Science Advisory Board in 1933, but rejected its proposals to "put science to work" against the Depression. In his second term, Roosevelt established a rudimentary capacity within the White House to monitor technological developments and their effects: the science and technology committees of the National Resources Planning Board (NRPB). Like Hoover's committees, the NRPB's reports raised the visibility of key technology policy issues but did not advance or implement solutions. The NRPB never developed into the planning apparatus that Roosevelt's reorganization plan for the executive branch envisioned; it was highly unpopular among Congressional conservatives, who finally killed it in 1943.[3]

Two revolutions radically diminished the significance of technology policy planning with respect to economic growth during the 1940s. One was the military revolution of World War II, in which the nation's scientific and technological capacities were fully mobilized for the first time. This mobilization owed much to the brilliant policy entrepreneurship of Vannevar Bush. With the full backing of the president, Bush devised innovative arrangements for engaging academic scientists and high-technology firms in the development of new weapons and instrumentalities of war. Along the way, he became the arbiter of all science and technology policy issues, including efforts to build up the government's capacity to manage civilian technological development in the postwar period. Vice President Henry Wallace, for instance, hoped that the war emergency could be used to break up technological monopolies, to extend technical assistance to small manufacturers, and to justify direct investments in the development of new industries, such as synthetic rubber. But Bush opposed these efforts, and they therefore came to little. The second revolution was the Keynesian revolution, which identified fiscal and monetary causes and solutions for economic problems, and ignored microeconomic factors such as the pace and direction of technological innovation. Authority for macroeconomic policy in the executive branch rested in the Bureau of the Budget (BoB), which had inherited the remnants of the NRPB, and the Council of Economic Advisors (CEA), which was established in the Executive Office of the President (EOP) in 1946.[4]

For much of the postwar period, economic policy meant macroeconomic policy; microeconomic policy, including civilian technology policy, was given short shrift. National security concerns dominated the federal technology agenda. Successive presidents developed management capacities in order to adjudicate technical disputes among the national security agencies and to formulate, legitimize, and promote new technological initiatives that they hoped would help to win the Cold War. These developments culminated in the appointment of a special assistant to the president for science and technology (a position which became known colloquially as the president's science advisor) and a President's Science Advisory Committee (PSAC) in 1957, and in the establishment of the Office of Science and Technology (OST) in the EOP in 1962. The authority of the science advisor, PSAC, and OST rose, and ultimately fell, primarily on the basis of their relationship with the president on national security issues, although they could and did get involved in other issues from time to time. Occasional efforts to focus federal technology policy on economic issues in the 1950s, 1960s, and early 1970s typically (although not always) ran into insuperable opposition from the BoB (renamed the Office of Management and Budget [OMB] in 1970), or from Congress.[5]

President Richard Nixon abolished the White House special assistant post and PSAC and transferred OST's duties to the National Science Foundation in 1973. Nixon wanted his scientific advisors to be loyal to the administration's policy positions and was infuriated by public criticisms of the supersonic transport (SST) program and the Anti-Ballistic Missile (ABM) program by some members of PSAC. The president's reorganization of the science advisory apparatus prompted vigorous objections from the scientific community, a reaction that contributed to the establishment by statute of the Office of Science and Technology Policy (OSTP) in the EOP in 1976. Under President Jimmy Carter and his science advisor, Frank Press, OSTP began to take a more active interest in technology and the economy than had OST. Press, for instance, recommended the interagency policy review that produced two major packages of industrial innovation initiatives that President Carter submitted to Congress in 1979 and 1980.

President Ronald Reagan, by contrast, had little interest in this sort of microeconomic intervention. His economic revitalization program was built around broad tax cuts; technological dynamism was expected to flow from the incentives to private enterprise that this policy supplied. Reagan tapped a relatively obscure physicist from the defense laboratory system, George Keyworth, as science advisor. In keeping with Keyworth's strengths and the president's priorities, OSTP returned to the traditional emphasis on national security issues in the Reagan years.[6]

President George Bush appointed a science advisor, D. Allan Bromley, who was more inclined to take the initiative in civilian technology policy than Keyworth or William Graham (who had followed Keyworth in the post). Bromley established an Industrial Technology Division of OSTP for the first time. He also revived the Federal Coordinating Council for Science, Engineering, and Technology (FCCSET), composed of representatives of the major science and technology agencies. Bromley's FCCSET devised the "crosscut" process, in which the Council identified program areas of interest to several agencies, developed interagency coordinating structures for them, and recommended budget increases. Crosscut program areas included high performance computing and communication, advanced materials, biotechnology, and advanced manufacturing, among others. However, most of President Bush's senior advisors, particularly Richard Darman, the director of OMB, were far less enthusiastic about these initiatives and far more powerful than Bromley. Darman and his colleagues agreed that technological innovation was critical for economic growth, but they bridled at pressure from the Democratic majority in Congress to identify and target "critical technologies," a term that Bromley endorsed. To the extent that Bromley succeeded in getting the FCCSET technology crosscuts included in the administration's budgets, the senior White House staff considered them to be preemptive concessions to Congressional Democrats, rather than true expressions of administration policy. A similar dynamic enveloped Bromley's attempt to issue a formal technology policy. A document entitled "U.S. Technology Policy" came forth from OSTP, but its influence was modest.[7]

The First Clinton Administration's Ambitions

Governor Bill Clinton's 1992 presidential campaign issue strategy was famously summarized as "it's the economy, stupid." The Democratic candidate accused the Bush administration of apathy and inactivity across a wide economic policy front. Drawing heavily on ideas that had already been advanced in Congress, including many that were championed by Senator Al Gore, the Clinton-Gore campaign added technology policy to its national economic strategy in September, 1992. The campaign statement said: "America can compete and win, but only if we have a positive vision guiding our economic policies. Leadership in developing and commercializing new technologies is critical to regaining industrial leadership." After the election, the campaign promises were refined into an official policy document, titled "Technology for America's Economic Growth: A New Direction to Build Economic Strength" and issued by the new president and vice president just a month after their inauguration.[8]

The Clinton-Gore policy proposed major shifts in the composition of federal research and development (R&D) spending, most notably by raising the share of civilian and dual-use R&D spending to 50 percent of the total. Among the favored programs were the Advanced Technology Program (ATP) of the National Institute of Standards and Technology (NIST), the Technology Reinvestment Project (TRP) of the Defense Advanced Research Projects Agency (DARPA, which was to drop the word "Defense" from its name and become ARPA), the Manufacturing Extension Partnership (MEP), a variety of computing and communications projects comprising much of the "national information infrastructure" (NII) initiative, and SEMATECH. (These programs are discussed in more detail in chapters 6, 7, 10, 13 and 15 of this volume.) The policy also promised a range of non-spending initiatives, in such areas as taxation, antitrust, trade, education, and environmental and safety regulation, to speed the pace of technological innovation.

To carry out these plans, "Technology for America's Economic Growth" proposed "major changes in the way we manage our efforts ... to ensure the highest possible return on our investments and to ensure that tax, regulatory and other efforts reinforce instead of frustrate our work." One institution that the policy aimed to take advantage of was the National Economic Council (NEC). Established at the very outset of the administration, the NEC would, its designers hoped, ultimately rival the National Security Council (NSC) in stature. Composed of Cabinet and ranking White House officials and chaired by the president, the NEC had a mandate to integrate international and domestic economic policy issues, coordinate policy development, set the economic agenda for the president, and ensure that his decisions were carried out. Like the NSC, the NEC was managed by an assistant to the president who had wide authority and direct access. Robert Rubin of Goldman Sachs was appointed to this position in December 1992. The "charter" of the NEC, an executive order issued on January 25, 1993, explicitly included technology policy in its jurisdiction, a domain that was affirmed in "Technology for America's Economic Growth." The NEC staff comprised some twenty professionals (the NSC, by contrast, had well over 100), hired primarily for their political and policy process management skills.[9]

The new administration also promised to "reinvigorate" OSTP. President Clinton appointed a science advisor, John H. Gibbons, four months earlier in his administration than Bush had appointed Bromley. Gibbons' appointment "shattered tradition" (according to the *Washington Post*), because he had spent the previous decade in Washington, directing the Congressional Office of Technology Assessment (OTA), rather than in a research university, national laboratory, or corporate R&D operation. Gibbons was seen as more politically savvy, for better or worse, than his predecessors. He was closely linked to the vice president, who was assigned overall responsibility for directing science and technology policy. The new science advisor retained the basic organizational structure and staffing pattern for OSTP that Bromley had established, including designating one of OSTP's four divisions to focus on technology. It was widely assumed that this division's duties would absorb much of Gibbons' attention.[10]

"Technology for America's Economic Growth" stated that FCCSET would be "strengthened." In November 1993, after a major investment of political capital by the science advisor, FCCSET was officially upgraded to become the new National Science and

Technology Council (NSTC). The NSTC paralleled the NEC and NSC in form as well as in its initials; it was composed of Cabinet officers and agency heads, chaired by the president, managed by an assistant to the president (Gibbons), and authorized to formulate Presidential Review Directives (PRDs) and Presidential Decision Directives (PDDs). Gibbons pictured the newly-established Council as a "virtual agency." Its work was to be done mainly by nine subcabinet interagency committees, which were co-chaired and supported by OSTP and agency personnel. The Technology Division of OSTP was given responsibility for four of these committees, which covered civilian industrial technology, education and training R&D, information and communication R&D, and transportation R&D. Given the tight fiscal environment, the most significant implicit goal of the NSTC was to settle interagency disputes over R&D spending before they reached OMB in the normal budget process. As Associate Director of OSTP for Technology Lionel Johns put it in late 1994, "NSTC is inventing new ways of establishing R&D priorities."[11]

OMB retained its broad-ranging influence in the new administration. The budget struggles that characterized the Bush years had, if anything, enhanced OMB's power. Its authority stretched far beyond the budget, officially encompassing proposed legislation, regulations, and Congressional testimony by administration officials, and actually encompassing just about anything. OMB's professional staff, which does not turn over with the change of administrations, has a deep knowledge of federal programs; as the EOP's main institutional memory, OMB had informational as well as structural advantages over other EOP organizations, particularly at the start of the new administration. Leon Panetta, whom Clinton appointed to direct OMB, had no particular interest in technology policy, but his organization was sure to be involved in it.

By contrast Laura Tyson, Clinton's choice as chair of the CEA, had (like her predecessor, Michael Boskin) a long-standing interest in the linkages between technology, public policy, and economic growth. Although Tyson frequently acted as an advocate for the administration's technology program, the institutional responsibilities and *modus operandi* of CEA were not slated to change, limiting Tyson's engagement in technology policy.

The entire process of reorganizing the technology policy-making apparatus was affected by the president's promise to reduce the White House staff by 25 percent. This reduction, depending on how it was defined and implemented,[12] had two potential effects. One possibility was that the White House would be less capable of making and overseeing technology policy. Another was that it would be forced to rely more heavily on the operating agencies for this work. In the latter case, much of the work would fall to the Technology Administration in the Department of Commerce, which was headed up by Undersecretary for Technology Mary Good. In this job, Good was responsible for implementing some of the main programmatic elements of the Clinton-Gore policy, including ATP and MEP, and could draw upon a forty-person Office of Technology Policy (OTP). In the NSTC framework, Good co-chaired the Committee on Civilian Industrial Technology with Johns.

With this set of management and coordination bodies in place, the new administration appeared to have undertaken a reform of the technology policy process as extensive as its reform of the content of that policy. Its larger commitments to economic growth and the specific campaign promises on technology policy's role in economic growth motivated these undertakings. The new institutional framework, however, was never fully utilized, nor, in my view, was it likely to have worked well if it had been fully utilized. Some of its components, on the other hand, seem to have been successful experiments that deserve to be carried on.

The First Clinton Administration: A Tentative Assessment

Although the president abandoned much of his ambitious investment agenda in 1993 in order to bring down the deficit and interest rates, he was, like most presidents, careful to follow through (or at least to attempt to follow through) on most of his specific campaign promises. In the first two years of the Clinton administration, programs like ATP, TRP, MEP, and the information infrastructure-related programs did experience the large budget increases that had been proposed in February 1993. The president went to the mat for his technology policy in the conflict with the Republican

Congress over the budget in the winter of 1995–96. Perhaps the biggest unkept promise was equalizing the ratio of federal non-defense (including dual-use) and defense R&D spending; after moving toward 50:50 through fiscal 1996, it slipped back to favor defense as the Republicans exerted their legislative authority. Overall, though, given the stringency of the discretionary budget, R&D spending did relatively well in the first term in the eyes of observers on both sides of the political aisle.[13]

The process by which the campaign promises were redeemed and by which new initiatives in civilian technology policy were developed as the initial agenda items were completed was, however, far from the model outlined at the outset of the administration. By all accounts, the chaotic nature of policy-making in the Clinton White House has not been confined to technology policy. This "adhocracy" (to borrow a term from Roger Porter) reflected the president's decision-making style, the unusually turbulent politics of the 104th Congress and, perhaps, the self-inflicted wound of White House staff cuts.[14] Vice President Gore, to whom technology policy was delegated, might have preferred a more structured decision-making process but, if so, he was swept up in the tide. On a few initiatives with which the vice president was personally affiliated, such as the NII and the Partnership for a New Generation of Vehicles (PNGV), his office played an integral role in all phases of the policy process. More typically, however, its participation was sporadic.

The NEC may plausibly be compared to the NSC, although it certainly never acquired the breadth of jurisdiction over economic policy issues that the NSC had over security issues. The president relied heavily on a process organized by the NEC in making the key decisions on the 1993 economic package, for instance, but the Council was largely shut out of the development of the president's health care plan, despite the plan's enormous economic and budgetary implications.[15] The NEC principals, who meet regularly, have rarely, if ever, addressed civilian technology policy issues. Meetings convened by NEC deputies have effectively resolved some issues in this area, for instance, at the intersection of technology and trade policy. The NEC's most important impacts on technology policy, however, have been the result of the sustained interest of a few members of its 20-person staff. These staff members act more as policy entrepreneurs than as convenors or "honest brokers" of agency interests, as the economic assistant and his or her (Tyson replaced Rubin in this job in 1995) deputies have sometimes been described. They have connections on Capitol Hill and to the political side of the White House, which assist them in devising strategy and gaining allies. They can also draw on the clout of their superiors at NEC. Backed by this authority, the NEC staff was able to exert some leverage on OMB and the operating agencies. Several of the first-term initiatives were spearheaded at this level. However, a few professionals, no matter how hard they work, can only do so much. As the need grew to conceive, develop, and execute new agenda items, beyond those inherited from the pre-Clinton Congress, the NEC's lack of analytical capability and staff support became an increasingly severe constraint.

Early in the term, OSTP, too, seemed to be very influential in technology policy-making as it related to the economy. A report in *Science* claimed that Gibbons met with the president nearly every day. OSTP took the leading role in the establishment of the PNGV, the administration's first major technology policy initiative, which involved negotiations at the very highest levels. But OSTP has not lived up to its early billings. Gibbons is not perceived to wield much clout in the White House. OSTP has focused much of its energy on the federal R&D budget, but its influence has been modest by most accounts. The guidance issued annually at the beginning of the budget process under the signature of the science advisor and the director of OMB is so general as to justify almost anything the agencies are doing. A great deal of OSTP staff time has been absorbed administering the NSTC committees, which have not generally been able to exert influence on the R&D budget commensurate with this effort. OSTP's participation in reviews of agency budgets, which is largely at the discretion of OMB, has been more effective, and OSTP deserves a share of the credit for the good showing of the R&D accounts in the Clinton budget proposals, including its technology R&D programs. The complaints that OSTP has been less than vigilant on behalf of R&D spending, which sometimes issue from the research community, are not shared by those inside the policy process; if anything, OSTP's views are sometimes discounted as those of a special pleader representing this community.[16]

A critique more commonly offered by observers outside OSTP is that it lacks the entrepreneurial capabilities necessary to succeed in an "adhocracy." It is not oriented enough toward problems that ought to be of pressing concern to the president; it has little feel for political strategy; and it lacks the ideas and clout to bring the relevant players to the table. To some extent, this critique misses OSTP's unsung achievements, particularly in heading off (or trying to head off) the adoption of technically misconceived ideas. Avoiding mistakes is an essential goal of OSTP, but is as difficult to take credit for as avoiding budget cuts. However, given its weak structural position in the EOP and its feeble political constituency, OSTP's effectiveness depends largely on its ability to work with more powerful organizations, such as the NEC and OMB. Despite some important successes operating in this mode, such as the NII and the educational technology initiatives, OSTP's credibility with these important players seems to have declined precipitously over the first Clinton term.

Ironically, one major cause of this decline was the NSTC, which was supposed to enhance the authority of OSTP and the science advisor, but has not developed into a high-level policy-making body. Despite its grandiose claims, the NSTC does not merit serious comparison to the NEC or the NSC. It has met just once as a council of departmental secretaries and agency heads, a meeting that was scheduled at the last minute and which involved the president for only half an hour, according to news reports.[17] The science advisor's formal authority to draft Presidential Review Directives (PRDs) and Presidential Decision Directives (PDDs) on behalf of the NSTC has not been exercised very much, either, as Table 17-1 shows. Few of the PRDs or PDDs bear on technology policy as it relates to the economy, and even fewer pertain to major issues in this policy area.

Since top agency officials are rarely involved in the NSTC's deliberations and the science advisor is unable to take its work directly to the president, the products of the nine NSTC subcabi-net-level committees and its 60-odd working groups[18] must be advanced through OMB, another policy council, or through informal persuasion of senior members of the administration. The committees got badly bogged down in the attempt to manage the

Table 17-1 NSTC Presidential Review Directives and Presidential Decision Directives

NSTC Presidential Review Directives (PRDs) (through 12/31/96)
1. Federal Laboratories
2. Space Policy
3. Global Positioning System Policy
4. University-Government Partnership

NSTC Presidential Decision Directives (PDDs) (through 12/31/96)
1. Establishment of Presidential Review and Decision Series
2. Convergence of U.S. Polar-Orbiting Operational Environmental Satellite Systems
3. Landsat Remote Sensing Strategy
4. National Space Transportation Policy
5. Guidelines for Federal Laboratory Reform
6. U.S. Global Positioning System Policy
7. Emerging Infectious Diseases
8. National Space Policy

Source: NSTC Home Page, <http://www.whitehouse.gov/WH/EOP/OSTP/NSTC/html/1996_Accomplishments.html>, March 20, 1997.

federal R&D budget, which one insider labels a "$73 billion cross-cut." This effort ignored the reality of the budget process, in which each agency is reviewed by OMB in a separate "stovepipe." OMB makes most of the decisions within the "stovepipes" and, unless special procedures are put in place, does not trade off the R&D programs of one agency against those of another. Although by some accounts OMB was initially enthusiastic about NSTC, it quickly became disillusioned by NSTC's cumbersome style and its pretentious claims. Without OMB's commitment and without an alternative channel to the top, the committees have largely been unable to make priorities and enforce them on the agencies. The NSTC committees' strategic plans, which consume staff time and energy, lack bite, too. They seem to deserve the epithet of "strategic description" that one observer applied to them.

Despite this bureaucratic burden, which has reduced the level of agency participation in the NSTC process, some NSTC committees have become effective devices for organizing interagency discussion and policy coordination at the deputy level or below. This is an important achievement; mutual ignorance among agencies engaged in related tasks is still far too common. The NSTC Committee on Civilian Industrial Technology[19] (CCIT), with Undersecretary Good in the lead, for instance, has overseen the implementation of PNGV (although it did not initiate or develop this program), an effort that involves seven departments and independent agencies as well as the NEC, OMB, OSTP, and the Office of the Vice President. The Committee on Information and Communication R&D (CIC) saw to conclusion the High Performance Computing and Communication (HPCC) initiative begun by FCCSET in the Bush administration and is now overseeing the Next Generation Internet initiative, which won scarce new dollars in the administration's initial fiscal 1998 budget proposal. In transportation, the NSTC supported the vice president's review of aviation safety and is now monitoring the implementation of its recommendations. As Table 17-1 shows, two of the four NSTC PRDs and five of its seven PDDs have related to space policy, in which it has been instrumental in brokering agreements between defense and civilian agencies. The NSTC rubric has also been used to reach out to constituencies concerned about science and technology policy, in order to gather input and marshal support for administration initiatives.[20]

Overall, however, rather than mobilizing agency resources to develop and advance the president's technology policy agenda, the NSTC often engendered confusion and blocked communication. The CIC, for instance, at least by one account, disrupted the functioning of the existing HPCC interagency process at first, although this problem was later rectified. Similarly, although the CCIT has carried out some significant tasks, it is not perceived (at least by some of its participants) as an effective means to advance their ideas. It is certainly true that agencies have parochial interests in their own programs and constituencies and will by their nature complain about the reception they receive in the White House. Nonetheless, the Clinton White House seems to have missed opportunities to take more effective advantage of the rest of the federal government's technology policy-making apparatus.

The same criticism applies to advisory and analytical resources. OSTP's two auxiliary organizations, the President's Council of Advisors on Science and Technology (PCAST) and the Critical Technologies Institute (CTI), have largely been neglected. Clinton's PCAST did not hold its first meeting until October 1994, and few resources have been devoted to it. Although PCAST has had some important achievements in other areas, such as the management of weapons-grade fissile material, it has been little involved in civilian technology policy. CTI, which was established by Congress in 1992 to serve as an institutional memory and analytical resource for OSTP, seems to have been absorbed, like NSTC, largely in attempting to manage the R&D budget. CTI, for example, developed the RADIUS database, the first comprehensive, real-time accounting system for all federal R&D projects, to this end. CTI has not been used as much for long-term policy analyses as its designers expected.

The Second Term: Suggestions

The American people passed favorable judgment on President Clinton in November 1996. The White House has not, however, taken the president's reelection as a signal simply to continue business as usual. The president has put together a new management team, and the new team has, in turn, begun to tinker with organizational structures within the EOP. Such tinkering cannot take the place of presidential discipline in decision-making nor can it substitute for good chemistry and trust among the key decision-makers around the president. Moreover, the pressures are so great and the range of issues and interests so varied and interrelated around the Oval Office that to attempt to specify precisely (much less legislate) the exact jurisdictional boundaries of the various organizations that serve the president would be foolhardy. Nonetheless, organizational changes may well enhance the capacity of the president to manage the nation's technology policy effectively. I have three suggestions to this end: strengthening the connections between NSTC's technology policy committees and the NEC, focusing the budget and oversight roles of these committees more tightly, and enhancing OSTP's analytical and advisory capacities.

NSTC and NEC: Stronger Connections

The NSTC has not and cannot become a strong policy council. Too much of the turf that might provide a claim on the time and energy of its principals is already staked out by the economic, security, and domestic councils and by OMB. The remaining issues on which NSTC might conceivably exercise jurisdiction in policy development are rarely important enough to merit presidential attention. If the science advisor were more entrepreneurially minded than Gibbons has been, one can easily imagine NSTC decisions leading to conflicts among the policy councils and end runs to the president. In a more structured White House, the NSTC would probably fragment the policy process unnecessarily. In the current setting, however, the NSTC may usefully generate an occasional PRD or PDD on issues that would otherwise slip through the cracks of the other policy councils.

The NSTC, then, is not the main channel for most technology policy issues that bear on economic growth. The NEC, as its "charter" holds, is the proper venue to consider policy options that aim at accelerating technological innovation and to evaluate them in the light of other approaches to economic policy. There may be tradeoffs between technology programs and other means of achieving prosperity that ought to be considered; there may also be complementarities, for instance, between trade policy and technology policy or between economic regulation (or deregulation) and technology policy, that ought to be taken advantage of. International economic relations increasingly involve technological issues, such as intellectual property and standards, and NEC has the mandate to blend international and domestic concerns, as the global market demands.

The NSTC and OSTP had some of their best moments in the first term when they fed into the NEC process, particularly in the area of information technology policy. The NEC connection brings technology policy initiatives to White House staff members who can mobilize political resources and helps make them credible to the Cabinet officers who will be asked to carry them out. This connection should be strengthened. Although the NEC does not have an institutionalized commitment to technology policy, the science advisor does have a seat on the council. He could act more assertively to claim this seat and direct the NSTC's technology policy committees to orient their output to the NEC. Implementing the Carnegie Commission's proposal of "double-hatting" the director of the OSTP Technology Division as a staff member of the

NEC might facilitate this reorientation.[21] OSTP staff would still be able to convene interagency committees under the NSTC label. With the science advisor speaking for it in the NEC process, the NSTC would operate more like the "virtual agency" that some claim it to be than it does now.

It is true that this structure politicizes technology policy-making. I believe this is inevitable. The NEC is a creature of the president, and if the president rejects technology policy, the NEC will ignore it. But this is equally true of the NSTC. It is probably impossible to institutionalize any particular economic policy option in the White House. We may hope that technology is now recognized to be so vital to economic growth that economic policy-makers will be unable to ignore it. Perhaps it is no accident that several of the recent CEA chairs have had an established professional interest in the economics of innovation.

NSTC and OMB: Tighter Focus

Many in the science and technology policy community initially saw NSTC as a "glorified FCCSET," with a primary focus on interagency program coordination and budgeting in support of OMB. In this role, NSTC has not worked as well as FCCSET, because it tried to do too much and spread its resources too thin. The NSTC's efforts to manage the federal R&D budget as a whole were misguided. Its approach assumed that the decisions that were necessary would trade off one science and technology program against another. This assumption is flawed; R&D programs are traded off against other programs in the same agency or appropriations cluster, some of which may be R&D programs, but many of which are not. What is needed is a structure that compares scientific and technological approaches with other means of achieving particular ends. In the case of economic growth, technology policy should be compared or combined with deficit reduction, traditional infrastructure spending, export promotion, deregulation. and other economic policy mechanisms. The NEC might be able to do this, given its broad mandate. The NSTC can not.[22]

Nonetheless, in a few priority areas, in which agency programs overlap or can be made more complementary, the White House needs something like the NSTC committees, convened by OSTP, to arbitrate and provide advice to OMB and the president. Although it has the power to make most of the relevant decisions, OMB lacks the technical sophistication to perform these budget and oversight functions as effectively as they ought to be performed. To be sure, this aspect of the NSTC committees' work is likely to be less pleasant, in the fiscal environment for domestic discretionary programs that is expected in the second Clinton term, than it was in the first term. The committees should not be asked to do too much, perhaps no more than a couple of tasks at any one time. There is too little staff capacity and, more importantly, too few carrots to offer (and sticks to shake at) the agency participants. Nonetheless, despite the budget situation, there is still room for policy entrepreneurship on the margin, as suggested by the recent educational technology initiative, which aims to connect schools and libraries to the national information infrastructure and to give students and teachers training and tools to take advantage of it. Properly focused, the NSTC committees can be effective instruments for identifying and realizing opportunities for policy innovation.

OSTP: Enhanced Analytical and Advisory Capabilities

OSTP is in a structurally weak position in the White House. It gets clout either by having allies or by having unique knowledge. Yet quite powerful allies such as Vice President Gore have not accorded OSTP very much authority over the past twenty years. Like CEA, OSTP might more effectively "earn its way into the deliberations" (as one old science and technology policy hand put it) in both policy formulation and program oversight if it did more to cultivate its expertise.[23]

The analogy between CEA and OSTP is imperfect: OSTP has management responsibilities that CEA lacks, and it cannot be quite as selective in choosing issues to focus on. Nonetheless, OSTP ought to aim to match CEA's reputation as an office that can convince the president to say "no" to ideas that its analysis reveals to be misguided. (In fact, the science advisor, PSAC, and OST once had such a reputation with respect to the defense agencies in the late 1950s and early 1960s.) It might be advisable for OSTP to conduct technical evaluations that have the potential to torpedo significant R&D programs. A technically-based negative appraisal of one or more such programs would help to bolster OSTP's credibility in the budget process and counteract the impression that it is merely the representative of the research community. On the other hand, through its close contact with the cutting edge of science and technology, OSTP has in the past had and can still have particular value as an "early warning system" for policy problem identification.

There are several sources of expertise that OSTP might draw upon. One is a staff that is freed up from some of the administrative burdens now laid on it by the NSTC. OSTP might also attempt to emulate, with scientists and engineers, CEA's practice of recruiting the top young academic economists in the country to spend a year or two in residence. Such an early socialization into science and technology policy would be very valuable in building a corps of contributors in this area over the long term. The science advisor would have to make a concerted effort to get such a rotation accepted by the young researchers' academic advisors; a stint at OSTP might eventually be seen as a sign of distinction (as a stint at CEA is for economists), rather than time wasted "away from the bench." At more senior levels, of course, it is crucial that OSTP have political knowledge and skills that these young hotshots are unlikely to have.

A second potential source of expertise is PCAST. The resuscitation of PCAST, begun in the last two years of the first term, could fruitfully be extended to technology policy. PCAST provides a mechanism to secure selective input from the private sector at a level higher than that secured by the agencies in their management of technology programs. Such advice might provide both helpful perspectives and political clout, although this advisory process would have to be managed with special care, given the strictures of the Federal Advisory Committee Act (FACA) and the controversy over White House fund-raising practices. The president's recent request that PCAST help to review and evaluate the federal technology partnership programs[24] is a step in the right direction, but it must be backed up with more resources than PCAST has received thus far in this administration.

The Critical Technologies Institute is a third possibility for enhancing OSTP's analytical capabilities. Rather than supporting the White House's management of the federal R&D budget, CTI could be tasked with longer-range analyses, which OSTP cannot conduct given the day-to-day demands of the EOP. The measurement and evaluation issues mentioned by Adam Jaffe in Chapter 3 are potential subjects of such work. CTI can also access expertise outside government without the constraints of FACA. Similar analytical work might be commissioned from the Office of Technology Policy in the Department of Commerce, which aims to track the nation's entire industrial technology base, and from the National Science Board, which has the mandate to oversee the nation's entire scientific program. Although such analyses would probably be perceived as biased within the White House, this perception might be reduced over time with careful management.

Of course, expertise will not by itself win invitations to meetings or open doors. It must be wielded with savvy and with the authority that comes from having direct access to the president. If OSTP hires a chief of staff, as the Carnegie Commission on Science, Technology, and Government recently recommended,[25] the science advisor will be freed up from administrative duties to become more entrepreneurial and exercise those skills that the Clinton White House demands.

Conclusion

The formal organizational structures of the EOP are, by all accounts, less important to effective policy-making than the capabilities and intentions of the people who work within (or around) them. However, a poor organizational scheme can present obstacles to even the most talented and best-intentioned of appointees. The suggestions that I have made attempt to create opportunities where there are now obstacles, within the overall constraints of the president's style. The integration of technology policy with economic policy is not an easy task, and continued organizational evolution on the basis of lessons learned seems to me necessary, defensible, and appropriate.

Acknowledgments

I am particularly grateful to those interviewed for this paper for their time and cooperation, including in many cases extensive comments on drafts. My co-authors in this volume also provided comments, as did Michael Boskin, David Robinson, and Eugene Skolnikoff. Harvey Brooks' comments were, as always, especially helpful. Jeff Livingston and the Competitiveness Policy Council provided research support.

Notes

1. This paper is based on 22 interviews and on published sources. The interviews were conducted on a not-for-attribution basis. I interviewed participants in and observers of the technology policy process from both political parties and from a broad range of organizations within and outside the White House.

2. Harvey Brooks, comment on draft of this paper, March 16, 1997.

3. Ellis W. Hawley, "Herbert Hoover, the Commerce Secretariat, and the Vision of an 'Associative State,' 1921–1928," *Journal of American History*, Vol. 61, No. 1 (June 1974), pp. 116–140; Karl T. Compton, "Put Science to Work!" *Technology Review*, January 1935, pp. 133–135, 152–158; David M. Hart, *Forging the "Postwar Consensus": Science, Technology, and Economic Policy in the United States, 1921–1953* (Princeton, N.J.: Princeton University Press, in press), chaps. 2–4.

4. David Hart, *Forging the "Postwar Consensus,"* chaps. 5–7.

5. John Hart, *The Presidential Branch*, 2nd ed. (Chatham, N.J.: Chatham House, 1995), pp. 96–98; Harvey Averch, *A Strategic Analysis of Science and Technology Policy* (Baltimore: Johns Hopkins University Press, 1985), pp. 56–65.

6. Bruce L.R. Smith, *American Science Policy Since World War II* (Washington, D.C.: Brookings Institution, 1990), pp. 91–93, 116–118, 125–141; Frank Press, "Science and Technology in the White House, 1977–1980, Part I," *Science*, Vol. 211, No. 4962 (January 9, 1981), pp. 139–145.

7. D. Allan Bromley, *The President's Scientists: Reminiscences of a White House Science Advisor* (New Haven: Yale University Press, 1994), chaps. 2–6, 9.

8. "Technology: The Engine of Economic Growth, A National Technology Policy for America," Clinton-Gore Campaign Headquarters, Little Rock, Ark., September 18, 1992; President William J. Clinton and Vice President Albert Gore, Jr., "Technology for America's Economic Growth: A New Direction to Build Economic Strength," February 22, 1993.

9. Clinton and Gore, "Technology for America's Economic Growth," p. 4; I.M. Destler, *The National Economic Council: A Work in Progress* (Washington, D.C.: Institute for International Economics, 1996), pp. 8–10, 24–27; Kenneth I. Juster

and Simon Lazarus, *Making Economic Policy: An Assessment of the National Economic Council* (Washington, D.C.: Brookings, 1997), pp. 5, 65–67; Hart, *The Presidential Branch*, p. 46.

10. "Gibbons Confirmed as President's Science Advisor," *Washington Post*, January 29, 1993, p. A21; Christopher Andrews and Colin Norman, "Jack Gibbons: Plugging Into the Power Structure," *Science*, Vol. 259, No. 5098 (February 19, 1993), pp. 1115–1116.

11. Clinton and Gore, "Technology for America's Economic Growth," p. 9; "A Year as Clinton's Science Adviser: John Gibbons Gives His Account," *Chemical and Engineering News*, April 11, 1994, pp. 20–26; Jeffrey Mervis, "Clinton Moves to Manage Science," *Science*, Vol. 261, No. 5129 (September 24, 1993), pp. 1668–1669; National Science and Technology Council, "1994 NSTC Annual Report" <http://www.whitehouse.gov/WH/EOP/OSTP/NSTC/html/nstc-an.html>, p. 2; Wil Lepkowski, "National Council to Revamp Federal Science and Technology Policy Process," *Chemical and Engineering News*, October 10, 1994, p. 21. The genesis of the NSTC is located by several people that I interviewed in the Carnegie Commission on Science, Technology, and Government; NSTC itself traces its origins to the vice president's National Performance Review. My characterization of budget management as NSTC's "implicit goal" was challenged by several people that I interviewed and supported by several others.

12. Hart, *The Presidential Branch*, pp. 120–122, notes that there was substantial ambiguity in the meaning of the president's promise. Comparing ibid., p. 46, with Bromley, *President's Scientists*, p. 42, suggests that the OSTP staff was not reduced under Clinton; however, such figures are notoriously inaccurate. Several people that I interviewed commented on the effect of the White House staff cuts, although they had no direct basis of comparison with prior administrations so far as I know.

13. National Science Board, *Science and Engineering Indicators 1996* (Washington, D.C.: U.S. Government Printing Office [U.S. GPO], 1996), appendix table 4-29; Kei Koizumi, Albert H. Teich, Stephen D. Nelson, and Bonnie Bisol Cassidy, *Congressional Action on Research and Development in the FY1997 Budget* (Washington, D.C.: American Association for the Advancement of Science, 1996), p. 41; Pete V. Domenici, "The Reality of Science Funding," *Science*, Vol. 273, No. 5280 (September 6, 1996), p. 1319; John H. Gibbons, "FY98 R&D Budget Overview," press release, Office of Science and Technology Policy, February 6, 1997.

14. Roger B. Porter, *Presidential Decision Making: The Economic Policy Board* (New York: Cambridge University Press, 1980), p. 25.

15. Destler, *National Economic Council*, pp. 13–24.

16. Anderson and Norman, "Jack Gibbons"; Harvard University, John F. Kennedy School of Government Case Program, "Partnership for a New Generation of Vehicles," draft of January 16, 1997; Andrew Lawler, "OSTP: A Mixed Midterm Report," *Science*, Vol. 268, No. 5208 (April 14, 1995), pp. 192–194; Wil Lepkowski, "Science Adviser Gibbons Staying Put for Now," *Chemical and Engineering News*, January 20, 1997, p. 10.

17. Jeffrey Mervis, "Clinton Inaugurates Science Council," *Science*, Vol. 265, No. 5169 (July 8, 1994), p. 182.

18. This figure comes from Carnegie Commission on Science, Technology, and Government, *Science and Technology and the President: A Report to the Next Administration* (New York: Carnegie Commission, 1997), p. 18. I thank David Z. Robinson for making an unpublished draft of this study available to me.

19. The CCIT was later rechristened (and is still known as) the Committee on Technological Innovation (CTI), but I will keep the original acronym here to avoid confusion with the Critical Technologies Institute (also known as CTI). Good had prior experience in both the private and public sectors, including service as chair of the National Science Board and on the Bush PCAST.

20. NSTC, "Calendar Year 1995 NSTC Accomplishments," <http://www.whitehouse.gov/WH/EOP/OSTP/NSTC/html/CY95accomp.html>; NSTC, "Accomplishments of the NSTC 1996," <http://www.whitehouse.gov/WH/EOP/OSTP/NSTC/html/1996_Accomplishments.html>, both accessed on March 20, 1997. It should be noted that the NSTC absorbed the National Space Council when it was formed in 1993.

21. Carnegie Commission on Science, Technology, and Government, *Science and Technology and the President*, pp. 20–21.

22. The same argument regarding the divorce of means and ends can be made against a "Department of Science and Technology" and against a unified federal science and technology budget.

23. Philip M. Smith, *The NSB and the Formulation of Science Policy* (Washington, D.C.: National Science Board, 1981), p. 30.

24. President to John A. Young, co-chair, PCAST, January 14, 1997.

25. Carnegie Commission on Science, Technology, and Government, *Science and Technology and the President*, p. 19.

18

Towards a Research and Innovation Policy

Lewis M. Branscomb and James H. Keller

Technology policy is as broad as it is deep. It spans diverse industries, organizations, sectors and processes, as well as a largely disconnected set of policy mechanisms. This project began as an effort to evaluate the Clinton-Gore technology initiatives, a bold, if imperfect, effort to advance economic growth through investment in innovation. In the process of this evaluation, we have constructed a set of six high-level principles for supporting the development of research and innovation for the public good, in support of both federal agency missions and larger national economic objectives.[1] These principles, which are the focus of this chapter, are intended to provide a politically robust platform on which policy development can be based. They are designed to strengthen what has been a difficult effort to balance between maximizing economic objectives and not interfering with private markets. These principles underlie many of the Clinton administration technology programs and policies, but they were not always borne out in the politicized context of program authorization and administration. This concluding chapter seeks to articulate and explore these principles and the tools available to carry them out as a basis for policy development, management, and evaluation.

As described in Chapter 1, the context in which technology development occurs has shifted significantly over the past decade. Globalization, restructuring of industries, and the current political and fiscal climates all give rise to a need for a fundamental rethinking of the federal role in supporting research and fostering innovation. Government policy must look beyond supporting research to providing incentives for private innovation, using the full range of policy tools that we have seen arrayed in promoting information infrastructure (described in Chapter 13 by Brian Kahin). A new, more sophisticated, and more complex role for government is emerging, one that makes better use of resources, and that shares more decision making with states and with the private sector. New policies should focus on long-term investments in knowledge-based infrastructure—the capacity of the entire system of private entrepreneurship, human resources, investment, and advancing frontiers of technical knowledge—using tools that encourage and enable rather than direct the deployment of these assets. Government should look for opportunities to enhance the social capital of our society, to make the emerging networks of firms, universities, states and federal laboratories and agencies into a dynamic, trusted efficient system of creative enterprise (see especially Chapter 4 by Jane Fountain).

The goal of this concluding chapter is to move the debate over the federal role in advancing technological development beyond partisanship, and to focus on defining a basis for federal activity, for both mission needs and economic objectives, that is market-oriented and equitable. The chapter explores the questions: what are the appropriate areas for federal investment? What are the proper roles of the various stakeholders in technology policy—states, universities, national labs, federal agencies, and industry? What are the institutional mechanisms through which technology policy can be managed? These questions are addressed in the form of six principles for a research and innovation policy which we present to guide both a reexamination and restructuring of existing policies and programs and the design and development of new technology initiatives. Following a discussion of each of these principles, we describe how the principles can be applied to guide federal funding, and then turn to the Advanced Technology Program to give a specific example of what such an enabling, research-driven approach to innovation would look like.

The Six Principles

We offer six principles to help policy makers determine useful answers to questions related to program structure and purpose.

- *Encourage Private Innovation.* Government should leverage private investment in innovation to spur economic growth, improve living standards, and accomplish important government missions by creating incentives for and reducing barriers to technology development and research-based innovation.

- *Emphasize Basic Technology Research.* Government direct investment in science and technology should focus on long-range, broadly useful research—in basic technology as well as basic science—that can produce benefits far in excess of what the private sector can capture for itself.

- *Facilitate Access to New and Old Technologies.* Policy-makers should promote use and absorption of technology across the economic spectrum, with special attention to the role of higher education, the states, and networks of firms and other institutions.

- *Use All Policy Tools, Not Just R&D.* Policy-makers should utilize the full range of relevant policy tools, such as economic policy, regulatory reform, standards, procurement, and intellectual property rights, in varying mixes, as appropriate for different industries, technologies, and regions.

- *Leverage Globalization of Innovation.* The U.S. government should encourage U.S.-led innovation abroad as well as at home, enabling U.S. firms to get maximum benefit from worldwide sources of technical knowledge, while keeping the United States the preferred location for investments in research and innovation.

- *Improve Government Effectiveness in Policy Development.* Government should work to become a stable and reliable partner in a long-range national research effort, by creating more effective institutions for policy development, strong and stable nonpartisan support, and stronger participation by the states in policy formulation and execution.

Encourage Private Innovation through Public-Private Partnerships

Private firms perform three-quarters of all the R&D in America.[2] They transform new scientific and engineering ideas into the products and services from which wealth is created, and are prime sources of innovation when the government is the primary consumer of the innovation. Technology policy should be structured to foster an economic climate that favors private investment in R&D and the effective and innovative use and absorption of technology by firms and organizations. With this in mind, federal interventions must encourage private investment, rather than substitute for it. They should favor the use of market mechanisms, such as tax incentives and creating markets for non-market entities (e.g., tradable permits for sulfur emissions), and not rely solely on direct government funding of R&D. However, substantial direct investments in research by government are also required, because private firms tend to underinvest in both long-range research of economic value and research to meet public purposes.

Many of the policies for encouraging private innovation are indirect. These policy tools are discussed below. But there is an important middle ground in policy, especially when the government has a job to do that calls for innovative solutions, such as promoting good health, protecting the national security, or cleaning up the environment. In the past, government has funded the total cost of research in the captive defense industry, while using regulation to impose the cost of more benign environmental technology on commercial industry. More recently policy makers have been looking for ways to leverage private investment to get the public's needs fulfilled in both of these areas, and perhaps in others as well. The use of public-private partnerships (as in the Advanced Technology Program described in Chapter 6, the Technology Reinvestment Project described in Chapter 7, the Partnership for a New Generation of Vehicles described in Chapter 15, the Environmental Technology Initiative described in Chapter 11, and Cooperative Research and Development Agreement programs described in Chapter 9) has begun to fill that middle ground.

The Defense Department's dual-use technology acquisition strategy (discussed in Chapter 7 by Linda Cohen) is a particular form of public-private partnership in which the DoD shares the cost of development of defense-relevant technology in private firms, thus leveraging the firm's incentive to develop the technology for competitive markets. This strategy can be applied to the technology missions of other agencies as well. Instead of government paying one hundred percent of the cost of technologies it may need to fulfill its own operational needs, government should leverage private investment that most nearly satisfies those needs. This can be done through cost-shared investment in technology in anticipation of both public and private use. This strategy does raise difficult problems of accounting for the distribution of public and private costs and benefits. It requires careful management of cost-sharing policy. But if America is to continue to embrace smaller, more agile government and is to rely more on private innovation for addressing public issues, it will have to be able to manage the financial arrangements in public-private partnerships.

Cost Sharing Arrangements

Cost-sharing should be a basic precept of federal technology initiatives where both public and private value is produced. The division of investment between public and private sources should reflect the relative public and private interests in the work. Basic science and technology research performed in universities and in independent laboratories, which rarely share in the economic benefits, should be fully funded by government in most cases. In contrast, public-private partnerships, especially those from which the private partner expects to derive a near-term commercial benefit, should require investment by both parties. Requirements for industry cost-sharing might be reduced in those cases where firms allow or even encourage the technology to be made widely available, for example through a consortium of participating institutions or by treating research results as non-proprietary. Industry cost shares will be greater when the investment area is closer to early commercialization.

In the public-private partnerships created by various federal agencies, these arrangements have been established *ad hoc,* with little uniformity as to cost-sharing policies. Overall federal guidelines for the establishment and management of public-private S&T partnerships are needed to ensure that cost-sharing is equitable, that technological development goals are given the best chance for success, and that intellectual property and diffusion issues are properly addressed. These guidelines should cover appropriate conditions for use of partnerships, criteria for degrees of cost sharing, policies for recapture of public investment, criteria for partner selection, criteria for allowing federal partnerships with single firms (rather than consortia), policies for disposition of intellectual property, policies for participation of partners with significant foreign ties, and policies obligating partners to cooperate with outcomes assessments after the partnership is dissolved. These policies should be designed so that they can be tracked by an entity within the federal government, such as the Office of Management and Budget, to ensure that abuses do not occur.

The funding ratios of federal technology programs should reflect the minimum public investment needed to entice private participants to develop technology that serves the public interest. The optimum ratio will shift from project to project and in some cases during the life cycle of a project. If, as we recommend in the next section, government shifts its emphasis to more basic technology, firms may be more willing to share the results and the funding ratio may reflect the increasing public stake in the outcome.

Emphasize Basic Technology Research

Long recognized as an important and appropriate role for government, investments in basic scientific research have made the United States the preeminent scientific power in the world. However, the creation of new industries and new tools, materials, processes and systems thinking takes more than science. These capabilities, and indeed all technical progress, are enabled through research in "basic technologies," a concept explored by Lewis Branscomb in Chapter 5. Creative research on new kinds of materials, new processes and ways of exploring and measuring, new ways of doing and making things: this is the world of basic technological research. It includes activities such as the research behind the blue laser, the exploration of biosensors, and the process of polymer cross-linkage. Basic technological research also creates tools and data about properties of matter, and about materials and processes on which the progress of both science and of technology depend. It defines an area for federal investment that starts early in the innovation process and leads to knowledge that is often non-proprietary and widely diffusable, though it will clearly lead, eventually, to industrial applications. Basic science and basic technology are inextricably linked and dependent upon one another.

When the political debate divides the world into "R" and "D," putting basic scientific research on the one side and lumping applied research and development together on the other side, a huge and vitally important area of basic technology is left out of consideration. Many people assume that if the work is not basic science, it must be commercial development and that therefore government has no business investing in it. This assumption leaves out a large gray area we are calling "basic technology research," in which both government and industry have an interest.

Companies have become increasingly reluctant to put resources into basic technological research that is long term, high-risk or both, even though this research might eventually pay handsome returns to the firm and to society as a whole. Increasingly, as product development cycles shorten and competitive pressures rise, companies look outside for the innovations that basic research makes possible. As they "outsource" innovation to their supply chains and downsize their corporate research laboratories, the focus shifts to nearer time-horizons, perhaps increasing short-term profits, but at the expense of intellectual assets for future growth. If the United States is not the most fertile seed bed for such innovation, companies will—and do—look overseas.

As discussed in Chapter 5, and again at the end of this chapter, government should invest in research— both scientific and technological—where the expectations for long-term public benefit exceed expectations for private returns to the research performer. This is the correct answer to the question, "When is it appropriate for the government to subsidize research?" How such research investment is allocated between more theoretical and speculative (opportunity-driven) research and need-driven (but not privately appropriable) research will depend upon the missions of the research funding agencies and the decisions of the Congress and the president about the relative urgency of those needs. The discussion of these topics will be easier to understand if, instead of debating about government roles and investments in science versus those in technology, we discussed resources and goals for publicly funded research, versus a variety of incentives for promoting innovation.

Facilitating Access to New and Old Technologies

The best science in the world is of little economic value if it cannot be accessed, understood, and put to use. Thus a cornerstone of any policy to promote innovation must be helping users acquire technical knowledge and skill. Firms need access to all available technology, not just the most recently created knowledge. They also need access to a workforce capable of utilizing available innovations. The development of a capable and competitive workforce is a key factor in any nation's business climate and is a vital area of public concern. Many small firms have only limited access to the science that would help them choose wisely among technologies and to make effective use of them. Public investments in technology utilization, usually made at the state and local level, have proved to have high economic leverage. The federal government, working closely with states and regions, should develop closer links between technology policy and workforce training and development. This will help spur the diffusion and use of technology and create strong links between technology and the creation of high-wage, high-skill jobs.

A historical strength of U.S. science and technology policy has been the decentralization of initiative both among and within federal agencies, and—more importantly—to universities, government, and private laboratories and industry. Today, state governments are better prepared than in the past to play a growing role in this decentralization of initiative and of program management (as Christopher Coburn and Duncan Brown describe in Chapter 16). As choices, guided by national goals, are made within that decentralized decision process, we urge more attention to input from the intended beneficiaries of federal policy.

Firms in specific industry sectors tend to cluster regionally, generating an opportunity for alliances between state governments and industry consortia for collaboration with federal agencies in technology-based development activities. States vary greatly in their needs and approaches to technology-based development.

Federal collaborations with states should have enough flexibility to respond to these local and regional differences. The U.S. Innovation Partnership, which links federal research and innovation policy-making to states through the National Governors' Association, provides an important new mechanism for coordinating federal and state-level policies. Increasing recognition of the significance of regional economic specialization makes the idea of geographically defined programs of development rational for economic as well as political reasons.

The Manufacturing Extension Partnership (MEP) is an example of an effective federal-state partnership in technology diffusion and regional economic development (see Chapter 10 by Philip Shapira). Federal policy-makers should learn from the success of this model when developing or redesigning other federal technology efforts, particularly those conducted in collaboration with the states. Following the principles for cost-sharing outlined above, the federal-state funding ratios and the income from user charges should reflect the benefits each sector can expect to enjoy in pursuit of national and local public interests and the private interest of the assisted firms.

Employing Consortia to Accelerate Diffusion and Public Benefits

Cost-shared partnerships between government and industry require a delicate balance in allocating costs to the participants, and a similar balance must be struck in the flow of information. Where one side gains almost all the benefits, the balance is easily obtained: for example, when government funds the entire cost of basic science it expects the results to be published, while a firm that develops technology for specific commercial products will normally keep the technical knowledge to itself. Where both government and the firm will benefit, both the costs and the knowledge may be shared in proportion to their interest, investments, and willingness to share results with others. Since the government's interest is strongly biased toward diffusion and utilization of the knowledge on a broad basis, government will expect the results from its partnership investment to produce broad public benefits. This can be accomplished through sharing the results with other firms, or at least commercializing them in ways that rapidly bring benefits to society and not just to the participating firm. Consortia can be used to share costs and to stimulate the absorption and use of science and technology in a manner that mitigates the problems of market distortion and fairness.

Congress encouraged the formation of R&D consortia through the Cooperative Research Act of 1984 and provided for their participation in the Advanced Technology Program in the 1988 Omnibus Trade and Competitiveness Act. Consortia stimulate the diffusion of technology through the movement of people and the sharing of information among firms. They may also generate competitive pressures which tend to keep research less proprietary and more long-range in nature. Networks of firms and other research institutions will be more likely to diffuse research results rapidly and will generate less concern that federal R&D expenditures might disrupt markets or respond to political pressures. Government participation in such networks also reduces the danger of anti-competitive behavior within the consortium.

Some other countries, even many that are smaller than the United States, have much more experience with industrial consortia, usually in form of industrial associations that operate R&D organizations for the common benefit of their members. In some highly developed smaller countries like Switzerland, firms' membership in these organizations is virtually compulsory. In Europe, the Framework Programs encourage trans-national consortia, including university participation in many cases. There are time-honored examples of horizontal consortia in the United States (American Gas Association, Electric Power Research Institute, Portland Cement Association, etc.), and more recent cases where there is significant government involvement (SEMATECH and PNGV/USCAR[3]), but overall the U.S. experience with such organizational structures is limited.

Horizontal consortia connect firms who have similar needs for base technology but who compete in the end product market; vertical consortia connect firms in a chain of innovation.[4] Horizontal consortia are useful for diffusing and sharing the costs of research leading to more efficient uses of new technology. Vertical consortia are useful for accelerating diffusion and can be a powerful mechanism for engaging the high-tech, first and second-tier, small and medium-sized firms. In both types, the sharing of information among firms helps to ensure that the government is not funding the development of products.

Apart from the practical advantages of engaging consortia in partnership programs, there is a political advantage of some importance. When the government contracts with single firms in projects like ATP, it is very difficult to reveal for purposes of evaluation the public benefits that may accrue. The use of an institutional arrangement, such as federal collaboration with a consortium that might include not only firms but state agencies and perhaps universities or national laboratories, itself provides the diffusion mechanism through which public values are realized.

By working within a network of firms and perhaps other institutions, the private sector can accelerate the diffusion of the innovations and assure the breadth of industry interest in the work, while the government focuses its investment on opening up new technical possibilities. There are situations in which such consortia can best be realized by relying on state authorities to assemble all of the relevant institutional commitments to maximize the likelihood of economic benefits where economic development is the objective. We discuss an example of this principle below where we discuss the ATP program.

Research and Innovation Policy Is More than R&D

A "one size fits all" research and innovation policy is almost certain to be unsuccessful. Every industry is different and government agencies must be sensitive to these differences, which may call for different policy tools and different mixes of science, technology, and systems research. For example, strong patent protection is essential to business success in pharmaceuticals, but less so in the computer industry, where most large firms are cross-licensed internationally. Biotechnology firms draw directly on forefront basic science, while chemical and materials firms are more dependent on advanced process technology. Industry structures are also very different. In some, scale economies are vital (chemicals, energy, communications). In others, small and new firms are an essential source of vitality (software, materials, instruments). These realities require that government acquire much more effective means of informing itself about the conditions, needs, and opportunities of many sectors of service and manufacturing industry (as recommended in Chapter 15 by Daniel Roos, Frank Field and James Neely).

There are two broad types of policy tools: those involving the direct provision of federal funds for R&D and those that use indirect means, such as tax and economic policy, regulations, standards, procurement, and the like. These indirect tools may be used to provide incentives for private sector investment in research and development, and to enhance the accessibility and utility of research results, both new and old. The effective use of the full range of science and technology policy tools can stimulate and encourage private investment and make those investments more effective. A variety of policy instruments can also help ensure that technology strategies meet the distinct needs of different industries, regions and missions.

The administration has demonstrated the coordinated use of a broad set of tools in its management of the National Information Infrastructure (NII) (see Chapter 13 by Brian Kahin). The Internet originated in two decades of government-funded R&D activities at universities and other laboratories. As computer networking matured and other telecommunications services proliferated and converted to digital technology, private investment grew and the government relied increasingly on deregulation and other indirect policy tools for the further development of the NII. Today private investment is generating expectations of very large economic payoff, and public policy for the National Information Infrastructure makes use of a wide array of direct and indirect policy mechanisms. The NII has been a unique departure from prior forms of physical infrastructure development, which were typically government-defined, government-led and, to a significant degree, government-financed. Here, the government role is cautiously defined and is comprehensive in scope. Almost every organ of government is in a position to foster (or impede) healthy NII development in the public interest.

The development of the Global Information Infrastructure is far from complete, and the administration has yet to define a mechanism to ensure that all of the federal policy tools—research, standards, trade policy, intellectual property, privacy, security, legal jurisdiction, and taxation—are properly coordinated. Despite this shortcoming, the Internet has done more for knowledge sharing and collaboration than any prior government effort. As such, it is identified by Jane Fountain (Chapter 4) as a promising element of social capital underlying U.S. innovative capacity. The Next Generation Internet Initiative can be a key element in advancing the technological edge and strengthening U.S. leadership in information infrastructure. The organizations in the president's executive office (discussed in Chapter 17 by David Hart) will have to be strengthened if the needed policy development and coordination is to be achieved.

Performance-Based Regulations and Other Regulatory Alternatives

Experience has shown that prescriptive or coercive regulations are an expensive and inefficient tool for forcing private investment in technology. So too are regulations that erect barriers to competition, in the absence of compelling reasons for a regulated monopoly service. As has been demonstrated on a limited scale, output-based regulations, which specify the goal of the regulations rather than the process of achieving that goal, can produce results consistent with the public interest while at the same time encouraging creative, less-costly, market-based solutions to the problem.[5] In environmental regulation, for example, incentives for new processes for reducing harmful emissions may be more effective than requirements to use "best practice" processes (as Chapter 11 by George Heaton and Darryl Banks explains).

Competition and Anti-trust Policy

Although anti-trust policy is not seen by many people as a tool of technology policy, its importance is illustrated by the National Cooperative Research Act of 1984 . The willingness of anti-trust authorities to define markets in global terms has given more freedom to U.S. firms that, though they might be well positioned in the United States, are hard pressed by foreign competitors. There is a strong connection between anti-trust policy and public-private technology partnership in that the participation of government officials in an industry consortium can provide protection against some anti-trust abuses. At the same time, new forms of monopoly power may be arising with new technology, and government must continue to ensure that market power is not used to suppress useful innovations.

Creating and Mediating Markets: Standards Policy and Procurement

The government plays a unique role in creating markets where they have failed to form and in harnessing the power of the market in the public interest. Examples include issuance of tradable permits in the regulation of air pollution, and the use of market power arising from its own massive purchasing activities to influence voluntary industrial and product standards. These functions present important opportunities to influence and advance innovation. Government should, wherever possible, set performance rather than design standards. Similarly, it should use both procurement and regulatory authority to encourage innovative solutions that, in the long run, have the most promise to achieve federal objectives at minimum cost.

In almost all of private industry's industrial standards processes, including international but non-governmental bodies such as the International Standards Organization (ISO) and its sister body the International Electrotechnical Commission (IEC), governments do not set standards but do play a facilitating role. A government can ensure that its own procurement standards are commercially compatible wherever possible, as the DoD has undertaken in its reform of its military procurement specifications (MILSPECs). It can also contribute personnel and resources directly to advance standards processes, as it did through participation in the Internet Engineering Task Force (which sets consensus standards for the Internet). This participation did much to hasten Internet growth and flexibility.

Tax Incentives

Tax policy has many direct and indirect effects on private sector investments in innovation, ranging from the way corporate R&D costs are allocated to foreign-source income, to depreciation rates for new scientific instruments and production tools. The most widely debated tax issue, however is the Research and Experimentation tax credit. (See Chapter 8 by Scott Wallsten). Although many consider it to be an attractive idea, others identify flaws, and it has never won permanent enactment by Congress. The R&E tax credit is a blunt and expensive instrument which seeks an overall rise in the level of R&D across all industries and regions. It rewards firms that are rapidly increasing their R&D investments, but does little for those industries most severely challenged by international competition.

A more effective use of the tax code to encourage innovation might be to design a more specifically targeted tax credit that encourages the diffusion of existing technology, encourages the purchase of research from universities, or lowers the cost of sending employees to mid-career training programs. Targeting industries and selected technologies at specific stages of development for tax incentives could also foster innovation.

Intellectual Property Policy as a Technology Driver

Intellectual property policy may be the most troublesome but important "indirect" tool in the toolbox. The way in which the United States develops its patent law to conform with other nations as required by the General Agreement on Tariffs and Trade (GATT) can have profound influence on U.S. innovation rates. The U.S. Patent and Trademark Office recognizes this fact, but tends to define innovation as synonymous with patent filing, when many of the most dramatic innovations have evolved with only modest recourse to patents. In some industries, for example computer hardware, patent policies are largely defensive; the larger firms worldwide are linked by cross-license agreements. In other areas such as biotechnology, however, rigorous patent protection is absolutely critical.

Similarly, changes are sweeping over copyright protection and trade secret and trademark protection, both because policy and enforcement internationally are not uniform and because many experts feel that some new form of protection, with features of both patent and copyright law, is needed.[6] The executive branch and Congress must recognize that balancing intellectual property protection and acceptable use—that is, incentives to put knowledge in the public domain or license it free of charge—is an essential element of technology policy and should be developed in concert with the other tools in the toolbox.

Technology Roadmaps

Since, as noted above, different industries, different technologies, and even different regions of the country follow different patterns of innovation, the federal government must have a clear understanding of these differences (as argued in Chapter 15 by Daniel Roos, Frank Field, and James Neely). This understanding can only come from outside the Washington beltway—technological and market understanding from the private sector, workforce needs from labor, and the promise of emerging science from the universities and other laboratories. But it is not enough for these groups to share their knowledge; the government must have the institutional capacity to absorb and use it.

To that end, the technology roadmap—a consensus articulation of a scientifically informed vision of attractive technology futures— offers an interesting tool with which to organize and shape the technology needs, both of government and industry.[7] Roadmaps are informed by research capabilities, the state of technological development, market trends, and public sector and industry needs and priorities, to assist policy makers and the research community in resource allocation and agenda setting. The technology roadmap designed by SEMI/SEMATECH offers a ready template for ways to join the interests of the federal agencies, the university research structure, and the research capabilities of the private sector.[8] More than performing a census and making surveys, the roadmap requires applied policy analysis and design, and an informed and open debate about alternative technology policies and strategies for every sector of the economy. Modification of some of the legal constraints against officials seeking advice from individuals outside of government might be appropriate in this circumstance.[9]

Roadmaps have value not only in fostering communications and common purpose among a variety of research organizations working toward similar objectives, but can also be helpful guides as technologies evolve over time. Very few exciting innovations come to practical fruition in a single effort. Many more modest steps are taken, each raising new possibilities whose exploitation requires solution of new problems. Thus government projects of limited duration rarely create radical new technological capabilities. Indeed, both the TRP and the ATP programs suffered from unrealistic expectations in this regard, since neither program was designed for a time sequence of ever more ambitious steps towards highly valued goals. Technology roadmaps can track those development trajectories and provide more realistic bases for program evaluation than can the examination of results from single projects, one at a time.[10]

Technology roadmaps have another useful function as guides to research opportunities of value to industrial and other user communities. As noted in Chapter 14, roadmaps tell researchers where intellectual effort is most likely to bear practical fruit, but do not constrain the researchers' choices. The creation of such roadmaps requires the collaboration of well-informed technologists with scientists, and is a valuable role for industry consortia, working in collaboration with universities and national laboratories. Other nations, particularly Japan, the United Kingdom, and Germany, have made use of a related technique, the Delphi survey of technical opinions, to construct a map of research opportunities of value to society for use in budget planning and project selection by researchers. In the United States the analogous activity has been the identification of lists of "critical technologies," for which the Critical Technologies Institute (CTI) attached to the Office of Science and Technology was created. Technology roadmaps generated in collaboration with industry would be much more useful as a guide to government research investment priorities.

Leverage Globalization of Innovation

Innovation opportunities in the United States increasingly require access to foreign resources and markets and compatibility with the policies of other countries. Information infrastructure, where U.S. firms and institutions enjoy a commanding lead today, illustrates the need for U.S. leadership in developing a harmonious international environment. While trade conflicts tend to capture more public attention, trans-national collaboration and cooperation in the development of new science and technology can bring even bigger benefits.

U.S. technology policy should encourage and facilitate globalization and trans-national collaboration. The United States must learn to cooperate as well as compete, given the rapidly growing technical assets in other countries (assets which are in many cases the product of public investment). The criterion for participation should remain the U.S. self-interest, but not defined in a zero-sum fashion. In most cases, the United States will prefer to leave such collaborations to firms, universities, and technical associations without government involvement. But the U.S. government should consult with U.S. firms, and should take the lead in defining the forms of trans-national technological cooperation that will be most useful to both business interests and the U.S. public interest.

This strategy suggests that the United States should aim for an international code of investment policy, such as that being developed by the Organization for Economic Cooperation and Development (OECD), that allows the United States to permit foreign-owned R&D establishments in the United States to participate in domestic technology programs, such as public-private partnerships, by ensuring that foreign subsidiaries of U.S. firms enjoy equivalent and comparable access.[11] The United States Trade Representative should take increasing responsibility to press for the multilateral elimination of foreign direct investment constraints under the World Trade Organization, and for establishment of a Multilateral Investment Agreement. Such an agreement would provide equal treatment for international investors with regard to market access and legal security.

The United States should also press for multinational agreements (discussed later in this chapter) to design, construct, and use the very large facilities required for modern science, such as accelerators, telescopes, and fusion research reactors, as well as global scientific monitoring projects, such as bio-assays of the seas and monitoring of the global environment.

Improve Government Effectiveness in Policy Development

Strong, stable, and continuing federal support for a research and innovation policy is of critical importance to the contribution of research and innovation to economic growth, job generation, and rising living standards, and also to the long-term, cumulative nature of the pay-off in those areas from government investment. This is especially true under the policies recommended here, which generally move away from public funding of proprietary commercial technology (except in cases where the government expects to be the purchaser of the resulting products, as in defense procurement). Just as nonpartisan support for science is essential to give scientists time to pursue unexpected opportunities, so too basic technology research needs continuity of support to maximize public returns over short-term private gains. Multi-year continuity in appropriations for research investments are crucial, and Congress must sustain a consensus policy through the ups and downs of political change. It is an unavoidable dilemma of technology policy that for the most appropriate federal role—investing in basic technology research—the time required to realize economic benefits is longest and least visible, while it is quickest and most visible for the least desirable investments, such as federal subsidies to product development.

The American science and technology system thrives because it is pluralistic. There are many sources of support, many types of performers, and a maze of linkages amongst funders, performers, and users of science and technology. This pluralism was intended by the nation's founders, who included a patent clause in the Constitution, rejecting monopolies protected by the Crown. Pluralism has grown with the nation, through the Morrill Act establishing the land grant colleges in 1862, the development of corporate R&D laboratories in the early decades of this century, and the defense, energy, space, and medical research complexes of the past fifty years. Pluralism is necessary because the outcomes of technological innovation cannot be predicted; they can only be discovered through real-world trials of competing ideas and institutions.

Making policy which can target and stimulate, not constrain or stifle, this diverse, loosely coupled environment requires the ongoing participation of stakeholders. There is not and should not be a single centralized technology policy process that undermines pluralism. The mix of technology policy tools must be adapted across regions and industries in accordance with particular needs and established patterns. Attempting to specify the exact mix from the center would be both foolhardy and counterproductive.

While the market provides a relatively demanding environment for selecting the most promising private sector organizational and technological innovations, the policy process in the public sector has generally not lead to equally sharp selection mechanisms. In part this is because of the difficulty of finding sufficiently measurable and objective indicators of success for public policy goals that work as well as profitability works for corporate goals (as Adam Jaffe explains in Chapter 3). Nonetheless, it is essential that policymakers attempt to define their goals, to measure the effectiveness of technology policy in reaching them, and to use these measures as feedback for improvement. Efforts at comparison—with other nations, across missions and regions, and with private sector innovation processes—are essential. Intentional experiments, in which different arrays of tools are voluntarily employed by different agencies and their state, non-governmental, and private partners, should be encouraged. Every program should have an explicit element for evaluation and learning.

Stakeholders Must Be Involved in Technology Policy
Development and Delivery

The federal government must have access to advice, data, and analysis that will help it tailor technology policy to fit particular industries and regions. Involving all the stakeholders—scientists and technologists, state and local governments, industry, labor, professional associations, and public interest groups—will bring new perspectives to the development of technology policy options and new rigor to testing them. The federal government often lacks information about actual practices and relationships on the ground as well as about scientific and technological opportunities. Especially now that the U.S. Congress Office of Technology Assessment (OTA) is no longer available as a source of analysis, a gap remains in the area of informed policy assessment. The White House Office of Science and Technology Policy (OSTP) should serve as the nerve center for this advisory process in support of the president and the NEC. The President's Council of Advisors on Science and Technology (PCAST), if better financially supported, and a restructured Critical Technologies Institute (CTI) (a Federally Funded Research and Development Center dedicated to the support of the Executive Office of the President and other federal agencies) should be viewed as valuable resources for OSTP in this regard. Since PCAST also advises the president on science policy, it may be useful to link technology policy-making to the National Science Board's (NSB) responsibility for both science and technology basic research by appointing the chair of the NSB to PCAST.

One important requirement is that the president have direct access to experienced technical professionals and innovators from the private sector. In addition to a better supported PCAST, this can be provided by reliance on the DOC Technology Administration's direct channels of communication with private sector technology decision-makers on issues related to innovation and commercialization of R&D. A Research and Innovation Board, advising the secretary of commerce and staffed by the Technology Administration, could strengthen those private sector linkages, as indeed the Commerce Technology Advisory Board did in the 1960s and 1970s. The Board could oversee the development of technology roadmaps and the department's sectoral industry studies (as recommended by Daniel Roos, Frank Field and James Neely in Chapter 15), and offer a potential venue for coordination and information sharing between government policy makers and private industry.

State-Federal Relationships

State governments are increasingly responsible for the delivery of technology and training services and, more generally, for technology diffusion and utilization. Furthermore, innovation-based development strategies, especially those that are regional in nature, call for integration of innovation programs with training and education, as well as with other areas of policy for which the states are better equipped than are federal agencies. If state-federal collaboration is to combine the best capabilities of both, the states need earlier and more influential access to federal technology policy-making processes while adjustments are still possible (see Chapter 16 by Christopher Coburn and Duncan Brown).

The Executive Office of the President, in collaboration with the National Governors' Association, has established the U.S. Innovation Partnership.[12] This joint effort of administration technology policy officials and governors is staffed by the Technology Administration in the Department of Commerce and seeks to ensure better coordination between state and federal efforts in the encouragement of innovation. This effort should be encouraged and supported as a mechanism for policy coordination in those areas where the states have important roles and assets, such as state-federal investment in technology-based economic development, the construction by state and municipal governments of the Intelligent Transportation System, and strategies for environmental containment, monitoring, and remediation.

The Role of Congress

Congress is central to the policy development process. Members of Congress have narrower constituencies and, as a group, face the electorate more regularly than does the president. It is understandable that many members will be eager for immediate results. Given the pressures members face, the administration should support them by advancing policies that recognize more fully both the importance and unpredictability of technological innovation and the necessity for the federal government to play a facilitating role in it. One key to this is establishing a basis for federal investment which clearly defines the federal role and offers a mechanism through cost-shared partnerships that does not cause inequity or market distortion. Congress has valuable knowledge to add to the technology policy process. For example, members can identify key stakeholders and ensure that their voices are heard. The Congressional support agencies perform needed program evaluations. Congress also has a central decision-making role, adjudicating among technology policy experiments. Policies that have failed must be killed; policies that succeed must be maintained or expanded. But most importantly, policy experiments have to be tried for a sufficiently long time and under sufficiently reasonable conditions in order to be judged. In its first term, the Clinton administration pursued aggressive expansion of its technology agenda. The 1994 reaction by the majority in Congress, aiming to hamstring or halt these experiments, was equally aggressive. A more patient, long-term approach by all parties can make second term efforts more stable and productive.

A White House Advocate for Technological Innovation, Linked to Economic Policy

The president and the White House staff must serve as advocates for research and innovation policy and coordinate the array of federal S&T activities. The Executive Office of the President must also provide the locus for linking the technology agenda with broad national policy objectives, such as economic and security policy (as David Hart discusses in Chapter 17). The president has the long time-horizon and national purview that justifies an intense interest in innovation that will advance the quality of life in the United States. The president has the strongest incentive and the authority to promote change in the face of vested interests bent on preserving the status quo. This does not mean that the White House should advocate every R&D program. Instead, the White House should be the arbiter for policy options that encourage technological innovation in the pursuit of agency missions (including non-R&D options), particularly in times of tight budgets when investments in the future tend to be squeezed out. Such options should be compared to and traded off against non-R&D alternatives for encouraging innovation in the pursuit of the same mission.

The major White House policy councils—the National Economic Council, National Security Council, and Domestic Policy Council—are the most appropriate forums for framing technology policy options and integrating them into the larger issues with which they are concerned. The council staffs should play major roles in developing these options, but should rely on OSTP (and where appropriate the committees of the NSTC) for the technical judgments on which the efficacy and practicality of those options rest. OSTP should have close linkages to all of these councils, as well as to OMB, at the staff level and through the science advisor's service as a principal member in many of their deliberations. The National Science and Technology Council, through which OSTP reaches out to the research and innovation units of federal agencies, can serve as a channel to the major policy councils for agency technology policy ideas.[13] NSTC should coordinate multi-agency programs and identify a few key budget priorities.

Applying These Principles to Determine When Government Should Invest in Research

These six principles for a research and innovation policy are intended to provide a clear and politically robust framework to aid in program and policy development. They do not lead to discrete answers, but instead are intended to inform decisions and provide a litmus test for program evaluation and improvement. Before any investment of federal moneys in technology can be made, one must ask: is there a significant public problem that needs to be addressed by the federal government? Are there no other entities, such as private firms, that are better positioned to offer a solution and are motivated to invest in it? Implied in this second question is the idea that any federal research investment should not only be of net benefit to the nation—the benefits will exceed the costs—but also that public benefits will substantially outweigh private returns when the government addresses the problem through public-private partnerships. If the problem passes these tests, one must then ask, is the federal government in a good position to solve the problem? Does it have the skills, experience, and political legitimacy to bring about the desired results in a manner acceptable to all those affected? Beyond satisfactory answers to these primary questions comes the realization that our federal government increasingly faces a future of finite resources. Priorities must be set and difficult choices made.

Two historical priorities should remain at the top of the list: (1) basic scientific and technological research: investments in the long-term future scientific and technological capacity of the people of the United States (in knowledge and human resources), for which there is no other resource than government; and (2) mission research: investments in research whose urgency derives from a high-priority public function, such as defense, health, environmental protection, and raising the standard of living, and where the work is of top priority within that function. The first, basic research, although consuming a minor fraction (about 21 percent) of federal R&D resources, often produces striking long-term benefits.[14] Mission research, the second historical priority, receives larger investments, but it remains important in fulfilling critical social needs. Where commercial interests are aligned with the technology development interests of the federal government, public investment can and should be highly leveraged by private investment.

When the primary goal of public investment in technology is the stimulation of private sector innovation, government should concentrate most of its investment at the most creative points in the innovation process.[15] The appropriate mix of federal investment in basic science and technology research enables creation of new technologies and informs choices among technical strategies. When developing products for its own use, as in the military and space programs, it is appropriate for government to fund not only research but development as well. However, product development is not an appropriate area for government funding when the goal is general economic development. Thus, while funding of basic science and technology research to support all areas of government activity is appropriate in principle, how far government goes beyond this toward commercialization should depend on the extent to which there is a public stake in the production of the end products. Rigorous program evaluation, based on metrics designed for the purpose, is of course indispensable. But there is a basic limitation on the quest for metrics that will quantitatively express economic outcomes in terms of appropriable returns. When such calculations can be made, that fact may suggest that private investors could, and should, capture these returns. The case for government investment may be highest in just those situations in which the benefits are hardest to quantify in dollar terms: basic research, education, and investments in social capital generally.

Finally, let us emphasize that determination of the government role is not to be made on the basis of the kind of research being performed. For this purpose it is not relevant whether the investigator is motivated by curiosity about nature or the satisfaction of solving a problem in which a sponsor may be interested. The criterion rests on the type and magnitude of returns to the public interest, in relation to any private benefits that may have been created.

Choosing Research Performers

How should agencies choose among firms, their own laboratories, independent laboratories, and universities when funding research? We believe they should select the institutions most competent to perform the work at a high level of excellence and able to diffuse the new knowledge to those who can best use it, thus ensuring that public benefits will exceed private revenues. Thus the public interest in the work matters, and so too does the effectiveness of the means for diffusion of the results to society.

The paths by which public value is created must be considered when selecting performers. Firms engaged in federally-funded research only need to move the ideas from laboratories to business units to see them put in practice, but until the research reaches many other users, public benefits may not be realized. In contrast, students trained in universities take the new knowledge with them to their jobs. Government-funded national laboratories may be particularly capable of interdisciplinary work, exchanging ideas across disciplinary boundaries, and working with industry through CRADAs. There is no single right answer to the selection of performing institutions. Indeed, a mix of institutional performers may be best, since industry, universities, and national laboratories each have their unique ways of ensuring that new work reaches the users.

Where the government funds one hundred percent of the work, the university, national laboratory, private firm, or consortium that performs the research must be committed to effective diffusion of the results. Universities that refuse to let collaborating firms restrain the right to publish, and whose students are free to use all the knowledge they have gained, will meet this requirement automatically. National laboratories should, as recommended by the Galvin Commission for the DOE, restrict themselves to work conducted under university-like conditions (both basic science and technology research) and to mission-related work in which the beneficiaries (the users of the technology) are identified and adequate mechanisms for diffusion are planned and provided for.[16] The CRADA mechanism is one such tool (as David Guston explains in Chapter 9).

The more difficult issue arises when government provides cost-shared funding to private firms, either individually or as part of consortium.[17] In this case the consortium may be preferred, since the effective diffusion of results is more nearly assured when a number of firms collaborate. In the case of those consortia made up of potential rivals, natural competitive pressures will tend to keep the research less proprietary and more long-range in nature, thus more "basic." However, as Linda Cohen observes in Chapter 7, the failure of the Technology Reinvestment Project (TRP) flowed from just this situation. One group of competitors (defense prime contractors) objected to cost sharing work intended to enhance, at their expense, the market opportunities of commercial firms in the same consortium.

A balanced portfolio of publicly-funded research leading to new science and new technology is the right approach to federal research funding, not only for the National Science Foundation (NSF) and the National Institutes of Health (NIH), but also for the long-term investments supporting the missions of agencies such as the Department of Commerce (DOC), the Department of Energy (DOE), the Department of Defense (DoD), and NASA. It should also be a focus of much of the government's funding for research in public-private partnerships such as the Advanced Technology Program, the Program for a New Generation of Vehicles, and the Environmental Technology Initiative, recognizing that industrial partners will also be investing in research and development addressing their specific commercial interests. Thus when government funds research in industry, government may take a share of the technical risks, but firms should take most of the market risk. If this is the division of labor, much of the concern about government R&D programs distorting markets, substituting for private investment, or causing anti-competitive impacts on individual firms should be allayed. In addition, basic technology research, while longer-range in nature than product development, will generally be less expensive than large-scale technology development and demonstration, allowing some additional resources to shift from development to research.

When federal agencies collaborate with consortia or individual firms, it is appropriate for the government to focus its investment on that part of the program which has a potentially high payoff to society, based on an attractive, if risky, technical opportunity. This has been the primary emphasis in NIST's ATP program. Keeping the technical goals ambitious and attractive means a move away from technologies likely to be quickly commercialized. To the extent that a substantial part of the work is not proprietary, the rate of diffusion of benefits would increase, and concerns about anti-competitive effects (which may arise regardless of the rigor of the competitive selection process) might be reduced. But political expectations for quick commercialization and evidence of immediate economic returns from partnership programs provide a strong incentive to program managers to invest in just those kind of research subsidies to which the Congress quite properly objects.

National Laboratories

One of the most successful institutional innovations of the Cold War period was the government-owned, contractor-operated national laboratories (GOCOs). Most of them have highly qualified staffs; many of them have pressing missions. But though they dominate the R&D funding portfolio of the federal government (receiving twice as much federal funding for R&D as the universities), they have had considerable difficulty in adjusting to the changing needs of the nation. This is not necessarily a failure of laboratory management, but more often results from the rigidity of agency authorities and Congressional committee charters. The Clinton administration attempted, with little success, to come to grips with the realignment of mission and the possible down-sizing of these laboratories during its first term in office. Managing priorities for funding of national laboratories and providing effective mechanisms for linking the laboratories to potential beneficiaries of their work requires collaboration with both Congress and the states.

Cooperative research and development agreements (CRADAs) solve some of the problems faced by national labs. These agreements and related mechanisms were initiated in the 1980s and, while already viewed favorably by most observers, can be made more effective. One way is to encourage the sharing of personnel so that the deep cultural canyons that often separate technology producers from users, and federal researchers from industrial researchers, can be crossed.

Very Large Technology Projects

In the past, technology policy often centered upon taking a few large risks, pouring large sums of money into a few technologies (e.g., synthetic fuels, the supersonic transport) in the hope that such a concentrated investment would ensure success.[18] These projects were often politically attractive but rarely achieved their goals. A better strategy is to make numerous, smaller technology bets, and to do so with a project selection mechanism that is market-based, wherever possible. The federal government should follow the NSF/NIH model of relying primarily on relatively small grants spread out among many performers, awarded competitively but funded over multiple years. It should fund a variety of technology areas chosen with input from technical experts from the private sector as well as from research institutions, as is done in ATP. It should achieve scale, where it is needed, by encouraging groups of institutions to collaborate in formulating plans for diversified research and the diffusion of the results.

Of course, there are some specialized research facilities—telescopes, oceanographic ships, accelerators, and the like—which, by their nature, require large capital investments, and without which science cannot progress. Many of these projects will, in the future, have to be planned and executed as international collaborations.

Such large-scale international collaborations can prove effective, given sound scientific and economic—rather than political—justification, and resilient institutionalized funding mechanisms (conceptually the same type of criteria we would advance for funding of national-level, industry consortia). To address the issue of commitment and accountability, there must be an international institutional context for which the U.S. Congress and president feel ownership and in which they have confidence, perhaps by means of a multi-year appropriation of funding, subject to performance review against agreed milestones.[19] Where the need for federal help arises from a commercial technology of such extreme cost that firms and their sources of finance are unable to accept the risks, such as might arise in a future supersonic transport aircraft, government should look to the array of policy tools discussed earlier in this chapter. One such tool could be for government to share part of the capital risk, leaving it to the private investment community to evaluate the commercial merits of the venture.

Having explored in general terms the application of our six principles for a research and innovation policy, the chapter now turns to the specific case of the ATP program.

Applying Research and Innovation Policy Principles to ATP

The NIST Advanced Technology Program (ATP) is a federal program that uses cost-shared, competitively selected support of advanced technological research as a stimulus to industrial innovation, and a means to benefit the economy (see Chapter 6 by Christopher Hill). Government expects to see measurable economic outcomes in due course, but must avoid interfering with competitive markets. As described earlier, this tension makes cost-shared technology investment an inherently uncomfortable area of policy development. Despite this, ATP has weathered ongoing scrutiny from policy-makers. The technical quality and applications potential of the work are the primary measures of ATP success. Government and industry goals for the program differ, but are not mutually exclusive, or even necessarily at odds. Commercialization, in which the government does not directly participate, is important to the participating firms. Diffusion of the technical achievement is of special interest to the government.

Applying the principles outlined here to the ATP program structure and funding guidelines can result in clearer definition of legitimate roles for the program participants, public and private. This could serve to strengthen the program, expand its economic benefits, provide clarity of mission to increase political support, and maximize the diffusion potential of technology outcomes. Such an effort would include an emphasis on basic technology; a commitment to consortium-based, cost-shared investment; and strong links to state and local economic development institutions. The model we suggest takes a more active economic development approach than the current program, through significant institutional reform. It contrasts with Christopher Hill's recommendations in Chapter 6, which leave the program framework intact, and offer improvement on the margin. Both approaches are consistent with our research and innovation policy principles, as are the set of program refinements announcements by Secretary of Commerce William Daley on July 10, 1997.[20] There is no one right structure that manifests from these guidelines. Instead, they are intended to provide a broadly agreeable conceptual basis from which program specifics can be developed.

The structure of the NSF State Systemic Initiatives Program offers a model for repositioning ATP with an emphasis on diffusion and regional development.[21] Such a model suggests inviting states—or regional groups of states—to compete for selection by NIST as a regional technology-based economic development program. To qualify for selection, the states would identify an industry sector— perhaps including the main elements of the supply chain as well— and create a non-profit consortium of institutions representing state agencies, the selected industries, labor, finance, education, and research. State-funded technology and economic development programs might participate and share the costs. The consortium might also produce technology roadmaps to guide the selection of basic technology research opportunities to be pursued through ATP projects, enhancing the opportunity for universities, national laboratories and small to medium-sized firms to participate. The proposal would not only make a case that the chosen sector is ripe for dramatic technical progress, but would also outline the consortium's commitments to investment, exports, worker training, and other activities that would maximize the economic leverage to be gained from ATP research support. The consortium might take responsibility for choosing specific firms for participation, subject to evaluation by NIST of technical merit. The consortium would also agree to make post-project evaluations for NIST of the economic outcomes of the total program.

This approach gets more economic leverage for NIST dollars, preserves the national standard for technical excellence, devolves to the states the task of selecting among individual firms, and creates a broadly-based constituency for the ATP program. Since ATP already invests most of its funds through "focus" areas—specific industry sectors with a compelling case for technology support—this would simply extend the principle by sharing responsibility with the private sector and the states. In short, collaboration by the states, firms, and laboratories participating in the consortium would strengthen the social capital that underlies the U.S. capacity for innovation. (See Jane Fountain's discussion of social capital in Chapter 4.) Incentives in the ATP program to encourage this type of networking and collaboration would alone provide a valuable economic contribution.

Conclusion

Just as the principles described here can be applied in a non-partisan framework to NIST's Advanced Technology program, they can be applied one by one to the full portfolio of technology programs. As with ATP, the principles do not lead directly to specific program agendas and definitions; rather they guide program development within a politically and economically rational framework. Our six principles can be seen reflected in the specific program evaluations in each of the chapters.

The administration set the right tone in the president and vice president's 1993 policy statement, which advocated a research-based investment strategy to help "private firms develop and profit from innovations," recognizing that the right incentives can direct the private sector's powerful innovative capacity to broad public purposes, including a rising standard of living and quality of life. If the federal government's policy gives new emphasis to its own participation in the network of universities, laboratories, and firms that is rapidly developing under world economic forces, its investment in research can create the world's strongest base of shared technical knowledge.

For too long both the political and the scientific communities have squabbled over narrow distinctions between "science" and "technology" as targets for federal investment. These distinctions fail tell us what the proper roles are for the public and private sectors, and lead to neglect of investments in the nation's knowledge base and innovation capacities. What is needed instead is a research and innovation policy that can continue to build America's innovative capacity through good times and bad, and through the ebb and flow of political philosophy. The nation is nearing the end of the century in which it has demonstrated the most creative and productive scientific and technological enterprise in the world. The driver was the threat of war. It is now time to establish the principles that can sustain this progress, not for fear of war but in anticipation of rising quality of life, a clean environment, and a healthy citizenry. If both scientific and technological research are strongly supported and the full range of other policy tools are applied to encourage innovation, public policy can safely leave to industry the realization of economic progress.

Notes

1. The principles in this chapter were anticipated in the unpublished working "Investing in Innovation: Toward A Consensus Strategy for Federal Technology Policy," prepared by the steering committee for this project and released on April 24, 1997. Summaries of the ideas were published in Lewis M. Branscomb, "From Technology Politics to Technology Policy," *Issues in Science and Technology*, Vol. 13, No. 3 (Spring 1997), pp. 41–48; and in L.M. Branscomb, "Technology Policy: Resolving the Ideological Confusion," *The Bridge*, Vol. 27, No. 2 (Summer 1997), in press.

2. Industry, including industry-managed national laboratories, performed 73 percent of the nation's R&D in 1996. See NSF Science Resources Division, *Data Brief*, Vol. 1996, No. 11 (October 25, 1996), p. 3; <www.nsf.gov/sbe/srs/databrf/sdb96328.htm>.

3. The United States Council for Automotive Research (USCAR) is an organiza-

tion formed by Chrysler, Ford and General Motors to strengthen the technology base of the domestic auto industry through cooperative precompetitive research; <http://www.uscar.org/>.

4. SEMATECH, the Semiconductor Manufacturing Technology consortium, is an example of a vertical consortium, created by semiconductor manufacturers to accelerate innovation by firms supplying the manufacturing tools. The Object Management Group is an example of a horizontal consortium, through which over 100 software firms set standards for object-oriented programming.

5. For example, in the regulation of sulfur emissions through the Clean Air Act.

6. See Pamela Samuelson, Randall Davis, Mitchell Kapor, and J.H. Reichman, "A manifesto concerning the legal protection of computer programs," *Columbia Law Review*, Vol. 94, No. 8 (December 1994), pp. 2308–2431.

7. For an excellent example of a technology roadmap see *The National Technology Roadmap for Semiconductors*, sponsored by the Semiconductor Industry Association <http://www.sematech.org/public/roadmap/index.htm>.

8. SEMI/SEMATECH is the organization of U.S. semiconductor process tool manufactures working with the semiconductor producers in SEMATECH; both were established by act of Congress in 1986. See <www.sematech.org/semi-sematech/general.htm>.

9. The Federal Advisory Committee Act discourages industry and other experts from giving confidential -advice to the government.

10. This point was made by Anita Jones, former Director of Defense Research and Engineering, at a seminar sponsored by the Governing Board of the National Research Council at Woods Hole, Massachusetts, on August 8, 1997.

11. See "Multilateral Agreement on Investment," Organization for Economic Cooperation and Development, <http://www.oecd.org/daf/cmis/mai.htm>.

12. Creation of the USIP was recommended by the State-Federal Technology Partnership Task Force, co-chaired by former governors Richard Celeste of Ohio and Richard Thornburgh of Pennsylvania. "The State-Federal Technology Partnership," Final Report, Partnership Task Force, August 1995.

13. An informal report of the Carnegie Commission suggests making the NSTC the primary policy body for science and technology, but it seems unlikely that the broader responsibility for research and innovation policy will reside there rather than in National Economic Council, the Domestic Policy Council, and the National Security Council. Carnegie Commission on Science, Technology and Government, "Science and Technology and the President: A Report to the Next Administration" (New York: Carnegie Commission, January 1997).

14. NSF estimates that basic research will represent about 21 percent of federal R&D obligations for FY1997. See NSF Science Resources Division, *Data Brief*, Vol. 1997, No. 5 (May 15, 1997), p. 1; <www.nsf.gov/sbe/srs/databrf/db97308.htm>.

15. Concentrating public funds on the "creative points in the innovation process" does not mean that government should restrict itself to "precompetitive"

research. Research on "downstream" activities such as manufacturing processes or quality control can improve performance or quality, reduce costs, or eliminate polluting effluents. The notion of "basic" research refers to the exploration of untested ideas of potential value, and is not restricted to the first stages of the classical "linear model" of innovation.

16. Secretary of Energy Advisory Board Task Force on Alternative Futures for the Department of Energy National Laboratories, "Alternative Futures for the Department of Energy National Laboratories," February 1995, <http://www.anl.gov/OPA/local/galvin.html>.

17. In certain cases, a partnership with a single firm which is granted an exclusive license for any patents may be an acceptable mechanism for creating public value in excess of private profit. This arises when the product that results carries the benefit to end users (a miracle drug, for example) or when intellectual property rights are sufficiently weak that others can quickly find a way to offer competing products. This was the principle behind the Bayh-Dole Patent act, which allowed federal agencies to grant exclusive licenses. How effective this policy has been, however, is only now being rigorously studied by economists.

18. Linda Cohen and Roger Noll, *The Technology Porkbarrel* (Washington, D.C.: The Brookings Institution, 1991).

19. President William J. Clinton and Vice President Albert Gore, Jr., "Science in the National Interest" (Washington, D.C.: The Executive Office of the President, August 1994).

20. ATP changes include an increased emphasis on support for partnerships and consortia; an expanded role for states and universities; a stronger emphasis on the program's support for small and medium-sized firms; and a greater cost-share requirement for large company single applicants.

21. NSF's State Systemic Initiatives Program is a regionally-based consortium approach to the reform of K–12 science and mathematics education. NSF encourages states to submit evidence that a consortium of education stakeholders, including state education authorities, teachers' unions, school boards, teachers' colleges, and business and citizen interests, is prepared to work under an agreed plan for education reform, using primarily their own resources. Winning plans receive a multimillion-dollar grant from NSF to help implement the plan. Even states that failed to win the grant have benefited from their planning efforts.

Index

4. Carnegie Commission, *Science, Technology, and the States*; Coburn and Berglund, *Partnerships.*

5. Coburn and Berglund, *Partnerships.*

6. Bill Clinton, Letter to Hon. Bob Miller, Chair, National Governor's Association (Washington, D.C.: The White House, February 3, 1997); National Governors' Association, *United States Innovation Partnership*, draft manuscript, February 6, 1997.

7. Carnegie Commission, *Science, Technology, and the States.*

8. Roy Rothwell, "Successful Industrial Innovation: Critical Factors for the 1990s," *R&D Management*, Vol. 22, No. 3 (July 1992), pp. 221–239.

9. Mowery and Nelson, "The U.S. Corporation and Technical Progress"; Richard S. Rosenbloom and William J. Spencer, "The Transformation of Industrial Research," *Issues in Science and Technology*, Vol. 12, No. 3 (Spring 1996), pp. 68–74.

10. See, for example, Charles M. Vest, "The Transformation of U.S. R&D," in *Competitiveness Index 1996* (Washington, D.C.: Council on Competitiveness, 1996).

11. Rothwell, "Successful Industrial Innovation."

12. National Science Board, *Science and Engineering Indicators 1996* (Arlington, Virginia: National Science Foundation, 1996), p. A-8; NSF Report 96-1.

13. Rosenbloom and Spencer, "The Transformation of Industrial Research."

14. Gary Anderson and Irwin Feller, *New York State Centers for Advanced Technology Program: Evaluating Past Performance and Preparing for the Future* (Washington, D.C.: SRI International, Center for Economic Competitiveness, April 6, 1992).

15. Battelle Memorial Institute, *Virginia's Center for Innovative Technology: An Economic Impact Assessment* (Columbus, Ohio: Battelle Memorial Institute, December 5, 1995).

16. Nexus Associates, *Evaluation of the New York Manufacturing Extension Partnership* (Belmont, Mass.: Nexus Associates, March 18, 1992).

17. Battelle Memorial Institute, *The Edison Technology Centers: An Economic Impact Study* (Columbus, Ohio: Battelle Memorial Institute, December 1996).

18. Kei Koizumi, "President Proposes $75.5 Billion for R&D in the FY 1988 Budget," *Science and Technology in Congress* (Washington, D.C.: American Association for the Advancement of Science, March 1997).

19. Clinton, Letter to Hon. Bob Miller; National Governor's Association, *United States Innovation Partnership.*

20. State-Federal Technology Partnership Task Force, *The State-Federal Technology Partnership Task Force, Final Report* (Washington D.C., 1995).

21. Coburn and Berglund, *Partnerships.*

22. Lawrence Reed, "Time to End the Economic War Between the States," unpublished manuscript, Mackinac Center, Michigan, 1996; available on World

system. The administration and Congress should sponsor a comprehensive assessment to describe the national innovation system objectively and quantitatively, and to recommend ways that the public sector can most efficiently contribute to economic growth based on technology. This study should characterize the role of each element of the public sector (the federal government, states, localities, universities, nonprofits, and foundations) in the changing innovation system; and characterize the economic development activities of federal, state, and local governments: How do they relate to one another? What are their costs and benefits? What are government's legitimate roles? What roles are illegitimate ?

Fundamental change is sweeping the national innovation system. Getting the most from scarce science and technology resources in the coming decades will require leadership and vision from the Executive Branch, beginning with the president, from Congress, and from the states. Government at all levels must attune itself to the needs of the market, working more flexibly and creatively with industry, universities, and nonprofit organizations to harness the private-sector sources of economic growth. States in particular are a valuable source of expertise and originality in responding to this challenge, through new kinds of partnerships with industry and the federal government. Every element of the system requires fresh approaches, based on a clear understanding of how the system works and how it is developing.

Notes

1. David C. Mowery and Richard R. Nelson, "The U.S. Corporation and Technical Progress," in Carl Kaysen, ed., *The American Corporation Today* (New York: Oxford University Press, 1996); Niren M. Vyas, William L. Shelburn, and Dennis C. Rogers, "An Analysis of Strategic Alliances: Forms, Functions and Framework," *Journal of Business and Industrial Marketing*, Vol. 10, No. 3 (1995), pp. 47–60.

2. Carnegie Commission on Science, Technology, and Government, *Science, Technology, and the States in America's Third Century* (New York: Carnegie Corporation, September 1992); Christopher Coburn and Dan Berglund, eds., *Partnerships: A Compendium of State and Federal Cooperative Technology Programs* (Columbus, Ohio: Battelle Memorial Institute, 1995).

3. State Science and Technology Institute, *State Funding for Cooperative Technology Programs* (Columbus, Ohio: State Science and Technology Institute, 1996).